Psychological Sciences:
A Review of Modern Psychology

Psychological Sciences:
A Review of Modern Psychology

JOHN BELOFF

Crosby Lockwood Staples   London

Granada Publishing Limited
First published in Great Britain 1973 by Crosby Lockwood Staples
Frogmore St Albans and 3 Upper James Street London W1R 4BP
Reprinted 1975

ISBN 0 258 96873 7 hardback
     0 258 97040 5 paperback

Printed in Great Britain by
Fletcher & Son Ltd, Norwich

To Zoe and Bruno

Contents

Preface

The word 'psychology' is familiar, the expression 'psychological sciences' is not. Yet, as soon as one attempts to say what psychology is about, it becomes clear that one is dealing, not with a single unified science, but with a collection of more or less loosely affiliated disciplines each with its own peculiar concepts and laws, its own methods and techniques. Thus, while we are already used to talking of the 'social sciences', the 'life sciences' or even the 'behavioural sciences', reference to the 'psychological sciences' still calls for comment.

There was a time, not long ago, when psychology was a battleground for various rival schools. Associationism, Gestaltism, Behaviourism, Psychoanalysis, etc., each in turn claimed to be the only truly scientific psychology. With the deflation of their imperialist claims we can now see them for what they really were: partial and provisional contributions to the infinitely complex and many-sided study of man. It is to the essential plurality of this study that my title draws attention.

As the term will be used in this book, a psychological science, as distinct from a behavioural science, is one that is either directly or indirectly concerned with man's inner life or subjective experiences. This does not mean, however, that a psychological science necessarily depends on introspection. On the contrary, as psychologists had to discover the hard way quite early on its history, the amount that one can hope to learn about a person's thoughts and feelings by introspection alone is severely limited. By far the greater part of all the psychological knowledge we now possess is based on inferences derived from the observation of behaviour. The point is, however, that this knowledge is inferential. If we were to confine ourselves to a strictly positivistic account of behaviour, as if we were dealing with robots which had no inner life, then, though we might succeed in establishing some kind of a behavioural science, it would not amount to a psychological science as we are here using this term.

This point is best illustrated by what, following the late E. G. Boring, the historian of psychology, I have called here 'Behaviouristics' (*see* Chapter 4). In contradistinction to all our other psychological sciences, behaviouristics is concerned not with the person but with his organism and with the effects of stimulating and manipulating it in various ways. By a strict operationist reanalysis of mental terms and concepts it strove to obviate the need for any kind of mentalistic approach. That eventually it failed in this bid, that its theoretical shortcomings eventually became too blatant, should emerge from the ensuing pages. Nevertheless, its practical achievements in the sphere of controlling behaviour, whether for medical or social purposes, must not be underrated. In brief, though it may be the joker in our pack, the pack would be sadly incomplete without it and it will serve, moreover, to throw into relief what is peculiarly psychological about our other sciences.

It should be clearly understood that there is nothing either exhaustive or definitive in my list of psychological sciences, still less in the series of topics which I have chosen to illustrate them. Another author, no doubt, would have produced a different list and his choice would equally reflect his own personal interests and predilections. Accordingly, readers must not be surprised to find here no discussion of developmental psychology and no mention of such an influential figure of contemporary psychology as Jean Piaget. Similarly, despite the dramatic progress of brain research during the past two decades which has undoubtedly enhanced our understanding of human behaviour, there is no chapter devoted to physiological psychology. For this latter omission I can only plead that it would not have been possible to do justice to so large a topic, one that is implicit in virtually every question in psychology, within the scope of the present volume.

But, while some will complain about what I have left out, others, no doubt, will criticise me for what I have put in. In particular, the inclusion of a chapter on parapsychology is bound to raise a few eyebrows among the conservative. Yet, in view of the profound philosophical and methodological issues raised by the persistence of this wayward science, and in view of my own personal involvement in the field, I do not think this calls for any apology.

Within each of my eight specimen sciences, my general plan has been to ask, first, what are the main problems of that area, to sketch out something of their historical background and origins and then to discuss some of the more important attempts which have been made to tackle them. Throughout, my primary aim has been to arouse the reader's interest rather than simply to furnish him with a ready digest of facts or theories. Accordingly, I have dwelt more on basic psychological ideas and controversies than on specific empirical findings. However, by making full use of the copious annotations provided at the end of each chapter together with an extensive bibliography, the serious student can use the book as a convenient jumping-off point for a more intensive study of any of the particular topics which interest him.

John Beloff

Edinburgh
October 1972

Introduction: The Idea of a Psychological Science

Objections

Right from the outset considerable confusion has prevailed over the question of what psychology is supposed to be about. During the 19th century the accepted answer was that it was the science of 'mind', taken by some to mean the content of consciousness, by others to mean mental acts. During the 20th century it has usually been defined as the science of behaviour, of human behaviour in the first instance, of course, but, by a natural transition, of animal behaviour also. In retrospect these rival answers may no longer appear quite as far removed from one another as they once appeared to their respective proponents.

Let us start with the concept of behaviour. In its widest connotation, in the sense in which one can speak about the behaviour of metals under stress, anything whatever may exhibit behaviour when considered in relation to its environment. Behaviour in this sense refers simply to the functional properties of objects exposed to stimulation. Now in physics these external functional properties of objects can be studied using much the same sort of concepts and techniques as are used to study their internal structural properties. In the biological sciences, on the other hand, the existence of the nervous system endows organisms with a degree of autonomy which so complicates their interaction with the environment that the case for a special science of animal behaviour becomes a matter of urgency. It is not however the mere fact of being alive that makes behaviour a problem. Take the case of machines. For the user there is always some uncertainty as to how a given machine will actually behave. It is seldom that this can be predicted with any exactitude from a knowledge of its design and structure plus a knowledge of the conditions under which it will have to operate. And the more delicate the interplay between artefact and environment the less is it possible in practice to predict its behaviour. The only way that, say, a yachtsman can find out about the behaviour of his yacht is by sailing it in all waters and all weathers. Yet, even so, compared with any living organism the transition from structure to function in the case of a machine or artefact is relatively trivial if only because its specification is fully known to start with and it stays unchanged in all essential respects for the duration of its existence. In living organisms, on the contrary, the nervous system differs in unknown ways from one individual to the next, its fine structure is never accessible to inspection and—a crucial distinction in this context—it is perpetually being modified as a result of its encounters with the environment. For all these reasons if we want to find out about the behaviour of organisms we have no option but to study them *in action*.

But, if behaviour were all that was involved, the study of animal behaviour could easily be accommodated as a mere extension of zoology. It is only because when we consider our own behaviour we realise that something more than just behaviour is involved, for example the fact that we are *aware* of what we do, that the case for a psychological science presents itself at all. Whether this awareness makes any difference to our behaviour is, of course, another matter; our answer to that question will depend on what view we take of the mind-body relationship. Whether intelligent behaviour could have evolved without consciousness supervening at any point or whether consciousness emerged because matter had reached a level of complexity at which it could no longer be self-regulating, is a question on which we do not even know at present how a decision could be reached. What, however, we shall here take as axiomatic is (a) that we know ourselves to be conscious, (b) that we cannot help but believe that our fellow humans are likewise conscious, and (c) that we suspect that, in some degree or some form, consciousness is a property of all animal life. In the opening sentence of his historic *Principles of Psychology* William James defines psychology as 'the science of mental life', offering as samples of mental life such items as our thoughts, feelings, desires and so forth. As a quite general definition of psychology I do not think it has been or indeed can be bettered. This does not mean that we must revert to a 19th century conception of psychology and confine our attention only to what is introspectible. Considerations of a phylogenetic and ontogenetic kind may carry us very far indeed from this central experiential core; similarly, the concept of the unconscious may force us to extend our terms of reference. But, unless the object of our inquiry has some bearing, direct or indirect, upon those processes which are, by definition, mental, it is gratuitous to describe such an inquiry as psychological. For example, the study of invertebrate behaviour may be of the greatest intrinsic interest, it may be of the highest importance for zoology and physiology, but it will lead only to confusion if we call it psychology.[1] Let us agree, then, that psychology is, indeed, the study of behaviour (even private experience cannot be communicated without behaving) but let us add that it is first and foremost the study of that special kind of behaviour which is the outward, observable expression of our inner mental life (or, if you prefer it, of that behaviour of which our mental life is the inward reflection).

Granted that we have now correctly located the proper domain of psychological phenomena, the next question we must ask is what can the scientific approach contribute to our understanding of them? Every discipline tries in some way to explain the phenomena that come within its purview; the distinctive feature of a science seems to lie in the kind of explanations it offers. A discipline does not become a science simply because it adopts some of the more salient appurtenances of a science: the use of instruments, the emphasis on measurement, the introduction of a technical vocabulary and so on. These are no more than means to an end. The test of a science lies in its capacity to generate hypotheses that can be confirmed or falsified. If, therefore, the epithet 'scientific', in that overworked expression a 'scientific psychology', is to have anything more than an honorific status two conditions will have to be satisfied: (1) it must have something to tell us about behaviour that goes beyond the deliverances of unaided commonsense or of the traditional insights of humanistic studies, and (2) its explanations must possess genuine predictive power.

With regard to (1) it is worth noting that psychology has had to operate from a higher baseline than was the case with the physical sciences. It is true that man acquired considerable practical knowledge of the physical environment without benefit of theory and, thanks to his perennial inventiveness, he acquired considerable control over it. Indeed had this not been the case he could never have survived long enough to create science. In fact science made little impact on technology prior to the 19th century, by which time an advanced industrial society had already come into being. Nevertheless, when it comes to an understanding of fundamental physical processes, man's untutored intuitions proved of small avail. One has only to think of the time it took before even the elementary laws of motion were correctly understood; the reason why Aristotelian physics persisted so long has less to do with the prestige of Aristotle than the fact that it represents the physics of commonsense. Modern physics began with the recognition that the physical world is an alien domain where neither our intuitions nor our anthropocentric assumptions can be trusted. Obviously, the same cannot be said, without an air of paradox, where man himself is the object of inquiry. It is therefore scarcely a matter of surprise that whereas the physical sciences have already revolutionised our technology, the behavioural sciences have as yet had little effect on our social institutions. The problem of psychology is that the domain of the psychological has already largely been pre-empted by non-scientific modes of thought.

As regards (2), the predictive power of a science, a brief digression is necessary on the meaning of 'explanation'. In its widest sense, explanation consists in the bringing together under a single orderly system of concepts and relationships facts and observations that would otherwise be disconnected. Here I shall distinguish two basic types of explanation in science which I shall call respectively (a) explanation in breadth, and (b) explanation in depth. The former seeks an answer to the question: what-goes-with-what? That is to say, concepts of the same type or level are brought into relationship with one another. This relationship may be either statistical, as when nothing more than a contingent association between the two entities is asserted, or it may be causal, either in the weaker historical sense of the one being a causal antecedent of the other or in the tighter nomothetic sense of the connection being necessitated by some general law. In the case of (b), an explanation in depth, concepts of one type or level are brought into a relationship with concepts belonging to a different type or level. Here we are looking for an answer to the question: what-underlies-what? In this case the lower level concept constitutes an explanation of the higher level concept. Sometimes the lower level concept is a pure hypothetical construct that may have no correspondence to anything empirically identifiable; sometimes, however, it can be identified with some entity that can be observed at a different level of observation. When this latter situation obtains we are entitled to speak of a full reductive explanation being achieved. The point is, however, that both basic types of explanation, in breadth or in depth, are indispensable in their appropriate contexts and both are to be found in every branch of science, physical, biological or behavioural, although depth-explanations, being characteristic of the more advanced sciences, are usually thought of as being the ideal type of explanation in science.

These, then, in very broad outline, are the major categories of explanation used in science on which hypotheses can be based and predictions made. In the psychological sciences, physiological psychology provides the main locus for explanations in depth although hypothetical constructs are used freely in various fields of psychological inquiry. In general, however, we shall expect to find the emphasis placed on explanations in breadth and, in a few cases, of which the Skinnerian school of operant conditioning is probably the most salient example, this is the only type of explanation recognised and all theoretical commitments as to the nature of the organism itself are sedulously avoided. But this is unusual. For the most part psychologists consider that their theorising has been most successful when it can be firmly anchored in the known facts of brain physiology.

We have now discussed both the question of what psychology is supposed to be about and the question of what it must accomplish to qualify as a science. We are ready, therefore, to consider the sceptical objections that purport to show either that psychology cannot be a science or, if it is a science, then it is not psychological! At first it may seem that such objections are frivolous; the fact is that a presumptive scientific psychology has now been part of the academic scene for so long that few people, other than professional philosophers, bother to question its credentials. Yet the rapid rise of an autonomous science of psychology at the end of last century represented a revolution in Western thought which it would be unwise, even now, to take for granted. Science, after all, had been developed to deal with the physical world. It is true that the 19th century also witnessed the rise of the social sciences, notably sociology and economics, but these were non-experimental sciences and could hardly constitute much of a precedent for the new psychology which, in emulation of physiology, claimed to be a laboratory science, rigorous, deterministic and exact. It was the feasibility of such a science as this that aroused so much controversy among the learned men of the time. Few doubted that a science of the brain was a perfectly legitimate objective, indeed an impressive start had already been made in that direction, and it could be assumed that by means of it a reductive explanation of complex behaviour patterns or of subjective mental processes might eventually be achieved in terms of the brain mechanisms through which they were mediated. But an independent psychological science was quite another matter; Helmholtz, the foremost physiologist of his day, whose great work, the *Physiological Optics*, consists in large part of what we would today call perceptual psychology, saw no need for such a discipline, which his pupil Wundt was then in process of trying to establish.[2]

As for the philosophers, they were deeply divided on the issue. In general, those who belonged to the Empiricist-Associationist tradition, like Spencer or John Stuart Mill, were sympathetic to the idea; those belonging to the Idealist-anti-Associationist tradition, like Green or Bradley, were openly hostile. Here we shall not attempt to follow the debate as it was waged between these two opposed and irreconcilable schools with their totally different conceptions of mind—the terms of that debate are no longer of relevance today—but an imposing body of recent philosophical literature testifies to the fact that opposition to the idea of a scientific psychology is by no means a dead letter.[3] It will, I believe, repay us if, at the outset of our inquiry, we examine some of the more persistent objections that have been voiced against the claim that human behaviour can, in anything more than a trivial or superficial sense, be the object of scientific investigation. In what follows I have attempted to extract what I take to be the most serious objections. No attempt is made to attribute them to particular authorities; I have preferred to state them in my own way as cogently and concisely as I can. For convenience I have given each a label and, after enumerating them all, I will, in my next section, examine each in turn.

(1)   The Teleological Argument

Science is deterministic in its mode of reasoning since only deterministic assumptions give us the licence to make predictions, and this we have already taken to be a distinguishing feature of scientific explanation in general. Even the weaker probabilistic prediction normally presupposes an underlying deterministic framework, the distinction being only with regard to the greater area of ignorance which it implies. Now the salient fact about animal behaviour in general is that it is adaptive, purposive and meaningful. It follows that it can be understood only in terms of the ends that it is designed or adapted to bring about, never in terms of the causes that may have brought it into being. The point is perhaps most clearly expressed in the distinction between an 'action', defined as the minimum intelligible unit of behaviour, and a 'movement', defined purely as a sequence of events in space and time. To perform an action it is of course necessary to make *some* movement but this can be any one of an indefinite range, since the action is defined in terms of its goal, not in terms of the specific path taken to reach that goal. A sufficient explanation of a movement is given once the forces acting upon the object in motion have been fully specified; a sufficient explanation of an action is given when the goal to which it is directed has been ascertained. In short, whereas a movement demands a causal explanation, an action demands a teleological explanation. But this is not to say that we can never predict in advance that a given action will ensue; if the situation is a familiar one we can often predict correctly on inductive grounds what the other person is going to do. The point is that such prediction is not the same as that which figures in a deterministic science where it follows deductively from some theory.

It is important to realise that the argument we have just stated does not, as is sometimes supposed, amount to a refutation of determinism, the doctrine that all events follow necessarily from prior events, on the grounds that actions, at any rate, are not determined. For actions are not, as such, events but rather ways of describing certain classes of events. Conceivably, an omniscient physiologist (that convenient fiction) knowing the state of my nervous system at some given instant could correctly predict, on deterministic principles, that I would execute a certain movement. And, given the context in which this movement will occur, I would be entitled to describe it as, say, the action of picking up a pencil. In this sense the action would have been predicted and determinism vindicated. Nevertheless, on a conceptual level, actions and movements are mutually exclusive: when one focuses on the one the other disappears. It follows that, inasmuch as psychology is concerned with actions, it cannot be a strictly deterministic science; inasmuch as it is concerned with the physiological processes associated with actions, it ceases to be psychological.

(2) The Rationality Argument

The Teleological argument is meant to apply not just to human actions but to those of animals as well. The Rationality argument applies uniquely to human actions where it can be assumed that the agent understands what he is trying to do, where he can recognise when he has achieved his aim and, in particular, where he can if called upon to do so justify his action as the appropriate one for bringing about the ends he intended. Now the reason why this subclass of actions presents additional arguments against the possibility of a deterministic analysis is that in this case the action is obviously governed by certain acknowledged rules and is designed to satisfy certain well developed criteria. We cannot, for example, explain the actions of a skilled workman without reference to the requirements of his craft. To try and explain such actions in any other way, more especially in the sort of way we would apply to purely physical processes, would be to void the action of its meaning. Rational actions, we may conclude, demand rational, i.e. non-causal, explanations.

(3) The Free Will Argument

Neither of the two preceding arguments strikes at the root of determinism; their aim is to show only that causal explanations are incompatible with a meaningful interpretation of actions. If, however, there are, as some philosophers would claim, genuinely free actions, in the strong contra-causal sense, then deterministic science faces yet another barrier inasmuch as the ultimate cause of such an action resides in the free decision, volition or intention of the agent to perform that action. The case for supposing that there are any actions that are free or undetermined in this sense rests largely on the claim that we know intuitively that we are free to perform this rather than that action. It is also sometimes further claimed (and as often contested) that such freedom is a necessary assumption if we are to retain the concept of moral responsibility, since if our actions were in fact determined by extraneous forces we could no longer be held responsible for them.

All rational actions, we may suppose, are free, though not all free actions will be rational since my freedom includes the possibility of my performing some manifestly non-rational or even irrational action. It is noteworthy, but often ignored by the defenders of determinism, that free actions do not need to be unpredictable. A man playing chess is acting both rationally and freely. Yet, knowing the situation on the board and knowing my opponent to be a strong player, I might well be able to predict that he will mate me in a given number of moves. My prediction here, however, is based on the logic of the situation; it is not based upon causal factors of the kind that an objective science seeks to establish. The fact that the player chose the most rational move, and that we expected him to choose it, does not make his choice any the less free.

Care must be taken to distinguish between 'free' actions, in this strong sense, and mere voluntary actions. Every action is voluntary, in the sense of being composed of voluntary movements; an involuntary movement such as a knee-jerk would not be called an action. And there are perfectly good objective criteria for distinguishing between voluntary and involuntary movements and adequate grounds therefore for saying, in the case of an animal, that it is performing some voluntary action. But it would not generally be conceded that an animal can exercise free will since an animal lacks the conceptual capacity presupposed when we attribute responsibility to an agent.

(4) The Argument from Socio-Cultural Relativism

An experimental science of animal behaviour is unobjectionable because the experimenter has the power of selection or control over the relevant variables, i.e. the innate characteristics of the organism, the properties of the external environment, etc. Man, however, is first and foremost a social being; his every thought and action reflects the society in which he has been reared and the cultural influences to which he has been exposed. Human behaviour, accordingly, can be understood only within its appropriate socio-cultural context and each action must be seen in its correct historical perspective. But neither the historical process nor the social milieu is open to experimental manipulation. It follows that, except with regard to certain primordial psycho-physiological processes which we share with the lower animals, the idea of an experimental science of human behaviour is a chimera. Psychology can never become a natural science, it is at best a social or an historical science.

(5) The Argument from the Uniqueness of Personality

The foregoing argument can now be taken one step further. Not only is man the product of certain unique historico-cultural factors but he is in himself the possessor of a unique mental history and a unique personality. Science, however, is necessarily indifferent to the unique particular as it is to the unique occasion. Its concern is with lawful regularities and repeatable effects. Faced with individual variation science can only take refuge in the statistical norm. So long as we are entitled to treat individual differences as trivial or irrelevant, as we can in most animal experimentation, a statistical analysis is perfectly in order. But, in all that concerns human beings, differences are all-important; the average man may or may not be a useful fiction in economics but he has no place in a humanistic psychology. Human behaviour may provide the data for biography; it cannot provide the data for an experimental science.

(6) The Interaction Paradox

A necessary precondition of the experimental method is that the phenomenon being investigated should not be materially affected by the procedure used to investigate it. With animals this condition by and large appears to be satisfied. This is not to say that we are entitled to extrapolate from the behaviour of the animal under the artificial conditions of the laboratory to its behaviour in the wild but, at any rate, we can generally assume that our findings have not been influenced by the fact that our subject knew he was being used as a 'guinea-pig'. No such assumption is possible, unfortunately, with human subjects. At best the human subject may be kept in the dark about the real purpose of the experiment but it is virtually impossible to conceal from him that he is participating in an experiment. He knows this is so and the experimenter equally knows that he knows. The result is a typical game-situation of the two-person kind and is quite unlike the observer-object relationship that obtains in the typical experimental paradigm of the natural sciences. It follows that what emerges from a psychological experiment is a fact about a particular interpersonal encounter rather than a fact about the subject's behaviour as such. And the more subtle and sophisticated the behaviour we are concerned with the more it will be liable to become distorted by the experimental treatment.

(7) Two Sceptical Objections

A. All important facts about human nature have, over the centuries, already been discovered and lie enshrined in the world's literature. There is, consequently, nothing left for a scientific psychology to discover other than details, trivialities or information of a quantitative kind.

B. Despite all that has been said and written we still know very little about human nature and are for the most part helpless when it comes to understanding why people behave as they do or to doing anything about it. However, the inherent complexities of the subject-matter coupled with the ethical restrictions that govern any attempt to experiment with people make it unreasonable to expect any help from the direction of scientific psychology. In the last resort we shall probably always have to fall back either on our own commonsense intuitions or on the insights of those creative writers who are capable of an imaginative understanding of the human condition.

This completes the list of objections that I propose to discuss. They do not add up to a demonstration that science cannot be brought to bear on human affairs or that an experimental psychology is an absurdity, but they do, I shall suggest, bring out certain important limitations which any future psychology must respect and they do indicate that the kind of a science that psychology can hope to become is different in certain important respects from that of the familiar natural sciences.[4]

Rejoinders

In my capacity as counsel for the defence the line I would favour would be to accept, by and large, the objections we have listed but to insist that they are directed against a conception of psychology which bears little relation to reality. They conjure up the spectre of an all-powerful science of man which is destined to rob our every action of its last semblance of spontaneity. While such a conception may be flattering to the psychologist, it remains a fantasy. As will, I think, become increasingly clear as our inquiry progresses, there is no such science; what we have instead is a more or less loosely knit collection of psychological sciences. Each is strictly limited with respect to its appropriate domain and with respect to its explanatory potentialities. Each rests upon a different set of pre-suppositions and exploits a different set of methods and procedures. Failure to recognise this situation accounts for most of the notorious controversies that have dominated psychological history and for the fact that, in place of a series of complementary sciences, one finds instead an array of embattled schools locked in mutual hostility and mutual incomprehension. Bearing this in mind, let us turn again to our seven objections and examine them each in turn.

1. Our first two objections represent conceptual difficulties. On

the whole they have in recent years been overplayed by the philosophers while the psychologists themselves have not taken them
sufficiently seriously. The first point to note about the Teleological
argument is that it is by no means restricted to the realm of
behaviour. Basically, what it is concerned with is the familiar
distinction between a 'why-question' and a 'how-question' and the
fact that an answer to the former must not be confused with an
answer to the latter, and conversely. Now a 'why-question' is
appropriate in many contexts besides that of behaviour. Perhaps
the clearest example of teleological analysis in science is to be found
in connection with evolutionary biology. Here the why-question
is answered when we identify the particular advantage accruing to
a species by the evolution of some new characteristic. This does
not of course preclude us from asking about the biological
mechanisms by means of which this adaptation was possible, which
is a causal question, but it is no less legitimate. What applies in
biology applies equally in engineering. Before we can sensibly
attempt to explain *how* a particular machine works we want to
know what it is *for*, that is to say what function it was designed
to fulfil.[5] When it comes to behaviour the teleological argument is
perfectly right when it stresses that the primary question to ask
about any given meaningful action is the why-question; if we
understand why a particular action was performed then we understand its meaning *qua* action. But of course this by no means
exhausts all the questions we might want to ask about a given
action. We might ask, for example, what were the necessary preconditions which made the action possible? In what circumstances
would one expect it to occur? An action, after all, is never an
isolated event. It takes place along with other events which delimit
it or circumscribe it. It follows that there is much more to the
explanation of an action than merely identifying its purpose as the
teleological objection would seem to imply.

What, I suggest, makes the philosophers uneasy is that when we
shift from the why-question to the how-question we no longer seem
to be asking a specifically psychological question. Very often the
relevant conditions which make possible the action turn out to be
physiological conditions with the result that we end by asking
physiological questions. This is true enough but it need not be
embarrassing. The psychologist who studies some behavioural
phenomenon does not abdicate when he attempts to coordinate his

findings with those of the physiologist. On the contrary he thereby achieves what many regard as the ultimate aim of any science: a reductive explanation. But the causal mechanisms involved are not by any means the only aspects of the action which interest the psychologist. An action may also be related to other actions; explanation in breadth may be sought as well as explanation in depth and, indeed, what we call a psychological type explanation is necessarily an explanation in breadth.

2. More subtle is the objection raised by the Rationality argument. For, on the one hand, there seems no reason why we should not inquire, concerning art, music, drama, religion, sport and so forth, how such activities originated, on what dispositions and abilities they depend for their continued existence, what satisfactions they afford their devotees, what functions they fulfil in the life of society as a whole and a host of similar questions. And if we can inquire into the history or sociology of such activities, we can discuss, surely, their psychology. On the other hand, these questions are all extrinsic to the activity in question; only when we discuss the activity in its own terms are we able to say anything that is of intrinsic interest. A special danger lies in supposing that in giving a psychological account of some activity we dispose of it in the sense that we no longer require to understand it from the inside. This is the well-known fallacy of 'psychologism', and the rationality argument is designed to put us on our guard against committing it.

Does this mean that psychology must abandon forthwith its claim to deal with rational activities and confine its attention to non-rational or pre-rational processes? Certainly the literature leaves us in no doubt that it is on this aspect of behaviour that psychology has had the most to say. Even if we consider only the field of cognitive psychology we shall find that it has been mainly concerned with the basic processes involved in perceiving, learning, remembering and thinking. But, as I shall try and show in a later chapter, there is reason to suppose that it can go further. In particular, the advent of the computer, and of its attendant computer sciences, has already brought about a radically new approach to the problem of rational behaviour. In the first place it has served as a reminder that a causal type of explanation is not by any means the only one which a scientific approach engenders. Such developments of applied mathematics as have given us cybernetics, information theory, game-theory and so on are clearly independent of the causal concepts that underlie the physical sciences. Of course these formal, mathematical sciences can tell us nothing about how people actually reason or solve problems or resolve conflicts, and so on, but they can be used to provide an ideal or standard against which actual human behaviour can be assessed and evaluated just as logic has traditionally provided the standard by which we validate deductive inferences.

Another consequence of the computer revolution is that we now no longer find ourselves the only rational creatures in the universe; our own artefacts have begun to compete with us on our own ground. The effect has been to liberate the concept of intelligence from an exclusive dependence on a living brain. The question we can now ask ourselves about some intelligent or skilled perform- ance is what would be required to program a computer which would be capable of a comparable performance? Simulation has thus become a species of explanation.[6] For example, if we were in a position to design an artificial intelligence having the power both to comprehend and produce correctly a natural language it is hard to see what more a psycholinguist could demand as evidence that we now understood the critical operations involved in the use of language.[7] We may conclude at any rate that science is not wholly irrelevant to the understanding of rational activities.

3. The Free Will controversy represents the archetypal unsolvable problem of the metaphysical kind and no attempt will here be made to offer a solution. Historically, however, it would probably be true to say that the libertarian objection has contributed more to the antipathy felt towards the idea of a psychological science, whether from theologian, philosopher or layman, than any of the other objections we have mentioned. Rightly or wrongly it was feared that if man ever came to be regarded as in all respects a proper object for scientific investigation and if his actions ever came to be regarded as, in principle, no less determined than the move- ments of inanimate physical objects, then the lynch-pin of our moral universe of praise and blame would have been removed. Moreover, even though one could never prove that determinism was true, each new success which the psychological scientist was able to chalk up would represent a further curtailment of the scope of our freedom.

These fears cannot be dismissed as the product merely of confused thinking. It is noteworthy, moreover, that those who have been most vociferous in advocating a scientific control of behaviour agree that their aims *are* incompatible with the assumption of free will. Since, however, they equate free will with such concepts as chance, caprice, indeterminacy, etc., they have no regrets in abandoning this assumption. There are also those who, anxious to have the best of both worlds, take comfort in the argument that there is a logical limit to the predictability of behaviour. This logical indeterminacy resides in the fact that I can always falsify any prediction made to my face about my future actions. Suppose, for example, a scientist could have exhaustive knowledge of the state of my nervous system at a given instant on the basis of which he could calculate what my behaviour would be during the next minute then, merely by enunciating his prediction in my hearing he would in some degree alter the state of my nervous system thereby upsetting the very calculations upon which the prediction was based.[8] In practice we know intuitively that such is the cussedness of human nature that such predictions are likely to be self-annulling. Yet this argument fails to get at the root of the malaise which the idea of determinism tends to arouse. For it is not the fear that in practice the scientist will one day be able to predict in detail our future actions which worries the libertarian, but rather the thought that the real determinants of our behaviour lie not within our mental life at all—not, that is, in our conscious wishes, desires, etc.—but rather in the various physical facts that govern these mental processes.

The issue often comes to a head in arguments about the nature of crime. Is crime an evil to be condemned or just a social illness which needs remedying? Those who take the 'progressive' line dismiss the moralistic attitude as no better than a pre-scientific superstition and differ among themselves only with respect to the relative emphasis they give to hereditary causes on the one hand or to social background on the other, whether the delinquent is to be regarded as a victim of his genes and his glands or of a rejecting home and a hostile society.[9] How far does this go towards disposing of the libertarian objection? Obviously it deals with only one very special kind of behaviour; moreover the determinants with which the criminologist is concerned determine only in a rather loose statistical sense. However, if predictability is possible for even one area of behaviour, where freedom of choice was once assumed to operate, it is presumably possible for others as well, and even if the level of probability is still low there is no reason why it should not increase. Suppose, therefore, to take a fanciful but not entirely unrealistic illustration, it could be shown that virtually one hundred per cent of adult males possessing an extra chromosome were given to acts of violence, or that some socio-psychological index enabled us to predict with almost one hundred per cent accuracy which six-year-olds would later develop criminal tendencies, would we still feel that man's moral autonomy was inviolate?

To sum up, the objection we have been discussing is less of an argument for doubting that a deterministic psychology is a possibility than a reason for hoping that it may fail or, at least, remain incomplete. Its appeal is based on our intuitions of freedom which are undoubtedly real enough but are not necessarily veridical. More-over, science has in the past often had to run counter to man's deep-seated intuitions. The objectivity of the secondary qualities had to be sacrificed to make possible a scientific account of perception, and science would have no more compunction in sacrificing our intuitions of freedom if this was necessary for the explanation of behaviour.

4 and 5. The next two objections are both directed at the idea of psychology as an experimental science and they can be taken together. Experimentation presupposes the possibility of situations which, for all practical purposes, are reproduceable. In the physical sciences this presents no problem. In the biological sciences a complication arises from the fact that no two specimens are identical but in practice there are well understood ways of allowing for this. In the human sciences, however, the whole concept of repeatability is open to question. In what sense can we assume that, even for the special purposes of the experiment, one human subject is inter-changeable with another? Can two separate occasions ever be truly comparable where human beings are concerned? It might be thought that the vast literature that has come into being on experimental psychology constitutes in itself an adequate answer to these doubts, but on second thoughts this may seem more doubtful. The bulk of this literature has very little to do with real life behaviour; it is con-cerned mainly with the basic psycho-physiological processes that

underlie behaviour. On the other hand, those studies that do claim to say something about real life, the work on personality development, the study of interpersonal behaviour, and so forth, are precisely those whose experimental basis is least secure.

These objections, as we have stated them, are deliberately overstated. Clearly there are many facets of human behaviour that are more or less invariant with respect to culture and history. Equally, while no two individuals are the same, people always have enough in common to make some generalisations tenable. Nevertheless these objections do serve to remind us of the danger in extrapolating from observations on people belonging to one particular society at one particular period of history to people of all societies at all periods, a danger that becomes the more serious the more the behaviour in question is susceptible to cultural influence. Likewise there are phenomena, the study of prodigies of one sort or another provides examples, where the whole interest rests on the fact that they are exceptional or unique and where the psychologist may have to settle for an intensive examination of the individual case instead of attempting to extract what may be valid in the general case. All the same, neither an extreme historicist nor an extreme idiographic position appears to be justifiable.

6. The interaction paradox raises an objection of a somewhat sophisticated kind, but the situation to which it draws attention is a familiar methodological headache. An experiment can be considered valid only so long as the phenomenon under investigation remains unaffected by the method of investigation. Where this condition does not hold we have to acknowledge that we are no longer dealing with a genuine natural phenomenon but with an effect that is at least partly of our own making. Perhaps the most celebrated instance of this paradox arose in quantum physics when it was realised that the behaviour of a particle was partly determined by the method used to observe it and the well known principle of uncertainty can be regarded as an attempt to cope with this state of affairs by showing that either the position or the velocity of the particle could be exactly determined, but not both. In psychology there are numerous situations where it becomes highly problematical as to what precisely is natural and what is artefactual. Does learning come about in the first instance as a result of differentially reinforcing blind trial-and-error responding or does it entail,

right from the start, a certain cognitive grasp of relationships? Critics of the trial-and-error theory were not slow to point out that if you confine your observations to rats inside Skinner-boxes or enclosed multiple-T-mazes you may well demonstrate trial-and-error learning, since you have virtually excluded any alternative kind of behaviour, but was your experiment a test of your theory or was it merely an illustration of what is meant by trial-and-error learning?

Now, when your subject is another human being like yourself instead of a laboratory animal, a new factor arises that still further increases the risk of forcing the issue by unwittingly allowing your own preconceptions to impose themselves on what takes place. The old quip about the analyst's patient who dreams the kind of dream that illustrates his analyst's theories has a moral that goes far beyond the pitfalls of psychoanalysis. It could, I think, be said without unfairness that every psychological laboratory tends to produce the results it expects. It was once thought that this was a danger peculiar to the practice of introspection and would disappear once psychology adopted objective methods. But, although the risk may be greatest where introspection is involved, since in that case subject and experimenter are, in a sense, the same person, it is now realised that bias is possible even with an ostensibly objective set-up.[10]

The fact is that the intrusion of bias is an extraordinarily subtle and elusive affair. We know, for example, that in any face-to-face situation far more is communicated than just the verbal message. The extent to which one person may be influenced or even indoctrinated by another in the course of a confrontation is always open to question. Much of the research on hypnosis now appears to be vitiated because the experimenter failed to consider the extent to which his own expectations plus the general 'demand characteristics' of the situation may have influenced the behaviour of his hypnotised subject [cf. Barber (1969)]. Even so this objection is not fatal. Bias may never be completely eliminable but it can be reduced. The use of the 'double-blind' technique is already mandatory for many experimental situations to which exception could be taken. Similarly, the deliberate use of deception in order to disguise from the subject the real aim of the experiment is already a common device of the social psychologist, although any too frequent reliance on such ruses is likely to backfire on the experimenter once word gets around. Finally the fact that one worker's findings must in the long run stand up to corroboration by other workers who will include critics as well as disciples provides science with its ultimate guarantee against personal bias and experimenter effects.

7. There remains for us to consider those objections that stem from a kind of commonsense scepticism about the pretensions of science to add anything important to our existing knowledge of what people are like. As I have suggested, such scepticism may take its stand on two opposing premises: on the one hand it may be said that we know so much already about human behaviour there is simply nothing left for a scientific psychology to do beyond dotting the i's and crossing the t's of this traditional wisdom; on the other hand it may be said that although there is so much we still do not know, the obstacles in the way of finding any definite answers are so formidable that we have got to be satisfied with our own conjectures. The first of these need not, I think, be taken too seriously as a reason for defeatism. It rests upon a confusion between two different kinds of knowledge. What might colloquially be described as knowledge of the human heart, such as we hope to derive from life or from literature, is not systematic knowledge of the kind which science seeks to establish and it carries with it no precise implications. There is, however, inevitably some overlap between traditional, commonsense or armchair psychology and laboratory psychology. As I have already pointed out, psychology has had to operate from a higher baseline than that of the physical sciences. Indeed it is debatable whether, during its century of existence as an independent science, psychology has yet discovered one single fact of any fundamental importance about human behaviour or the human mind. A great many facts have, during this same period, been discovered about the workings of the brain; whole regions of the brain whose functions were until recently unknown or misunderstood have been successfully charted. But the history of psychology, as distinct from the history of physiology, has been more a succession of shifting viewpoints than a series of revelations. Its most surprising development, that which we associate with the name of Freud, was unfortunately precisely the one that has least claim to be considered scientific. When, for example, Freud declared that all dreams are wish-fulfilments in disguise he really believed that he had made a genuine discovery. Modern dream research has shown this to be yet another non-discovery. Had he said that

some dreams are wish-fulfilments, his statement might have stood the test of time but would not have been particularly surprising or interesting. All too often psychologists have made their impact more by exaggerating to the point of paradox some unexceptionable claim than by disclosing some striking new fact. This is not to say that psychology is condemned for ever to choose between enunciating dull truisms or exciting falsehoods. It can profoundly affect man's image of himself. But it does so less by supplying him with a new set of facts than by forcing him to take a new point of view.

A much graver problem are the sheer practical difficulties that stand in the way of psychological progress. Consider, for example, the study of the emotions, surely a central topic for any understanding of man's mental life. As Koestler [1964] has recently had to remind us, there is no literature worthy of the name even on such a basic emotional response as that of weeping. The reason is not far to seek: the atmosphere of the laboratory is inherently antagonistic to the production of genuine emotion. Moreover, unlike conditioning, this is not an area in which one can profitably resort to the use of animals. And, if this is true of such basic responses as laughter and crying, the mind boggles at the thought of attempting to experiment on such subtle emotions as, let us say, falling in love. Perhaps the closest ingenuity has come to solving this dilemma is by using hypnotism to obtain hypnotically simulated emotions.

Or consider the purely ethical barriers which impede research. None of the really pressing social problems on which psychology might be expected to give a lead lend themselves to the sort of experimental manipulation that would be necessary before a scientific answer were forthcoming. Consider any of the controversial problems that are discussed daily in the press: How dangerous is it to permit the consumption of soft drugs? Does the exploitation of violence in the mass media contribute materially to the spread of violence in real life? Does a permissive upbringing contribute to the later alienation of youth from society or to student unrest? How can we best educate the young to foster their latent talents and creativity? Any of these questions (at any rate after they had been more precisely rephrased) could be settled by appropriate experiments even if some of them might take a rather long time to complete. Such experiments would not even require any special ingenuity to design. But although commissions are periodically set up to inquire into these problems, they cannot resort to experiment for the simple reason that this would demand an intolerable degree of interference in the lives of private citizens (the subjects would have to be conscripts rather than volunteers). No authority short of an absolute dictator would ever be in a position to do what was necessary.

Or consider the perennial controversy between hereditarians and environmentalists. This is not just an academic issue; it penetrates almost every psychological topic we shall consider as well as having important practical implications for education in connection with the use of intelligence tests, a topic that rarely fails to arouse strong feelings. I like sometimes to indulge in a daydream about some Brave New World where every pair of identical twins as soon as they were born became the property of the Ministry of Science. For we have known, ever since Galton, what must be done to disentangle the relative contributions of heredity and environment, namely to keep the hereditary component constant while varying the environment. What makes this a daydream is that our ethical code forbids us to treat human beings as if they were experimental animals. The result is that, while our knowledge of the genetics of behaviour in animals continues to increase, in the case of our own species the best we can hope for is the devious and elaborate application of statistical analyses to data culled from appropriately selected samples of the population.

So much, then, for the objections. Some were more serious than others but none could be dismissed as wholly frivolous. Their combined weight has, I hope, served as a salutary reminder of the sheer audacity which the idea of a psychological science implies. At the same time the point I have tried to bring out is that the idea is audacious, not fallacious.

How the Idea Took Effect

The eventual emergence of psychology as an independent empirical science from having been a branch of speculative philosophy was no doubt inevitable, given that faith in scientific method that is the mark of our civilisation, but the way it came about may be traced to a number of separate developments during the 19th century which in due course converged. Five of these call for special comment:

(1)   The growth of sensory physiology and psychophysics past the point where they could be conveniently contained within the framework of conventional physiology.

(2)   The Darwinian revolution which made it feasible to think of human behaviour in a biological context.

(3)   The emergence of a science of statistics especially as associated with the work of Galton.

(4)   The growing humanitarianism of the late Victorian era which gave a new urgency to the care and treatment of the sub-normal, the handicapped, the insane and other social misfits, thereby creating challenging fields of application for an aspiring psychological science.

(5)   The spread of hypnotism which, by the end of the century, had overcome the main opposition from orthodox medicine and which, in its train, had brought to light a whole new range of mental phenomena that upset traditional philosophical theories of mind.

We will proceed to consider each of these developments in turn.

1.   It has been aptly said that experimental psychology is the off-spring of a marriage between British philosophy and German physiology. Certainly the atomistic analysis of mind provided by the British Associationists of the 19th century from James Mill to Bain provided a convenient philosophical background for the work on the physiology of the sensations from Johannes Muller to Helm-holtz.[11] Three landmarks stand out on the road to Leipzig where, in 1879, Wundt established the first psychological laboratory: first, the publication in 1856 of the first volume of Helmholtz's *Physiological Optics*, a mine of information on the psychology of perception which even today has not yet been exhausted;[12] second, the publication in 1860 of Fechner's *Elements of Psychophysics* which some authorities take to be the true point of departure of the new psychology; and third, the publication in 1873-74 of the first edition of Wundt's *Physiological Psychology*, the first general text-book of the new psychology and, according to the late E. G. Boring,

'the most important book in the history of psychology'. It was the second of these that provides the key to the emergence of psychology as a separate discipline from physiology. Let us look, therefore, at what it was that Fechner was trying to do.

In its broadest sense psychophysics is concerned with the relationship between the objective properties of the external stimulus and their phenomenal representation in consciousness. In less technical terminology one could say that it is an attempt to provide a precise quantitative answer to the age-old problem of the relationship between reality and appearances. It must be distinguished both from the study of the mechanisms which mediate perception, which is the province of the neurophysiologist, and from the study of the specifically psychological factors that determine how we see the world which includes our past experience and present expectancies. In psychophysics we postulate a normal observer operating under ideal conditions and what we look for are the equations that express the way in which variations in the stimulus relate to variations in the perceptual experience. This science was the brain-child of one man alone, Gustav Fechner, mathematician, physicist and philosopher of pronounced mystical leanings. It was he who introduced the basic methods still in use today of testing a subject's powers of sensory discrimination and it was he who gave precision to the concepts of absolute and differential threshold with respect to a given sensory dimension. In particular, and this was in fact the crowning achievement of Fechnerian psychophysics, he showed that the subjective intensity of a sensation could be quantified if one took the just-noticeable-difference (j.n.d.) at any given point on the scale of physical intensities as the unit of subjective intensity. One could then express the subjective intensity of any given stimulus as the number of j.n.d.s above the absolute threshold (i.e. the point below which no conscious sensation is experienced). Proceeding on the basis of Weber's earlier discovery that the increment in physical intensity necessary to produce a discriminable difference is always a constant fraction (the Weber Ratio) of the physical intensity of the initial stimulus, Fechner went on to derive the 'Weber-Fechner Law', as it is now known, which states that 'the subjective intensity of a stimulus increases as the logarithm of its physical intensity', or $S = k \log R$ where R is the physical intensity, taking the absolute threshold as unity, k is the appropriate Weber fraction and S is the subjective intensity.

The Weber-Fechner Law is no longer sacrosanct. It was always thought to be suspect as regards the upper and lower limits of the scale and in recent times it has been superseded by other laws of sensory scaling that do not depend on the dubious assumption of the additivity of j.n.d.s.[13] Historically, however, it would be hard to exaggerate the importance of this law in promoting belief in the possibility of a psychology that could be at once lawful, experimental and quantitatively exact. In passing, we may note that Fechner, in his *Vorschule der Aesthetik* of 1876, was also the sole founder of experimental aesthetics where he extended the methods of psychophysics to deal with form preferences, especially in connection with the problem of ideal proportions of rectangles or other geometric shapes. Fechner, however, went no further than to lay the foundations for the new psychology. He himself was more interested in the philosophical implications of his work, believing, as he did, that it held the key to the mystery of the relationship between mind and matter, a mystery which he sought to solve in terms of a 'pan-psychism', the view that there is a psychic component to every physical process in nature. It was left to Wilhelm Wundt to build on the Fechnerian foundations and, in doing so, make the new psychology a going concern.

Wundt was a physiologist by training who had worked under Helmholtz at Heidelberg but who, unlike his master, harboured strong philosophical leanings. Eventually, in 1875, he was appointed to the Chair of Philosophy at Leipzig and it was there, four years later, that he set up his historic laboratory and, in 1881, founded the first journal to be devoted exclusively to experimental psychology which provided a forum for the work of the laboratory: the *Philosophische Studien*. Wundt was a man of prodigious productivity. His published output, which is said to exceed that of any other psychologist, extends over a wide range of topics, many of them far removed from the preoccupations of the laboratory. Throughout a very long career he dominated the new psychology, often in a high-handed dictatorial manner. But his determination and initiative bore fruit and within a few years similar laboratories sprang up at many other German universities, usually with his own pupils occupying the Chair.[14] It was not long, moreover, before his example caught on in the United States, where laboratories were started by Americans who had learnt their trade in Germany.[15] Britain was much slower to respond although it was an Englishman, Titchener, who became the most renowned exponent of Wundtian psychology in America from his centre at Cornell. But, by the close of the century, experimental psychology had become an accepted feature of academic life at most of the major seats of learning in Europe and America.

Apart from the psychophysics of the sense-modalities, especially of vision, two other areas of research feature prominently in the work of the early laboratories: (a) the introspective analysis of experience including feelings and emotions, and (b) the study of reaction times. It was the former, which we shall be considering more in detail in the next chapter, which was the most distinctive feature of the Wundtian school as it was also the one that invited the most criticism and even derision from his contemporaries but, given the view of psychology which he held, this emphasis on introspection was entirely rational. As Wundt himself put it: 'Psychology has to investigate that which we call internal experience—i.e. our own sensations and feelings, our thought and volition—in contradistinction to the objects of external experience which form the subject-matter of natural science.' Like the modern 'Identity Theorist', he regarded conscious mental events as, at bottom, identical with their corresponding brain-processes but knowable in a different way or from a different angle. Hence, in the last resort, physics and psychology were complementary sciences: the primary data of each consist of sense experiences but whereas physical observation treats them as referring to events in the external world, introspection concentrates on the experiences themselves and attempts to analyse their composition. Wundt took a basically Humean view of mind, but where he went far beyond Hume or any of the philosophical Empiricists was in the relentless rigour with which he and his pupils actually practised introspective analysis. That, in the end, little of any permanent scientific or philosophical importance came of this endeavour cannot detract from the Herculean nature of the undertaking.

In comparison, the study of reaction times was something of a side issue. It all started with the discovery of individual differences in the observation of stellar transits. It was the astronomer Bessel who, in 1822, first drew attention to this source of error and discussed ways of combating it. Then, in 1850, Helmholtz succeeded in making the first measurement of the speed of a nerve-impulse which showed that, contrary to what was commonly supposed as a result of the misleading analogy of electrical conduction along a wire, this speed was remarkable for its slowness (less than 100 feet per second) though the actual speed varied somewhat depending on the particular type of nerve fibre involved. It followed that the minimum time required to elicit some response to a stimulus would be of an appreciable duration. In fact, as we now know, most of this interval is occupied by the transmission of the nerve impulse across the synapses that link one neurone to another rather than along the axons of the neurones themselves, but that is by the way. The point is that if minimal reaction-times could be empirically established to different kinds of stimulation it was hoped that a complete chronometry of mental processes could be worked out, ranging from simple reflexes up to complex cognitive tasks. The complexity of the task could then be measured as a function of the increasing latency of the response.[16] In fact this chronometric approach proved on the whole to be yet another abortive attempt to objectify the data of psychology based on oversimplified assumptions. Yet reaction times still have an important if modest part to play in the present day laboratory in research on information processing and perceptuo-motor skills.

At first little attention was paid to what were eventually to become the central topics of experimental psychology: learning, remembering, thinking, or what, in general, are called the higher mental processes. Wundt, himself, was sceptical about what could be accomplished in this direction along strictly experimental lines and although he wrote about them at length it was not in his capacity as an experimentalist. The notable exception at the time was Hermann Ebbinghaus who, after reading Fechner's *Elements*, decided that quantitative methods could equally be applied to the study of memory. He thereupon single-handed, using himself as his own subject, set about investigating the basic laws of retention and forgetting. As his unit of quantification he introduced his celebrated nonsense syllables (consonant-vowel-consonant) which he considered to be neutral and interchangeable verbal items which also had the advantage of being pronounceable. With these he proceeded to plot the now familiar curve of acquisition as a function of the number of presentations and the curve of forgetting as a function of the time elapsed since learning. He discusses the now standard methods of measuring memory such as 'the method of recall' and the 'method of recognition' and he also introduced the very sensitive 'method of savings' which makes it possible to measure retention in terms of the reduced number of trials needed to relearn some given material. His monograph on memory, which he published in 1885,[17] became at once the classic work on verbal learning and rote-memory, and the nonsense syllable has still by no means exhausted its usefulness.

2. Darwinism produced a number of rather different repercussions on the development of psychology. In the first place it gave birth to the new science of comparative psychology. Although Darwin's own work had mainly been concerned with the problems of comparative anatomy, both his *Descent of Man* of 1871 and, still more, his *Expression of the Emotions in Man and Animal* of 1874 dealt, in part at least, with problems of comparative behaviour. But, even before the publication of the *Origin of Species* in 1859, Spencer, in his *Principles of Psychology* of 1855, had already purveyed an evolutionary approach to human behaviour, an approach he was to take much further in the revised edition of his book of 1870-72. The Darwinian initiative was carried forward by such eminent British naturalists as Romanes and Lloyd Morgan, about whom we shall have more to say in a later chapter.

With the advent of a comparative psychology the case for regarding introspection as the *sine qua non* of psychology became harder to sustain. The way was thus open to the rise of Behaviourism which, after World War I, became the dominant school of psychology in America at a time when America was wresting from Germany the leadership in experimental psychology. Although Wundt published lectures on 'Human and Animal Psychology' as early as 1863, he never considered it worth while to undertake research on animals. Probably the first *bona fide* psychologist to conceive the idea of bringing animals into the psychological laboratory was the American, E. L. Thorndike, whose work antedates by a few years that of his Russian contemporary, Pavlov. But, whereas Pavlov never claimed to be other than a physiologist, whose technique of conditioning was supposed to be a means of finding out about the functions of the cerebral cortex, Thorndike was primarily an educational psychologist who studied cats struggling to get out of puzzle-boxes because he believed that this set-up represented a simple but generally valid paradigm of the learning process.[18] The combination of Thorndikean trial-and-error and Pavlovian conditioning eventually provided Watson with the

scientific ammunition he needed to launch the Behaviourist movement. Latterly, the influence of the European Ethologists has made
us more wary about extrapolating from one species to another or
from the artificial conditions of the laboratory to behaviour in the
natural environment, with the result that there has been reversion
to the naturalistic traditions of the early Darwinians. But, even
though Behaviourism was no more than a by-product of the Darwinian revolution, the whole subsequent trend towards making
psychology a predominantly biological science which brought about
such a dramatic shift in the original meaning of psychology is an
indubitable legacy of Darwinism.

One of the more immediate effects of the new biological orientation was to popularise the idea of human instinct. Traditionally,
a sharp distinction was drawn between animals who were essentially
creatures of instinct and man who was endowed with reason which
enabled him to choose between one course of action or another.
Although man could be swayed by his natural passions, in the
last resort these, too, were under the dominion of reason. The only
theory of motivation which enjoyed serious consideration up to
this time was the hedonistic theory according to which a man's
action was the outcome of his effort to maximise his pleasures or
minimise his pains. Now, in the aftermath of Darwin, the question
was raised as to whether reason and intelligence played more than
a superficial part in shaping men's lives and whether there might
not be deep-seated biological forces outside conscious awareness and
control that really determined the overriding goal towards which
we strove. It was William McDougall who took this idea to its
furthest limits (and some would say to its *reductio ad absurdum*).
He was a medical man by training, strongly influenced by Darwinian teaching, and he became the first person to practise the
new experimental psychology in Britain. He proposed what he
called a 'hormic' theory of motivation to replace classical hedonism
and he attempted to identify an instinctual basis underlying every
major human activity as well as every principal emotion and sentiment.[19]

Instinct theory was vehemently repudiated by the Behaviourists
who reverted to the extreme environmentalism of Locke and the
Associationists. Apart from certain innate reflexes, everything in
mammalian behaviour was to be accounted for henceforth in terms
of conditioning. But the concept of instinct has proved more durable

than it once seemed. The influence of ethology has done much to counteract the tenets of behaviourism, and what might be loosely called the 'naked ape' school of human ethologists has been vocal in holding that our animal inheritance cannot so easily be ignored when it comes to understanding such matters as the role of aggression in human society. Hence, even though the theories of McDougall are now only of historic interest, the once popular notion that human nature was infinitely pliable now looks like dangerous utopianism.

Darwinism was also the inspiration behind the first of the psychological schools to challenge the supremacy of Wundtian Introspectionism, namely the American school of Functionalism whose chief spokesman was William James. James was the first to introduce experimental psychology into America, in fact the laboratory which he started when he was still a lecturer in physiology at the Harvard Medical School antedates even Wundt's own laboratory in Leipzig; but in the end he rebelled against the narrowness of what he called the School of 'Structuralism' on account of its preoccupation with the structure of consciousness. The prime fact about behaviour was that it was adaptive and to understand it the first requirement was to find out what *function* it fulfilled in the life of the individual or of the species. Consciousness itself, he insisted, must have originally emerged, at some point in evolution, to fulfil some particular function; it could not be reasonably conceived as a superfluous appendage of the brain, as the epiphenomenalists wanted us to believe.

3. Statistics could be called the charter of the inexact sciences. Certainly, psychology as we know it would have been unthinkable without its statistical apparatus. There are in fact several different ways in which statistics enters into psychological discourse. In the first place, the kind of variables which the psychologist deals with—abilities, traits, attitudes, dispositions and the like—are, from the metrical standpoint, inherently fuzzy concepts. All measurement, of whatever sort, is subject to a certain understood margin of error, but whereas in the physical sciences this error is assumed to arise from the actual operation of measuring, in the behavioural sciences, in addition to the unreliabilities of the measuring instruments themselves, the variables being measured are assumed to fluctuate constantly in a random fashion. In the second place,

psychological laws, such as they are, always express tendencies, never uniformities. In elementary mechanics, for example, it would be ridiculous if we were to say that longer pendulums *tend* to have longer periods than shorter pendulums because of course we can express the duration of the period as an *exact* function of the length of the pendulum given the gravitational constant. In the behavioural sciences, on the contrary, exact functional dependence has to be replaced with probabilistic concepts such as correlation and contingency. Finally, whereas in physics a prediction can usually be confirmed in an all-or-nothing fashion according to some critical observation, it is a characteristic of all the inexact sciences (medicine and agriculture no less than psychology) that hypotheses can be confirmed only to a certain level of confidence equivalent to the odds against the particular result of the experiment having been due purely to chance.

Statistics may be regarded as the practical application of probability theory to empirical data. At the beginning of the 19th century probability theory had already reached a high level of development. Gauss worked out the mathematics of what we now call the 'Normal Distribution' or 'Gaussian Curve of Error', showing its relationship to the familiar binomial distribution and arguing that random errors of observation or measurement in science should tend to distribute themselves around their true mean according to this bell-shaped curve. But it was a Belgian astronomer, Quetelet, who first applied the concept of the normal curve to biometric data and demonstrated that such variables as the height or chest-girth of army recruits did in fact conform to the normal distribution. When Galton came along, with his passionate interest in quantifying individual differences, especially variations in ability, he reasoned that such a characteristic as intellectual ability should distribute itself normally over the general population with genius representing the upper tail-end of the curve and imbecility the lower. Galton then went on to take an even more important step in the application of statistics to mental testing. Given two variables, each of which was normally distributed around its respective mean, it was possible to estimate the degree to which these variables co-varied and express this as a correlation coefficient having a value between zero and one. Knowing to what extent two variables were correlated one could then, given some specific measurement, say the mean intelligence of a set of fathers, predict the most likely value for the mean intelligence of their sons. It was not, however, until the 20th century that the tests of significance now in use in psychology were introduced. These were largely the work of R. A. Fisher who was attached to the Rothamsted agricultural laboratories.

4. New sciences as often arise in response to new practical needs as to new theoretical developments. The awakening of the social conscience during the 19th century, which was to find expression in so much new legislation for the benefit of the weak and defence-less, had important repercussions for our present theme. After so many triumphant demonstrations of the power of science and technology to alleviate the lot of man, it was likely that some thought would be given as to what science might be able to do for the social misfit and the victim of natural disabilities. Medicine began to extend its scope to the diagnosis and treatment of the mentally sick and, before long, mental testers were attempting to detect as early as possible those whose innate deficiencies would make them incapable of benefiting from ordinary schooling. In our own time applied psychology and mental testing has extended to every major arena of social life, to industry, commerce, admini-stration, etc.

5. I have left to last the strangest development of all: the story of hypnotism, as it unfolded in the century between Mesmer and Charcot. This was a development which took place entirely outside the confines of official science and medicine, was beset with tragic misunderstandings, was continually exploited by the unscrupulous and yet, in spite of it all, probably did more to extend the concept of mind than any of the previous developments that we have dis-cussed. It revealed, in the first place, the extraordinary power which mere suggestion can, given the right conditions, exercise on the behaviour of an individual and the extent to which it can temporarily transform his consciousness. The whole idea of the unconscious which, for good or ill, has been such a powerful influence in modern psychological thought would never have got off the ground had it not been for the bizarre discoveries of the hypnotists, with their secondary personalities, dissociated states, motor automatisms and the like. In effect: no Mesmer, no Freud. We may also note, in anticipation of our final chapter, that it was in the practice of hypnotism, especially during its early mesmerist

phase, that parapsychological phenomena were first reported under controlled conditions.

The diverse origins of modern psychology are in line with its inherently diversified character. At the present time psychological research is cultivated under a wide variety of auspices, makes use of a wide variety of specialist techniques and pursues a variety of problems that seem to bear little relationship to one another or to any wider conceptual scheme. The one thread that unites all these separate inquiries is a belief in the value of the empirical approach and in the virtue of trying to think scientifically about human beings.

Notes

1   Yet one should not be too dogmatic even about this. After making this statement I came across the following passage written by a biologist: 'The idea of an extreme dichotomy that sets insects so far apart from vertebrates as to be qualitatively different is founded as much on a fear of anthropomorphism ... as on a paucity of data. Perhaps these insects are little machines in a deep sleep but, looking at their rigidly armoured bodies, their staring eyes and their mute performances, one cannot help at times wondering whether there is anyone inside.' [Dethier (1964)]

2   *See* Boring [1950] p. 297. 'Unlike Wundt, Helmholtz held no brief for the formal establishment of psychology as an independent science, nevertheless the weight of his work and the effect of his prestige were such as to make him, with Wundt and Fechner, a "founder" of the new science.'

3   *Cf.* Hearnshaw [1964] p. 211. 'It was, we may surmise, the doubts and inhibitions engendered by this long philosophical debate during the first half of the twentieth century which retarded the development of British psychology and blocked its academic growth.' For example, R. G. Collingwood, a latter-day Idealist, considered that psychology should concern itself exclusively with 'sensations, appetite and the emotions' or else with 'Freudian or other forms of treatment'. At all events, psychology could never be the science of mind since that title was pre-empted by logic, by

ethics and, above all, by history, conceived in its Collingwoodian sense as the 'self-knowledge of mind'. To pretend otherwise was to make of psychology 'the fashionable scientific fraud of the age'. [Collingwood (1939)]

Another Oxford philosopher who, as it happens, was Collingwood's successor in the Wayneflete Chair of Metaphysics, though belonging to a quite different school of philosophy was no less sceptical of the pretensions of psychology. Thus, Gilbert Ryle regretted that the word psychology had not been restricted to its medical applications, especially to those associated with 'its one man of genius: Freud'. Psychologists, he argued, had no business trying to explain normal behaviour and should stick to aberrations: 'Let the psychologist tell us why we are deceived; but we can tell ourselves and him why we are not deceived.' [Ryle (1949) Chap. 10, 'Psychology'] Nevertheless, his characterisation of psychology as 'a partly fortuitous federation of inquiries and techniques' consorts well enough with the plan of this book.

Wittgenstein's much quoted aphorism that 'in psychology there are experimental methods and conceptual confusions' [Wittgenstein (1953) II, xiv] has been a recurrent motif among his followers, cf. Hamlyn [1953], Peters [1958], Louch [1966], Mischel [1969]. Taylor [1964] makes a bold bid to defend teleology as the basic type of explanation in the behavioural sciences. His book reveals an acquaintance with the experimental literature unusual in a philosophical work.

4 It is by no means only the philosophers who have questioned the pretensions of scientific psychology; latterly not a few psychologists, after a lifetime spent in the laboratory, have taken to confessing their doubts and perplexities. One such case is Joynson [1970], [1974], but perhaps the most striking case of all is that of Sigmund Koch. For the first ten years of his career, he tells us, he was an enthusiastic follower of Hull: 'a dauntless and virile rat-runner concentrating on the differential testing of rival theories of learning'. Then, at the behest of the American Psychological Association, he undertook to edit the multi-volume compilation entitled *Psychology: The Study of a Science*. [Koch (1959/1963)] He emerged from these labours purged of his enthusiasm not only for Hull, whose system he had already criticised exhaustively [Koch (1954)], but for all behaviouristic psychology and even for

the whole conception of psychology as a science: 'I think it is by
this time utterly and finally clear that psychology cannot be a
coherent science, or indeed a coherent field of scholarship, in any
specifiable sense of coherence that can bear upon a field of inquiry.'
[Koch (1974)] The long delayed seventh volume of his *Psychology*,
which he had undertaken to write himself, is meanwhile awaited
with some apprehension! While I do not wish to be associated with
his more nihilistic conclusions I do find myself in some sympathy
with his plea for the essential diversity of psychological knowledge:
'Students should no longer be tricked by a terminological rhetoric
into the belief that they are studying a single discipline ...' [*idem*]

5   The point has been argued at length by Polanyi [1958] Chap. 11.

6   *Cf.* Fodor [1968], Part 4, 'The Logic of Simulation'.

7   Whether it will ever be possible to simulate, in the strong sense
of the term, any of our higher mental faculties, let alone our
capacity to use natural language, is still a matter of fierce controversy. Dreyfus [1972] argues from the inherently holistic nature
of mental processes that any attempt to translate them into programs
for digital computers is bound to end in failure. Meanwhile, however, machine-intelligence enthusiasts show no more sign of pay-
ing attention to the doubts of the philosophers than did the original
pioneers of experimental psychology.

8   This particular solution of the free will problem has been advocated by MacKay [1960] who is himself a notable authority on
computer simulation.

9   It is not so often that one hears the determinist argument applied
to meritorious behaviour, but a consistent determinist, like Skinner
[1971], readily admits that praise is just as meaningless as censure
however useful it may be as a means of reinforcing behaviour.

10   *Cf.* Rosenthal [1966]. Although some of Rosenthal's own
evidence for unwitting experimenter effects has in turn been
severely criticised by Barber and Silver [1968], there can be no
doubt that his work created something of an upheaval in psychology
and has led to a new level of methodological sophistication.

11 'The Germans knew how the receptors worked; the British knew why they were important. Given the positivistic spirit of the times it was inevitable that the two lines of thought should converge. When this happened, psychology became a science.' [Miller (1964) p. 14]

12 'His *Physiological Optics* is still the most important work on the subject; indeed disappointingly little has been added since.' [Gregory (1966) p. 90]

13 For the modern approach to problems of sensory scaling *cf.* Stevens [1957] or Galanter [1962].

14 After Leipzig, some of the more important centres were: Göttingen (from 1881 under G. E. Müller), Berlin (from 1894 under C. Stumpf) and Würzburg (from 1894 under O. Külpe). But during this period there was still no sharp separation between experimental psychology and sensory physiology. Thus, E. Hering, best known as the champion of Nativism in perception in opposition to the dominant Empiricism of Helmholtz, occupied the Chair of Physiology at Prague between 1870 and 1895.

15 The laboratory at Johns Hopkins, Baltimore, founded by G. Stanley Hall in 1883, has been cited as the first of the American psychological laboratories. Other important centres in the United States were: Harvard (where James had in fact been engaged on experimental psychology since his appointment to a lectureship in physiology in 1876 and where, in 1892, he installed H. Münsterberg whom he specially brought over from Germany to run the laboratory), Yale (from 1892 under E. Scripture), Columbia (from 1891 under J. McK. Cattell) and Chicago (from 1894 under J. R. Angell). Garvey [1929] lists 117 American laboratories in order of their foundation and with the names of the first directors.

16 *See* 'The Timing of Mental Processes' in Humphrey [1968] pp. 285-90.

17 *See* Ebbinghaus [1964].

18 His influential monograph *Animal Intelligence* of 1898 was

his Ph.D. Thesis. It was later published in book form in an expanded version. [Thorndike (1911)] From 1901 to 1942 E. L. Thorndike was at Teachers College, Columbia, New York, where he established himself as a pioneer of mental testing as well as of learning-theory.

19 In his *Social Psychology* of 1908. This immensely popular work ran to many editions, the 28th was printed in 1946. [*see* McDougall (1946)]

CHAPTER ONE

Introspective Psychology

Although introspection has every right to be considered the psychological technique *par excellence*, it is arguable whether there exists any such thing as a distinctive introspective or phenomenological psychology. Such studies as appear to fall under this designation certainly appear to be lacking in one vital ingredient of a science, namely, any sort of theoretical or explanatory framework. Nevertheless, if only for historical reasons and because of the stress we have already laid on consciousness in defining the scope of psychological inquiry, we make no apology for commencing our review of the psychological sciences with a discussion of 'introspective psychology'.

It is common today, especially among philosophers, to dismiss introspective psychology as a misconception on the grand scale both as to the nature of experience and as to the rationale of psychology. It has even been suggested that the introspective psychologists were really performing a species of conceptual analysis under the delusion of engaging in empirical research. My own view, which I shall try to make clear in the course of this chapter, is that the failure to create a viable science of experience is due to empirical rather than logical reasons; that, whereas the *a priori* objections to introspection can, in general, be met, it is not so easy to justify pragmatically the attempt to produce a systematic analysis of consciousness.

Let us look briefly at some of these *a priori* objections which have been raised against the practice of introspection in particular over and above the general objections we have already considered against the idea of a psychological science. The most radical of these objections was simply that there was no such thing as a private inner world of experience to which each of us has a privileged access. What purports to be introspection, therefore, must either consist in observations of events in the external world, or at least inside the observer's body, or else deal with purely mythical and fictitious entities. This popular modern heresy is one which I have discussed elsewhere and which I regard as being entirely groundless. [*see* Beloff (1962) Chap. 2] Such plausibility as it can muster relies on our adopting a naïve-realist view of perception according to which perception is supposed to afford us direct knowledge of the external world. But, in fact, perceptual experience is no less subjective than any other kinds of experience and the only difference between observation and introspection lies in the ends they are made to subserve.

A somewhat less radical objection, one that has been made much of by behaviouristic psychologists, while not denying that we have inner experiences insists that these can never become the data of a science since science can deal only with what is public and objectively verifiable.[1] This objection would be valid, however, only if it were true that the experience of any one individual was not only private but had nothing at all in common with that of any other individual. And, of course, such is not the case, indeed it would be hard to conceive of a world in which this would be the case. The question therefore comes down in the end to one of inter-subjective agreement and there is no reason in principle why there should not be a measure of inter-subjective agreement between subjects exposed to similar stimulus conditions. There is, indeed, a subjective element in all observation though with the help of instrumentation and automation the physical sciences contrive to reduce this to a minimum. In the field of aesthetics, inter-subjective agreement is the only basis on which the expert can validate his own personal response to the work of art. It is true, however, that introspection, as practised by the founders of introspective psychology, is a methodologically deviant technique if only because it means that the role of subject and experimenter have to coalesce in the same individual, and such a situation is bound to be specially vulnerable to experimenter bias.

Another allied objection concerns the language used to describe subjective experience. Would this not entail a private language? Yet, as Wittgenstein insisted, a private language is a contradiction since words can only be learnt and understood with reference to the public world of the language users. [cf. Pears (1971) Chap. 8] And it is surely no accident that when we do try and talk about our sensations and feelings we tend to fall back on a public-object vocabulary; thus we may describe a headache as 'splitting', a noise as like dripping water, a texture as 'velvety', a scent as of heliotrope, etc. But too much can be made of this. Natural languages, after all, were evolved for practical reasons, not as vehicles for enabling introverted aesthetes to discuss the finer nuances of sensuous experience. Nevertheless, when a need arises in science a specialised technical vocaulary can always be devised. Those professionally concerned with colours or with smells have no trouble in devising such a vocabulary to cover the full range of discriminable hues or odours. Similarly musicians have developed a musical notation which in effect assigns a proper name to every discriminable interval along the pitch continuum. In brief, there is no reason to doubt that, so long as we have anything worth saying about our subjective experiences, we shall not be restricted by the limitations of language.

Finally, a minor objection of a more practical kind hinged on the question of whether introspection requires us to do two things at once: to undergo an experience and at the same time to examine and report on it. Such a task would certainly appear to be impossible in a literal sense and becomes the more absurd as the experience in question becomes more subtle and complex. This objection, however, was always admitted by the exponents of introspection. Titchener himself declared that 'introspective examination must be a post-mortem examination'; in other words, introspection was in fact retrospection. Of course this in turn raises fresh problems concerning the validity of memory, but the kinds of experience Titchener had in mind were those that could be produced under controlled laboratory conditions and so could be assumed to be repeatable where necessary.

It would seem, therefore, that none of the arguments so frequently cited to show that introspection is invalid for logical or conceptual reasons really stand up to analysis and the only question that really need concern us in what follows is whether the practice can be defended on pragmatic and scientific grounds.

Analytical Introspection

The earliest of the psychological schools, that which came to be known variously as 'Structuralism', 'Content Psychology' or, as I shall be calling it, 'Introspectionism', was an abortive attempt to create a pure science of consciousness. But it was also one of those failures in the history of ideas which has, perhaps, more to teach us than many successes. It rested upon at least four epistemological assumptions which it had taken over from the philosophy of Empiricism, all of which were open to question. The first, or 'sensationist', assumption was that, given a particular experience, it was always in principle possible to isolate the sensory core and to consider it independently of the meaning with which we imbue it when we describe it as an experience *of* something other than itself. The second, or 'elementarist', assumption was that in principle it was always possible to decompose it into a finite number of simple, irreducible and identifiable sensory elements. The third, or 'associationist', assumption was that these sensory elements combined with one another according to certain regular and ascertainable laws so as to produce the complex experiences with which we are immediately familiar. The fourth, and final, assumption was that all experience was by definition introspectible and that, in particular, the atomistic structure of experience was open to inspection if one followed the proper mental procedure.

Introspection, as understood and cultivated by this school of psychologists, was given a Humean rather than a Lockean interpretation. By this I mean that we were not to regard it as the operation of what Locke called an inner sense which could contemplate and reflect upon the deliverances of the outer-senses, rather it was itself just a further sequence of conscious events. Titchener is quite explicit on this point: 'This looking into one's mind or observation of one's own mental processes must not be understood literally, as if consciousness were one thing, existing of itself, and the "I" or observer could stand apart and watch it from the outside. The "I", the watching and the conscious phenomenon observed are all alike conscious processes; so that when "I observe myself" all that happens is that a new set of processes is introduced into the consciousness of the moment.' [*cf*. Titchener (1897) Chap. 2]

Yet, in spite of all this, it was not held that introspection was an infallible source of knowledge or even that it was at all easy to perform. For, even though no distinction was admitted between the having of an experience and knowing that one was having it, more was implied here than just a sheer awareness. In particular, introspection was of no use unless it could issue in precise, accurate description and this, clearly, was something that demanded no less exacting discipline and application than other forms of scientific observation. No untrained observer could ever hope to distinguish in all cases between what is actually given in experience, the sensory core, and the inferential structure we place upon it. The natural tendency is always to commit what Titchener called the 'stimulus error', the error, that is, of describing an experience in terms of the object which occasions it instead of in terms of the sensations out of which it is composed.

There was some difference of opinion, however, among introspectionists as to the potential scope of introspective psychology. Wundt, on the whole, took a moderate line and thought of it as applying mainly to the more elementary aspects of passive awareness or, at most, to the volitional processes involved in such standard situations as the reaction-time experiment. His pupil, Titchener, however, went much further and claimed that virtually all the higher mental processes were amenable to this approach since they were all, in the last resort, reducible to elementary sensations. Titchener, in fact, was not only the most extreme proponent of this approach in psychology, he was also its most articulate spokesman and apologist, a position he may well have been pushed into just because he was such an isolated figure on the American psychological scene. In his later years he had to meet a strong challenge from the Gestalt school, a challenge all the more serious for being launched by his fellow experimentalists in the name of introspective accuracy. What the Gestalt psychologists criticised most strongly was the reductionist and associationist assumptions of Introspectionism. These they opposed with their holistic assumption according to which all experience is, by its very nature, both inherently meaningful and inalienably organised. Accordingly the attempt to divest it of meaning in search of the pure stuff of consciousness, or to analyse it into its sensory elements in the belief that this would reveal its fundamental structure, could only result in destroying the very aspects of experience which should be of primary concern to the psychologist.

Later in this chapter we shall have more to say about the kind of psychology that arose from these alternative holistic assumptions but, for the present, it is necessary to point out that this attack betrayed a certain misunderstanding of what the Introspectionists were trying to achieve. Wundt had always acknowledged that all our familiar experiences are indeed of a composite nature and that pure sensations are nothing more than the end-product of analysis and abstraction. It was in fact he, and not, as is often assumed, any of the Gestaltists who coined the dictum that the whole is more than the sum of its parts. He was prepared to admit that the synthesis of these experiential wholes might well give rise to new emergent properties of an unforeseen kind, a view that was already implicit in the concept of 'mental chemistry' which was John Stuart Mill's special contribution to the Associationist tradition, a concept he thought no less necessary for an understanding of the operations of mind than the 'mental mechanics' which had preoccupied earlier associationists such as his father.[2] But Wundt, and still more Titchener, argued that analysis and abstraction are essential features of the scientific method in general. After all, the analysis of matter made no progress so long as people were content to base their inquiries on the categories of commonsense; even the ancient doctrine of the four elements took unanalysed concepts as fundamental, modern chemistry was born only with the introduction of an atomic theory of matter. The analogy was to be taken seriously: pure sensations might have no more reality than atoms so far as commonsense experience was concerned but they might be equally indispensable as theoretical constructs so far as a scientific analysis of mind was concerned. And this, they insisted, must be the first objective of the new psychology. Titchener resolutely refused to be sidetracked into speculating about the larger issues surrounding experience and behaviour which so intrigued William James. The Functionalists, he considered, were little better than commonsense psychologists of the old armchair tradition.

But in the end it is not intention, however impeccable, that can make a science, but achievements. What, after the dust of controversy had settled, had Introspectionism to show to its credit in terms of positive achievement? Its main success, I suggest, was to lay the foundations of a taxonomy of the phenomenal world. This may now strike us as only a very small corner of psychological science but is still a problem that has to be faced by every psychophysicist and phenomenologist. The problem was complicated from the start by the difficulty of agreeing as to the proper elements for such a taxonomy. Were sensations alone sufficient? Were mental images just faint copies of sensations occurring in the absence of stimuli, as Hume had intimated in his distinction between 'sense-impressions' and 'ideas'? And what was to be done about feelings? Were they to be treated just as aspects of sensations, as Wundt, following the classical tradition, had at first supposed, or were they to be treated as elements in their own right, as he later came to think? Külpe took an important step by clarifying the distinction between an element and an attribute. Thus, any constituent of an experience which could be conceived as existing independently of any other constituent would qualify as an element; any constituent that could *vary* independently of any other constituent though it could not exist independently of it would qualify as an attribute. Originally, every sensation was assigned the twin attributes of 'quality' and 'intensity', to which Külpe also added 'duration'. Eventually Titchener arrived at a list of five attributes which every sensation was supposed to possess. These five attributes were: 'quality', 'intensity', 'extensity' (every sensation however minimal must occupy some finite portion of the sensory field), 'protensity' (= subjective duration; i.e. every sensation, however minimal, must occupy a finite segment of the temporal continuum) and, lastly, 'attensity' (= vividness). This last was a product of Titchener's somewhat desperate efforts to give a purely sensationist account of the facts of attention.[3]

The concept of an attribute or dimension, as we would now usually call it, has proved to be a useful one for descriptive purposes over a wide range of phenomena. The problem of dimensional analysis—of determining, that is, the minimum number of co-ordinates necessary to describe any member of a given domain—is one that crops up in a variety of contexts and, provided quantification is possible, there are mathematical techniques available, such as factor analysis, which can be applied in solving the problem. An early example, based purely on introspective analysis, was Wundt's tridimensional theory of feelings. In addition to the familiar dimension of pleasure-unpleasure (what the psychophysicist would now call 'hedonic tone') Wundt claimed that two other independent dimensions could be discerned with reference to which every feeling could be located, namely 'excitement-calm' and 'tension-relief'. To the casual reader these last two might sound curiously similar but Wundt appealed to the findings of his introspectionist experts as evidence that both were necessary. Given, then, this three-dimensional matrix every emotion, at least as regards its effective component, could be assigned a unique position.

Wundt's methodology may now strike us as archaic but there can be no doubt that the sort of problem he was tackling was real enough and the question of classifying the emotions is still a live one. A comparable modern example of dimensional analysis applied to the problem of subjective or associative 'meaning' would be Osgood's 'Semantic Differential'. This is a test in which the subjects have to rate a number of arbitrary concepts on pairs of anonymous adjectives such as 'hot-cold', or 'fast-slow', etc. On the basis of these ratings Osgood carried out a factor analysis which showed that any arbitrary concept could be located in a 'semantic space' defined by no more than three independent axes which he labelled 'Evaluation', 'Potency' and 'Activity'. Although the data which Osgood uses are based on snap intuitive judgments in response to verbal stimuli, rather than on painstaking introspections, the result bears more than a fortuitous resemblance to Wundt's analysis of the emotion. [cf. Osgood, Suci and Tannenbaum (1957)]

It would not, I think, be too far fetched to regard the elaborate descriptive science of colorimetry, which today has many practical applications, as a legitimate descendant of Introspectionism. Indeed the world of colour nicely satisfies most of its basic requirements and presuppositions. Thus colours can, with the aid of a reduction-screen or similar device, be detached from the surfaces of objects to which they would normally be perceived to adhere and thereby viewed as pure sensory qualities in their own right. The bewildering variety of colours in nature can, by dint of careful matching procedures, be reduced to a large but finite number of discriminable shades. The entire domain of colour can be dimensionalised in terms of the four primary hues together with such attributes as saturation and brightness. The colour atlas, with its orderly progressions of varying shades, illustrates well the structure of this self-contained universe. Moreover colours, more especially coloured lights, combine with one another lawfully to produce other colours according to ascertainable formulae.[4] Finally, there is more than just an analogy between the introspectionist trained to detect the sensory elements of his experiences and the artist whose trained eye enables him to pick out the constituent colours of a natural scene.

It is tempting to see in the contemporary art movement that came to be known as Impressionism an exemplification of the same essential outlook as that which inspired Introspectionism. Both are concerned with the world of immediate appearances as opposed to the world of enduring objects. A Monet landscape in which cathedral and railway station alike dissolve into mosaics of colours and light effects is no less an aesthetic *tour de force* than the descriptions of experiences obtained in the laboratories of Leipzig or Cornell were scientific *tours de force*. Monet is reported to have once told an American pupil that he wished he might have been born blind and then of a sudden regained his sight so that he could have begun to paint without knowing what the objects were that he saw before him![5] This is the purest Titchenerianism. The parallel seems to hold even down to the historical roles of the two movements in art and psychology respectively. The first Impressionist Exhibition was held in Paris in 1874 and the work of the leading Impressionists, Monet, Sisley, Pissarro, represents probably the highest point ever attained in European Art with respect to sheer fidelity to visual impressions. Yet, already soon after the turn of the century the movement had been overtaken by a variety of avant-garde schools such as Fauvism, Cubism, Futurism, etc., which renounced the whole aim of naturalism in art though they exploited some of the aesthetic discoveries of Impressionism. In like manner, Wundt and his followers, having given birth to the new psychology, were, before Wundt died in 1920, superseded by the newer schools of psychology, Gestaltism, Behaviourism, Psychoanalysis, etc., which entirely repudiated his conception of mind and pursued quite different aims. The fact that Impressionism was an artistic success while Introspectionism was a scientific failure in no way vitiates this comparison.

In retrospect, the deficiencies of Introspectionism are so glaring and have been so often dwelt upon that there is no need here for yet another detailed critique. In general it could be said that it succeeded well enough within its own terms of reference so long as it concentrated on certain well-defined regions of sensory experience, but that not even the efforts of the indomitable Titchener could endow it with much plausibility when it ventured beyond these limits. Here I will mention three aspects of cognitive experience which defeat any strict introspective analysis. Consider, first, what is involved in an ordinary perceptual judgment: e.g. 'A sounds louder than B', 'C looks further away than D'. Now, the processes whereby these judgments are arrived at are not open to inspection. This is especially obvious in the case of stereoscopic depth-perception. This, as we all know, depends upon there being certain discrepancies in the two retinal images. But the fusion of these images to give us the characteristic depth-effect is a process which takes place in the brain; no amount of introspection could ever reveal it. The same applies of course to the stereophonic phenomenon on which auditory localisation depends. Once again we distinguish the effect but the underlying process is perfectly opaque to direct analysis. Nor are these special cases. Consider the way in which we are aware, even with our eyes closed, of the approximate relative position of our two hands, so that if we were to touch the two sides of an object using our hands as a pair of calipers we could judge its approximate thickness. Now, a moment's reflection is all that is required to make us realise what an enormous number of separate variables enter into what seems like a quite simple judgment. We have to take into account each of the joints in our body that come between the one hand and the other and the relative setting of our limbs at each of them. [cf. Gibson (1966) Chap. 7] Yet not one of these variables is represented in consciousness! Somehow or other the brain is able to compute the resultant for us taking all this information into consideration. Such examples could be multiplied indefinitely. What they prove is that perception is, in the first instance, a function of brain processes most of which have no counterpart in consciousness, so that any introspective analysis can at most yield only a fragmentary and disjointed account of what is involved.

The situation becomes even more acute when we come to the problem of thinking. Consider only what is involved in replying appropriately to some question. We are conscious of hearing the question, of uttering our answer and, if the question is a difficult one, we may be aware of the mental effort involved in searching for the answer, but what takes place in the critical gap between looking for an answer and supplying one is not an event which anywhere figures in consciousness. The retrieval of the information from the memory store is an operation which the brain accomplishes in silence, as it were. This, in effect, is the crux of what Külpe discovered the hard way when he actually attempted an exhaustive introspective analysis of the thinking process. Külpe was a contemporary of Titchener and, like him, had been a pupil of Wundt's trained on strict introspectionist lines. After he had been appointed to the Chair of Philosophy at Würzburg in 1894 he inaugurated a celebrated series of experimental studies on the nature of thought in which a team of psychologists participated. The Würzburgers eventually arrived at the conclusion that thinking cannot be fully described in terms of conscious contents, i.e. sensations or images, but requires the introduction of such purely dispositional concepts as set, attitude, or 'determining tendency', etc. Titchener, steadfast to the last, refused to accept these conclusions as final. He argued that the unaccountable gaps might well be filled with kinesthetic imagery of a quality so elusive that it had escaped detection even by the trained introspectionists of the Würzburg laboratory. But the tide of history was moving against him and his arguments sounded too much like special pleading. At all events, this 'imageless thought' controversy contributed heavily towards the downfall of the whole Introspectionist school.[6]

Finally, Introspectionism proved powerless to cope with the ubiquitous problem of meaning. All conceptual thinking depends in the last resort upon our capacity to use symbols. Now, symbols may be verbal or pictorial, they may be given physical embodiment or they may be purely mental, in the form of mental images, but what in every case enables some entity to function as a symbol is the special relationship which we ourselves establish between it and its *referent* in the real world. Furthermore, when we treat any item of experience as an experience *of* something other than itself, i.e. as a meaningful as opposed to a purely sensuous experience in its own right, we are assigning it a symbolic function. Titchener realised that, having divested experience of its meaning for the purpose of analysis, he was then faced with the task of giving an account of how the meaning got there in the first place. His solution was to offer a 'core-context' interpretation of meaning whereby the context of associated imagery in which the sensory core was embedded furnished the meaningful aspect of the experience. The solution, however, could not transcend the logical gap that separates an entity from a relationship. If meaning resides in the relationship that holds between a symbol and its referent or between a percept and an external object, it is clearly useless to enlarge the inventory of conscious entities in the hope that, by providing the core of sensations with a context of images, what is intrinsically meaningless will become automatically meaningful.

Starting from a set of dubious premises Introspectionism led eventually to an inevitable dead end. But, while the movement did not survive the demise of Titchener himself, the practice of introspection continued weathering even the blasts of Behaviourism and remains an integral albeit minor part of psychological science. One could even say that it is still the one distinctive technique which the psychologist can call upon. We shall next consider how it was used in a quite different way for quite different ends.

Phenomenology

Once the reductionist assumptions of Introspectionism are jettisoned what remains of a science of experience? The answer, in one word, is 'phenomenology', defined here as the descriptive science of conscious experience as it is *in itself*: that is, when treated as an object for examination and not as information to be acted upon or as raw material for theoretical interpretation. That such an enterprise is worth undertaking, or even that it makes sense, are themselves assumptions which have by no means escaped criticism. But the assumptions are quite different from those which governed the practice of Introspectionism. There is no longer any question of the subject having to be trained in order to avoid the 'stimulus error'. On the contrary, he is encouraged to adopt an attitude of ultimate naïvety towards his perceptual world. It is the investigator who has to take care to distinguish between the perceptual world of the subject and the corresponding public, geographical world of the stimulus. One reason why the perceptual illusions figure so prominently in the phenomenological literature, though they are rare enough in real life, is that in the case of the illusions there is no temptation to confuse what is perceived and what is actually there. Watching a film, for example, is not so very different from watching events in real life and yet the stimulus situation, in the case of the cinema, is nothing more substantial than a changing pattern of illumination on a flat screen.

It is important to understand that pure phenomenology makes no claims to explain behaviour. The phenomenologist is interested in the nature of experience insofar as this can be elucidated by accurate and refined description but he is not, *qua* phenomenologist, interested either in its causes or in its consequences. It is the phenomena or appearances alone that matter, not what they portend nor even what they are composed of. Phenomenology is not psychology, at most it provides a point of departure for psychology. But, why, one may well ask, does it demand a special discipline if it takes its stand on a direct naïve account of experience? The answer lies in the fact that a consistent phenomenological approach is difficult and requires cultivation. The ordinary subject is first and foremost a pragmatist; he is little concerned with the *quality* of his experiences, he is concerned with practical success and failure in action. He is likely to be as little able to stand aside and take a detached view of his experience as a fish would be able to take a detached view of water. Equally, the scientific observer is unconcerned about the quality of experience; for him it is the world which is revealed *through* experience that matters. To some extent the attitude of the phenomenologist is more like that of the artist; both are capable of contemplating experience for its own sake but for the artist this is only the first stage towards transforming it into the work of art. The problem which confronts the phenomenologist is how to describe an experience in such a way as to make it intelligible without, at the same time, distorting or falsifying it by forcing it into any abstract theoretical framework.

The subject-matter of phenomenology is illustrated by such questions as: When are two successive events perceived as manifestations of one and the same object as opposed to manifestations of two different objects? What is involved in doing something voluntarily as opposed simply to doing it? On what basis do we come to distinguish between what is phenomenally objective in experience, e.g. the colours, sounds, odours, etc., which we refer to an external world, and what is phenomenally subjective, e.g. aches and pains, feelings of remorse, cravings for affection, etc., which we refer to the 'self'? Are we directly aware in experience of the flow of time or is this something we know at one remove on the basis of memory? Here, then, we have a mixed bag of arbitrarily chosen problems which demand a phenomenological solution. They can be tackled either on a philosophical plane, by reflecting upon one's own intuitive knowledge, or they can be answered by means of controlled observations in a laboratory. The latter is of course the method of the phenomenologist who is also an experimental psychologist, but a phenomenological experiment is more in the nature of a demonstration by means of which a particular problem can hopefully be settled by a single crucial observation rather than by the laborious collation of data as in the conventional psychological experiment. It is with the phenomenology of the laboratory that we are here concerned, but since, of all the psychological sciences, the science of experience is the one that impinges most on questions of a philosophical kind, it is necessary to say something first about the role of phenomenology conceived as a method in philosophy.

Broadly speaking there are, one could say, two alternative approaches that one can adopt in pursuing epistemology and the philosophy of mind. There is, on the one hand, the *linguistic* approach which consists essentially of attempting to clarify our mental concepts by examining the way in which certain key words are used in ordinary language and, on the other, there is the *phenomenological* approach which bases its arguments on an appeal to concrete experience. On the whole the philosophy of mind as it has developed in the last few decades in England and America has tended to rely more on the linguistic approach, while the philosophy of mind that has developed during this period on the Continent has tended to rely more on the phenomenological approach. The phenomenological movement in Continental philosophy has also been closely associated with the Existentialist movement; the latter, with its insistence on man's moral autonomy, has taken an anti-behaviourist stance in psychology and has naturally welcomed the phenomenologist's concern with the reality of man's inner life.

The distinction between Phenomenology and Introspectionism has its roots in the two rival traditions of European philosophy since Descartes: the Rationalist and the Empiricist. And, if Hume represents the fountain-head of Empiricism and Associationism in psychology, Kant's critique of Hume may be taken as the starting point for the various holistic and phenomenological currents that are to be found in the work of the anti-associationist schools of psychology. The bridgehead between philosophical and psychological phenomenology was Brentano who, as it happens, published his *Psychology from the Empirical Standpoint* in the same year, 1874, as Wundt completed his *Foundations of Physiological Psychology*. In this work Brentano attacked the idea that psychology was concerned with the analysis of the conscious *content* of mind which, he argued, yielded a misleadingly passive conception of the nature of mind. In its place he proposed that psychology should concern itself with mental or psychic *acts*, the characteristic of an act being the relationship it implied between the subject or self and the mental object which it 'intended'. He distinguished three fundamental classes of 'acts': ideating, i.e. sheer sensing or imagising; judging, which included all the cognitive acts involved in perceiving, recalling, believing, apprehending, etc.; and, thirdly, the gamut of the effective-conative acts such as loving and hating, desiring, willing, etc. These alone, he contended, qualified as 'psychological phenomena', not the sensory elements, the colours, sounds, odours, etc., that preoccupied Wundt and his followers which, misleadingly, Brentano classed as 'physical phenomena'. The way was thus opened for a bifurcation of psychology into a study of the acts, processes and experiences of the mind on the one hand and their mental objects or contents, be they percepts, images, thoughts or whatever, on the other. [*cf.* Rancurello (1968)]

Unfortunately, acts do not readily lend themselves to experimental investigation with the result that act-psychology was developed more by the philosophical psychologists than by the experimentalists. Brentano's influence was strongest in the work of his two Austrian disciples, Meinong and von Ehrenfels, who were his students at the University of Vienna where Brentano held the the Chair from 1874 to 1894. Meinong, the more important of the two as a philosopher, was primarily a theorist and systematist in psychology but he encouraged experimental studies and indeed founded the first psychological laboratory in Austria at Graz in 1894. Von Ehrenfels is now mainly remembered as the originator of the concept of 'Form-qualities' (Gestaltqualität) which he introduced in a paper he published in 1890. The point about a form-quality was that it could remain invariant when all its constituents varied. It could be spatial, a given contour or shape, or it could be temporal, a given melody, a sequence of speech-sounds, but, in whatever modality it appeared, it existed as an independent entity in its own right. The theory of form-qualities, which was further developed and elaborated by Meinong, is often taken as the starting point of Gestalt psychology, as it eventually came to be known. It was, however, anticipated by another thinker of a very different background and philosophical allegiance, namely, Ernst Mach.

Mach was, in fact, an extreme positivist or phenomenalist who believed that all the entities alike of physics and of psychology derive in the first instance from what he called sensations but what, following the later Logical Positivists, we would now call 'sense data'. However, in his book, the *Analysis of Sensations*, which he wrote in Prague in 1886,[7] he parted company with orthodox Introspectionism by denying that sensations necessarily correspond with the punctate elements recognised by the physiological psychologists and he made free play with such notions as 'space-sensations' and 'time-sensations'; his discussion of the perception of spatial and temporal forms and patterns has much in common with later Gestalt psychology. As a prominent physicist as well as one of the pioneer philosophers of science, Mach exercised a powerful influence on his contemporaries, not least on his friend William James whose 'Radical Empiricism' owes much to Mach.[8]

The actual term 'Phenomenology' first gained currency through the writings of Husserl, a former pupil of Brentano, around 1900 when he was working under Stumpf. Unfortunately, he appropriated the term for his own peculiar metaphysics of 'Pure Being' which are of no concern to us in this context. Stumpf himself, however, who was deeply influenced by Brentano whom he succeeded to the Chair at Würzburg in 1874, introduced the term phenomenology in his papers of 1906 to designate the study of the introspectible contents of mind. This, he considered, was 'propaedeutic' to psychology proper which, following Brentano, he defined as the study of mental acts or, as he preferred to call them, psychical *functions*. Stumpf, as it happened, was a gifted musician and his most important contributions to experimental psychology lay in the field of psycho-acoustics and the psychology of music. His two-volume *Tone-psychology* (1883/1890), which dealt with the question of tonal fusions, became a classic text in its field. Stumpf eventually settled in Berlin where he occupied the Chair from 1894 to his retirement in 1921 and where he took over the psychological laboratory that had been started there by Ebbinghaus. Among his students were two of the future leaders of the Gestalt school, Köhler and

Koffka, both of whom completed their doctoral theses under him; eventually, Köhler succeeded him to the Chair at Berlin which thereupon became the centre of the Gestalt movement until its dispersion under Hitler, when Köhler emigrated to the United States.

The Gestalt School began when Wertheimer joined Köhler and Koffka at Frankfurt. Wertheimer went there in 1910 and embarked on an investigation of the stroboscopic effect in movement-perception using Köhler and Koffka as his subjects. His principal method was to expose two vertical lines at a fixed distance apart which could be made to alternate on and off at a variable rate. He demonstrated that, as the time interval between their successive appearances increased, various changes could be observed at the phenomenal level. When the time interval was very long the lines were perceived as two separate stimuli presented one after the other. When the time interval was very short, below the threshold for flicker-fusion, the two lines were perceived as standing simultaneously side by side. Somewhere between these two extremes one obtained the optimal conditions for perceiving an apparent movement-effect as if a single line was jumping to and fro. What Wertheimer called the pure 'phi-phenomenon' was the effect which occurred when the interval was lengthened beyond that which gave optimal apparent movement, at which point the subject would report that, while there was an indubitable movement, yet nothing could be seen to move across the gap which separated the two end-positions. This paradoxical movement-effect, movement without a moving object, became the prototype of all gestalt phenomena. Actually, from the standpoint of Gestalt psychology, the phenomenon of real movement perception makes the point just as cogently. For, although to the physicist motion can be analysed as a function of distance over time, to the phenomenologist it is a phenomenon in its own right: to be aware that an object has been displaced during a period of time is not the same thing as seeing it move. We can be aware that the minute hand of a clock has been displaced 30° in the course of five minutes but, since its speed falls below the threshold for movement perception, we never see it as a moving object. Phenomenological analysis has recently been corroborated by the physiological discovery that there are cells in the visual cortex that specialise in detecting movement.[9] However, in the case of the stroboscopic effect, no physical motion whatever is involved; an impression of movement is created by purely static stimulation. Wertheimer typically chose to demonstrate the meaning of a gestalt phenomenon with reference to an illusion, and the 'phi-phenomenon' itself (which is a special case of the stroboscopic effect) is that phenomenological nicety, an illusion that is also a visual paradox!

From these beginnings Wertheimer went on to study the phenomenology of forms, patterns and configurations. He enumerated a number of factors which were said to determine the way in which a set of discrete objects, dots, dashes or whatever, came to be organised into perceptual wholes: factors such as 'proximity', 'similarity', 'continuity', 'closure', 'simplicity', etc. It was never very clear whether these so-called laws of formal organisation were intended to be laws in the same sense as the older psychophysical laws. These had attempted to relate in an orderly way the independent physical variable to the dependent psychological variable whereas, in Wertheimer's case, his factors could never be defined independently of the perception. But, as descriptive principles of the way in which parts and wholes are related to one another in complex visual objects, Wertheimer's analysis may be taken as an unexceptionable piece of phenomenology. But phenomenology was only one aspect of the Gestalt programme which, like its opposite number Behaviourism, was offered as a comprehensive programme for psychology or, at any rate, for cognitive psychology, and it is as well to remember that practically all the research on perception and on problem-solving between the First and Second World Wars was carried out by those who were either directly or indirectly influenced by the Gestalt outlook.[10]

The distinctive feature of Gestalt theory was not so much its concern with phenomenology as its holism. Not only was the whole more than the sum of its parts, as Wundt had already acknowledged, but the parts depended for their characteristics upon the whole to which they belonged. In a sense, therefore, the whole was regarded as epistemologically prior to its parts. There was, however, an important difference here between the pre-Gestalt followers of von Ehrenfels and the official Gestalt school represented by Wertheimer, Köhler and Koffka. The former took the organised nature of perception as evidence for the creative-synthetic powers of mind, the latter regarded sensory experience as 'self-organising' according to the laws of field theory. This difference reflected a profound difference in philosophical orientation between the two parties. The 'Austrian Gestalt School' had their roots not only in Brentano but in the whole Idealist tradition in 19th century philosophy with its pronounced anti-associationist stance. The 'Berlin School' took their holism, not from Idealist philosophy, but from the field theories of the physicists. As Boring says: 'Köhler was always a physicist in his thinking, indebted for stimulus in his student days at Berlin to Max Planck rather than to Stumpf.' One could say that their approach was at bottom no less mechanistic than that of the Behaviourists even if the mechanics they invoked was one more in tune with Maxwellian electromagnetism than with the old Newtonian dynamics.[11] This comes out clearly in Köhler's 'Isomorphism' postulate which became an important part of Gestalt doctrine. Köhler put forward the intriguing idea that the brain itself acted as a physical gestalt so that the brain traces formed in perception were governed by the same kind of field forces as were found to operate with respect to the phenomenal field. Thus, if, in the 'phi-phenomenon', static stimuli appear to be in movement, this is presumably because there is actual movement across the electrostatic field of the visual cortex. If, in the 'figural after-effects' phenomenon, the test figure appears to be distorted this is because the traces produced by the inspection figure have been subjected to field forces in the brain. In this way there was no need for any kind of organising 'self' or 'ego' to account for the order we find in experience, it could all be explained in terms of automatic processes in the nervous system. This mechanistic, anti-personalistic bias in Gestalt doctrine proved to be both its strength and its weakness. It offered a much better leverage for experimental attack than the more metaphysical teachings of the Austrian school; at the same time it produced a psychology of a somewhat narrow and arid kind. What was more serious from the scientific point of view was that little independent evidence was forthcoming for Köhler's hypothetical field-effects in the brain and it ran directly counter to the accepted facts of neural transmission and brain function. Indeed from the modern cybernetic standpoint there is something rather quaint in this idea that the brain should encode information in a way that preserves a formal resemblance to the structure of the message itself: the dial of the speedometer does not have to be moving in order to indicate motion! Thus, little in the end remained of the isomorphic assumption[12] and in retrospect one can say that the most lasting contribution the Gestalt school made to the development of modern psychology, apart from the stimulus it gave to research in a variety of fields, was its phenomenology.

Here, by way of concrete illustration, are some of the phenomenological discoveries made by those who came within the orbit of Gestalt psychology. I will start by mentioning three perceptual phenomena that were brought to light at about the same time as Wertheimer was working on the 'phi-phenomenon'. As it happens they all originated in the work of three young psychologists then at the Göttingen laboratory whose director was the great pioneer psychologist-psychophysicist, G. E. Müller. These were (a) the size-constancy phenomenon which, according to Boring, can be traced to E. R. Jaensch's monograph of 1911 on visual depth-perception; (b) the figure-ground effect first discussed by the Danish psychologist Edgar Rubin in a publication of 1915; and (c) the diverse modes of colour-manifestation as described by David Katz in his paper of 1911.[13] As regards (a), it has since become an axiom of perceptual psychology that the percept, i.e. what we actually *see*, corresponds more closely in all respects to the real world, i.e. to what is actually *there*, than it does to the 'proximal stimulus', i.e. the particular pattern of excitation on the sense-organ. Thus, if we observe someone walking away from us he does not normally appear to shrink in size even though the image he casts upon our retina halves in size every time his distance from us doubles. This simple phenomenological fact is difficult to explain so long as one assumes that perceived size is a straightforward function of retinal size. But it becomes intelligible if one takes into account the scale and perspective of the retinal image in relation to which the receding figure remains invariant. There is still a problem of explaining how the brain transforms the fluctuating sensory inputs into a stable perceptual environment but it is one that demands an appropriate brain-model; all that phenomenology can do is to establish the facts and the extent of perceptual invariances.

As regards (b), the figure-ground effect, this is perhaps the most ubiquitous of all perceptual phenomena. It refers to the fact that in any given percept it is possible to distinguish between (1) the 'figure', which comprises everything that pertains to the object being attended to, and (2) the 'ground', which includes everything else and corresponds to the undifferentiated mass against which the figure is perceived. Such a statement sounds unexceptionable but it is apt to cause some uneasiness among positivistic scientists and philosophers. How else, they may ask, could we conceivably perceive an object except in terms of figure and ground? It must be admitted that the statement does have a disconcerting air of the obvious about it and yet, as Rubin's classic demonstrations show, more is involved here than just a tiresome verbal tautology. Ordinarily, the distinction between figure and ground in perception corresponds to differences in depth, that is to say the contour of some object in space represents a kind of visual precipice in the depth-dimension. Rubin, however, characteristically chose to study the illusory case where the contour is simply a line on a flat piece of paper and he invented ambiguous compositions in which the contour could be seen either as defining the portion of the picture on its right, in which case the right-hand side became the figure and the left-hand side the ground, or *vice versa*. In this situation the observer experiences an alternation depending on which portion of the picture is seen as the figure. Moreover, with each shift in perception every subsidiary detail undergoes subtle transformation depending on whether it is seen as part of the figure or part of the ground. It is of some interest to compare the phenomenological distinction between figure and ground with the dichotomy between signal and noise which is a central concept of information theory.

Lastly, with regard to (c), it was Katz's achievement to have shown that the perception of colour and the perception of space are bound up with one another so that more is needed for a full analysis of colour than just the classic psychophysical dimensions of hue, saturation and brightness. In real life colours are nearly always seen as adhering to the surfaces of objects and their quality is duly affected by the texture of those surfaces. An exception is the expanse of a clear blue sky which lacks not only texture but any definite spatial location which is a characteristic of ordinary textured objects. However, by holding a screen with a small aperture in front of any coloured surface it is possible to detach the colour from its surface location and to see it as a textureless film or suspension bounded only by the aperture. There is thus an important phenomenological distinction to be made between surface-colour and film-colour. The mistake which Introspectionism had made was to suppose that film-colour alone required analysis since it alone represented pure colour-quality. Following this primary distinction many other modes of colour perception could likewise be singled out for examination, for example, the 'lustrous' colour of a gloss surface has a different quality from the matt colour of a rough surface; similarly the 'luminous' colour of a stained glass window has a different quality from the colour of a painting or mosaic that is lit from the front, and the 'volumic' colour of a glass of red wine differs from a luminous red that merely extends in two dimensions but does not fill a region of space. Today a phenomenologist would have to take note of the special quality of fluorescent colours (which can reflect more light than illumines them) and would observe their tendency to 'jump out at us' from the plane to which they belong.

But the most interesting of the perceptual psychologists whose work was predominantly phenomenological was, in my opinion, the late Albert Michotte of the University of Louvain in Belgium. He made his name internationally with his painstaking studies of what he called the 'causality effect'. By this he meant that, whatever Hume may have said about causation being inferred and not perceived, phenomenological analysis reveals that a given object A *can* be perceived as causally modifying a second object B and that this is *not* the same thing as perceiving a sequence of events involving A followed by a sequence of events involving B. To demonstrate this Michotte used markings on a disc that could be made to rotate behind a slit in a screen at a known speed. In this way A and B appeared as small rectangles moving to and fro relative to one another along the slit. The resultant causality effects that could be demonstrated by this means, and there were many subtle variations, could be compared to the phi-phenomenon for, just as apparent movement cannot be reduced to mere displacement in space, so apparent causality cannot be reduced to a mere sequence of two independent events; it could be shown simply to supervene as a phenomenon in its own right once certain critical physical conditions obtained.[14]

Using a similar technique where the stimulus situation is simplified or schematised down to its bare essentials, Michotte and his associates went on to investigate other phenomenological problems connected with our basic categories of thought. [*cf.* Michotte *et al.* (1962)] For example, the problem of permanence: under what conditions will an object be perceived as continuing to exist when it is no longer present in the sensory field? Or the problem of identity: what transformations can an object undergo and still be perceived as the same object? Or the phenomenology of space:

under what conditions will a drawing or photograph appear merely to *represent* objects in three dimensions and under what conditions will they actually appear to *occupy* three-dimensional space? One concept which emerges from these and similar studies is the important concept of 'amodal perception'. Modally, that is in terms of strict sensory content, we can perceive at any instant only a very limited portion of our surrounds, in vision only those surfaces which form the base of a cone whose apex corresponds to our optic centre. Yet it is clear that our perceptual experience includes far more than this: we perceive one object lying *behind* another; we perceive an object as possessing solidity, that is as having a back as well as a front, an inside as well as an outside; we perceive events as temporally related to one another, and so on. Admittedly these are tacit dimensions of perception; we are not normally aware of them unless some deception is practised on us so that our expectations are frustrated and we receive a 'perceptual shock'. Previously it would have been argued that these are really *inferences* which we automatically make *on the basis of* our perceptual experience, rather than aspects of perception as such. Perhaps, in the last resort, it is a question of semantics whether we say that we *believe* a given object, seen only from the front, is a complete object or whether we amodally *perceive* it to be so; the point is however that a phenomenological analysis shows that there is no sharp distinction between the modal and amodal aspects of perception. [*cf.* Michotte, Thinés and Crabbé (1964)] The distinction is rather at the physical level; presumably the brain makes certain rapid calculations on the basis of the sensory inputs it receives and these determine the amodal properties we then actually perceive.

A great deal of unnecessary confusion arose over the Michotte demonstrations as regards what it was they were meant to demonstrate. This was because insufficient care was taken to distinguish between the phenomenological and the ontogenetic aspects of the phenomena. Like most of his Gestaltist predecessors Michotte tended to take a nativistic view of the ontogenetic question, almost as if to admit that the phenomenon was dependent upon certain prior experience rather than upon the innate structure of the brain was to trivialise it. And yet there is no logical reason why a holistic phenomenology should have to go with a nativistic ontogenesis or why, for that matter, an atomistic phenomenology should have to go with an 'empiricistic' ontogenesis. An emergentist theory of development, according to which new perceptual wholes would come into existence at certain critical junctures of the developmental process, would have served the holists just as well. But, historically, the fact is that by and large the Gestalt school embraced nativism while the Associationists and Introspectionists embraced empiricism. [*cf*. Hochberg (1962)] Now whereas it is almost certain that the ability to perceive movement is an innate property of the brain, it is by no means certain that this is the case with regard to the ability to perceive causation or any of these other effects which Michotte liked to demonstrate. Indeed on a commonsense basis it seems much more likely that the idea of causality originates, ontogenetically speaking, from our infantile discovery that we are able to control our own limbs and that our limbs in turn can be used to control objects in the external world. It further seems likely that our conception of causation as a relationship obtaining between inanimate objects was in the first instance an animistic projection from our own experience of our transactions with other objects. Accordingly, Michotte's critics claimed that in viewing his causality demonstration we are merely importing into the situation ideas that have been fashioned by our commerce with our everyday environment, as if to make this claim was to dispose of the validity of the demonstration. But in fact it is irrelevant from the phenomenological point of view whether the Michotte demonstration is seen as a schematic representation of a real life situation or whether it is seen as a self-contained perceptual phenomenon in the sense in which a patch of colour is self-contained. What matters is only to recognise that, once we have learnt to see things as causally related, our perceptual world has thereby acquired a new feature. Unfortunately Michotte himself exacerbated the confusion by insisting that causality must be a self-contained effect. He further added to the confusion by arguing that his findings disposed of Hume's analysis of causation. However, this latter claim confounds phenomenology with metaphysics. Whether we adopt the positivist, Humean view that, in nature, there is nothing beyond a constant conjunction of certain events or whether we adopt the realist view that nature comprises a necessitating principle which the observed sequences of events merely exemplifies, is independent of how we actually perceive the Michotte effect.

I have discussed here only the phenomenology of perception, but there is nothing in principle to prevent one from developing a phenomenology of memory, of imagery, of thinking, dreaming, speaking, or any other process which involves conscious experience. In a still broader context the term 'phenomenological' has come to be applied to the use, in psychology or in the social sciences, of the subjective standpoint. Thus, certain contemporary schools of psychotherapy adopt what is called a 'phenomenological approach', by which is meant that they take, as their point of departure, how the patient sees himself and his world in the here and now as opposed to the objective facts of his case-history. Various questionnaire techniques have been developed to this end which purport to reveal the subject's 'personal constructs', or 'level of aspiration', or 'self-image', etc.[15]

*　　*　　*

After its eclipse during the behaviourist revolution, introspection has once more come into its own and today psychologists are again taking an interest in various facets of inner experience ranging from types of imagery to altered states of consciousness. Introspection is now likely to retain a permanent if subordinate role in most of the psychological sciences. In general one could say that any truly psychological problem will have at least four aspects: the social or interpersonal, the individual-behavioural, the physiological and the subjective or experiential. None of these can be neglected in any comprehensive approach but it is the last of these which, in the end, makes the problem a specifically psychological one.

Summary

Analytical Introspection

The first of the psychological schools was one which attempted to make of psychology a science of pure consciousness. Its key assumption, which it had taken over from the associationism of the Empiricist philosophers, was that the whole of experience could be analysed into a finite number of irreducible sensory elements. What was new in its approach was its professionalism, its belief in the possibility of actually achieving this goal using specially trained subjects in control situations, and its claim that this constituted the entire programme for a scientific psychology. The supreme exponent of this Introspectionism was, not Wundt, but the Anglo-American E. B. Titchener. For Titchener analytical introspection meant detaching the pure sensuous content of an experience from all objective reference and meaning and thereby avoiding the 'stimulus error' of naïve introspection. The parallel is drawn here between the attitude of mind of the Titchenerian introspector and of the Impressionist artist. Contrary to what many critics have alleged there is nothing inherently impossible or absurd in the practice of analytical introspection but, as a programme for a science, Introspectionism was a monumental failure. Even so it was not completely without issue; in certain areas of psychophysics concerned with mapping the different dimensions of sensation (e.g. colorimetry) the analytical approach still has its function.

Phenomenology

When the sensationist and atomistic assumptions of Introspectionism were discarded, what remained of the practice of introspection was phenomenology. This may be defined as the descriptive science of pure experience divested of all theoretical and pragmatic implications. It never purported to be more than a point of departure for the explanatory sciences of psychology. The phenomenologist is essentially a naïve realist who treats raw experience just as it comes in all its irreducible wholeness and meaningfulness. Indeed, these aspects become themselves the object of phenomenological inquiry. The only expertise involved lies in the attention paid to the nuances and complexity of experience and this, like all expertise, comes with practice and exposure. The history of phenomenology is here traced from Brentano and his Act Psychology to the Gestalt School of Wertheimer and his followers. It is here argued that, contrary to what Köhler supposed, it is not the doctrine of Isomorphism which represents the chief contribution of the Gestalt School to perceptual psychology, but its descriptive phenomenology. The work of Michotte, as the outstanding representative of this tradition, is singled out for special discussion.

Notes

1   *Cf.* Mischel [1969] p. 24. Writing about what he calls the 'Wundtian impasse' he asks: 'What are we to do if two observers describe their experiences differently under the same experimental circumstances?' and goes on to say: 'When I describe an insect or a mineral I can check my description by consulting others or by looking at it again; I can try and remember what it looked like, and I can check my memory by renewed observation, or by looking at a photograph and so on. But none of this is possible when I am describing my immediate subjective experience.' It should be clear, however, from his reference to 'an insect or a mineral' that he has succumbed to the naïve-realist epistemology which vitiates so much of modern linguistic philosophy, as if ordinary scientific observation is simply a matter of seeing things *as they really are*. In fact, of course, his insect or mineral are just stimuli like any other objects. Naturally, the accounts which these objects will elicit from trained observers will show a high degree of concordance whereas an account of the sensations or, still more, of the feelings and emotions which they arouse would not be expected to show any comparable degree of consensus. This, however, has nothing to do with the fact that, whereas we can pass round for inspection such things as beetles or crystals, we cannot swap sensations or emotions!

2   *See* J. S. Mill's *System of Logic* of 1843 [Mill (1875)] Bk 6, Chap. 14, sect. 1, 'What is meant by laws of mind?' Mill's point of departure was the extreme associationism of his father James Mill whose *Analysis of the Phenomena of the Human Mind* first appeared in 1829 and was subsequently re-edited with an introduction by his son in 1869. [*cf.* Drever (1968)]

3   Perhaps the best introduction to Titchener's views is to be found in Boring [1950] pp. 410-20. Boring was a student of Titchener at Cornell though never a disciple.

4   For a general introduction to colour theory and colorimetry *cf.* Evans [1948].

5 *See* Kenneth Clark, *Landscape into Art* (Murray: London 1949) p. 94. Lord Clark calls it 'the most extreme and most absurd statement of the sensational aesthetic'.

6 For an authoritative account of the 'imageless thought' controversy *see* Humphrey [1951] Chaps 2-4.

7 Its full title is *The Analysis of Sensations and the Relation of the Physical to the Psychical*. It has been reissued in English by Dover Publications in a paperback edition (New York 1959) with an introduction by T. Szasz.

8 James met Mach in Prague in 1882. He said of him afterwards: 'I don't think anyone ever gave me so strong an impression of pure intellectual genius' (quoted in Allen [1967]).

9 *Cf.* 'Some cells fire best to a moving stimulus and in these the direction and even the rate of movement are critical.' [Hubel and Wiesel (1962)]

10 The classic texts of the Gestalt School in English are Koffka [1935] and Köhler [1929], [1938], [1940].

11 Köhler was a student of Max Planck and was specially interested in the field concepts exemplified in Clerk Maxwell's *Electricity and Magnetism* or in Kirchhoff's laws of the flow of electric current along a wire. While marooned in North Africa during the First World War he wrote a book about this aspect of physics and about its possible application to the laws of psychology and brain function. When it appeared in 1920 it was greeted with enthusiasm by Wertheimer and by Koffka. Köhler mentions these facts in a paper he wrote shortly before he died in answer to a request by the American Psychological Association to address its annual convention of 1967 [*see* Köhler (1967)] where he writes: 'In a sense Gestalt Psychology has since become a kind of application of field physics to essential parts of psychology and of brain physiology.'

12 *Cf.* Gregory [1966] p. 7. 'This doctrine known as Isomorphism has had unfortunate effects on thinking about perception. Ever

since, there has been a tendency to postulate properties to these hypothetical brain fields such that visual distortions and other phenomena are "explained". But it is all too easy to postulate things having just the right properties. There is no evidence for such brain fields and no independent way of discovering their properties.' Actually, in the last years of his life, Köhler went to considerable trouble to obtain independent evidence for these brain-fields using EEG recordings from the subject's visual cortex. [see Köhler (1969)] To the best of my knowledge, however, nothing much has come of these efforts so it may well be that Gregory has pronounced the epitaph on the theory of Isomorphism. For the application of Köhler's theory to figural after-effects see McEwen [1958] Chap. 2.

13 (a) and (b) are discussed in almost every introductory textbook of psychology; for (c) see Katz [1935].

14 See Michotte [1963]. Michotte has been sharply attacked by Joynson [1971] for concentrating exclusively on his stimulus-variables to the exclusion of individual differences among his subjects. Certainly, considered as experiments, Michotte's work is open to criticism on many counts. However, whatever Michotte himself may have thought he was doing, his experiments are really demonstrations. They serve the same purpose as the illustrations to be found in a Gestalt textbook, in other words they enable the spectator to verify the effect for himself and thus obviate the necessity for a statistical confirmation. This is typical phenomenology and as such Michotte's demonstrations possess great elegance.

15 For a discussion of phenomenology in this wider connotation see MacLeod [1964]. Among the pioneers of the phenomenological approach in clinical psychology were Carl Rogers and George Kelly. The latter devised his 'repertory grid test' which purported to elicit the subject's 'personal constructs', i.e. the concepts through which he views his world.

CHAPTER TWO

Comparative Psychology

The expression 'comparative psychology' will be used here in the conventional way to refer to comparisons between rather than within species. Etymologically, there is no reason why it should not have been used to signify any study of psychological differences between different sections of the human family, between races, classes, nations, cultures or between the sexes, the age-groups and generations and so on. The fact is, however, that such studies have come to be subsumed under such headings as 'social psychology', 'social anthropology', 'developmental psychology', 'differential psychology', etc., leaving 'comparative psychology' to cover differences between the human and the infra-human mind. Unfortunately, in the titles of journals and textbooks, the term is too often stretched to cover any investigation of animal behaviour, regardless of whether comparisons are drawn or implied and regardless, even, of whether anything of psychological interest is involved. It is necessary therefore to stress at the outset that here we shall be using the term in its literal sense, not just as a synonym for animal psychology.

In one sense, comparative psychology stands in no need of any special apology. Today a large proportion of all research carried out in departments of psychology the world over involves experiments on animals. Yet, from another point of view, its study raises some of the most vexatious questions regarding the nature and purpose of a psychological science. For example, is psychology about *people*, as the humanistic psychologist would have us think, or is it about *organisms*, as the psychobiologist would prefer to put it? Does our possession of language and all that goes with it in the way of symbolic activity and self-awareness make us different in kind from other species? And, if so, can comparative psychology teach us anything except about the biological preconditions for being human? It is true that we each start our life-cycle with no special advantage over other species and that it is only by due process of socialisation that the metamorphosis takes place which turns an infant into a person. It is true, likewise, that as a species we are a product of evolution and that whatever social superstructure we may have erected on our biological foundations the basic processes involved in perception, learning motivation and so on are all such as can be discerned throughout the phyletic range. Nevertheless, temporal continuity does not imply conceptual continuity and we can never take for granted that the conceptual framework that may be adequate for an understanding of animals and pre-verbal infants can be applied to the understanding of adult human behaviour.

Even from the standpoint of temporal continuity the situation is unfortunate since the various hominids or sub-human species have long been extinct and have left so little trace. Neither the study of the anthropoid apes nor that of our few surviving pre-literate societies can do much to bridge the chasm which this has left in the evolutionary story, much of which has to be filled out with mere conjecture. It is almost as if we had to construct a developmental psychology while being unable to test any child between the ages of three and thirteen! Another limitation which confronts us is that nature offers us no counterparts to so much that we consider characteristic of homo sapiens. It is an intriguing intellectual exercise to imagine what kind of a comparative psychology would emerge if we were ever to establish contact with other articulate beings on other planets instead of being restricted to the products of terrestrial evolution. Perhaps the nearest we shall ever come to a comparative psychology of the higher mental processes is through the design of artificial intelligences. Take, for example, the concept of memory, surely a key concept for any psychology. Memory in its widest sense is concerned with the storage and retrieval of information irrespective of how this may be realised in the particular case. Hence any general comparative psychology of memory would need to take account not just of the biological memory systems as found in nature but also of the various artificial memory systems such as may be used to equip a computer. And what is true of memory is true of any other psychological function which can be expressed in informational terms. This opens up the prospect of a comparative psychology of a quite general kind which would include not just man and animals and any hypothetical extra-terrestrial beings which may or may not exist but also the entire new race of robots, automata and intelligent machines which human ingenuity may devise.[1] But this is to look towards the future; we must turn next to the past.

Animal Minds

There can never have been a time when man did not feel a certain sense of community with the brute creation. That animals are sentient creatures like ourselves with minds which, though no doubt cruder than our own, yet bear a family resemblance to it, is part of our commonsense heritage. Indeed pre-scientific thinking on this question tended to exaggerate this affinity much as children still do today. The initial impact of science, from Descartes up to the 19th century reflexologists, was all in the direction of showing how much of animal behaviour could be explained by purely mechanistic assumptions. Modern comparative psychology can fairly be said to begin with Darwin. The evolutionary hypothesis gave a new urgency to the comparative approach by insisting that mind, along with everything else in the cosmos, could only be understood when viewed in its evolutionary setting. Three distinct periods can be discerned in the rise of comparative psychology and although there is inevitably some degree of overlap between them, this division will help us to appreciate the main currents that have gone into its making.

The first period, which we may call the 'mentalistic phase' of comparative psychology, is exemplified in the work of the eminent British naturalists who followed closely the lead of Darwin himself. Their aim was to explore the nature of the animal mind, to elucidate the principles of mental evolution and to stress the continuity between human and animal consciousness. The second period, which I shall call the 'behaviouristic phase', is exemplified in the work of the American school of learning theorists and its aim was to show that human behaviour could be treated from the same objective standpoint as we apply to animal behaviour. As experimental psychologists they favoured laboratory experimentation as against field observation and they stressed the principles of conditioning and of trial-and-error learning as against the innate determinants of behaviour. The third period which began only after World War II with the work of Lorenz and Tinbergen in Germany may be called the 'ethological phase'. Ethology, as the new science came to be known, claimed to be no less objective in its approach than 'behaviouristics' but it stressed the importance of studying behaviour in the animal's natural habitat and it rescued the discredited concept of instinct by offering a new analysis. In what follows I shall discuss each of these three movements in the history of comparative psychology.

The principal protagonists of what I have described as the 'mentalistic' period were, in the order both of birth and of priority in the field: G. J. Romanes, C. Lloyd Morgan and L. T. Hobhouse.[2] Romanes, who may be credited with introducing the term 'comparative psychology', has been saddled with the reputation of being an anecdotalist of anthropomorphic inclinations and there can be no doubt that, in his more popular writings, he was sometimes insufficiently critical of the evidence he cites and too prone to look for human analogies. As Hearnshaw [1964] has wittily remarked: 'In attempting, as he claimed, to bridge "the psychological distance which separates the gorilla from the gentleman" he scaled the gorilla up rather than the gentleman down.' At the same time he was also an imaginative and versatile experimenter who pioneered many new areas of animal psychology. His work on the structure and function of the nervous system in the jellyfish, starfish, and sea-urchin, at a time when there was still some doubt as to whether such organisms possessed a nervous system, earned him a solid scientific reputation. In the light of a much publicised recent attempt to teach a chimpanzee to use sign language [cf. Gardner and Gardner (1969)] it is of interest to learn that Romanes claimed to have taught a female chimpanzee at the London Zoo to count up to five, which she demonstrated by producing from her mouth the requisite number of straws in response to the appropriate word. It is also of interest to learn that long before Harlow challenged orthodox motivation theory by declaring that, for monkeys at least, problem-solving could be self-rewarding so that the animal would continue to tackle such tasks without primary reinforcement, Romanes made a very similar observation with respect to a pet monkey he kept in his own house.

Lloyd Morgan was an influential figure, especially in the United States where he spent some time lecturing. His most important experimental contribution to comparative psychology was made early in his career and it concerned the pecking abilities of newly hatched chicks and other species of fowl in an attempt to assess how much of their behaviour was innately determined and how much was acquired. He drew attention to the extent to which such behaviour could be modified by experience and it was he who coined the expression 'method of trial and error learning' which was to play such a prominent part in the next phase of comparative psychology, especially as developed by Thorndike. To the present-day student of psychology he is best known as the author of the 'canon' which bears his name and states that: 'In no case may we interpret an action as the outcome of the exercise of a higher psychical faculty if it can be interpreted as the outcome of the exercise of one that stands lower in the psychological scale.' This maxim was offered as a corrective against the temptation to which his predecessor, Romanes, whom in general he much admired, occasionally succumbed. In the hands of his successors, however, this modest caution became something of a rallying cry to justify the elimination of all psychical faculties whatsoever, higher or lower; it became, in effect, the Occam's razor of behaviourism. This was far from being its author's intention, for Lloyd Morgan himself never wavered in his conviction that psychology begins from the introspection of our own mental processes and that 'introspective study must inevitably be the basis and foundation of all comparative psychology'. The case for imputing mental processes to animals was basically the same, he argued, as the case for imputing them to other people; both rested on the inductive argument based on analogy. The fact that animals cannot speak to us and describe their mental state does, admittedly, place the 'zoological psychologist' at a disadvantage but language, after all, is not the only known means of communication; he still has sufficient cues on which to base plausible inferences about the mental processes that underlie an animal's actions and expressions. Hence, says Lloyd Morgan, 'we are not only justified in extending our comparative psychology so as to include within its scope the field of zoological psychology but we are logically bound to regard psychological evolution as strictly coordinate with biological evolution'. On this latter point Lloyd Morgan was emphatic that he was a firm scientific monist, not a dualist, and that the mind and the organism were but two sides of the same coin. The trouble about this position is that it inevitably prompted the question: why, if psychological evolution is coordinate with biological evolution, need we waste time on unverifiable speculations concerning the subjective states of animals; why not concentrate instead on their overt observable behaviour and, if possible, on the state of their brains?

Hobhouse, the third member of this trio, was a philosopher and a sociologist, and his investigations of animal behaviour represent only one episode of a distinguished academic career. The outcome of this work is to be found in his book *Mind in Evolution* of 1901 which was an ambitious attempt, in the Spencerian tradition, to see mind as a developing system of increasing complexity starting with reflex action and culminating in systematic thought. Its most original part, however, is the account he gives of the experiments on animal problem-solving which he himself carried out using cats, dogs, monkeys and even an elephant. His experiments anticipate both in method and conception the later 'insight' experiments of Köhler with his apes and the still later work of Harlow with his Rhesus monkeys. Like them, he was already critical of Thorndike's view, based on the behaviour of cats in puzzle-boxes, that all problem-solving could be reduced to a matter of random trial-and-error searching. He was the first to describe the 'two-stick' problem in which a monkey is able to use one stick to reach a longer stick which can then be used to retrieve a banana. [*cf.* Köhler (1957) Chap. 5] He also discusses the detour problem as an example of insight and the fact that an animal can be shown how to solve a given problem and so learn by copying after failing to do so of its own accord.

After Hobhouse Britain lost its lead in the field of comparative psychology. But a new and enthusiastic generation of comparative psychologists was springing up in America. The most outstanding of these was Robert Yerkes who is best remembered for his studies of primate behaviour; the Yerkes Laboratory of Primate Biology, set up at Yale in 1919 and transferred to Orange Park, Florida, in 1930, became the main centre for primate research in the United

States. In 1929 he published, together with his wife, a monumental opus entitled *The Great Apes: A Study of Anthropoid Life*. On his retirement in 1941 the directorship of the Yerkes Laboratories went to Karl Lashley, one of the most important figures in modern experimental and physiological psychology. Yerkes's interests were by no means confined to the primates. Boring tells us that 'he worked successively on various lower animal forms, then on the crab, the turtle, the frog, the dancing mouse, the rat, the worm, the crow, the dove, the pig, the monkey and man'. [Boring (1950) p. 628] The final item refers to the fact that during World War I it was Yerkes who supervised the intelligence testing of recruits to the American armed forces, the first mass application of mental testing in history. It is noteworthy that Yerkes never joined the ranks of the behaviourists and his outlook and approach makes him the last great representative of our first period of comparative psychology which still came under the influence of the all-embracing evolutionary tradition begun by Darwin and Spencer.

The behaviouristic phase which followed owed little to the evolutionary tradition beyond the precedent it had set for studying animal behaviour. It can best be understood as the product of two other independent traditions: the psychological associationism that was the legacy of British Empiricist philosophy and the physiological associationism that attained its highest development in the work of the Russian school of reflexology whose founder was Sechenov. To the former it owed its extreme environmentalism; to the latter, which became influential after Pavlov's work started to become known in America during the 1920s, it owed its unremitting objectivism. Everything in behaviour, apart from a few innate reflexes and the physiological mechanisms necessary for generating drive-states, had henceforth to be explained in terms of the previous interactions between organism and environment. Moreover learning itself could now be conceived in the quasi-physiological terminology of conditioned reflexes; there was no longer any need to talk of the animal 'profiting from experience'. The behaviourist revolution produced a profound change in the prevailing conception of comparative psychology. Behavioural differences between species were now considered of little interest to the psychologist since they could all be regarded as incidental consequences of their anatomical differences or of the specialised way of life to which they had become adapted. All that matters in the last resort are the essential principles which govern the modification of behaviour in all species. Hence the overwhelming emphasis on learning theory that we find in this period. The following quotation from Thorndike, writing in 1911, illustrates clearly this new attitude: 'If my analysis is true, the evolution of behavior is a rather simple matter. Formally the crab, fish, turtle, dog, cat, monkey and baby have very similar intellects and characters. All are systems of connections subject to change by the law of exercise and effect.' [Thorndike (1911)] Skinner, writing half a century later in 1966, expresses a very similar point of view. Defending himself against the charge levelled by Beach who pointed out that the book which Skinner brought out in 1938 was entitled *The Behavior of Organisms* but was in fact 'based exclusively upon the performance of rats in bar-pressing situations', he argues that the biological sciences offer many precedents for a similar preoccupation with a single species: Mendel with his peas, Morgan with his fruit-flies, Pavlov with his dogs, and so on. 'Although species differences exist and should be studied,' says Skinner, 'an exhaustive analysis of the behaviour of a single species is as easily justified as the study of the chemistry or microanatomy of nerve tissue in one species.' Furthermore, Skinner denies that any particular advantage accrues from studying organisms in their natural environment, even if we could be sure what really is their natural habitat from an evolutionary standpoint: 'What an organism does,' he points out, 'is a fact about that organism regardless of the conditions under which he does it. A behavioral process is none the less real for being exhibited in an arbitrary setting.' [Skinner (1966)]

Given, then, these assumptions that species differences are unimportant and that virtually all behaviour is learned behaviour, it becomes a mere matter of convenience what sort of organism you decide to use as data. The rat or the pigeon become simply a useful stand-in for the human subject and bar-pressing or disc-pecking a paradigm of human learning. Indeed, the simpler the organism and the simpler the response the less the risk of becoming confused by irrelevant complications. Naturally, we may expect differences in the rate of learning from one species to another or differences in the complexity of problem that can be learned, but these quantitative differences need not prevent us from constructing a theoretical system based on the essential uniformity of all behaviour. It is noteworthy that the comparative psychology of this second period was the work of experimental psychologists, not biologists; animals were studied seldom for their own sake, as distinctive forms of life, but as substitute human beings.

Ethology was largely the creation of German zoologists, as opposed to American psychologists, and it represents among other things an attempt to restore comparative psychology to the field of evolutionary biology from which it had originally emerged.[3] Although none of the leading ethologists were behaviourists in the dogmatic sense—the influence of German psychology, which had never been behaviourist, was too strong for that—they insisted that ethology was every bit as much an objective or positive science as behaviouristics. Where it differed mainly from the latter was in the prominence it gave to inborn patterns of behaviour. This innate aspect, they argued, had for too long been obscured by an exclusive preoccupation with animal behaviour under artificial laboratory conditions. Under natural conditions it at once becomes obvious that an animal is geared to seeking out particular forms of stimulation, and genetically predisposed to respond to this stimulation in certain characteristic ways. In this way they reopened the entire question of instinct which had become all but a dead letter during our second phase of comparative psychology. Whereas, in the first phase, instinct and habit had served as the twin pillars upon which mental evolution rested, during this second phase habit had all but swallowed up instinct. Even such congenital responses as pecking in the newly hatched chick had to be explained in terms of a conditioning process taking place in the egg rather than as a case of genetically determined behaviour. The ethologists introduced four new concepts which not only gave rise to a new conception of instinct but which had far-reaching repercussions for psychology in general.

First, came the introduction of 'Fixed Action Patterns', which are defined as coordinated motor actions that occur as units in the appropriate situation and are assumed to be genetically programmed, inasmuch as they do not presuppose any prior practice on the part of the organism or any opportunity for the organism to imitate the pattern from another member of the species. On the physiological side they cannot be reduced to a mere chain of reflexes but have to be considered integrated and adaptive units in their own right. Secondly, came such concepts as 'Sign-Stimuli', 'Releasers', 'Innate Releasing Mechanisms', etc., all of which referred to the way in which the fixed action patterns were elicited. Of special interest were the shapes, colours and markings belonging to predators, prey or rivals that entered into the animal's ecology as, for example, when the red breast of the male robin acts as a releaser for the attacking response of another male robin. Similarly, the fixed action pattern of one animal could itself function as a releaser for triggering off another fixed action pattern in a second animal. Tinbergen analysed along these lines the elaborate courtship rituals of the stickleback. These 'sign-stimuli' were thus a special class of unconditioned stimuli and their effects could be studied experimentally in the laboratory; they could even be manipulated so as to elicit responses stronger than those found in nature ('super-optimal stimuli').

The third concept, and one that seems to have captivated psychologists, was that of 'Imprinting' which we owe to Konrad Lorenz. [see Sluckin (1965) Chap. 1] It was observed that, among certain species of ground-nesting birds such as chickens, ducks and geese, the newly hatched young tend to follow automatically the mother bird, a behaviour which is, incidentally, vital for their survival. This following response, however, is not, like pecking, congenital; it comes about as a result of the organism being exposed, during a brief critical interval following birth (extending usually for about 24 hours after hatching), to some prominent moving object. It is this special kind of one-trial learning which thereafter gives all the appearances of being an instinctual response which has been given the name of 'imprinting'. Like the innate releasing mechanism, it can be studied in the laboratory where conditions can be arranged so that the critical object is not the mother bird or even another animate object, in which case the fledgling will be duly imprinted on this inappropriate object. What specially interested the development psychologist about this phenomenon was not so much the fact of imprinting itself which, in its classic form, can, after all, be demonstrated only in a few species of birds, but rather the idea of there being a critical period for learning and socialisation which does seem to apply in some degree quite widely across species. The fourth and final ethological concept we must note here is that of the 'Hierarchical Organisation of an Instinct', which is specially associated with the name of Tinbergen. Any total instinctive display, whether it is a case of nest-building, courtship, fighting, migrating, etc., commences with certain appetitive behaviours and concludes with certain consummatory activities. The aim of the ethologist is to construct an appropriate hierarchy or 'ethological grammar' which allows him to specify what options are possible at any particular stage of this display. Seen in this way it is no longer necessary to think of an instinct as a single stereotyped performance, for although the ultimate consummatory acts may be relatively fixed and stereotyped the initial appetitive moves may be highly variable and adaptive. [cf. Tinbergen (1951) and Thorpe (1963)]

It may at first seem strange that a zoological science so closely tied up with innate behaviour patterns in birds and fish should have any influence at all on psychology. Yet the fact is that its influence during the past couple of decades has been considerable and is still continuing. Various reasons may be suggested for this state of affairs. I have already alluded to the idea of the 'critical period' which came out of the work on imprinting and which to some appeared an independent corroboration of certain psychoanalytic insights. Another reason of a negative kind may be found in the disenchantment which began to be felt with the behaviouristic approach by the early 1950s. The beguiling simplicities of stimulus-response psychology began to look too much like an artefact of its own restrictive methodology. In these circumstances a fresh look at nature, such as the ethologists seemed to offer, with its reminder of the diversity and complexity of the real world, came as a welcome relief. At the same time, as we shall have occasion to note in our next lecture, the pendulum had swung so far over in the environmentalist direction that a reaction was inevitable and the genetics of behaviour once more came to seem important. Finally, ethology and physiological psychology began to draw closer together. Hebb had already prepared the ground by showing that the central nervous system could not be regarded as an inert machine waiting to transform sensory inputs into motor actions, but was itself a centre of autonomous activity. The experiments of von Holst demonstrated that the locomotory activity of fish was controlled and coordinated centrally and was not like a chain of reflexes dependent on sensory stimulation. Further experiments in the late 1950s by von Holst and von St Paul showed that complete fixed action patterns could be elicited by stimulating electrically specific points in the brains of chickens. These and similar experiments 'gave strong support', in the words of E. H. Hess, 'to the long-held opinion of ethologists

that there must be a structural organization within the central
nervous system which parallels the lawfulness of behaviour observed
by ethologists, and particularly the hierarchical organization of
behaviour as shown by Tinbergen.' [Hess (1962) p. 214] In the
long run it may be that it is through the fresh light that ethology
will be able to shed on the nature of the brain and nervous system
that its main contribution to human psychology will be made. In
the short run, however, the more urgent question was whether
anything corresponding to the instinctive behaviour, which ethologists had observed with so much care in the animal kingdom,
existed in man. It is to this question that we must now address
ourselves.

Instinct in Man

The place of instinct in human nature is a question that continues
to agitate psychologists and social psychologists and in recent years
has once again come to the boil as a result of a number of best-
selling books by ethologists, or popularisers of ethology, purporting
to reveal the instinctual roots of various facets of man's behaviour
and, in particular, of his aggressive behaviour.[4] The latter claim
has especially incensed the critics who find it ominously reminiscent
of the doctrine of original sin. Thus, the anthropologist, Ashley
Montagu, launching his counter-attack against Ardrey, Lorenz and
their followers, feels it necessary to reiterate the hallowed articles
of the behaviourist faith in the following words: 'There is, in fact,
not the slightest evidence or ground for assuming that the *alleged*
"phylogenetically adapted instinctive" behaviour of other animals is
in any way relevant to the discussion of the motive-forces of human
behaviour. The fact is that, with the exception of the instinctoid
reactions in infants to sudden withdrawals of support and to sudden
noises, the human being is *entirely* instinctless' (my italics).
[Montagu (1968) p. 11]

As with so many controversies in science that arouse fierce
passions, one suspects that more than just theoretical positions are
at stake; ideological commitments are engaged. To cast doubt upon
the malleability and hence perfectability of the human race has,
ever since the Enlightenment, been regarded by progressive thinkers
and social reformers as a kind of treason. Moreover, since the con-

cept of instinct is capable of a variety of interpretations, it is hardly surprising if the two sides often found themselves speaking at cross purposes and if the controversy continued to resist a definitive settlement.

The idea that instinct might be relevant to human behaviour is one of the direct legacies of Darwin. McDougall, writing in 1908, states: 'It would be difficult to find any adequate mention of instincts in treatises on human psychology written before the middle of last century,' and adds, 'but the work of Darwin and Herbert Spencer has lifted to some extent the veil of mystery from the instincts of animals and has made the problem of the relationship of instinct to human intelligence and conduct one of the most widely discussed of recent years'. [McDougall (1908)] And although Drever [1917], writing ten years later, in his *Instinct in Man* traces the notion of human instinct to the vaguer notion of 'natural inclinations' as discussed in the writings of Descartes, Malebranche or Hobbes, we are probably safe in taking our stand with McDougall and accepting Darwinism as the source of the idea. Before that, the contrast between human actions as being guided by reason and animal behaviour being under the governance of instinct was too salient to allow much scope for a special category of human instinctive behaviour.

Among the founding fathers of the new psychology, the first to champion the doctrine of human instinct was William James, to whom Darwinian ideas were in general congenial. He defines instinct in a way that would be hard to fault, as 'the faculty of acting in such a way as to produce certain ends, without foresight of the ends, and without previous education in the performance'.[5] When he comes to the question of instinct in man, however, the clause about performance is quietly dropped and the instinct is made equivalent to a mere unlearned impulse to action. Accordingly, such examples as 'greediness and suspicion, curiosity and timidity, coyness and desire, bashfulness and vanity, sociability and pugnacity', which we would now regard as a mixed bag of traits, dispositions and types of behaviour, are all cited as examples of human instincts. No wonder that James was able to claim that man had more, not less, instincts than any other mammal. But James did make one important point that set the stage for subsequent discussion, namely that there was no incompatibility between instinct and intelligence; instinct could be modified by learning and there was in fact a continual interplay between instinct and learning. The point has again been emphasised in the context of animal behaviour by modern ethological research. From James onwards, instinct theory in psychology became mainly a theory of human motivation and it was taken for granted that the overt expression of the instinct could take whatever form learning imposes.

The most systematic and ambitious of the instinct theorists was, of course, McDougall. When he came to write his *Social Psychology* of 1908 he found in instinct theory the dynamic he needed as a basis for his psychology of social life which he failed to find in the hedonistic assumptions of the earlier associationists. 'What could be more absurd', he asks, 'than Professor Bain's doctrine that the joy of a mother in her child, her tender care and self-sacrificing efforts on its behalf, are due to the pleasure she derives from bodily contact with it in the maternal embrace?'[6] To McDougall (if not to Freud) the question could only be rhetorical. Nothing could well be more self-evident, he thought, than that a woman's maternal behaviour was an expression of an inborn maternal instinct. Nor do I think McDougall would have argued differently had he then known about hormones; he would have said that the endocrine mechanisms are just another of the inborn devices by which nature insures the fulfilment of the instinctual aim. Of course this does not commit us to saying that the human female is born with a ready-made knowledge of child care; here, as elsewhere, the core of the instinct, for McDougall, was in its conative-affective source, not in its external manifestations. This aspect is emphasised in his much quoted definition where he writes: 'We may then define an instinct as an inherited or innate psycho-physical disposition which determines its possessor to perceive, and to pay attention to, objects of a certain class, to experience an emotional excitement of a particular quality upon perceiving such an object, and to act in regard to it in a particular manner, or, at least, to experience an impulse to such action' (*idem* p. 65).

Here we see that, apart from the clause about acting in a particular manner towards the stimulus-object, the definition is couched in the language of experience rather than behaviour. Drever went even further in distinguishing clearly between instinct as an objective biological fact and as a subjective psychological reality; in the latter connection he introduces such expressions as 'instinct-experience' and 'instinct-interest' to denote the feeling of 'worth-whileness' that attaches itself to objects that arouse instinctive emotions. In the face of criticisms and misunderstandings McDougall came to attach more and more importance to this moti-vating aspect of instinct for human psychology, as opposed to its usage in animal psychology to stand for a kind of inherited skill. In the final supplementary chapter which he wrote for the twenty-third edition of his *Social Psychology* of 1936 he has this to say: 'It is this central part of the instinct, both affective and conative in function, which we need to distinguish and define as clearly as possible; and since we can properly and very advantageously regard it as a functional unit of structure, we need for it some special designation. I have, therefore, proposed to speak of this central part of the innate disposition which is an instinct as a *propensity*, making use of a good English word used by many of the older authors in almost the same sense' (author's italics) (*idem* p. 502).

The behaviourist attack on instinct theory, an attack which was so far successful that during the inter-war years it practically dis-appeared from academic psychology and, as my quotation from Ashley Montagu shows, has, even now, never properly recovered, had both its positive and negative aspects. On the negative side, much the most damaging criticism that was voiced concerned the alleged sterility of the instinct concept. The instinct theorists, it was said, succumbed to the same fallacy as that which vitiated the earlier 'faculty psychology' of the phrenologists, that of supposing that to invent a name for some phenomenon is tantamount to explaining it. A fruitful concept in science is one that helps us to understand better the causal processes that underlie a given pheno-menon; an instinct, however, can be identified only by its aim, not by its causal conditions, and hence can never yield anything more than the spurious satisfaction of a pseudo-explanation. There was some substance to this complaint but, in the main, it betrays a misunderstanding of the logic of taxonomy. Thus the concept of 'instinct' may be compared with the concept of 'disease' in medical science. Normally a disease-entity is postulated on the basis of a particular symptomatology before any specific micro-organism has been identified as the causal agent of that disease. Indeed, histori-cally, the concept of disease was an indispensable tool of medicine long before any knowledge of micro-organisms existed. In just the same way one may postulate a particular McDougallian instinct on the basis of certain behavioural or experiential facts before one knows anything at all about the neurological structures that, supposedly, constitute the 'innate pyschophysical disposition'. In fact that taxonomic aspect of instinct theory was carried to its logical conclusion by R. B. Cattell who, on the basis of a factor analysis of questionnaire data, attempted to identify certain fundamental factors in human motivation which he called 'ergs' and which he explicitly tried to relate to McDougall's instincts or propensities.[7]

The other major argument against any too free indulgence in instinct postulation was that, in default of any known instances of complex behaviour common to all human beings, it was more parsimonious to assume that the goals we seek in life are all culturally determined rather than laid down for us by nature. This argument was reinforced by the work of the social anthropologists which stressed the sheer diversity of customs, mores and traditions and pointed as an example to the absence in some societies of anything we would describe as 'competition' which, in Western civilisation, is so widespread that it gives all the appearances of being one of the inherited features of human nature. Here, again, we may recognise the sound heuristic sense in dwelling on the actual ways in which, whether through upbringing or other special mechanisms of cultural transmission, values, goals, modes of life, are inculcated among members of a given society rather than appealing to some universal inborn disposition. Yet, when all has been said, there remain certain aspects of behaviour that are so ubiquitous that it would be hard to attribute them simply to common cultural influences. I have in mind especially the eruptions of violence that have been such a notorious accompaniment of human history in almost every age and place. It is hardly sufficient in refutation to point to a few small, isolated and highly atypical communities, of the sort that anthropologists delight in bringing to our attention, where all overt expressions of hostility are successfully inhibited from an early age.

So much for the negative case. But, if we go along with the behaviourists in repudiating all genetic determinants of behaviour as opposed to structure, what alternative dynamic can we offer in place of instinct theory? The answer seems to be 'drive theory'. As with instinct theory, drive theory took various forms but seems to have reached its fullest and clearest expression in the writings of Clark Hull.[8] It is based essentially on a homeostatic conception of the living organism which may be expounded as follows: an organism if left to itself will remain in a state of rest until eventually some internal metabolic deficiency or chemical imbalance (i.e. a drive) goads it into a state of general restlessness which, in the first instance, is quite undirected. This condition then persists until, initially quite by accident but later as a result of learning, the organism engages in some activity (i.e. consummatory behaviour) which restores the equilibrium, whereupon the organism returns to its initial state of inactivity until this cycle is ready to recur. Only a few primary drives were thought necessary to explain all behaviour, notably those of hunger, thirst, sex and pain-avoidance; all other motives, including even such elemental ones as fear, were acquired; thus fear is originally brought into play by external cues that have become associated with pain.

At first reading it might be thought that the primary drives were merely another name for instincts or at least for that conative-affective core of an instinct which McDougall called the propensity. But there is an important distinction. For the instinct theorist, what was innate was the pre-programmed disposition of the nervous system which insured that energy would be channelled in some particular direction under appropriate conditions. For the drive theorist the only innate properties of the organism that affect behaviour, other than certain innate reflexes involved in consummatory activity such as sucking, swallowing, urinating, defecating, copulating, etc., are the specific mechanisms, hormonal or other, involved in the production of hunger, thirst, sexual excitation, etc. A corollary of this view was that, so far as the animal's behavioural repertoire was concerned, any drive was as good as any other. So long only as a certain level of drive or arousal is attained, any response whatever, no matter how irrelevant to the drive in question, will be acquired provided it results in a diminution of the level of arousal.

Some confusion has arisen in the past from this failure to distinguish between the concepts of drive and of instinct. While both issue in a specific goal-state, the concept of drive is a strictly causal concept while that of instinct is essentially teleological. There is nothing in the concept of drive which corresponds to McDougall's innate tendency to 'pay attention to objects of a particular class' or to 'experience an emotional excitement' in its presence or 'to act in regard to it in a particular manner'. All these aspects of instinct theory are relegated instead to learning theory. The one crucial feature of the drive-state is that it goes on building up as a direct consequence of some physical privation until eventually it finds an outlet in the relevant consummatory activity like a river finding a path to the sea. This outlet then provides the reinforcement which, in Hullian theory, is both the necessary and sufficient condition to insure that the behaviour leading up to it will be learned. Such, then, is the drive-reduction theory of learning; it does not deny, of course, that anatomy imposes certain limitations on what an animal can or cannot learn; obviously one cannot teach pigs to fly; furthermore, the size or complexity of the animal's brain will impose certain further limitations on his repertoire; but, within these very broad limits, species differences count for very little and so for the drive theorist it became a mere matter of convenience which particular species, be it man or rat, was used to demonstrate the universal principles of motivation.

Eventually, drive theory in turn came in for attacks from one quarter or another. On the physiological side, Hebb and his followers with their experiments on sensory deprivation showed how implausible it was to conceive of the organism as a homeostat, inasmuch as a certain level of arousal is necessary for the optimal functioning of the CNS (central nervous system) so that, if deprived of it, the organism *seeks* stimulation. At the same time the new knowledge of the role of the reticular activating system in sustaining this level of arousal further contributed to a new conception of the functions of the CNS. [*cf*. Hebb (1955) and Zubek (ed.) (1969)] On the behavioural side, Harlow and others drew attention to the importance of exploratory behaviour and showed how typical it was of so many species from rat to monkey. [*cf*. Harlow (1953)] That animals are naturally curious was a fact well known to Darwin, but it was never easy to reconcile this fact with the homeostatic assumptions of orthodox drive theory though, inevitably, some attempts were now made. [*cf*. Berlyne (1960)] At the human level there was a marked trend during the 1950s away from purely biological theories of motivation towards more positive and humanistic conceptions: Maslow's 'self-actualisation', McClelland's 'achievement motivation' are among the pointers of this new tendency in motivation theory. [*cf*. Maslow (1954) and McClelland *et al*. (1953)] There were also some attempts during this period to revive hedonism, and concepts such as 'affective arousal' began to supplant 'drive-reduction'. [*cf.* Young (1959)]

It was at this time of general dissatisfaction with the austerities of the behaviouristic approach that ethology began to attract notice. Tinbergen's *Study of Instinct* of 1951 went a long way towards rehabilitating instinct as a respectable zoological concept. At first ethologists were careful to avoid extrapolating their findings to the human case, but Lorenz's essay on aggression, first published in Vienna in 1963, set a new fashion [Lorenz (1966)] and, since then, many volumes have appeared by various authors presenting an ethological interpretation of human behaviour in its various aspects with special reference to its primate origins. These have been received with enthusiasm by the general public but psychologists have, on the whole, been highly critical and they have been dismissed as too speculative to provide much more than entertainment value for an understanding of human behaviour. It would be true to say that today the term instinct is very rarely used as a technical term with reference to human behaviour, at least outside the specialised context of psychoanalysis. And it may be pointed out, in passing, that the concept of instinct in psychoanalysis comes closer to that of the Hullian drive than it does to a true McDougallian instinct. Indeed, Freud's 'libido' may be thought of as something like the sex drive only with a more diffuse goal; copulation is not necessarily its natural terminus. Like a drive-state, the libido too was regarded as representing a definite quantity of vital energy or tension which would alternately accumulate and then discharge itself through various outlets and generally motivate behaviour in the course of doing so. But even in the sphere of animal psychology some notable authorities now regard instinct as too imprecise a term to be worth preserving. Thus, Beach [1955] argues that when the science of behaviour genetics is further advanced we shall be in a position to analyse each specimen of behaviour in terms of its hereditary or environmental contributions and we shall no longer require any such crude blanket expression.

But, even if this proves to be the case and if, with the increasing sophistication of the biological sciences, the term instinct finds less and less application, an argument could still be advanced for retaining it in the context of the social sciences,[9] at any rate in one of its more innocuous adjectival forms such as 'instinctive' or 'instinctual'. Certainly, it is difficult to take seriously any longer the view, so dear for so long to so many social scientists, which, in effect, reduces the individual to a mere neutral set of capacities which society can shape to any specification, as if man were a computer waiting to be programmed with any arbitrary set of instructions. We do not need to swallow the more far-fetched ethological notions in order to recognise that certain objects will be intrinsically more attention-getting than others, some kinds of behaviour more readily acquired than others, and that, beneath the veneer of civilisation, there exists within each of us certain ineradicable urges and impulses that we share with our simian ancestry.

In the last resort, though no doubt the whole question is ultimately one of semantics, the case for calling, say, aggression instinctive is neither worse nor better than the case for calling sex instinctive.[10] Indeed, in the male, at least, the two often go together and it can be shown that the same hormones that determine the typical male sexual behaviour in mammals also contribute to manifestations of aggressive behaviour.[11] It is true that the sex instinct has a more clearly defined goal—obviously the continuance of the species depends on it, whereas it is still a matter for some debate and speculation as to precisely what is the natural function of aggression. It has been argued that, for modern man, it is chiefly a hangover from the time when it was an indispensable part of defending one's territory or maintaining one's position in the dominance hierarchy of the tribe and that, in civilised society, its effects are purely destructive. On the other hand, it has also been claimed by psychologists that without an element of aggression none of the constructive and creative achievements which we owe to man's restless and ambitious nature would ever have come into being.[12] But, whatever its function, we may say of aggression, as we may say of sex, that the form it takes among human beings is culturally determined but the basic cravings, desires and emotions that go with it are part of our native endowment. In both cases its overt expression may, under certain circumstances, be entirely inhibited or, under other circumstances, erupt at the slightest provocation. To show, as some authorities have tried to do, that aggression occurs normally only as a reaction to some identifiable frustration does not, as has been too often assumed, dispose of its instinctual origins; it serves only to make more specific the conditions required to elicit or release such behaviour. The disputed question as to whether there is anything corresponding to innate aggressiveness in human beings devolves upon the question of whether violent, hostile and destructive actions are always acquired as a result of being reinforced in the first instance by extraneous rewards, or whether they may appear naturally under certain conditions even in defiance of extraneous punishment. Commonsense would suggest that in man, no less than in other species, anger and fight like panic and flight are instinctual reactions. But to call aggression instinctual does not imply, as critics have too readily assumed, that we are all potential killers, any more than to call sex instinctual implies that we are all potential rapists. When our frustration-tolerance becomes low enough we are easily provoked to anger and violent outbursts; in the same way, to the lonely sex-starved individual, objects which to the normal person would appear as no more than mildly erotic may be severely inflammatory.

The upshot of this brief discussion of instinct in man is that instinct, as a general concept in the behavioural sciences, has declined in importance as detailed knowledge of the determinants of behaviour, both internal and external, has increased and that, in any case, its importance diminishes the higher we ascend the phyletic scale. Hence, to some extent, we can separate psychology, as being predominantly concerned with learned behaviour, from ethology which is predominantly concerned with innate behaviour. At the same time it is suggested that the word instinct retains a certain residual usefulness in social psychology if only as a reminder that human nature has a certain grain and, however cunningly we manipulate human beings, we can only go either with the grain or against it. This reminder is sometimes needed as a corrective to the more insidious forms of utopianism which assume that human beings can be fashioned to conform to any arbitrary model.

* * *

We can now attempt to sum up the implications of these past two sections for the status of comparative psychology as a psychological science. That animal behaviour is worth studying for its own sake has never been in question; ethology would still stand irrespective of whether or not it had any relevance to psychology. But at least three positive reasons may be given for thinking that the study of animal behaviour is relevant to an understanding of human behaviour:

(1) Man's brain and nervous system is constructed on the same

basic pattern and with the same basic components as those of lesser organisms and, since there is obviously a strict limit to the amount of experimentation that can be done on the living human brain, comparative psychology becomes necessary as a testing ground for human physiological psychology. It is perhaps salutary to note that the most fundamental work that has been done so far on biological memory systems is that which has used the octopus as a subject.

(2) Though the human mind is unique in certain respects, in others, which include all the basic processes which underlie adaptive behaviour, the animal and human mind form a natural continuum just as the infant and adult mind form a continuum.[13] Furthermore, insofar as we still retain vestiges of instinctual behaviour patterns inherited from our pre-human past, ethological studies, especially those dealing with primate species living under natural conditions, may reasonably hope to throw some light on their nature and origins.

(3) Comparative psychology is important not just on account of the similarities it reveals in cross-species comparisons but, equally, on account of the contrasts it brings into relief. In this respect its justification is similar to that of other comparative studies, e.g. 'comparative institutions', 'comparative religion', 'comparative linguistics', etc.; in every case concepts initially derived from a single restricted domain are enriched by being extended to a wider field. If ever we are to understand our own natures it will only be by reference to and in contrast with the minds of alien species.

Summary

Animal Minds

The development of an animal psychology is here traced through three distinct historical phases: (i) a mentalistic phase which flourished in the late nineteenth century under the inspiration of Darwin and the British School of Darwinian naturalists; (ii) a behaviouristic phase which flourished during the inter-war period under the auspices of the American School of learning theorists; and (iii) an ethological phase belonging to the post-World War II years which was inaugurated by Lorenz and the German School of naturalists. This latter development has once more aroused interest in the innate determinants of behaviour and in possible instinctual bases for certain aspects of human social behaviour, notably aggressive behaviour.

Instinct in Man

Instinct theory was one of the legacies of Darwinism and it reached its climax in the writings of McDougall early this century. A reaction against its excesses led to its being ousted by Behaviourism which was dogmatically environmentalist and sought to explain all behaviour as the product of conditioning. With the decline of behaviourism and the advent of ethology, the question of instinct in man has been reopened. Here we have argued that the case for an instinctual basis for aggression is neither more nor less implausible than the case for an instinctual basis for human sexual behaviour. We have further suggested that whatever terms we use to refer to the genetic components of human behaviour the old utopian optimism which regarded human nature as infinitely malleable, and hence infinitely perfectible, is hard to sustain in the light of what we now know of our evolutionary past.

Notes

1 In my own university, at Edinburgh, a 'Theoretical Psychology Unit' was set up in 1972 under the chairmanship of Professor H. C. Longuet-Higgins in the School of Artificial Intelligence.

2 The principal works of these three founders of comparative psychology are: G. J. Romanes *Animal Intelligence* (1882), *Mental Evolution in Animals* (1883), *Mental Evolution in Man* (1888); C. Lloyd Morgan *Animal Life and Intelligence* (1890), *Introduction to Comparative Psychology* (1894); L. T. Hobhouse *Mind in Evolution* (1901). For a discussion of their work and influence *see* Hearnshaw [1964] Chap. 6.

3 According to Jaynes [1969], the term 'Ethology', to mean the

study of the behaviour of animals in their natural habitat, is due to Isidore Geoffroy-Saint-Hilaire, son of the eminent early evolutionist Etienne Geoffroy-Saint-Hilaire, who coined the term in 1859. It then fell into oblivion from which it was rescued by another French biologist, a specialist in marine biology, Alfred Giard, during the 1870s. Jaynes admits, however, that its present currency is due to the work of Lorenz and Tinbergen in Germany and now represents in part a protest against the artificialities of comparative psychology as developed by American behaviourists.

4 Notable examples of this genre are: Lorenz [1966], Ardrey [1967], [1970], Morris [1967], Russell and Russell [1968], Tiger [1969], Tiger and Fox [1972].

5 *See* James [1890] Vol. II, Chap. 24, 'Instinct', opening sentence.

6 McDougall [1908] p. 37n. *See also* pp. 56-69, 'The Parental Instinct and the Tender Emotion', where he argues that 'parental love must always appear an insoluble riddle and paradox if we do not recognize this primary emotion deeply rooted in an ancient instinct of vital importance to the human race' (p. 60). Yet, at the same time he saw no contradiction in admitting that 'there are women, happily few, whose attitude towards their children shows them to be devoid of a maternal instinct' (p. 61n.).

7 *See* Cattell [1950] Chap. 7, 'The Structure of Innate Drives'. The definition which Cattell uses to define his 'erg' is almost word for word McDougall's definition of instinct, as quoted on p. 80 above.

8 *Cf.* Hull [1943]. From his pivotal position at the Institute of Human Relations at Yale, Hull influenced deeply an entire generation of behavioural and social scientists.

9 *Cf.* Fletcher [1957]. It may be significant that Fletcher, who here puts forward a strong plea for retaining the concept of instinct, is himself a sociologist, not an experimental psychologist.

10 *Cf.* L. Tiger [1969]. 'Just as there is a valence between males and females, my suggestion is that there is also a valence between males.

In the way that males and females make love, males and males make war ... It is the social response of men in groups which is the infrastructure of aggression activity.' (*Encounter,* **33**, pp. 59-63.)

11   *Cf.* Vowles [1970]. 'In women it is known that androgens can be secreted by the adrenal gland and there is some evidence that if hormones become too concentrated in the pregnant mother her genetically female child may develop a partially male behaviour pattern with its associated aggressiveness.' It is noteworthy that nowhere in this lecture does Professor Vowles use the word 'instinct', though I gather he has nothing against it as a descriptive term.

12   *Cf.* Storr [1968] p. 62. 'It is highly probable that the undoubted superiority of the male sex in intellectual and creative achievement is related to their greater endowment of aggression.' The author, a well-known psychoanalyst, dedicates his book 'with admiration and affection' to Konrad Lorenz.

13   This is not to imply that the continuity is a smooth one. The old Aristotelian idea of a *'scala naturae'* or 'great chain of being' on which every creature could be graded on a single dimension of complexity or perfection, with man (or God) occupying the topmost rung, has recently been blamed for the tendency of comparative psychologists to ignore the 'discontinuities implicit in the theory of evolution as a result of the divergence of evolutionary lines and the extinction of many intermediate forms'. *See* W. Hodos and C. B. Campbell 'Scala Naturae: Why there is no Theory in Comparative Psychology'. *Psychol. Rev.*, **76**, 1969, pp. 337-50.

CHAPTER THREE

Differential Psychology

In every science one can distinguish a polarity between theory and application, between the pure scientist concerned with laws that hold over the entire domain of his science and the applied scientist who is interested in the particular case. Among the physical sciences the geologist and the astronomer use the laws and theories of physics and chemistry to explain the special properties of rocks or stars. Among the life sciences the botanist and the zoologist apply their knowledge of fundamental biology to the study of particular species of plants and animals. This distinction is not absolute: the applied scientist may wish to introduce special laws that hold only with respect to his own part of the wider domain; it is more a question of orientation: whether the focus of interest falls on the universal and the necessary or on the particular and the contingent. Thus, insofar as physics concerns itself with the properties of matter as such, as opposed to the properties of particular material systems, be they rocks or stars, plants or animals, it represents the theoretical pole of science in opposition to these other special sciences which deal with the accidental products of cosmology or evolution.

When it comes to the psychological sciences the same polarity reappears even though the theoretical pole now begins to look much less pure. Ironically, those who founded experimental psychology did so in the confident belief that psychology would provide the mental counterpart of physics and that certain universal laws of mind would soon emerge to match the universal laws of matter. The Weber-Fechner law attracted so much attention precisely because it once looked like being a model of just such a law. But with the shift of emphasis from consciousness to behaviour a more modest conception of psychology took its place. The behaviour of organisms, and of man as just one special kind of an organism, was clearly governed by a multitude of contingent factors, internal as well as external, and it seemed most unlikely that it would conform to any simple laws of wide generality. Hence, despite some attempts to propound such laws, especially in the field of conditioning and learning, psychologists have, for the most part, been content to pursue the path of the applied scientist tackling each fresh problem as it arose in a piecemeal empirical fashion and borrowing unashamedly from the older sciences whenever necessary. But, of all the psychological sciences, the one that most clearly exhibits this practical and applied approach is that which we are here calling 'differential psychology'.

The study of individual differences, also known in its quantitative aspects as 'psychometrics', has had three main objectives: (1) to specify the most important ways in which people differ from one another; (2) to identify the causes of these differences, whether biological or cultural; and (3) to plot the actual distribution of various mental attributes in the population at large. The tool which the psychometrist uses in pursuit of these three objectives is the 'mental test'. A mental test, whether it belongs to the simple pencil-and-paper variety or whether it requires elaborate instrumentation, has to satisfy three major criteria: (a) it has to be *standardised* with reference to certain known norms; (b) it has to be *reliable*; and (c) it has to be *valid*. The reason for this is that, unlike a census return or an opinion poll where, assuming the statements are truthful, they should be self-explanatory, the scores obtained from a mental test are meaningless in isolation. Thus, suppose we have a test of musical ability, we cannot interpret an individual's score unless we already know: (a) something about the distribution of scores in the population on which the test has been standardised; (b) how far we can assume that we would have obtained approximately the same score from that same individual under the same conditions on another occasion; and (c) on what grounds, apart from mere face-validity, we are entitled to claim that our test is in fact a test of musical ability. As regards (a), the two parameters of the distribution which are crucial for the purpose of standardisation are first, the mean or central measure and, secondly, the variance or degree of scatter. As regards (b), reliability, it is customary to express this in terms of a reliability coefficient which can vary between o and 1 where zero would imply that it is a matter of pure chance what score a given individual gets on a given occasion and unity implies that one can always rely on getting exactly the same score from a given individual under the same conditions. One way of estimating this coefficient is by means of the so-called 'split-half' correlation, which means that the overall score is divided into two parts based respectively on the odd and even items of the test and the two halves are then correlated over all subjects. As regards (c), validity, this can be measured either by reference to some external criterion—in the example we took one could find out how well the test discriminated between musicians and others—or one can fall back on some form of internal validation and show that the test agrees well with other tests that purport to measure musical ability. In any test the composition of suitable items often calls for considerable flair and ingenuity and is not something that can be reduced to a set of rules; the point that I am making here is that, given a set of items, there are well recognised procedures for evaluating them.

Granted, then, that mental attributes, no less than physical characteristics, can be measured using appropriate techniques, let us now consider how each of the three main aims of differential psychology can be realised. First, then, since the number of possible ways in which one individual may differ from another is clearly infinite, how are we to decide which of these to single out for special study? If we take the word 'personality' as the most general term to cover the totality of different ways in which any pair of individuals may differ from one another in the psychological sense, the first dichotomy that suggests itself in attempting to introduce order into the field is that between (a) the relative effectiveness with which people function in a given context and (b) everything else about them that goes to make them the kind of people they are. Thus we get on the one hand the problem of the abilities and, on the other, the traits of temperament and character that constitute personality in the narrower sense. We shall first confine ourselves to the abilities which, historically, were the first to gain attention but we should bear in mind that the division is one of convenience and that when it comes to predicting success in life it is useless to consider one and to ignore the other.

Abilities

The first fact of which we have to take note in discussing human abilities is that they are not independent of one another but fall into certain clusters and are otherwise interrelated in more or less complex ways. This being the case, the first problem which the psychometrist must face is one of sampling policy; in other words, given that he can obtain only a few measures from each individual, which of them are going to prove the best bet in the sense of having the greatest predictive power? Thus, one answer to the question of relative importance derives from the fact that not all items of information that pertain to a person are equally informative. But, quite apart from the economics of testing, a knowledge of the 'structure' of abilities is of obvious theoretical interest. Traditionally two opposite views have been held on this issue: on the one side there have been those who have argued that some people are just generally more capable than others and it makes no difference in what special direction they choose to apply their ability; on the other side there have been those who believed that we are born with an assortment of different gifts and that success in life depends on discovering where one's particular bent lies; the pseudo-science of phrenology did much to popularise this latter notion during the 19th century. Modern statistical developments, in particular the technique known to statisticians as factor analysis, have at last made possible a more or less definitive solution of this problem which shows that there was some truth on both sides, that is to say the abilities form an hierarchy according to their level of specificity or generality. The concept of general intelligence which has played so large a part in the history of differential psychology can now be identified with the apex of this hierarchy inasmuch as it enters to a greater or lesser extent into every cognitive task. At the next level below one can identify certain broad group factors such, for example, as those that enter only into tasks of a verbal as distinct from a spatial, numerical or mechanical sort, and below this again abilities of a still more specific nature can be identified.[1] The point to note about this sort of a classification is that if one knows how an

individual stands with respect to an ability at one level of the hierarchy it is possible to make certain inferences about his standing
with respect to other abilities lower down in the hierarchy, but not
vice versa. It follows, in particular, that an estimate of a person's
general intelligence constitutes by far the most important single
item of information about that person's cognitive capacities that is
available, even though there is enough leeway in the practice of
factor analysis for authorities to differ among themselves as to the
relative weight they attach to special abilities as against general
intelligence.

To what extent are these differences of ability the result of inborn
differences in the power and efficiency of our different brains and to
what extent are they due to environmental pressures and influences?
This is the traditional 'nature-nurture'[2] controversy which previously, in the absence of any clear evidence one way or the other,
tended to divide people along ideological lines. Those who could not
bear to think that nature might be indifferent to our democratic-
egalitarian sentiments dwelt upon the supremacy of nurture, those
who favoured an élitist approach in social affairs sought justification
in the natural inequalities of man. But today, while there is still
room for a difference of emphasis, there is already enough firm
evidence to remove the controversy from the arena of doctrinaire
allegiances even though it is too much to hope that from now on
purely scientific considerations will prevail. From an *a priori* point
of view it might be thought that, since the calibre of the brain is
as much subject to genetic determination as that of any other part
of our anatomy, an hereditarian conclusion could scarcely be
avoided. This, however, would be a rash assumption. We know, for
example, that a person's strength is closely bound up with the regular exercise of his muscles and there is every reason to think that of
all the organs of the body the brain is the most susceptible to
external influences; what, after all, is learning except a modification
of brain structure?[3] At most, therefore, what can be meant by
heredity in this connection is that our capacity for learning and the
upper limit of achievement to which we can aspire is set by certain
innate properties of the brain we inherit, much as the upper limit
of strength which we can attain depends upon certain innate properties of our musculature. In order, therefore, to ascertain how
important is the hereditary component in the actual determination
of ability and intelligence we must turn to the empirical evidence

which is no different from that for any other characteristic which geneticists study even if, for various reasons, the picture we get is rather more complicated than for most.

Just because the whole controversy has been so muddied by misrepresentation it is important to be clear from the start precisely what questions can meaningfully be asked in this connection and what cannot. We cannot, for example, in the case of a particular individual, ask to what extent his musical ability is due to his breeding and to what extent to his upbringing. Such a question is meaningful only when we are talking about populations rather than individuals, and what it means in this case can be expressed as follows: what proportion of the *phenotypic variance* (i.e. the observed variation of the characteristic in question within the given population) is due to *genotypic variance* (i.e. the putative variation due to hereditary differences)? This proportion, known technically as the 'heritability' of the characteristic, can be expressed as a quotient and appropriate formulae have been devised by means of which it may be estimated. It must be understood, however, that there is nothing immutable about a given heritability estimate; it is always relative to the variability of the environmental conditions involved. In the case of human intelligence, if society could insure exactly the same upbringing and treatment for each individual, the heritability would rise to 100 per cent since all the observed variation would now be attributable to hereditary factors; similarly, the more uniform the population of a particular society becomes, say as a result of generations of inbreeding, the more the heritability will sink to zero since all observed variation will be attributable to environmental differences. All that we can hope to do, therefore, is to arrive at an heritability estimate based on the conditions that hold for our own society.

What makes it difficult to estimate heritability at all accurately in the case of human beings is that we are debarred from the cross-breeding experiments which form the classical genetical technique for investigating the mechanisms of heredity in animals, nor are we free to manipulate the environment. Instead we have to fall back on comparing samples that differ either in degree of kinship or with respect to environmental background, and correlating the scores of appropriate pairs in each sample. Thus, at one extreme, one might examine the scores of pairs of identical twins reared together; at the other extreme, one would look at the scores of unrelated individuals reared apart. Between these extremes come samples composed of siblings reared together, unrelated children reared together (as in foster-homes) and siblings reared apart. There are, of course, a great many pitfalls to guard against in this approach if the final estimate is not to be biased, but enough different studies have now been reported where hereditary and environmental factors have been systematically varied in this way for some tentative conclusions at least to be possible.[4] On this basis an heritability quotient of around 75 per cent, leaving 25 per cent for miscellaneous environmental effects, would be a conservative estimate. It is significant that intelligence behaves in this connection much more like some physical attribute such as height than it does some more culture-bound variable such as scholastic attainment. None of this, of course, invalidates those studies that have appeared in the literature showing that strongly adverse social conditions can lead to a progressive lowering of the mean IQ of groups exposed to them or, conversely, that improved social conditions may lead to a progressive raising of this measure. This, after all, is what one would expect for height in children: slum conditions leads to stunting, free milk to increased growth, even though stature is generally regarded as largely genetically controlled.

In brief, then, it can no longer be seriously doubted that differences in ability are predominantly due to differences in heredity. Two arguments in particular have been repeatedly emphasised by Burt in support of this assumption: first, if we take intelligence as being a polygenic variable as it seems we must (i.e. one governed by a large number of different genes), a theoretical value can be computed for the correlation coefficient that one would expect as between pairs of individuals of some known degree of kinship. Thus, on the simplest assumption of random mating (which can be corrected to allow for assortative mating) the correlation between monozygotic twins should be 1·00, between siblings or between parent and sibling 0·5, between first cousins 0·125, etc., until one gets down to random pairs of individuals with an expected correlation of 0·00. The mean observed values come close to these theoretical values based on the assumption that heredity alone is relevant.[5] The other argument rests upon the occasional incidence of high ability in individuals who lack any of the initial advantages, whether social or natural. This is very hard to explain on an environmentalist hypothesis, but on the assumption that exceptional ability represents a rare combination of genes this is precisely what one would expect to find once in a while.

The genetic aspect of intelligence has important implications when we turn to what we may call the demography of individual differences. It means, for one thing, that we cannot depend on our educational system alone to supply the personnel that is needed if we are to prevent our complex technological civilisation from disintegrating. Even a slight dysgenic influence sufficient to bring about an overall decline in intelligence would create such a dearth of cases from the upper tail of the continuum that disaster could ensue. At one time psychometrists were seriously alarmed by the discovery that intelligence was negatively correlated with family size since it appeared that the differential fertility of the less intelligent constituted just such a dysgenic trend. Subsequent national surveys, however, failed to show up the predicted decline[6] and it now transpires that the statistical argument on which the original predictions had been based were unsound inasmuch as they failed to allow for the fact that at the lower end of the distribution many individuals never marry and have families.[7] But the danger remains real enough, human abilities are still our most precious of natural resources and should be tended accordingly.

Secondly, with respect to the class structure of society, the heritability of intelligence is a force tending to aggravate social stratification. Inevitably, in any complex society such as our own where there are large differentials in the pay and prestige of different occupations, the more intelligent will gravitate to the top and the less intelligent will sink downwards. Their children, in turn, will reflect the parental bias and, given the fact of assortative mating, the parent-child correlation will exceed the theoretical 0·5. In addition the more intelligent parents will provide more stimulating environments in which their children can grow up, the less intelligent parents less stimulating environments. The effect of all this will be the familiar state of affairs that prevails throughout the civilised world. Indeed the situation is no different in the Soviet Union where the official ideology denies the very existence of innate differences of ability and where intelligence testing is strictly forbidden; the same disproportionate number of students at the universities are found to emanate from the professional and managerial classes as in the West! None of this, of course, is an argument for class discrimination. On the contrary, equality of opportunity is the best guarantee that the reserve of talent in the community will be exploited to the fullest advantage; nothing is more detrimental to the interests of a society than a rigid caste system. It is ironical that those who condemn intelligence testing as somehow 'undemocratic' fail to realise that, since the IQ is a much more sensitive index of a child's real potential than either an attainment test or a teacher's rating, it is the best safeguard that his potential will be duly fostered. There is, moreover, a wide spread of ability within any given class or occupation and this spread increases as one goes down the social pyramid. At the same time, since the absolute numbers also increase, one can expect to find most of the ablest individuals from the lower strata.

Far more controversial, not to say inflammatory, is the difficult question of racial and ethnic differences in ability. The very suggestion that there might be innate differences between groups having a different racial composition tends to evoke horrified cries of prejudice and 'racism'. And yet, knowing what we now know about the genetic component of intelligence, it would be little short of miraculous if every group turned out to be *exactly* equivalent in IQ even when they were drawn from populations which had never interbred and even when they differed on every other measurable trait. Of course, without resorting to actual testing, one would never be able to declare in advance which of two such groups would yield the higher mean but, from the simple logic of the situation, it would be most surprising if there were no differences at all. As it happens there is no lack of data on certain race differences, in particular Negro-White comparisons in the United States where every type of test has been applied and where every kind of sampling procedure has been tried to make the comparisons valid.[8] The upshot is well known to all who have bothered to consult the literature, namely that there is a decisive advantage in favour of the Whites but that there is also a large overlap and that both populations span the entire range of ability. But, while the facts are not in dispute, the interpretations differ. Those who refuse to admit that this is evidence of any innate inferiority on the part of the Black population appeal to the fact that the tests have been standardised and validated on a White population and argue that their validity cannot just be taken for granted when applied to those from a markedly different culture.[9] Certainly this is a methodological limitation that psychometrists now generally recognise when it comes to assessing members of pre-literate societies. Alternatively it may be argued that the disabilities imposed on Negroes in the United States produce a stunting effect on their intelligence. But political passions have made it difficult to view the problem with suitable scientific detachment. However, men of goodwill may take heart from the fact that, thanks to the work of the mental testers, we now know that, apart from minor fluctuations, the reservoir of ability in all the major racial groups of mankind is very similar. Feminists may also be grateful to differential psychology for destroying once for all the age-old belief in the innate intellectual inferiority of women.

*　　*　　*

No other psychological technique, I suppose, has found quite so many practical applications in daily life as mental testing so that the mental test has today become a familiar (if sometimes resented or derided) feature of modern society. When we inquire into its origins we find that we can conveniently begin with the work of a single individual, that versatile scientific genius of late Victorian England, Sir Francis Galton.[10] Psychology was in fact only one of the many fields in which his ingenuity found an outlet[11] and even there his interests were characteristically varied and diffused; his studies of mental imagery are well known and he discovered the method of free-association as a means for uncovering long lost memories from childhood many years before Freud introduced it as the basis of his psychoanalysis. Here, however, we shall be concerned purely with his contributions to differential psychology, a field where his originality and achievements have insured him a permanent and unchallenged place among the founders of modern psychology. His interest in the field seems to have started following his reading of the *Origin of Species*, a catalytic experience which formed the turning-point of his career. It occurred to him that man might one day be able to take command of his own evolution, perhaps even give birth to a new race of supermen, if he learnt to apply to his own species the principles of selective breeding that he already applied to his domestic animals. This idea, which was to find practical expression in his founding of the Eugenics Society in 1907, exerted a quasi-religious hold over his imagination. As his biographer, Pearson, tells us: 'His researches in heredity, in anthropometry, in psychometry and statistics were not independent studies, they were all auxiliary to his main object—the improvement in the race of man.'[12]

It was this eugenic ideal again which inspired his first book, *Hereditary Genius*, of 1869, where he reports his researches into the genealogies of eminent men drawn from many different walks of life and shows that the chances of finding other eminent persons among their relatives is very much higher than could be expected from the incidence of gifted individuals in the population. As a demonstration of the importance of heredity, however, this 'pedigree' method has obvious limitations since the eminent man bequeaths to his posterity not only his genes but also a certain family tradition for it to emulate. Galton, however, tended to play down any environmentalist interpretations, arguing that geniuses are born and not made and that they will assert themselves under whatever circumstances; he draws attention to the many great men known to history who from humble origins and against formidable odds scaled the heights of human achievement. His hereditarian bias was, however, somewhat modified by reading de Candolle's *Histoire des Sciences et des Savants depuis deux Siècles* which appeared in 1872, and by the lengthy correspondence with its author which he entered into, so that when Galton brought out his sequel to *Hereditary Genius*, namely *English Men of Science: their Nature and Nurture*, of 1874 he was prepared to grant somewhat more credit to nurture. We must note that Galton never relied exclusively on the pedigree method in order to make his point about heredity; it was he who first appreciated the importance of examining the careers of identical twins in this connection.[13] If today Galton strikes us as having overdone his stress on nature we must remember that when he wrote he was trying to challenge the even more dogmatic preoccupation with nurture that was such a salient feature of British philosophy.[14] Likewise, if we now feel shocked by his naïve belief in the racial superiority of Europeans and in the right of the more favoured races to supplant those less well fitted to survive, we must not forget that, though a humanitarian and a staunch liberal in politics, he was a child of his age and he was writing in the heyday of British Imperialism.

As befitted the founder of psychometrics and a pioneer of statistics, Galton was possessed of a passion for counting. This sometimes found rather bizarre outlets as when he sat for his portrait for his sixtieth birthday and counted the exact number of strokes it took the artist to complete it or when, at lectures at the Royal Geographical Society, he counted the number of 'fidgets' per minute he observed in selected members of the audience as a quantitative measure of boredom.[15] But it was at the International Exhibition in London in 1884 that he got an opportunity to indulge his passion for counting and measurement to the fullest degree. At the Health Pavilion he got permission to set up an 'Anthropometric Laboratory' where, for the fee of threepence, visitors could have themselves measured and tested on a battery of assorted tests and measures both physical and mental. When the exhibition closed the laboratory was transferred to the Science Museum, South Kensington, where it remained until 1891 when it was again transferred, this time to University College, Gower Street, where it formed the nucleus of the future department of statistics. It must be admitted that this spate of measurement yielded little of lasting scientific value or importance. One of the few conclusions to which Galton himself thought it safe to commit himself on the strength of his data was that women were on all counts inferior to men! At the same time, as Pearson points out, it provided Galton with excellent material on which to try out his new-found technique of correlation.[16]

But, for all Galton's importance as the father of differential psychology, credit for the development of the first real intelligence test, the supreme achievement of the mental testing movement, goes to the French psychologist, Alfred Binet. Galton certainly believed in the concept of a general mental ability, he even anticipated the correct distinction between general intelligence and special abilities, but he was unfortunately misled by inadequate evidence into supposing that simple tests of sensory discrimination afforded a valid index of a subject's intellectual powers. This enticing but deceptive assumption was then taken over by the American, James McKeen Cattell, who, after getting his doctorate at Leipzig under Wundt, worked for a time with Galton in England and then became the first psychologist to introduce mental testing into the United States. As a result, the mental testing movement in America started off on the wrong foot. Eventually, in 1901, one of Cattell's students at Columbia, Clark Wissler, applied a battery of Cattell's tests designed to measure simple cognitive abilities involving attention, fluency, discrimination, immediate memory, etc., to a large sample of Columbia undergraduates and found to his dismay that there was only a negligible correlation between their scores on any of these tests and their academic grades. [Wissler (1901)] Moreover, whereas the intercorrelations among the mental tests were trifling, the different academic grades in fact gave sizeable correlations with one another. Actually, Wissler's findings had been anticipated a few years earlier by a woman student of Tichener's at Cornell: Stella Sharp. After this setback the mental testing movement in America, which had got off to a flying start when Jastrow had set up his own stall for testing visitors to the Chicago Exhibition of 1893, took some time to recover its momentum. But a new chapter began when Binet's work became known through translation, especially after Terman and his associates at Stanford University produced the Stanford-Binet test of 1916 which has remained the prototype of all subsequent individual tests of intelligence. By 1917 mass testing of recruits to the American armed forces began with the 'Army Alpha' and 'Army Beta' group intelligence tests, the latter a non-verbal test suitable for illiterates and foreigners.

Binet avoided the mistakes of his predecessors by the unswerving commonsense and practicality of his approach. In the article in which he and his collaborator, Théophile Simon, first describe the original Binet-Simon scale for diagnosing subnormality in children he explains what he understands by the term 'intelligence'. 'It seems to us,' he says, 'that in intelligence there is a fundamental faculty, the alteration or the lack of which is of the utmost importance for practical life. This faculty is judgment (*le jugement*), otherwise called good sense, practical sense, initiative, the faculty of adapting oneself to circumstances. To judge well, to comprehend well, to reason well, these are the essential activities of intelligence.' [Binet and Simon (1905)] He realised that it was useless to assess this faculty indirectly either by psychophysical tests of sensory acuity or by tests of memory; tests must be devised which presented the subject with tasks which required an intelligent response. In fact, since 1894, he had been using just such tests with children in the schools. Hence, when, in 1904, the French Ministry of Education set up a commission to look into the problem of retardation, with a view to sifting out those pupils who were congenitally incapable of benefiting from ordinary schooling, Binet was the obvious choice to head the commission. The outcome was the Binet-Simon Scale that was based on the brilliant idea of measuring the child's 'mental age'. At each age level there should be certain tests of reason or comprehension which the average child at that age should be able to pass. Their scale consisted of a graded series of such tests and, depending on the point at which the subject starts to fail, an estimate should be possible of that subject's mental age. The concept of an Intelligence Quotient or IQ, as the ratio of mental over chronological age, was introduced later, in 1912; this refinement is attributed to William Stern, a notable German pioneer of child psychology and of mental testing.[17] Of course this formula for estimating the IQ is applicable only up to adolescence, after which the mental age levels off; the equivalent IQ in the case of adults has to be estimated relative to the norms for adult performance.

At roughly the same time as Binet and Simon were compiling their epoch-making test, the English psychologist, Charles Spearman, was initiating a much more theoretical attack upon the whole problem of what intelligence is and how it can be measured. He asked what would be the implications of assuming that every cognitive test of whatever description could be regarded as composed of two ingredients: one that it shared with all other cognitive tests and one that was specific to that particular test. Suppose, now, we think of this common ingredient as a kind of hypothetical test or 'factor' with which every test correlates to some degree (which may vary between 0 and 1), then it follows that the degree to which any test correlates with any other test must be entirely accounted for by the degree to which each of the tests correlates with this universal factor since, *ex hypothesi*, the tests have nothing else in common. Expressed in technical terminology the observed correlation between any pair of tests is a simple product of their respective factor 'loadings'. Spearman then went on to show how from a given matrix of correlations such hypothetical factor loadings could be derived. [*see* Spearman (1904)] Actually, as soon became apparent, his assumption was a drastically oversimplified one, though convenient enough for didactic purposes. Between Spearman's general factor and his specific factors it was found necessary to postulate a number of group factors common to some tests but not to others. However, Spearman's insight had started the very important factor-analytic approach to the problem of intelligence and of its relation to the special abilities.[18] This mathematical technique was brilliantly developed by the British School led by Sir Cyril Burt and Sir Godfrey Thomson[19] and was then carried forward by the American School which included T. L. Kelley, L. L. Thurstone and J. P. Guilford.[20]

Something of a tug-of-war persisted for a long time between the British and American factor analysts concerning the relative importance of a general factor of intelligence favoured by the British School as against the group factors representing primary abilities favoured by the Americans. But, in the end, these differences came to be regarded more as a matter of interpretation than as fundamental disagreements. Factor analysis presents a curious instance of a statistical technique of very wide generality (it may be applied wherever one is dealing with large numbers of intercorrelations, not only with psychometric data), which was developed by psychologists for their own requirements and then taken up by the statisticians, rather than the other way round.

Debate on the meaning of intelligence and what exactly it is that intelligence tests measure has continued unabated ever since the possibility of measuring intelligence was first envisaged. However, the demand for intelligence tests continued to grow, especially in the United States, unhampered by the academic controversies. It now looks as if at last a definite decline has set in and the IQ no longer enjoys the status that it once held. Perhaps two reasons may be advanced for the loss of enthusiasm. First, it has shown itself much less satisfactory as a predictor of success and achievement in real life than it was once thought to be; even as a predictor of scholastic performance it has only limited value. Consequently, psychologists have been searching for other measures that might better account for what distinguishes the high and low achievers. The conventional intelligence test, after all, tested only the subject's facility for a certain kind of logical thinking; it told us nothing about the subject's originality, inventiveness, imagination, or general intellectual fecundity. In due course, under the heading of 'creativity', these neglected but vital aspects of ability began to receive attention. Latterly 'creativity' has supplanted intelligence as the focus of interest for students of individual differences and for those on the look out for talent, despite the fact that it is still a somewhat nebulous and ill-defined concept.

Secondly, although as I have already explained there is no difficulty in showing that heredity must account for at least 75 per cent of the variance of measured differences in intelligence among the general population, it can never be proved that, in a particular case, an individual's test score is a true measure of his innate capacity. Thus the way is always open to the sociologically oriented psychologist who rejects the Galtonian conception of intelligence to dwell upon environmental influences. The most that many such critics would now concede is that the IQ represents a rough-and-ready index of a person's current mental effectiveness while denying that it constitutes any sort of biological constant.[21] Yet, when all is said and done, the fact remains that an IQ, based on a suitable test properly administered, is still the most important single psychometric measure that one can obtain in assessing an individual's potentialities.

Traits

When we move on to the non-cognitive aspects of personality, differential psychology becomes so complex and so diffuse that we cannot hope to do more here than just to take a few bearings and discuss some of the more salient issues in this field. Some authorities, indeed, would argue that personality is so subtle, imponderable and indivisible a concept that it must for ever elude the psychometric approach. Be that as it may, the attempt to measure traits in the same sort of way as proved effective in the case of the abilities has been made and deserves consideration.

If the study of intelligence was the result of applying the methods of the psychological laboratory to the problems of the schoolroom, the study of personality has its origins in medicine. Starting with Galen, whose doctrine of the four temperaments reverberated down the ages so that echoes of it may still be heard today,[22] most of the inventors of personality typologies were medical men. These include Gall and Spurzheim, the early 19th century anatomists who created the immensely popular pseudo-science of phrenology, a number of psychiatrists around the turn of the century and, closer to our own time, such names as Jung, Kretschmer and Sheldon. But a systematic and comprehensive science of personality differences only finally got going when the insights of the medical men merged with the statistical and experimental techniques of the academic psychologist. In particular the technique of factor analysis which had been worked out to deal with the measurement of the abilities was ready and waiting to be used in connection with the traits. It is significant that both R. B. Cattell and Hans Eysenck, the two foremost exponents of the psychometric approach to personality, about whose work we shall have more to say in this chapter, graduated from London University where they learnt their factor analysis as students of Burt. The contrast between these two men is also revealing. Cattell, who subsequently emigrated to the United States, has worked entirely within an academic setting, namely at the University of Illinois; Eysenck has always worked in a clinical setting, first at Mill Hill and then at the Maudsley Hospital in London. It could be argued that having to relate his researches to the practical demands of the psychiatrist has given the Eysenckian system a certain edge of realism that many find lacking in the Cattellian corpus, where the proliferation of factors seems to become an end in itself.

Perhaps the first thing to be said about a personality trait is that, like an ability, it is a dispositional concept. Thus, in calling someone cheerful we do not imply that he is never downcast, only that he tends to look on the bright side of things and does not easily lose heart. The attribution of traits to people presupposes, of course, that human behaviour has a certain consistency, that it is not wholly a function of the specific stimulus situation, but there is ample evidence both from research as well as from commonsense observation to think that such an assumption is valid. However, commonsense would probably also agree that we tend to be less consistent in what concerns our personality than in matters of the intellect. The useful word 'mood' testifies to this fact; a moody person is precisely one who is inconsistent in his behaviour from one occasion to the next. Of course moodiness can itself be a trait having its own second-order consistency, indeed extreme fluctuations of mood are a familiar psychiatric syndrome; not that our abilities are completely constant: most people have days when they are on top of their form and other days when they cannot work or think so efficiently; some people are at their best in the morning, others do not reach a peak until late at night. Even so, traits are notoriously less stable dispositions than abilities and a reliable assessment of a given trait requires sampling over a period of time.

The second point to be made about a trait is that, again like an ability, it is a continuous not an all-or-nothing variable. It may not always be easy, in any given case, to suggest a suitable metric but it always makes sense to say of someone, with regard to a particular trait, that in him it is more or less pronounced. This is possible because one can always conceive of variations in the intensity of

the stimulus conditions necessary to elicit the characteristic behaviour. We call a man irascible because it takes so little to make
him lose his temper; the patience of Job became proverbial not
because it was inexhaustible (by the end of the story even Job had
had enough), but because of all that he endured without complaint.
Hence, whatever technical problems may arise in connection with
its actual measurement, a trait can, from the psychometric point
of view, be regarded as one possible dimension along which personalities may differ.

As compared with an ability, the measurement of a trait is much
less straightforward. To measure an ability one has to have a set
of tasks for the subject to perform or a set of small-scale problems
for him to solve and one can then proceed to count the number of
items he successfully completes. To measure a trait there are a
variety of procedures to choose from (Allport [1961] lists no less
than eleven of these), and we have no assurance that they will all
produce the same answer. Here we shall limit ourselves to the three
main psychometric methods: (1) ratings, (2) questionnaires, and
(3) objective tests. Of these the ratings method offers the most direct
approach. Here one person, the judge or rater, has to evaluate
another person, the subject, for a designated trait using some appropriate scale. Usually a five-point or seven-point scale is considered
quite fine enough for the degree of precision possible with judgments of this sort. The rater may be chosen because he has a
specially intimate knowledge of the subject in question or because
he is thought to be specially skilful at making such judgments on
the basis of interviews or other sampling procedures. But, to increase reliability and inter-subjective validity, it is preferable to use
a panel of judges rather than a single authority. There are two well
known snags that must be reckoned with in using the method of
ratings: (a) the 'halo effect', and (b) the semantic ambiguity of
trait names. The halo effect refers to the common tendency to let
one's judgment of a person on one trait be influenced by one's
judgment of him on some other trait, even when there may be no
logical connection between the two. Thus a person's appearance
may prejudice one in his favour, or against him as the case may be.
It is due to this halo effect that the public may be blind to the failings
or weaknesses of its heroes or that a biography may degenerate
into a hagiography. Semantic ambiguity comes about because one
can never be sure that every rater will understand the trait designa-

tion in just the same way. For this reason it is sometimes advisable instead of using a single adjective to append a brief description to each interval of the scale so as to give it a more concrete anchorage.

Of all the devices used in personality assessment the questionnaire is certainly the most familiar and widely used. A typical questionnaire or self-inventory will consist of a series of items or statements and the subject or respondent is called upon to say whether each statement is true or false when applied to him personally, at least if taken as a broad generalisation. Each response contributes to his overall score on one or more different traits according to some pre-arranged system. Other things being equal, the more items per trait the more reliable the overall score. Unlike the rating score, however, the scores on a questionnaire require interpretation. One cannot simply take each item as self-explanatory, it becomes a matter for empirical validation to show that responding in one way rather than another betokens a particular trait. One way of showing this is to cross-validate the questionnaire against a set of ratings for the same subjects. The danger of all questionnaires is that the content of the items is seldom sufficiently opaque to throw the subject off his guard and prevent him distorting the result in some desired direction. Edwards [1959] has shown that every questionnaire item has a certain 'social desirability' component to a greater or lesser extent. This offers ample scope for the respondent to 'fake good', as the testers call it, and if the result is to have any personal consequences for him there is, in addition, ample incentive for him to do so. To defend themselves against this source of bias, psychometrists invented the so-called 'lie scale'. This consists of a number of critical items interspersed inconspicuously among the other items which serve as a trap for the untruthful, since it can be assumed that no candid person would answer them in a positive sense. Respondents with too high a score on the lie scale may then be eliminated from the experimental population. Even so, questionnaires remain suspect because they must depend to some degree on the veracity of the subject.

Objective tests escape this particular defect of the questionnaire but at a price many may think excessive. There are two basic varieties of objective test: the behavioural and the physiological. The former tests some aspect of the subject's overt performance on the experimental task such as his speed, fluency, flexibility, persistence, perseveration, suggestibility and so forth. The latter measures his physiological reactions to some emotive stimulation by recording changes in his pulse rate, blood pressure, electrical skin-resistance, glandular secretions and so on. The drawback of both varieties of objective test, however, is not just that they are time-consuming and presuppose the facilities of a well-equipped laboratory and trained administrators but that, relative to the other two kinds of test, they lack both reliability and validity. The score is apt to be influenced too much by the accidents of the test situation, including the personality of the tester, which makes for a low reliability. It is also apt to have a large specific component as shown by the small loadings one gets from objective tests on any common factors. The upshot is that the amount one can infer about a given individual on the basis of his objective test scores is disappointingly small in proportion to the effort required to obtain such scores.

I have said nothing so far about either the 'expressive' tests or the 'projective' tests although both of these, especially the latter, have figured prominently in the literature on personality assessment. The former is based on the assumption that our personality is reflected in our movements, postures, gait, gestures, physiognomy, hand-writing and so on, an assumption which undoubtedly has some plausibility although all attempts to make it at all specific, as in the practice of graphology, have been arbitrary and lack validity. Projective tests derive their rationale from the so-called dynamics of the unconscious which postulates a tendency in each of us to externalise our own inner conflicts and preoccupations onto the outside world. In a typical projective test the subject is presented with either some ambiguous forms to which he is asked to attach a meaning, as in the Rorschach Inkblot Test, or with the picture of people in some unstructured situation, as in the TAT (Thematic Apperception Test), around which he is asked to weave a story.[23] Projective tests usually require a great deal of expertise to use and interpret appropriately and should be considered as broadly diagnostic rather than psychometric in nature. They are used mainly to probe the subject's inner mental life, his fantasies, aspirations, attitudes, and so on, and so they do not really compete with the other methods we described which attempt specifically to measure discrete traits. There is, however, no reason why either the expressive or the projective principles should not be exploited by the test constructor in designing objective behavioural tests, and in fact this has been done.[24]

One of the first problems that confronts the psychometrist who takes personality as his domain is the bewildering variety of different traits. Allport and Odbert who compiled a lexicon of trait names found that there were no less than 18,000 words in the English language that could be used to describe people, even if one omitted compound expressions like 'nature-lover'. After pruning this vocabulary so as to include only words that described semi-permanent traits they were still left with a list of between four and five thousand terms.[25] Now, obviously, a great many of these are more or less redundant, and by grouping together synonyms or near-synonyms a further reduction is possible. Even so, what remains is likely to be too numerous to provide a workable system of classification for scientific purposes. What the scientist seeks is a relatively small number of fundamental dimensions which can be used to account for a multitude of observed differences. It is for just this sort of situation that factor analysis was invented, and the first psychologist to attempt to apply factor analysis systematically over the entire domain of traits was R. B. Cattell during the 1940s. Taking his point of departure from the Allport-Odbert Lexicon, he first condensed this to 171 logically distinct traits, most of which could be specified by a single pair of polar opposites, and he then further distilled these to a set of 35 'nuclear clusters' on the basis of previous research which had shown empirically that certain traits went naturally together and could be subsumed under a single heading. Ratings were then obtained for 208 male subjects on each of these 35 nuclear traits, the rating scores were duly inter-correlated and the resulting correlation matrix duly factor-analysed. The final outcome was 12 distinct factors which Cattell called his 'source traits'.[26]

Such factors have to be identified by reference to the items which give the highest loadings on the particular factor. In this respect they are no different from, say, Thurstone's primary ability factors. One feature of trait factors that makes them different from ability factors, however, is that one expects to find both positive and negative loadings. The reason for this difference is that whereas all tests of ability inter-correlate positively, tests of traits will often correlate negatively since some traits are obviously mutually antagonistic; one cannot be both an optimist and a pessimist! If we examine a typical Cattellian source trait, such as his factor F which he calls 'Surgency', we find among the high loading $F+$ items such surface traits as: cheerful, sociable, energetic, humorous, talkative; while among the high loading $F-$ items we find their opposites: depressed, retiring, subdued, dull, taciturn. Some years after this factor analysis of ratings Cattell carried out a similar operation with respect to questionnaire data. This time he extracted at least 16 distinct factors which he then attempted to match, where possible, with his ratings factors. On this basis he proceeded to compile his '16PF (Personality Factor) Questionnaire' [Cattell and Stice (1949)] which has since been widely used in personality research. More recently he has attempted to factor analyse the data from batteries of different objective tests and this gave him a further 17 factors which posed their own problem of identification. Cattell hoped that by testing single experimental population on all three methods a smaller number of second-order factors common to all three media might emerge. These hopes were frustrated when it was found that many of the factors remained obdurately specific to one particular medium of testing.[27]

A more radical attempt to get at the underlying sources of variability beneath the endless diversity of superficial differences is that of Eysenck, a major figure in contemporary psychology whose many popular writings have made his views familiar to a wide public. His point of departure lay in the prevailing systems of classification or diagnosis used in psychiatry. He was impressed by the fact that, ever since Kraepelin (who received his psychological training under Wundt) psychiatrists have recognised two main categories of psychotic disorders: on the one hand the schizophrenias characterised by derangements of the intellect, on the other the manic-depressive psychoses characterised by affective disturbances. Similarly, with respect to the neurotic disorders, psychiatry since Janet has distinguished two main types of neuroses: the anxiety or obsessional type on the one side and the hysterical and psychopathic type on the other. It occurred to Eysenck that both these dichotomies might reflect in an abnormal form a fundamental dichotomy in the basic personality type of the patient. This fundamental dichotomy, he suggested, was that between the introvert and the extravert, using the terms first introduced into psychology in 1920 by Jung when he published his *Psychological Types* but which have since become as firmly entrenched in the English language as words like 'melancholic' or 'phlegmatic', legacies of the old Galenic typology. By this equation both 'schizothymes' and 'dysthymics' (anxiety types) were pathological expressions of introversion while 'cyclothymes' and 'hysterics' were pathological expressions of extraversion. Indeed, Jung himself had already identified the hysteric as a neurotic extravert although Jung's distinction between extravert and introvert was primarily concerned with the orientation of the individual towards the world: whether, as in the case of the extravert, external, objective reality took precedence or whether, as in the case of the introvert, the internal subjective world was the more real. Jung further linked his typology with four basic mental functions, namely thought, feeling, sensation and intuition, so that, depending on which of these predominated, eight different types could be distinguished. However, this part of Jung's speculative system has played little further part in empirical personality research and no further reference will be made to it.

Eysenck was thus left with three independent factors with which to account for all the observed symptomatology of the psychiatric repertoire: (1) Extraversion-Introversion, (2) Neuroticism, and (3) Psychoticism. The last of these has not so far had much relevance outside a clinical context and is, in any case, the least securely established from the empirical point of view, so we need say no more about it here. But the first two dimensions, especially extraversion-introversion, found far-ranging applications in places as diverse as the analysis of socio-political attitudes or of aesthetic preferences, or in problems of criminology or of student selection. Sometimes, in particular fields like that of socio-political attitudes, it was necessary to introduce some extra dimension of a specified kind such as 'radicalism-conservatism' but, otherwise, two and only two dimensions were needed to cover the entire gamut of personality differences.[28]

In making this sweeping claim, it may appear as if Eysenck were directly contradicting the findings of Cattell with his multitude of source traits. The fact is, however, that Cattell's factors were not meant to be 'orthogonal' (independent). Rather there was a slight correlation between one and another with the result that the factors could themselves be factor-analysed and made to yield second-order factors. Cattell indeed carried out such a second-order factor analysis on his data from ratings, questionnaires and objective tests respectively and found that the two principal second-order factors to emerge in each case were those he himself labelled 'Extraversion-Introversion' and 'Anxiety versus Integration' [see Cattell (1957) pp. 317-19]. Thus the difference between Eysenck and Cattell is perhaps more apparent than real. It re-enacts the earlier clash of viewpoint between the school of Thurstone and the school of Burt on the relative importance of the primary abilities as against the general factor of intelligence, and has arisen for much the same technical reasons.[29]

Eysenck's drastic simplification of the personality sphere, a remarkable achievement in its own right, paved the way for a renewed attempt at a biological explanation of personality differences, a goal that was scarcely feasible so long as one had to deal with a large array of different factors. Since the late 1950s Eysenck has himself been in the forefront of this endeavour. Put very briefly and with a minimum of technicalities his theory, as it now stands, may be stated as follows:

Individuals differ from one another in the first instance on account of certain innate differences in their nervous systems. Extraversion is related to the RAS (Reticular Activating System), a brain mechanism now known to control the prevailing level of cortical arousal in the organism which keeps it in an appropriate state of alertness. The introvert has a more active RAS with the result that for the same level of external stimulation he shows a higher level of cortical arousal and less stimulation is required for him to reach his optimum. From this it may be inferred that the introvert will avoid exposing himself to excessive stimulation and will tend to withdraw into himself to find peace and quiet; the extravert, on the contrary, untroubled by an over-active RAS, will seek out stimulation and enjoy plenty of noise, excitement and social interaction. It can also be deduced from this theory that the introvert will condition more easily and extinguish more slowly. In terms of the conditioning that constitutes the process of socialisation in childhood with special reference to the use of punishment, this means that the introvert grows up to be more cautious, timid, reserved, more worried about infringments of the social taboos, while the extravert, less easily conditioned, grows up to be impulsive, adventurous, active and generally more dominant. The second factor of Neuroticism, or 'Emotional Instability' as it may also be called, is linked by the theory to the limbic system, the brain mechanism known to govern the emotional life of the organism via the autonomic nervous system. The individual with an unstable limbic system is more liable to break down under stressful conditions and is also likely to be more suggestible.

So much for the bare bones of the theory. Like most theories in psychology it is, of course, highly controversial.[30] Almost every feature of it has been contested and criticised; authorities are by no means agreed, for example, whether there is any single trait of general conditionability. Eysenck, himself, admits that other mechanisms than the ones he suggests may in the end turn out to be the critical ones. The virtue he would claim for his theory is that it does at least allow for sufficiently precise predictions to make it worth anyone's while to try and overthrow it in favour of a better theory. Thus, Eysenck has committed himself to a large number of very specific predictions about the kinds of difference to be expected between groups selected in accordance with their scores on the EPI (Eysenck Personality Inventory) when tested on various performance tests of perception, conditioning, etc. Nor is it any longer a question of hypotheses. One would be hard put to mention any other explanatory theory in the personality field of comparable scope that can appeal to a larger body of experimental evidence, even if not all the evidence has gone in its favour. Considering that most previous theories in this field have been too vague to lend themselves to any crucial predictions, we cannot afford to set aside lightly a theory which, whatever its inadequacies, has not so far been bettered.

If we accept the Eysenckian framework with its two main orthogonal axes we are confronted with four main contrasting types corresponding to its four quadrants: the stable extravert who, given good ability, is the most likely to make a leader and man of action; the stable introvert who, again assuming adequate intelligence, is your potential scholar, researcher and man of ideas; the *un*stable extravert with his latent criminal tendencies and, lastly, the *un*stable introvert who is liable to end up a gloomy, guilt-ridden fanatic. But this is merely to illustrate the theory by reference to certain familiar social stereotypes; it is not intended to suggest any kind of biological predestination. For the theory is concerned essentially with certain constitutional predispositions. For the rest, it depends upon the particular life-history of the individual concerned and upon the laws of learning theory. Even so, Eysenck acknowledges that he has laid more stress on hereditary determinants than has been customary with most modern personality theorists, and admits that he has done so partly to compensate for their previous neglect. Certainly, most psychologists have hitherto assumed that, even if our abilities are inherited, our personalities are mainly acquired. And, of course, if by 'personality' we mean what is commonly called 'character' and if we take it to include everything that goes to make up our peculiar ethos, outlook and orientation in life, then there can be no denying that 'personality' is overwhelmingly the product of upbringing, education and general cultural indoctrination. But none of this is incompatible with the Eysenckian supposition of a certain inborn temperamental bias.

In the past, the main support for the belief in innate personality types has come from the 'body-build' school of theorists best represented in modern times by Kretschmer in Germany and Sheldon in America. Their aim has been to relate differences in temperament with measurable differences in physique. Such evidence is at best likely to be equivocal however. Even if we could demonstrate that fat men behave differently from thin men, could we infer that each inherits his peculiar personality along with the shape of his body? Or, might it not be more plausible to suppose that differences in behaviour are the consequence of having to go through life with a particular physique? The only acceptable way of trying to resolve the nature/nurture problem here as elsewhere is through the kind of genetic study which enables one to tease out the heritability quotient on the basis of correlations pertaining to groups differing in degree of kinship. And the simplest kind of survey which makes this possible is one which compares the correlation between pairs of identical twins with the correlation between pairs of fraternal twins (of like sex). On this basis, Eysenck claims to have found alike for Extraversion and for Neuroticism heritability quotients comparable to those claimed for general intelligence, that is to say something of the order of not less than 75 per cent of the variance.[31]

* * *

While the question of the hereditary basis of personality may be of great theoretical interest, how important is it as regards its practical implications? For, in the first place, the great majority of people, almost as a matter of definition, fall at neither extreme of the personality continuum but somewhere in the middle. They are neither extraverts nor introverts but common-or-garden ambiverts: neither 'dead neurotic' nor 'towers of strength' but ordinary vulnerable mortals. But even where the innate temperamental bias does happen to be very pronounced in a particular case, how much difference can it make in the long run by the time that such an individual has been exposed to all the influences that can affect his mature personality; to the differential reinforcement of his behaviour from an early age; to the adult models and father-figures with whom he is expected to identify and the culture-heroes whom he is expected to imitate? Surely the wide diversity of modal personality types to which social psychologists draw attention as between class and class, nation and nation, epoch and epoch, are reminders of how large a part tradition can play in moulding personality in one form or another.

Take the critical case of personality differences between the sexes. To the layman there can be few more salient contrasts than that between the typical male and the typical female personality. Nor is this just a case of popular stereotypes. Test constructors know to their cost that it is difficult to devise any sort of mental test, no matter how devoid of any sexual connotations, which does not discriminate to some degree between the sexes. And when it comes to real-life situations the differences become very marked. What is it, one wants to know, that makes men so much more dominant, ambitious and aggressive than women and, despite all that female emancipation has achieved, so much more creative? Psychometrists on the whole have been strangely silent on this issue[32] and it has been left mainly to the social psychologists, who have not failed to stress the wide variations that exist between one society and another in the prevailing conceptions of masculinity and femininity, depending on the differentiation in the respective sex roles that happens to obtain. Yet there remains a certain consistency through-out all these variations that leads one back again to the biological distinctions. Are the differences in temperament a direct function of differences in physique and constitution? Or are they functions of the different roles demanded in the interests of child-rearing and so forth? The difficulty of finding any firm answers to questions such as these illustrates the general difficulty that confronts all attempts to explain personality differences. Yet the complications that inevit-ably arise for differential psychology when it ventures into the thorny field of personality are not sufficient reason for restricting its terms of reference to the more amenable problems of the abilities.

Summary

Abilities

Abilities are viewed here as forming an hierarchy with general intelligence as the apex. Thus an estimate of an individual's IQ constitutes the most important single variable for predicting his overall cognitive efficiency. The controversial nature/nurture problem, as applied to intelligence, is here discussed and evidence is cited which would suggest a 'heritability' quotient of not less than 75 per cent in a modern Western community. The implications of this for the perpetuation of class differences is discussed and the vexed question of possible innate intellectual differences between racial or ethnic groups is also touched upon. The mental testing movement from Galton to Binet is then briefly surveyed, culminating in as it did in the concept of mental age and IQ. Finally some reasons are mentioned for the fact that mental testing has lost ground in recent years in the face of continued criticism.

Traits

For a number of reasons mentioned, the quantitative assessment of personality traits is a more complicated enterprise than the measurement of abilities. The three main psychometric techniques in this connection are (1) *ratings*, (2) *questionnaires*, and (3) *objective tests*. Some account of each, with their respective strengths and weaknesses, is given. At the present time the two main exponents of the psychometric approach to personality are (a) R. B. Cattell, working in the United States, and (b) H. J. Eysenck, working in Britain. Both rely on the statistical technique known as 'factor-analysis', but while Cattell prefers to operate with a large number of factors even if these are not wholly independent of one another, Eysenck has concentrated on just three orthogonal factors: 'Extraversion-Introversion', 'Neuroticism-Stability' and 'Psychoticism'. Since the late 1950s Eysenck has been seeking to extend differential psychology beyond its narrow taxonomic frame of reference into the realm of theoretical explanation. Thus he now links his Extraversion factor with the conditionability of the organism (the extra-vert being innately *less* conditionable than the introvert), and Neuroticism with the constitution of the subject's autonomic nervous system (the neurotic being someone with an innately un-stable ANS). This, however, is still speculative and places more emphasis on the biological determinant of personality than many psychologists would allow.

Notes

1   *Cf.* Vernon [1950] Chaps 2-3, or Burt [1949]. Also for a more recent overview *see* Butcher [1968] Chap. 2, 'The Structure of Abilities'.

2   The expression (as I discovered from reading Professor Broad-hurst) is due to Galton, though it was Shakespeare who, in *The Tempest*, has Prospero describe Caliban as 'a born devil, on whose nature Nurture can never stick'. [*See* Broadhurst (1967)]

3   There is now definite empirical evidence of such changes in the brain. Thus, Rosenzweig *et al.* [1972] state: 'The hypothesis that changes occur in brain anatomy as a result of experience is an old one, but convincing evidence of such changes has been found only within the past decade. It has now been shown that placing an experimental animal in enriched or impoverished environments causes measurable changes in brain anatomy and chemistry ... the most consistent effect of experience on the brain that we found was the ratio of weight of the cortex to the weight of the rest of the brain.'

4   A lucid analysis of the nature/nurture issue is to be found in Jensen [1969] in his controversial article: 'How Much can we Boost IQ and Scholastic Achievement?' or, at a more popular level, in Eysenck [1971].

5   Erlenmeyer-Kimling and Jarvik [1963] considered 52 such studies *see* Table 2 of Jensen [1969] or Table 4 of Burt [1966]. This latter table gives the fullest listing of the observed and theore-tical correlations for differing degrees of kinship based both on Burt's own surveys in London and on those of other investigators.

6 *Cf.* Maxwell [1949] which compares the results of massive surveys of schoolchildren in Scotland in 1932 and 1947 and shows that a small improvement in mean IQ had taken place.

7 *Cf.* Gottesman [1968] Tables 1.6, 1.7 and 1.8. The author takes his data from the extensive survey by Reed and Reed [1965] covering some 289 families over six generations, comprising in all some 82,217 individuals. Gottesman comments: 'The dullest group had the highest fertility within marriage but the lowest proportion married. However, he also points out: 'Five million of the six million mentally retarded persons in the United States are the offspring of a mentally retarded parent or of a normal parent with a mentally retarded offspring.'

8 Shuey [1966] surveys some 382 such studies in her 578-page review, *see also* Dreger and Miller [1968]. For a concise summary of this literature *cf.* Tyler [1965] Chap. 12 or Eysenck [1971] *op. cit.* Differentials of around 15 pts IQ (i.e. one standard deviation) have been widely reported.

9 Jensen [1969] favoured an hereditarian interpretation of these facts but not even a scholarly approach and the obscurity of a learned journal could save him from the storm of protest which his article aroused! Gottesman [1968] takes a more guarded line: 'The differences observed so far between Whites and Negroes can hardly be accepted as sufficient evidence that, with respect to intelligence, the Negro American is genetically less well endowed.'

10 Galton was a grandchild of Erasmus Darwin and hence a first cousin of Charles Darwin.

11 Among the many legacies of his versatility was the concept of the anticyclone in weather forecasting and the use of finger-printing by the police. Boring [(1950) p. 482] has suggested that the reason why his influence on psychology was not greater was that his attention was dispersed in so many other directions: 'After all, Galton was but half a psychologist and that for only fifteen years. Wundt was nothing but a psychologist for sixty years.'

12 *See* Pearson [1924] p. 86. This monumental biography by a disciple who was himself an eminent statistician is our main source of information on Galton. That Galton himself recognised this as the goal of his endeavours is apparent from the concluding paragraph of his *Inquiries into Human Faculty* of 1893, where he writes: 'The chief results of these Inquiries has been to elicit the religious significance of the doctrine of evolution. It suggests an alteration in our mental attitude and imposes a moral duty. The new mental attitude is one of a greater sense of moral freedom, responsibility and opportunity; the new duty ... is an endeavour to further evolution especially that of the human race.' [Galton (1907) p. 220]

13 His first contribution to the topic came in an article he wrote for *Fraser's Magazine* for November 1875, but *see also* his section on 'The History of Twins' in Galton [1907] *op. cit.*

14 The Benthamites, or philosophical radicals, for example, believed exclusively in nurture. That is why when James Mill undertook the education of his son John Stuart and got him to read Plato in the original Greek at the age of three he had no doubt that the credit was due to his own educational principles!

15 A reproduction of this portrait is given in Pearson [1924]. The passage in which Galton describes his method of counting fidgets is given in Broadhurst [1967].

16 Galton's paper on 'Co-relations and their Measurement' appeared in the *Royal Society Proceedings* for 1888. His biographer, Pearson, writes: 'I have sought in vain for any forerunner of Galton in this matter and feel convinced that he was the first to grasp not only the need for measuring associated variations but the first to provide any real measure of them.' The correlation coefficient most widely used today is the so-called Pearson-Bravais product-moment coefficient devised by Pearson on the basis of earlier work by the French mathematician, A. Bravais. Correlating measurements has nowadays become such an indispensable part of every science where statistics play any part that it is hard to think oneself back to a time before this technique had been conceived.

17   *See* Boring [1950] p. 574. Stern published his *Über Psychologie der Individuellen Differenzen* in 1900.

18   Spearman's mature views are presented in his book *The Abilities of Man* (1927), in Part I of which he discusses the rival doctrines then current. Spearman was professor of psychology at University College, London, and, a rare honour for a psychologist, a Fellow of the Royal Society.

19   The late Sir Cyril Burt, some of whose innumerable writings on intelligence have already been mentioned, succeeded Spearman to the Chair at University College in 1931. A 332-item bibliography spanning the years 1909 to 1965 is given in Banks and Broadhurst (eds) [1965] (a Festschrift volume in honour of Burt's eightieth birthday). Sir Godfrey Thomson was professor of education at the University of Edinburgh and the author of *The Factorial Analysis of Human Ability* (1939).

20   Kelley was the author of *Crossroads in the Mind of Man* (1928), *see* Wiseman (ed.) [1967], excerpt 4. Thurstone was the author of *Vectors of the Mind* (1935). Guilford, the junior member of this trio, has held the Chair of Psychology at the University of Southern California since 1940. His contribution to the problem of creativity is discussed in Chap. 5 below.

21   *Cf.* Hunt [1961], [1968] or Vernon [1969]. Vernon, an outstanding representative of the British Factor-Analytic School, has recently turned his attention to cross-cultural studies involving intelligence testing among pre-literate and non-Western societies and stresses the cultural influence on intelligence. On the other hand, McNemar [1964] and Burt [1968] lament the decline in prestige of the intelligence test and do not consider that 'creativity' tests offer an acceptable alternative.

22   Galen was a second century AD Roman physician. His doctrine goes back to Hippocrates, the 'father of medicine' of the fourth century BC. From Galen to Harvey, in the 17th century, both Western and Islamic medicine were, according to Allport [(1961) p. 39], 'written almost exclusively in terms of his theory', and he goes on to point out that 'among psychological writers who

have made extensive use of the fourfold division of temperament are Kant, Wundt, Höffding, Herbart, Külpe, Ebbinghaus, Klages, Pavlov'. To this list one could now add Eysenck, *see* below.

23 According to Semeonoff [1966], projective psychology really began with the publication of Hermann Rorschach's *Psychodiagnostics* of 1921, a year before Rorschach himself died. For an account of his famous ink-blot test see his article 'The Form Interpretation Test' in Semeonoff (ed.) [1966] excerpt 10. On the TAT Semeonoff has this to say: 'Among projective techniques the TAT alone approaches the Rorschach in popularity', but adds, 'The two techniques are not to be thought of as in rivalry with one another; rather their functions are complementary. The Rorschach aims at analysis of personality structure; the TAT throws light on the here and now, the specific interpersonal and other situations which are "pressive" or "significant" for the individual.' The chief architect of the TAT is Henry A. Murray of the Harvard Psychological Clinic, *see* excerpts 12 and 13 of Semeonoff [1966].

24 *Cf.* Eysenck [1970] Chap. 7, 'The Analysis of Projective Techniques', which is very critical of projective tests as conventionally used but claims that if used in a 'purely psychometric manner, results appear much more positive and favourable'. Vernon [1963] is likewise critical of projective techniques for diagnostic testing, despite 'their obvious value as exploratory instruments in therapy'.

25 These are listed in full in Cattell [1946] Table 15. Cattell argues that ordinary language must long since have reached a plateau with respect to all the words that are needed to describe personality so that the totality of these words represent what he calls the 'Personality Sphere', a permanent frame of reference for the psychometrist.

26 For a full description of these twelve source traits, *see* Cattell [1946] *op cit.* pp. 313-37.

27 The objective-test factors remained particularly hard to align with those from the two other media, *see* Cattell [1957] pp. 321-29. This, as Eysenck [(1970) p. 243] points out, remains 'a powerful

barrier to easy acceptance of Cattell's set of factors'. Cattell's own approach is most clearly set out in Cattell [1950] or, in his more popular recent exposition, Cattell [1965].

28 For the relevance of these two factors to politics, *see* Eysenck [1954]; to aesthetics, *see* Eysenck [1941] and [1947] Chap. 6; to criminology, *see* Eysenck [1964]; to student selection, *see* Lynn [1959]. An attempt to link psychoticism, Eysenck's 'P-factor', with certain varieties of sexual behaviour is made in Eysenck [1972]. For a comprehensive coverage of this area, *see* Eysenck (ed.) [1970/71].

29 Cattell adheres faithfully to the so-called 'simple structure' criterion in factor rotation which does not necessarily preserve orthogonality, but this whole controversy is of a highly technical nature so that the non-specialist can scarcely hope to be able to adjudicate between the parties.

30 The theory was first presented in Eysenck [1957] and is further developed in Eysenck [1967] esp. Chap. 5, but a more popular account can be found in Eysenck [1965] Chap. 2 or in Eysenck [1972]. For a criticism of the theory *see* Vernon [1963] pp. 185-94.

31 See Eysenck [1952] Chap. 5, 'Heredity and Environment', or Eysenck [1967] Chap. 4, 'Heredity and Personality'. As against critics who argued that his formula does not allow for the fact that monozygotic twins are not only more alike genetically than dizygotic twins but are liable to be treated more alike by their family or by society, so that the formula would exaggerate the contribution of heredity, Eysenck [(1967) p. 198] cites evidence to show that the correlation is not much affected even where the monozygotes are reared apart and that it makes little difference whether the parents are correct or incorrect about the zygocity of their twins [*idem* p. 103]. One of the first attempts to estimate the relative nature/nurture ratio for personality factors, using in this instance selected groups of children and a junior version of the 16 PF, was that of Cattell [*see* Cattell, Blewett and Beloff (1955)] but we had to admit that the results were anything but clear cut.

32   I have looked in vain for any discussion of the problem in the voluminous writings of Cattell and Eysenck and had to go back to the earlier work of Terman and Miles [1936] who devised a much used masculinity-femininity scale.

CHAPTER FOUR

Behaviouristics

There are many ways whereby one person can try to influence another person's behaviour, either for his own immediate ends or to bring about certain long term changes. He can try rational persuasion, i.e. he can try to show that it is in the latter's interest to adopt the course of action he recommends; failing that he can try exhortation or suggestion; he can, if need be, plead, threaten, cajole, bribe or resort to any of the other innumerable ways that have been practised since time immemorial for getting one's way by playing upon another's emotions and sensibilities. Similarly, should it be a question of changing behaviour gradually in some desired direction, there are a wide variety of strategies that come under the general heading of 'education'. The point about all such methods is that they all, to a greater or lesser extent, depend upon the willingness and cooperation of the individual whose behaviour is to be influenced. The point about the special process we shall call 'conditioning' is that it is assumed to act automatically, irrespective of the wishes or intentions of the subject and irrespective of whether he is aware of what is happening to him or not. To learn something or to obey someone are the sort of things which you can do or not do; to be conditioned is the sort of thing which either happens to you or else fails to take effect. It is the organism rather than the person which is the proper object of the conditioning process.

It has been necessary to insist upon this distinction because it has so often been disregarded by the exponents of conditioning. They firmly believed that conditioning represented the basic phenomenon underlying *all* attempts to modify behaviour. If, in certain cases, something more seemed to be required, namely the active participation of the subject himself, this merely showed that we had not yet brought all the relevant variables under a rigorous cause-effect analysis. This view, which was never more than a piece of unsupported dogmatism, has become increasingly difficult to defend against the criticisms levelled against it by the cognitive school of learning theory. At the same time the reality of conditioning as a phenomenon cannot easily be called into question and, as a technique, it has shown itself to be even more powerful than was once supposed. It now looks, therefore, as if learning theory, like so much else in psychology, will have to settle for a pluralistic basis that will allow room both for the automatic effects of conditioning as well as for intelligent learning. Unfortunately, it is never very easy to specify, in any given case, whether the one or the other kind of process is involved; usually both play a part. Conditioning is the more primitive kind of learning and has been demonstrated throughout the animal kingdom; insightful learning seems to presuppose a substratum of conditioning and is seen most clearly at the higher levels of the evolutionary scale. It is precisely because the two are so closely interwoven that, in spite of what we have said previously about persons being the subject matter of psychology and organisms the subject matter of conditioning, it is necessary to treat 'behaviouristics', the science of conditioning, as a psychological and not just a biological science.

Conditioning

Since the advent of Skinner it is customary to distinguish between two main types of conditioning: the first, which was the first to be explored, consists essentially of pairing some given neutral stimulus which initially elicits no special response from the subject with a special stimulus which, as a result of certain innate connections in the nervous system, invariably elicits a particular response. After repeated pairings the neutral stimulus begins to acquire some of the properties of this special stimulus so that, even when presented on its own, it is able to trigger off the response or 'reflex'. It is then said to be a 'conditioned stimulus'. The science of establishing or extinguishing such conditioned stimuli constitutes what is known in the literature as 'Classical' or 'Pavlovian' conditioning. Opposed to this we have what is now called 'Operant' or 'Skinnerian' conditioning. Here the accent falls on the response rather than the stimulus. Any arbitrary response can be conditioned using an operant technique, it does not have to be an innate reflex. All that is necessary is that every time the response is emitted in the appropriate situation it must immediately be followed by a suitable reward. Eventually the subject is found to emit the response whenever he is exposed to the original situation even when the reward or 'reinforcement' is no longer forthcoming. When this stage is reached he is said to be conditioned. The critical distinction between the classical and operant paradigms devolves on the role of the reinforcement. In the classical paradigm the reinforcement is identified with the unconditioned stimulus that elicits the reflex. In the operant paradigm it corresponds to the rewarding stimulus which ensues once the critical response has been made. Otherwise the two are held to be closely parallel and both are assumed to function automatically given the appropriate conditions.

The natural point of departure for any theory of conditioning lies in the concept of the 'reflex'. This we must now examine. At the present time physiologists know roughly what they mean by a reflex and have identified a vast number of distinct reflexes without which the body could not function properly. Only a few of the more noticeable of these, however, are likely to come to the attention of a layman. Yet, despite a deceptive simplicity, the term has in the past been used in a wide variety of connotations. Fearing [1964], who has made a thorough study of its history, lists eight criteria that have commonly been taken by different authorities to distinguish the reflex from other kinds of response, the four most frequently cited being that it is (1) involuntary, (2) unlearned, (3) predictable and uniform, and (4) unconscious. The trouble is that reflexes are seldom met with in isolation and a temptation arises to think of any regular stimulus-response relationship as a sort of reflex. The reflex comes to be loosely used to stand for a kind of behavioural atom out of which all other responses are composed.

As is well known, it was Descartes who first formulated the concept.[1] He used it, however, mainly to support his theory that animals were nothing more than natural automata whose behaviour was governed by a strictly mechanical cause-effect relationship. Man, on the other hand, was not an automaton because, thanks to his possession of a soul, he was free to influence the workings of his nervous system and override if necessary its reflex action. Descartes' successors, however, uninhibited by this dualist metaphysic, welcomed the concept of reflex action precisely because it promised to reveal man, no less than other animals, as a machine. Ultimately all behaviour, voluntary no less than involuntary, learned no less than unlearned, conscious no less than unconscious, must be shown to be merely variations and elaborations of the basic reflexes. Only thus could one hope to build a science of behaviour that would no longer need to invoke the concept of mind. The theory of conditioning was, in the first instance, an attempt to realise such a science. Curiously, while most of the work on the physiology of the reflexes was done in the West, especially in Britain, it was in Russia that the theory of conditioning eventually developed. Nor was this perhaps a mere historical accident. To the radical intelligentsia of 19th century Russia, science was imbued with something of the same mystique as that of the Orthodox Church for slavophiles and supporters of the Tsarist autocracy. And, since science signified, above all, materialism and determinism, the more materialist and determinist your outlook the more socially progressive you would appear.[2]

The father of what eventually came to be known as the Russian School of Reflexology was I. M. Sechenov. He graduated first from the St Petersburg School of Military Engineering (at almost the same time, incidentally, as the writer Dostoevsky) but then switched to medicine in which he took his degree from Moscow University. He then went to Germany where he engaged in physiological research under Helmholtz and Du Bois-Reymond and there he began a lifelong association with Carl Ludwig. He thus came under the influence of the leaders of the German materialist school of biology. Later he worked for a time under the celebrated Claude Bernard in Paris, whose outlook was similar. One of his discoveries was of an inhibitory centre in the frog's brain which, if stimulated directly, could be made to inhibit reflexes mediated by the spinal cord. He also carried out important original research on muscle sensations and discussed its implication for understanding the development of spatial awareness in man. On returning to Russia he published in 1863 the book for which he is best remembered, *Reflexes of the Brain.* [*see* Herrnstein and Boring (eds) (1965) excerpt 63]

Sechenov was intrigued by the fact that the occurrence of a reflex depends upon the current state of the organism. Thus, the same food which will make a man's mouth water when he is hungry will merely sicken him when he is sated. Today it is a commonplace of physiology that reflexes do not function in isolation but are integrated into the general activity of the nervous system.[3] Sechenov realised that cerebral processes must intervene between the peripheral stimulus and the ultimate reflex action but he argued that these brain events must be no less deterministic and no less dependent on external stimulation than the original uncomplicated reflex. In the last resort, 'all conscious movements (usually called voluntary) ... are reflex, in the strictest sense of the word' (!) He even coins the expression 'psychical reflexes' to cover all conscious ideation and suggests that thoughts are no more than 'inhibited reflexes'. In this way the word 'reflex', originally introduced to distinguish one special kind of involuntary movement, is extended to embrace the entire mental life of man. As with such statements as 'everything is an illusion' or 'everybody is mad', we see here a concept which has been voided of all meaningful content by being universalised. Yet, despite its semantic absurdity, the book had an important message to convey and one that had a profound influence on the future of psychology. In the first place, it was a plea for a fully fledged physiological psychology. Since all our knowledge of other minds comes from observations on their external manifestations and since all such manifestations, whether it be the case of a 'child laughing at the sight of toys' or 'Newton enunciating universal laws' comes down, in the end, to contractions of the muscles, the whole of psychology falls within the purview of the physiologist. Exactly ten years after his *Reflexes of the Brain* he brought out a second book entitled *Who Must Investigate the Problems of Psychology and How*. Then, in the second place, Sechenov was concerned to promulgate the view that all behaviour is externally initiated. Sechenov derided the notion that we are autonomous centres of activity as being 'the greatest of falsehoods'. In reality, he explains, 'the initial causes of all behaviour lie, not in thought, but in external stimulation, without which no thought is possible'. This view, as we shall see, was to become the cornerstone of behaviouristics and is no less fervently upheld today by Skinner [1971] who does *not* look to physiology to solve the problems of behaviour.

Sechenov, himself, never got much beyond propounding a programme for an objective stimulus-response psychology. It might even be said that he did not take the argument much beyond the point reached a hundred years previously by David Hartley when the latter attempted to present a physical interpretation of associationism.[4] It was left to an enthusiastic disciple, some twenty years his junior, to bring the programme to fruition. In the preface to the first Russian edition of his *Lectures on Conditioned Reflexes* of 1923, Pavlov testifies to the impact made on him in his youth by reading Sechenov's *Reflexes of the Brain*. The patriot in Pavlov was specially thrilled that at last a Russian should have made his mark on physiology.

Like Sechenov, Pavlov acquired much of his physiological knowledge in Germany where he spent the years 1884-1886. In 1890 he was appointed to the Chair of Pharmacology at the Military Academy of St Petersburg and in 1895 to the Chair of Physiology at the University of St Petersburg, a post he held through the turmoil of war and revolution until his retirement in 1924. His monograph 'The Work of the Digestive Glands' was published in 1894 and his discoveries in this field earned him a Nobel Prize in 1904. His transformation from being an eminent authority on digestion to being the inaugurator of a new system of psychology came about through a natural sequence of events. Already in 1894 he was saying, in one of his lectures: 'And so, above our expectation, besides the physiology of the salivary glands they were found to have a psychology ... we can see all the elements of what is called mental activity: feeling, desire and indifference, ideas of the properties of what is entering the mouth ...' [*see* Anokhin (1968)] The crucial observation which led to his theory of the conditioned reflex was finding that his dogs often began to salivate before food had reached their mouths; sometimes, indeed, it was enough for the dogs to hear the sound of the footsteps of the attendant who brought the food. Now, no doubt, similar observations must often have been made in the past, in fact Robert Whytt, the 18th century Edinburgh physiologist, who was among the first to study reflexes experimentally, had recorded just such an observation;[5] but, in the history of science, it is the context in which an observation is made that is all-important. Pavlov was uniquely equipped to develop its implications. In the first place he had a set-up which enabled him to measure the exact quantity of saliva excreted following a specific stimulus but, no less important, he had the background and attitude of mind which made such measurement meaningful coupled with unbounded faith in the beneficent power of science.

He thus began in 1902 to investigate the laws which govern the formation of these conditioned reflexes, as he called them, and the various factors that make for their facilitation or inhibition. This occupation lasted him the rest of his long and productive life. Despite his protestations that he was nothing other than a physiologist who happened to be interested in the cortical connections that occur when learning takes place, his *obiter dicta* make it abundantly clear that he believed he had found the key to all the basic problems of psychology and psychiatry. Actually, as Woodworth and Sheehan [(1964) p. 96] point out, his method did not afford him any special insight into what was happening at the level of the cortex: 'He observed stimulus and response and offered what seemed to him a reasonable theory of intervening brain processes.' Whether he clung to his role as a physiologist because this enabled him to avoid the political pressures which assailed his psychological colleagues in the Soviet Union one can only surmise, but ironically it was on psychology, both of the Eastern and Western variety, that his impact was felt, not on brain physiology. Thus his explanation of conditioned reflexes in terms of a supposed irradiation of excitatory or inhibitory waves emanating from specific loci in the brain was not supported by later physiological research. The psychologists, however, especially at first in America, seized eagerly on his work almost as soon as it became available in translation. Watson, in 1916, gave his presidential address to the American Psychological Association on 'The Place of the Conditioned Reflex in Psychology'. Watson believed that Pavlov's conditioned reflexes were a more precise formulation of the vaguer concept of 'habit' on which behaviourism had previously based itself and he took at its face value Pavlov's own claim that 'it is obvious that different kinds of habits ... are nothing but a long chain of conditioned reflexes'. Actually, as Hilgard and Marquis [(1961) p. 38] have stated: 'it is now clear on both theoretical and experimental grounds that simple chaining of conditioned responses will not produce the characteristics of complex habits'. However, this blurring of the distinction between habit and reflex gave to Pavlov's system far more prominence than if there had been no such confusion.[6]

Curiously, the Soviet psychologists, in spite of his having enjoyed the patronage of Lenin himself, found his teachings too restrictive in their mechanistic simplicity to furnish the ideological underpinning for a new psychology of Soviet Man. Then, in 1950, fourteen years after his death, for devious political reasons having more to do with chauvinism than Communism, Pavlov was officially elevated to the Marxist pantheon and thereafter for many years no psychology text could be printed that did not contain some obeisance in his direction. [see Woodworth and Sheehan (1964) pp. 95-97] Pavlov, of course, cannot be blamed for the posthumous stranglehold which he exerted on Soviet psychology from which it is only gradually emerging. He can, however, be criticised for the same semantic recklessness as was shown by Sechenov in his use of the term 'reflex'. In Pavlovian terminology every response becomes either a reflex or a conditioned reflex. In fact it has been seriously questioned whether a 'conditioned reflex' is, properly speaking, a reflex at all. There is evidence, for example, that a conditioned knee-jerk or a conditioned eye-blink correspond more closely, when analysed on a myographic recording for their temporal characteristics, to the voluntary form of these movements than to their ordinary reflex form. For such reasons many psychologists now prefer to use the more non-committal expression 'conditioned response' rather than 'conditioned reflex'.

Classical conditioning has also been interpreted as a special case of 'sign learning'. The bell that precedes the food becomes as it were a *sign* that feeding is due to commence. It never, as Pavlov's account would imply, becomes a *substitute* for the food stimulus. If it did, the animal would start to behave towards it as if it *were* the food, which is absurd. What the animal does in fact is to behave as if it *expected* food to appear; it becomes excited, or, if the food does not appear, exhibits frustration. The process is no different from hearing a familiar voice and expecting to see the face that goes with it. The only advantage of using a reflex like salivation is that it provides a ready means of measuring the strength of the association that has been formed at any given time. But the association itself is of the S-S rather than the S-R variety.[7] To understand how the latter type of association can be set up we must turn next to operant conditioning.

Operant conditioning, which deals specifically with the acquisition of new responses, was formally introduced during the 1930s by B. F. Skinner and was first given a definitive exposition in his book *The Behavior of Organisms* of 1938. Skinner owed far more to the work on trial-and-error learning, that had been the mainstay of the American school of learning theory from Thorndike onwards, than he did to the Russian reflexologists. Already in 1911 Thorndike had initiated an important departure from traditional associationist principles by propounding his 'Law of Effect', according to which, 'Of several responses made to the same situation, those which are accompanied or closely followed by satisfaction to the animal will, other things being equal, be more firmly connected with the situation, so that when it recurs they will be more likely to recur ...' [*see* Thorndike (1911) p. 241] This 'law' passed through a number of vicissitudes but, with the exception of one abortive attempt by E. R. Guthrie to assimilate it to the older law of contiguity, it remained a permanent adjunct of all subsequent learning theories. In Skinner's hands it became the principle of 'Positive Reinforcement' and it would be no exaggeration to say that the whole of operant conditioning is based upon this one supreme law.[8]

There was thus a direct link between Thorndike's 'connectionism' and Skinner's 'operant conditioning'. What Skinner did was to take trial-and-error learning and reduce it to its simplest expression so that the parallel with classical conditioning would be most apparent. To this end he discarded the use of the maze, which up to this point had been the main tool of the learning theorist, and designed what has come to be known as the 'Skinner-box'.[9] This ingenious little gadget consists of a small chamber bare of everything except a single 'manipulandum' (e.g. a lever for a rat to press or a disc for a pigeon to peck at) which, when operated upon, causes a pellet of food to be delivered down a chute. When the subject is first placed in the box nothing may happen for some time but eventually it is bound to stumble upon the manipulandum, make the required response and duly receive the reinforcement. Thereafter its rate of responding will increase and this will be registered automatically on a moving band. Skinner called this process 'operant conditioning'[10] because the subject is required to operate on his environment in some way, and he contrasted it with classical conditioning where the response has to be forcibly *elicited* by an appropriate stimulus rather than being at first spontaneously *emitted*. Given this basic paradigm, variation can then be introduced. For example, reinforcement can be given only intermittently instead of after each response or reinforcement can be made conditional upon the prior occurrence of some signal or cue (e.g. a pigeon may be required to peck only after a specific colour stimulus has been presented). By such means Skinner was soon able to show that virtually all the phenomena that could be demonstrated by means of classical conditioning could equally well, and far more effectively, be demonstrated by using operant procedures. In addition, operant techniques made it possible to condition whole sequences of different responses by insuring that the reinforcement of any one response in the sequence was made conditional upon the performance of the preceding response.

Skinner's position in psychology represents an extreme instance of the pragmatic approach in science. He has repeatedly emphasised that he is not interested in what goes on 'inside the skin'. It is simply not the business of the experimental psychologist to speculate, *à la* Pavlov, about the possible neural mechanisms that may underlie conditioning nor even to construct theoretical schemes *à la* Hull from which the phenomena can be deduced and the observations predicted. Still less, of course, does he need to invoke mentalistic explanations *à la* Freud. Skinner's sole concern, he insists, is with the observable regularities and consistencies in the overt behaviour itself. Implicit in this approach is the belief which Skinner holds, no less strongly than did Sechenov, that all behaviour is ultimately under the control of the external environment. It is the environment which provides the relevant schedules of reinforcement and so determines what responses become a permanent part of our repertoire. Unfortunately it does so in a very haphazard sort of way that is not always beneficial. Skinner has therefore made himself the advocate of a new utopianism in which behavioural engineering would be deliberately practised by the social planners to 'shape' behaviour along socially desirable lines.[11] The urge to harness science for the better regulation of human affairs has always been a strong element of behaviouristics; it was the motivation behind Pavlov's labours as well, but nowhere has it been expressed more explicitly than by Skinner:

When we have achieved a practical control over the organism, theories of behaviour lose their point. In representing and managing relevant variables, a conceptual model is useless; we come to grips with behavior itself. When behavior shows order and consistency, we are much less likely to be concerned with physiological or mentalistic causes. A datum emerges which takes the place of theoretical phantasy. [Koch (ed.) (1959) p. 375]

At first blush this advice to seek control without bothering about theoretical understanding may sound like the very abnegation of what science is about. Within the special context of conditioning, however, Skinner's pragmatism has something to recommend it. The stark fact is that no one knows as yet what structural modifications of the brain cells occur as a result of conditioning nor why reinforcement has the effect it appears to have. Moreover, attempts to build a learning theory using purely theoretical constructs unattached to known physiological facts, as Hull tried to do, tend to collapse under the weight of their own complications. All we do know for certain is that operant conditioning is an astonishingly powerful device for training animals to perform tasks for which nature never intended them[12] or for curing human patients of undesirable habits. In the event there is something to be said for Skinner's policy of sticking closely to the observed stimulus-response correlations and not trying prematurely to impose on them any arbitrary theoretical interpretation.

At the same time the danger of adopting a purely positivist attitude is that it may serve as a cloak to conceal certain theoretical assumptions that are never made explicit. Skinner, for example, never doubts that operant conditioning *is* a genuine form of conditioning, in the sense we are here using the term for a wholly automatic process of learning. Yet the question as to whether the reinforcement automatically stamps in the response is one that is hotly debated among learning theorists. There is some justification for saying that, in some situations at least, the subject makes the response *knowingly, in order to* obtain a reward or to avoid a punishment as the case may be. The fact that Skinner was glibly prepared to equate the teaching-machine (it is not the least of his claims to fame that he may be considered the father of programmed learning) with the Skinner-box situation makes one all the more suspicious of his interpretation of conditioning.[13] For, in the case of the teaching-machine, what corresponds to the reinforcement is the information the subject receives that the response he has just made is correct or incorrect. But can a piece of pure information be equated with a biological reward? And, if we can equate the two, then might not the real function of the reward, even in the Skinner-box situation, be that of *informing* the animal which is the right response for obtaining food rather than that of simply increasing the probability of its recurrence in some quite automatic fashion?

However, whatever view we finally take of either classical or operant conditioning, the idea, once widely canvassed and still defended by Skinner and his followers, that all learning is based on conditioning of one type or the other is hardly compatible with all that we now know about the role of cognitive strategies in the acquisition of knowledge and skills. At the same time there is no good reason to doubt that *some* forms of learning are indeed both automatic and involuntary and operate without the subject being aware of what is involved, and it is to these forms of learning that the conditioning model applies.[14]

There is one other distinction within conditioning theory, besides the classical/operant dichotomy, to which I would like finally to draw attention, especially in the light of our next topic. This distinction arises from the fact that reinforcement may be of one of two kinds: positive or negative. So far we have spoken only of positive reinforcement or reward. Now I wish to say something briefly about negative reinforcement or punishment. It is always tempting to suppose that reward and punishment, pleasure and pain, are simply the two sides of the same coin and that whatever effect the one may have the other must have the diametrically opposite effect. Hence, if positive reinforcement strengthens a response, negative reinforcement weakens it, and *vice versa*. But what might be called the first principle of conditioning tells us that it is the *absence* of reward which weakens and eventually extinguishes a response. What, then, is the role of punishment?

Punishment is defined in the terminology of conditioning as any stimulus that is demonstrably noxious or painful for a given organism. If, in the classical situation, a neutral stimulus is repeatedly paired with a painful stimulus, the former acquires the power to evoke the emotional reactions and avoidance reflexes connected with the latter. In certain cases punishment can be used to inhibit a previously acquired response. Thus, if an animal which has become accustomed to finding food or water at a particular spot is suddenly shocked when it arrives at that spot it may cease thereafter to go there. It would be technically incorrect, however, to say that its previous response had now been extinguished, rather we must say that the antagonistic response of withdrawal had now replaced the previous tendency to approach. Negative conditioning of this sort can be highly efficacious. Whether a response can ever be conditioned on a single trial using positive reinforcement is a matter of controversy but there can be no doubt whatever that, using negative reinforcement, a permanent conditioned response can be set up quite easily after a single presentation provided the punishment is sufficiently traumatic. Nor is it hard to understand why this should be so. In nature it may be literally a matter of life or death for the individual to be able to respond appropriately to the danger signals in his environment after a single warning. The extraordinary power of negative reinforcement may sometimes produce consequences of a paradoxical kind, so that a relatively mild punishment may suffice to inhibit an impulse of great biological urgency. Thus R. L. Solomon demonstrated that a group of puppies who were given a rap on the rump with a rolled newspaper just at the moment when they were about to partake of food from a container thereafter refused to eat in the experimental situation even after being deprived of food for many hours when they were literally starving![15] The persistence of taboos and irrational fears of a highly maladaptive kind in human beings presents something of a parallel.

How can negative reinforcement be applied to condition any arbitrary response as in operant conditioning? Here the secret is to administer a shock only on those trials when the required response is *not* forthcoming. Ordinarily, however, for this to work a two-stage process is needed. In the first stage the animal learns (in accordance with classical principles) to associate a particular cue, say the sound of a buzzer, with the onset of a shock. In the second phase it discovers, at first by accident, that making the response in question results in the shock being withheld. When eventually it continues to make this response on every trial whenever the buzzer is sounded, without the necessity of further shocks, the avoidance response is said to be conditioned. At this point, however, conditioning theory is confronted with an apparent paradox. What sustains the avoidance response? How is it that it can persist for hundreds of trials without any apparent reinforcement when, from all that we have said previously, it should follow that the absence of reinforcement results in the extinction of the response? One solution of this paradox consists of taking fear to be the missing variable. Fear then represents the drive whose reduction constitutes the reinforcement. Fear or anxiety is assumed to have been conditioned by the pairing of shock and buzzer during the initial classical phase of the process and the consequent alleviation of the anxiety that follows the critical response when the shock is withheld continues to reinforce this response during the second operant stage of the conditioning.[16]

The process thus becomes self-reinforcing and to such good effect that normally the animal never waits to find out whether a shock would still occur if the response were not given. Hence, unless the response is somehow forcibly prevented it can never be extinguished since, in order for it to be extinguished, the experimenter would have to arrange for the animal to experience the unconditional absence of shock following the critical cue. This aspect of avoidance conditioning likewise has its analogue among phobic patients who usually take care not to expose themselves to the object of their phobia and thereby prevent the possibility of deconditioning.

One further point calls for mention with respect to which reward and punishment are not symmetrical. This has to do with what is known as the temporal gradient of reinforcement. The power of a given amount of reinforcement in operant conditioning is an inverse function of the interval between the occurrence of the response and the onset of the reinforcement. Immediate reinforcement is much more effective than delayed reinforcement, and if delay exceeds a certain critical length the efficacy is entirely lost. Now the point is that negative reinforcement gives rise to a much steeper temporal gradient than positive reinforcement. Hence, even if punishment has a stronger effect when it follows immediately the response, its effect may be weaker than the corresponding reward after a certain interval has elapsed. This principle has been invoked to explain some of the paradoxes of human pathological behaviour.[17] Why, for example, does the alcoholic persist in an addiction that may bring him to the verge of self-destruction? Or the psychopath persist in committing petty crimes for which he is constantly caught and punished? On rational grounds there is no answer, but in terms of the conditioning model we would have to say that the immediate positive reinforcement which such behaviour affords outweighs the long term negative reinforcement. One could say that much of all traditional morality was concerned with trying to counteract this natural tendency to disregard deferred penalties in favour of present satisfactions.

Behaviour Therapy

Behaviour therapy represents, I suppose, the most advanced development yet in the application of science to the control of human behaviour. I do not propose, however, to try and evaluate its contribution as a branch of modern psychiatry or attempt to arbitrate as between it and other forms of therapy. Nor shall I expatiate on the ethical questions to which it gives rise, beyond remarking that, although to some it may sound suspiciously like 'brain-washing', mental illness is a source of so much suffering that almost anything, however distasteful, provided it helps, can, in my opinion, be justified.[18] What will concern us here is rather the implications of behaviour therapy for our understanding of the role of conditioning in human life and to what extent its very real practical achievements may be taken as confirming principles established in the laboratory.

The expression 'behaviour therapy' has come to stand for an approach in psychiatry which purports to deal directly with the patient's symptoms instead of regarding the symptoms as merely a manifestation of some underlying disturbance in his mental state, as in a 'psychodynamic' approach. Beneath this broad umbrella term of diversity of therapeutic practices have found shelter, not all of which, by any means, can be identified with conditioning techniques. What unites them is only the belief that abnormal and deviant behaviour is the product of maladaptive learning rather than the symbolic expression of repressed conflicts, with the corollary that the cure resides in a process of re-learning, not in the uncovering of unconscious complexes. Eysenck has distinguished two main categories of mental disorders: (1) where the patient has learned the wrong responses, and (2) where he has failed to learn the right ones. In either case a behaviour therapy implies a process of learning. The question we shall have to try and decide is how far is it also a process of conditioning.

In the first part of this chapter we defined conditioning as a learning process that is assumed to act automatically on the organism without presupposing any sort of an awareness or understanding on the part of the subject. Now, on the face of it, although the patient in a behaviour therapy is relatively passive, as compared, say, with his role in a psychotherapy, the treatment does depend on a certain degree of collaboration from the patient. In this respect the situation is very different from those physical therapies in psychiatry (e.g. brain surgery, electro-convulsive shock, drugs, etc.) where all that is required of the patient is that he should assent to the treatment. In behaviour therapy it makes all the difference whether the patient is well motivated to undergo treatment or whether, as may be the case with some sexual offenders, he is referred by a court of law. The behaviour therapist, moreover, no less than the psychotherapist, takes the patient into his confidence, explains to him the nature of the treatment he is to get and the reason for it and, finally, gives him all the reassurances and moral support that he needs. The treatment is thus far from being a simple routine affair that could just as easily be carried out by a machine. Nevertheless, the critical factors involved *are* assumed to operate irrespective of the patient's wishes or beliefs. Perhaps an analogy with ordinary medicine may help to clarify this distinction. It is common knowledge that recovery from any illness is affected by such imponderables as the patient's morale and his confidence in the treatment, nevertheless the critical factors in his recovery are certain biophysical events of which he has no knowledge or awareness.

In the history of conditioning the transition from laboratory to clinic was a particularly lengthy one. In spite of the interest shown by Pavlov, and still more by Bekhterev,[19] in psychiatric problems, in the West, at any rate, it was not until the late 1950s that conditioning techniques first began to make any sort of an impact on clinical practice. The actual term 'behaviour therapy', introduced in contradistinction to 'psychotherapy', did not become current until 1960 with the publication in that year of the volume *Behaviour Therapy and the Neuroses* edited by H. J. Eysenck. During the past decade, however, there has been a vigorous expansion of this new technology which has produced its own flood of specialist literature.[20] Today it looks like becoming the accepted form of treatment for a wide variety of mental disorders for which previously, ever since the advent of Freud, psychotherapeutic methods were the only recourse. Already it has to its credit many successful cures with cases that proved impervious to any other approach. When we reflect on the magnitude of the social problem which mental illness presents—about half of all hospital beds in the United States are occupied by mental patients and the figures for other countries are comparable—one cannot but welcome any development that gives promise of progress.

Three particular techniques that fall under the general rubric of behaviour therapy will here be considered both because they have by now been well tried and because they all purport to base themselves on conditioning principles. These are: (1) the technique of 'reciprocal inhibition' or 'systematic desensitisation' designed specifically to eliminate phobias and other symptoms of irrational anxiety; (2) aversion therapy, where the aim is to get the patient to relinquish some undesirable behaviour to which he was previously addicted (*cf.* Eysenck's Type I disorders); and (3) operant conditioning therapy, which is specially applicable to cases of behavioural deficiencies (*cf.* Eysenck's Type II disorders). These three major techniques can be used separately or in conjunction with one another as the individual case history demands. We shall start by examining each of these in turn with special reference to the way in which they are supposed to exemplify the principles of either classical or operant conditioning.

(1)   Reciprocal Inhibition

Reciprocal inhibition was the first of the behaviour therapies to reach maturity. Its pioneer was a South African psychiatrist, Joseph Wolpe, who has since emigrated to the United States. His book *Psychotherapy by Reciprocal Inhibition*, which came out in 1958, may be regarded as the first textbook of the new movement even though Wolpe retains the term 'psychotherapy' for his special form of treatment. The key term 'reciprocal inhibition' relates to the familiar fact that certain states of mind are logically incompatible with certain other states. One cannot, for example, at one and the same time, feel both elated and depressed; the one experience excludes the other. In particular one cannot simultaneously feel anxious, tense and agitated and yet remain perfectly calm and relaxed. This truism, in turn, can be related to the physiological fact that there is an antagonism between the sympathetic and parasympathetic parts of the autonomic nervous system: the former being activated by danger and stress, the latter by soothing and pleasurable stimulation. Wolpe's system consists essentially of trying to counteract anxiety by exploiting antagonistic reactions. In the experimental context of the animal laboratory this can be done most easily by bringing into play activities connected with food or sex; in the clinical context, however, the most convenient way of counteracting anxiety is to give the patient a training in systematic relaxation (this has also been used in the past as a therapy in its own right). Should the patient be incapable of achieving adequate relaxation of his own accord, hypnosis may be used to facilitate the process. When the patient is at last duly relaxed the critical stimulus connected with his particular phobia will then be presented. The more often the patient can experience its presence while still in a relaxed condition, the more will it lose its previous anxiety-arousing properties.

The special problem which this procedure poses is how to introduce the critical stimulus without it reactivating the very emotions that one is seeking to quell. Wolpe's solution was to approach the problem obliquely by operating with a series or 'hierarchy' of responses ranging from the most alarming to the least upsetting. This can be arrived at beforehand simply by questioning the subject concerning his relative fears with respect to various objects and situations. Then, by starting with stimuli which the patient can quite easily withstand, the therapist can work his way up gradually, over many sessions, until the patient can tolerate even the most dreaded item. The process of desensitisation is then complete. In certain simple cases, such for example as a spider-phobia, the anxiety hierarchy may consist of a series of concrete situations such as presenting the spider at different distances from the patient. In other cases, such as cases of impotence or frigidity, where the anxieties relate to sexual activities and situations, the therapist may have to resort to 'imaginal stimulation', that is to say the patient will be asked to imagine as vividly as he can the relevant activities or situations that arouse anxiety. Here again these can be taken in order of increasing intensity until the patient finds that he can freely contemplate any of these critical items with impunity.

Wolpe claims that his method is firmly based on facts that had been experimentally demonstrated in the laboratory. Certainly the classic work of Watson and his associates in the early 1920s on the conditioning and de-conditioning of fears in infants utilises the principle of the anxiety hierarchy and of reciprocal inhibition. The critical stimulus, say a rabbit, would be brought each time closer to the infant while the latter was engaged in eating until the infant was quite happy to stroke it with one hand while feeding itself with the other whereas, at the start of the experiment, the mere presence of the rabbit was enough to produce a paroxysm of fear.[21] Nearly twenty years later J. H. Masserman, a psychiatrist-cum-experimentalist, carried out a similar series of experiments using cats as his subjects. He trained them first, by the usual operant conditioning procedure, to obtain food in a special cage by operating a lever. Then, at the critical trial, instead of receiving food they would be given a sharp blast of air. The effect apparently was so traumatic that the animals became completely disturbed and intractable and, like Solomon's puppies mentioned earlier, could not be induced to eat again in that situation however hungry they might be. Masserman then experimented with various methods of curing their 'neurosis'. Forcing proved quite ineffective, but success was eventually attained by a combination of stroking and hand-feeding, at first outside the laboratory altogether and then, by degrees, closer and closer to the critical area until at last the animal would again take food inside the special cage itself. [see Masserman (1943)] From this account it would appear that the principles of reciprocal inhibition had been known to psychologists for a long time but it was left to Wolpe to discover their implications for the treatment of human patients.

(2) Aversive Therapy

Aversive therapy is based more directly on Pavlovian principles. The idea in this case is that if a given stimulus to which the subject is attracted is paired repeatedly with some noxious stimulus it will acquire in due course some of the aversive properties possessed by the latter. In this way an addiction can be replaced by an aversion or, failing that, can at least be neutralised. The noxious stimulus commonly used in a clinical setting is either some chemical agent such as apomorphine which acts as an emetic, or produces strong sensations of nausea, or else an electric shock of a requisite strength. On the whole the latter is now thought to be superior, partly because it allows for a more accurate timing between presentation of the critical stimulus and the onset of punishment, and partly because it is less messy and disagreeable, though both methods are of necessity unpleasant for the patient.[22] Among the first to use an aversion therapy of the Pavlovian kind was, fittingly enough, a psychiatrist belonging to the Leningrad Psychiatric Hospital, N. Kantorovich, around 1930. Consumption of alcohol was paired with electric shock. Some twenty alcoholic patients were treated by this method and it was reported that most of them abstained thereafter from alcohol for at least some months. Already in 1942, Voegtlin and Lemere published an extensive review of cases of alcoholism treated by aversion therapy, mainly of the chemical kind. They concluded that 'with proper application of the technique improvements could be expected in as many as 70 per cent of patients treated'. Then, in 1950, they reported their own results with more than 4,000 patients whom they treated using their own system of chemical aversion at a sanatorium in Seattle. An analysis of the abstinence rates for varying periods revealed a slow rate of attrition from 60 per cent for at least a year to 23 per cent for at least ten years but, as the authors point out, the results compare favourably with other methods of treatment, none of which could claim abstinence rates of more than 24 per cent. [see Rachman and Teasdale (1969) Chap. 3] Yet, in spite of this encouraging start, aversion therapy has never become the standard treatment for alcoholics. This is partly because there are so many other ways of tackling this problem and partly because physicians are naturally disinclined to prescribe so drastic a treatment in view of its uncertain prognosis. [see Kessel and Walton (1965) p. 144]

On the whole, the sexual disorders have proved a more promising field of application for aversion therapy. The most widespread problem here is that of male homosexuality. It is complicated from the start by the fact that in many cases there is, in all probability, a large genetic component involved. Of course it has never been suggested that pressure should be put on all homosexuals to undergo treatment; many are content to remain as they are. But, for those who desperately want to change their sexual orientation, aversion therapy has been able to help when all else has failed. For example, in one published case [James, B. (1962)] a man of fifty with an exclusively homosexual history from the age of fifteen was able to make a reasonably successful transition to heterosexuality after quite a brief course of aversion therapy. Of course, in cases of this sort, it is seldom sufficient to block one sexual outlet without helping the patient to find an alternative one so that alongside aversive conditioning directed towards the attractions of the same sex the patient is conditioned, or at least encouraged, to take an interest in members of the opposite sex; injections of a male hormone are also sometimes used to facilitate the transition. But, in any case, one can usually rely on nature not to leave the individual entirely divested of sexual appetites. The problem of what to use as the critical stimuli is not as straightforward, however, as in the treatment of alcoholism. Most commonly, slides of a sexually provocative kind will be presented, sometimes to the accompaniment of suitable tape-recordings. Otherwise imaginal rather than actual stimuli may be used; the patient would then be required to concentrate on creating a mental fantasy of himself indulging in some gratifying sexual activity and this would be duly followed by punishment. This procedure has now become more feasible since the introduction of a plethysmograph that can be fitted to the penis and so register the precise degree of tumescence attained at any instant. [see Rachman and Teasdale (1969) Chaps 7 and 8]

So much, then, for aversion therapy. Although much more takes place during a typical treatment than just a simple conditioning routine, the mere fact that behaviour of such a persistent and compulsive nature can, in a matter of a few days, be abandoned so completely is surely a remarkable tribute to the efficacy of classical conditioning principles. Nor does it belittle their significance to point out that the risk of a relapse is always present. In contravening what are often the habits of a lifetime this is the least we can expect and, from the practical point of view, the patient can always return for a booster course of treatment if need be.

(3) Operant Conditioning Therapy

We come, lastly, to operant conditioning therapy, also referred to, on occasion, as 'behaviour shaping' or 'behaviour modification'.[23] Here the emphasis is on promoting adaptive responses rather than inhibiting maladaptive ones. As it happens, it is in connection with the psychotic disorders, the most intractable of all psychiatric problems, that operant conditioning has achieved its most impressive results. This is because it is the psychotic who suffers most from behavioural deficits and stands most in need of enlarging his behavioural repertoire. Sometimes the patient has withdrawn so far from social life that he has lost the basic skills required for any form of social intercourse and requires something of the same training as an infant who is still in the process of being socialised. Considering how little we know still about the nature of a psychosis—there is still no general agreement as to whether it is due primarily to some organic malfunction of a biochemical kind or to psychogenic factors connected with the patient's life-history—it would be too much to expect that a brief course of operant conditioning was all that was needed to enable a certified patient to recover his sanity and earn a discharge. The stark fact is that there is no known method of curing most genuine psychoses. As things are at present the most we can hope for is to reduce some of the more distressing symptoms. Until very recently this usually meant either some form of chemotherapy or electric shock therapy applied to the brain. Since behaviour therapy, as we have said, focuses on the symptoms rather than on the causes of a given disorder, it was not deterred by the fact that we do not yet understand why people become psychotic but instead concentrated on improving the behaviour of the patient.

The essence of operant conditioning, as we saw earlier, is that the reward is made contingent upon the production of the desired response. But what kind of a reward is suitable in a clinical context? If a food reward is used, then, quite apart from the indignity of feeding adults in this way, there is the risk that the patient will be sated before the session is complete. Money or commodities are, of course, the normal positive incentives with adults in daily life but they may not be so meaningful to a lifelong inmate of an institution. Consequently, although material incentives are used on occasion, the most convenient and universally efficacious form of reward now used is what would be called 'social reinforcement', e.g. smiles, nods, praise, or suchlike signs of attention or approval. For, strangely enough, even the most withdrawn psychotic who, to all outward appearances, seems completely indifferent to what goes on, is not immune to the effects of social reinforcement. A nice example of the efficacy of such reinforcement comes from the case of a woman patient who was treated for *'anorexia nervosa'* (refusal to eat). In the nature of the case, food could not here be used as a reward. Instead, arrangements were made for the patient to take her meals in a special room together with a member of the hospital staff who had been instructed to converse with her on topics that were known to be of interest to her, but *only* when she gave signs of being about to eat. Later, TV and radio were brought into the situation to provide additional incentives of this sort. The treatment worked and the patient, who on being admitted to hospital was on the point of starvation, recovered well enough to be able to go back home and lead a normal life. [*see* Beech (1969) pp. 192-194]

An outstanding exponent of operant conditioning therapy at the present time is Irene Kassorla. She made her reputation by applying the technique to autistic children and other children suffering from gross behavioural abnormalities; the children would only receive food or attention when they gave cooperative rather than negativistic responses. But her most ambitious undertaking to date, she maintains, is the case of 'Mr B.' at a London mental institution in 1967. The case is well worth considering in some detail. In 1936, at the age of 21, Mr B. became mentally ill. The reason, as so often, is unclear, but it is known that the patient had suffered some distress beforehand including an unrequited love affair. At all events, he became more and more depressed and neither drugs nor ECS (Electro-Convulsive Shock) produced any improvement. For thirty years before Dr Kassorla met him he had been kept at the institution where, for the most part, he remained mute and inert. She decided to start by concentrating on his verbal behaviour. At first he was to be rewarded only when he imitated words that were spoken to him, very much as one might do for an infant learning to talk. The problem was, what form of reinforcement would be suitable with a patient who, as she put it, 'had shown no interest in money, books, entertainment or anything for so long'? In the circumstances she decided that it would have to be food but, in addition, a negative reinforcement was used consisting of deliberately ignoring the patient for a period of ten seconds whenever he lapsed into psychotic or uncooperative behaviour. Pictures from magazines were also presented to him which he was required to name. After 31 days of such treatment the patient was talking to the extent of being willing to name any object that was pointed out to him and, more important, his general demeanour had greatly improved. The treatment continued for a further 103 days. Six months later the occupational therapist in charge reported as follows: 'Mr B. isn't satisfied to sit back any more. He's interested and right up front now. We talk with him every day. No food—just nice talk.' Mr B. was not, of course, discharged, but he had become a very different sort of a person. [*see* Kassorla (1969)] What is of particular interest in a case of this description is its implications for our understanding of psychoticism. The fact that a patient so regressed as Mr B. was amenable to the therapeutic influence of a simple but astute manipulation of incentives suggests that even such a serious psychosis must be, in part at least, a case of maladjustment as opposed to some kind of organic imbalance.

The basic simplicity of an operant conditioning routine means that to a large extent it can be carried out by nursing staff providing they have been suitably trained and instructed in its use. This has already been tried with some success in psychiatric institutions in the US and Canada. It is specially useful in overcoming some of the more troublesome and disruptive behaviour on the part of certain patients which can create so much difficulty for those whose job it is to look after them. Similar experiments have also been attempted, in penal institutions in particular, in connection with the treatment of adolescent offenders.[24] Potentially the method offers great possibilities for dealing with some of our most pressing social problems. It is not, however, with its practical applications that we are now concerned but rather with the inferences we can draw from them for the theory of conditioning. For I shall take it for granted that such methods do get results. It is true that a properly controlled assessment of the long term efficacy of behaviour therapies is still needed, but it must be remembered that these methods are peculiarly well adapted for objective assessment—indeed the therapy often resembles more an experiment than a form of treatment—so that it is hardly possible to deny from the evidence we have so far that major modifications of behaviour are in fact produced by these means. What is specially striking, from a psychological point of view, is that the means turn out to be so surprisingly simple. Certainly, few authorities would have had the hardihood to predict such results had they been told about these methods before they had been put to the test. Yet now even the more grudging critics of behaviour therapy are forced to admit that it has opened up new prospects in the control of human behaviour. Where we find much less agreement is on the question of why it should be as effective as it is. On this point we cannot simply be content to accept the answer of those who have been foremost in developing such techniques.

Thus, Breger and McGaugh [1965] state that, while they have no quarrel with the techniques as such, they take strong exception to the construction that has been put upon them and, in particular, to the assumption that 'the concepts taken from conditioning, either as described by Pavlov or the operant conditioning of Skinner, can be used as explanatory principles'. They argue that, on the contrary, 'when we look at the way conditioning principles are applied in the explanation of more complex phenomena, we see that only a rather flimsy analogy bridges the gap between such laboratory defined terms as stimulus, response and reinforcement and their referents in the case of complex behaviour'. The gist of their criticism is that, in the laboratory paradigms of conditioning, a stimulus always means some specifiable external stimulus, a response means some measurable overt response, while reinforcement again means some identifiable stimulus. When we examine the usage of these terms in the clinical situation, however, we find that it is stretched out of all recognition. Thus, the 'stimulus', at least in desensitisation and aversion techniques, is often nothing more than an image in the mind of the patient but is no less effective than if it were a physical object. Likewise the response, though it may in some cases refer to some quite specific physiological reaction, a penile erection, a fluctuation in the patient's pulse-rate or electrical skin-resistance, etc., in other cases may be nothing more definite than just behaving cooperatively. This is especially so when it comes to estimating the success of the treatment when the concept of generalisation tends to be used very freely and loosely.[25] As for the concept of reinforcement, we have seen that one of the more powerful kinds of reinforcement is that which we called 'social reinforcement'. This is understandable if we take as our point of departure man's need for affiliation, but it is not so easily expressed in the objective terminology of conditioning. Indeed, learning theorists have given up trying to provide any descriptive definition of what constitutes reinforcement and have settled for the purely functional definition according to which a positive reinforcement is anything that facilitates learning, a negative reinforcement anything that impedes learning.

Breger and McGaugh, be it noted, are not denying that behaviour therapy is a species of learning but they complain that behaviour therapists too often ignore the importance of cognitive and central processes in learning.[26] In their view, 'Learning is the process by which information about the environment is acquired, stored and categorized'; in other words, they equate learning with memory rather than with the performances dependent on memory. They suggest, accordingly, that 'a neurosis is a set of central strategies (or a program) which guide the individual's adaptation to his environment'. In this connection it is of interest to note that Kassorla, strict Skinnerian though she be, writes, à propos of her Mr B., 'We viewed him as being responsible and decided that he was to work for his food (by being normal) as did people in the world outside the hospital.' [Kassorla (1969) p. 71] This is indeed a far cry from the conception of the reinforcement as automatically stamping in whatever response immediately precedes it. Instead, we have the conception of a person forced to realise what pays off and what does not. In crude terms, the patient has to be made to understand that it pays him to behave sensibly and does not pay him to play the fool.

However, if the conditioning model as applied to the treatment is suspect, it is even more rickety when applied to the origins of a given disorder. True, in the case of certain isolated phobias it has sometimes been possible to trace this to a single traumatic event as the precipitating cause and even then it is often far from clear why the event in question should have had such powerful consequences. In the case of such innocuous objects as ordinary spiders it is hard to understand the patient's anguish unless the object has a symbolic significance of some kind. Of course one can always invoke the 'contingencies of reinforcement' that may have operated in the outside world to have brought the patient to his present pass, but it is quite another matter to give a plausible account of how the aberration came to assume pathological proportions. Take, for example, the bizarre case of transvestism to which aversion therapy has been applied with good effect. It is not sufficient to point out that the patient has derived satisfaction from dressing as a woman, the problem is to explain how the practice ever came to obtain such a hold over him, how it is, in other words, that people become a slave to their vices. In point of fact, most behaviour therapists do not worry too much about how their patients came to be as they are or what led to a particular addiction or perversion. Wisely, perhaps, they are more interested in the cure than in the cause. But, from a theoretical standpoint, this is clearly unsatisfactory. In defending themselves against the criticisms of Breger and McGaugh, Rachman and Eysenck, while not denying that a cognitive interpretation of the neuroses is a possibility, insist that, as things are, the conditioning model is able to make more testable predictions and hence the behaviour therapist is justified in preferring it. [see Breger and McGaugh (1965) seq.] This, however, is to take a narrowly pragmatic view of the situation; after all, this may not always be the case and meanwhile we have the right to demand that a theory should be convincing, not just that it should be useful.

But to say all this is not to disparage the achievements of behaviour therapy. Breger and McGaugh go too far, it seems to me, in wanting to show that conditioning principles have no relevance to the therapeutic process. After all, at one level, the patient alreadys knows, at the outset of the treatment, that his present strategies are no use, otherwise he would not be seeking treatment. He becomes free to adopt a more rewarding strategy only after he has been subjected to a course of therapy in which a conditioning procedure appears to play an essential part.

*　　*　　*

The science of behaviouristics is one of the legacies of the doctrine of Behaviourism which itself was only the culmination of a movement which had its beginnings in the 17th century scientific revolution of applying to animal and human behaviour the mechanistic approach that had been found so successful with inanimate objects. [cf. Lowry (1971) or Mackenzie (1973)] At the present time it presents us with the curious paradox that, while its academic standing is weaker than ever before and its theoretical foundations more persistently under critical fire [cf. Chomsky (1971)], yet its social applications in such diverse fields as psychiatry, penology and even education are everywhere gaining ground. It is easy to dismiss, as largely bombast, Skinner's claim [1971] that his system now makes it practicable to refashion society and recast human nature (granted sufficient dictatorial powers); nevertheless we may agree with Eysenck [1972] that far more could be done for the benefit of the mentally sick, the delinquent or even the ordinary school dunce if we took advantage of the known principles of behaviouristic science. I suggest that the solution of this paradox can be found in the fact that behaviouristics incorporates within itself certain indubitable truths on which it has imposed a more dubious theoretical superstructure. These truths are, more specifically, two principles whose efficacy has been recognised since time immemorial: (1) the principle of association, and (2) the principle of hedonism. The crucial achievement of behaviouristics was to reinterpret them both in strictly objective and operational terms and, in so doing, to quantify them. In this way classical conditioning reaffirms the first principle while operant conditioning reaffirms the second. But, by dint of this translation, they brought out, in a way never before realised or suspected, the critical significance of the temporal intervals involved. This becomes particularly striking in the case of operant conditioning. The older hedonism, we now see, took a far too intellectualist view of the relationship between pleasure and behaviour and assumed that, in general, we simply act in such a way as to maximise our utilities or satisfactions in the long run. Operant conditioning has demonstrated that, in certain cases at least, it is the *short run* that counts. The tremendous efficacy of immediate positive reinforcement is something that could not have been anticipated by the older introspective psychology.[27] If there have been any genuinely novel discoveries in modern psychology (which in our introduction we took leave to doubt) this would surely qualify as well as any. The besetting weakness of the behaviouristic approach has been its rash assumption that these two principles provide an adequate basis for a comprehensive psychology.

Summary

Conditioning

Conditioning is here defined as a method of modifying behaviour which, in theory at least, is automatic and independent of the subject's attitudes and volitions. Two basic types of conditioning are distinguished: (1) *classical conditioning*, as associated with Pavlov, the crux of which is the pairing of two arbitrary stimuli until one stimulus alone can produce an effect similar to that of the other, and (2) *operant conditioning*, as associated with Skinner, the crux of which is to strengthen some arbitrary response by rewarding it immediately each time it is emitted in the appropriate stimulus situation. Both types of conditioning are based on the traditional associationist assumption that all complex behaviours are built up piecemeal from a set of behavioural atoms or 'reflexes'. The history of classical conditioning is here traced from Descartes, who introduced the concept of the reflex, to its culmination in the work of the Russian School of Reflexology. Operant conditioning, a product of the late 1930s, is here seen as the outcome of an attempt by B. F. Skinner to simplify and systematise the laws of trial-and-error learning, as developed by Thorndike and the American School of Learning Theory, by modelling them on the principles of classical conditioning.

Behaviour Therapy

Behaviour therapy is a psychiatric technique of recent origin based on the principles of conditioning. As opposed to 'dynamic' psychotherapy, which regards the patient's symptoms as no more than the expression of some underlying conflict which has to be resolved, it attempts to deal directly with the symptoms and to cure the patient by eliminating them. Three main varieties of behaviour therapy are discussed: (1) *desensitisation* or *'reciprocal inhibition'*, aimed primarily at the elimination of phobias; (2) *aversion therapy*, whose object is the elimination of undesirable habits; and (3) *operant conditioning therapy*, whose object is to promote desirable habits which the patient for some reason lacks. The strong and weak points of each of these three techniques are discussed and it is concluded that, all in all, behaviour therapy represents the most powerful application of science to the control of behaviour so far devised. Even its critics do not deny its practical achievements; what is still much more a matter of dispute is how far these achievements rely on pure conditioning theory and how far they rely on learning in a broader, cognitive sense.

Notes

1   The idea is first expressed in his *Passions of the Soul* (Paris 1649) published a year before his death. It was first worked out with concrete examples and diagrams in a posthumous treatise *L'Homme*

(Paris 1664, originally published in Latin as *De Homine*, Leiden 1662). The relevant passages from this latter work are reprinted as excerpt 57 of Herrnstein and Boring (eds) [1965] where the whole of Chap. 9 is there devoted to this concept. As the editors there remark: 'No physiological concept has influenced psychology so broadly and deeply as the concept of the reflex.'

2   This, at least, would seem to be the view of a Soviet author, M. G. Yaroshevski, who writes: 'Why was it that this model was created for the first time in Russia and not in some other country? There were quite definite social and historical reasons why this should be so. The deterministic, materialistic conception of the mind was developed in Russia by people who, in the service of revolution, sought to create a personality capable of opposing the existing order and of destroying it.' ['I. M. Sechenov—The Founder of Objective Psychology', Chap. 5 of Wolman (ed.) (1968)] While I cannot pretend to understand what his last sentence means, the sentiment is obvious enough. I am indebted to Yaroshevski's article for the facts concerning Sechenov's life given below.

3   At least since 1906 when Charles Sherrington, the great English physiologist, published his *Integrative Action of the Nervous System*. Sherrington remained, however, a convinced dualist and emphasised the distinction between reflex and voluntary action. He never sanctioned the extension of the reflex concept in Pavlov. He insisted, for example, that reflexes are not to be confused with habits. The latter are conscious, voluntary and often skilled acts which only gradually become unconscious and automatic as practice brings fluency. Pavlov's so-called 'conditioned reflex' he regarded as just another species of habit rather than as a real reflex: 'So with a dog whose mouth waters at the sound of a tuning fork, which training has associated for it with food. These trains of reaction have become automatic, though at first attended by acute and critical awareness ... the reflex is independent of consciousness even at first occurrence.' [Sherrington (1940) p. 195]

4   In his *Observations on Man* (London 1749). Drever [1968] remarks *à propos* of Hartley's theory that 'it illustrates a rather pervasive feature of associationism, namely that explicitly or implicitly it tends to assume a physiology. Sometimes, as in this case, the

processes assumed are speculative, sometimes ... they are old-fashioned. Commonly they are both.' There is a direct historical link between Hartley's 'vibrations in the medullary substance' and Sechenov's 'reflexes of the brain'.

5 Whytt was the author of *An Essay on the Vital and other Involuntary Motions of Animals* (Edinburgh 1751). [*see* Herrnstein and Boring (eds) (1965) excerpt 60] An American contemporary of Pavlov's, E. B. Twitmyer, established a conditioned knee-jerk in a human subject as early as 1902.

6 We have already mentioned Sherrington's views on this distinction in note (3) above. Recently an American biologist, R. Efron, in an article entitled 'The Conditioned Reflex: a Meaningless Concept' [Efron (1966)] sees the whole of conditioning theory as an attempt to 'escape the facts of consciousness and voluntarily initiated behaviour'.

7 For the concept of 'sign-learning' and the distinction between S-S and S-R conditioning, *see* Tolman [1932] or Hilgard and Bower [1966] Chap. 7, 'Tolman's Sign Learning'. Though a methodological behaviourist, Tolman took what would now be called a cognitive approach to the problem of learning.

8 For Thorndike, the law of effect was never more than one of several laws of learning, e.g. 'frequency', 'recency', 'belonging', etc. [*see* Thorndike (1966)] For Guthrie's attempt to assimilate all laws of learning to a combination of contiguity plus recency, *cf.* Mueller and Schoenfeld [1954] or Hilgard and Bower [1966] Chap. 4.

9 An amusing account of the stages which led to this invention has been given by Skinner himself in a revealing autobiographical article 'A Case Study in Scientific Method' in Koch (ed.) [1959] Vol. II.

10 The term 'instrumental conditioning' is also widely used, thus Hilgard and Marquis [1961] contrast 'classical' with 'instrumental' conditioning. The distinction was first introduced by Skinner in his article, 'Two Types of Conditioned Reflex and a Pseudo-type', *J. Gen. Psych.* 12, 1935, which has been reprinted in Skinner [1961].

11   Skinner's one excursion into fiction (as a young man he had ambitions to be a writer) was his utopian novel *Walden Two* (Macmillan: New York 1948) which was intended to represent a kind of benign 'Brave New World'. Against the critics who were appalled at the idea of a community whose members were scientifically manipulated from the cradle to the grave he defended himself in Part I of Skinner [1961]. He further develops his social engineering in Skinner [1953] but for his most recent defence of scientific utopianism *see* Skinner [1971].

12   Thanks to operant techniques it is now possible to investigate the perceptual and discriminatory powers of animals with a precision which, for human beings, would require a full-scale psychophysical test. As a *tour de force* of operant conditioning *see* Skinner's article 'Pigeons in a Pelican' in Skinner [1961] where he describes a wartime project which he undertook for the US Navy with the object of replacing the computer components of a guided missile with a live pigeon trained to peck at a window according to whether the target appeared on or off centre. Though never actually used, the project proved perfectly practicable.

13   *See* Skinner [1961] Part III, 'The Technology of Education'.

14   A striking illustration of this comes from the recent extension of operant conditioning which has led to the technique now often referred to as 'bio-feedback'. Here the subject, by dint of appropriate reinforcement, is able to acquire control over functions not normally under voluntary regulation, *cf.* Miller, N. [1969], using rats, and Shapiro *et al.* [1969], using humans. Thanks to this technique, patients suffering from high blood-pressure can now learn to control this pressure and epileptic patients can learn to control their own brain rhythms.

15   The best account of the Solomon experiment is to be found in Eysenck [1965] but *see also* R. L. Solomon, 'Punishment', in Haber [1966].

16   This interpretation of avoidance conditioning first appears in Mowrer [1950], but Miller, N. [1948] had already demonstrated that fear could function as an acquired drive. For the classic experi-

ment in active avoidance conditioning *see* Solomon and Wynne [1953].

17 The concept of differential gradients of reinforcement and its implication for the explanation of conflict behaviour is due to Neal Miller, *see* his 'Experimental Studies of Conflict' in Hunt (ed.) [1944]. It was, however, Mowrer who coined the term 'Neurotic Paradox', *see* Mowrer [1950].

18 The expression 'brainwashing' has no definite connotation in scientific usage. Eysenck [(1965) Chap. 5, 'Therapy or Brain-Washing'] suggests that we use the term behaviour therapy when it is practised in the interests of the patient and brainwashing when it is practised in the interests of the manipulator.

19 V. M. Bekhterev was second only to Pavlov as a pioneer of 'reflexology' (it was he who coined the term). He was himself a psychiatrist, not, like Pavlov, a pure physiologist, and, in 1907, he founded the Psychoneurological Institute of St Petersburg where he conducted his researches and treated patients.

20 A specialist journal, *Behaviour Research and Therapy*, under the joint editorship of H. J. Eysenck and S. Rachman was founded in 1963. For a convenient up-to-date survey and discussion of the field *see* Beech [1969], to whom I am much indebted for the contents of this section.

21 The celebrated case of 'Little Albert', in which an eleven month infant was given a conditioned fear response to a white rat, using a loud noise as the unconditioned stimulus, was first reported by Rosalie Rayner (later Mrs Watson) and J. B. Watson in *Scientific Monthly*, 1921. The fear response soon generalised to other similar objects, e.g. 'a rabbit, a dog, a sealskin coat, cotton wool, human hair and a false face' (this last item does not appear to have much in common with the rest; perhaps it was frightening for other reasons). The first systematic attempt to de-condition spontaneously acquired fears in infants was carried out by Dr Mary Coover Jones under Watson's direction, as reported in her article 'The Elimination of Children's Fears', *J. Exptl. Psych.* 7, 1924, p. 382. An account

both of the Little Albert case and of the cases dealt with by Dr Mary Coover Jones is given in Watson [1930].

22 A simple device for administering shock treatment is described by R. J. McGuire and M. Vallance in their article 'Aversion Therapy by Electric Shock: A Simple Technique' *Brit. Med. J.*, Jan. 1964, 151-53. They state that 'the strength of the shock should be adjusted so that it is as painful as the patient can bear', but add, 'The patient, himself, decides how severe the shock should be. After initial instruction he can treat himself and may take the apparatus home to continue treatment there.' They point out the advantage of this for cases involving masturbation to perverse fantasies since the patient can use the apparatus whenever he is tempted to masturbate. For a general discussion of aversion therapy *see* Rachman and Teasdale [1969].

23 This, of course, stems directly from Skinner's work with animals. He himself discussed its applications to human behaviour disorders in, for example, his chapter on psychotherapy [Skinner (1953)] and in a 1955 paper, 'What is Psychotic Behavior?' reprinted in Skinner [1961].

24 *Cf.* Ayllon and Azrin [1968]. Eysenck [1972] pp. 119-25, has discovered a remarkable forerunner of the token economy technique in Alexander Machonochie, who was superintendent of a penal settlement in Australia during the early 19th century and who practised it on the inmates with considerable success, despite the suspicion with which he was regarded by his superiors in Britain. His account is taken from J. V. Barry's *Alexander Machonochie*. Oxford Univ. Press: Melbourne 1958.

25 Beech, himself a practitioner, points out that it is not sufficient to explain an all-round improvement in the patient's condition by saying that it was a certain *class* of behaviour that was being conditioned, rather than some specific behaviour, unless one is in a position to state beforehand *which* class. [*see* Beech (1969) p. 192]

26 *Cf.* also A. Lazarus, a prominent behaviour therapist. Arguing against theorists such as Wolpe, he says: 'I do not think that all learning is conditioning; the term conditioning should be restricted

to the description of laboratory experiments in which clearly defined conditioned and unconditioned stimuli are presented in known temporal relationships with each other' [CIBA Foundation (1968) p. 194].

27 Hume gets close to recognising the importance of the time factor when he writes: 'A trivial good may, from certain circumstances, produce a desire superior to what arises from the greatest and most valuable enjoyment; nor is there anything more extraordinary in this, than in mechanics to see one pound weight raise up a hundred by the advantage of its situation.' (*Treatise of Human Nature*, Bk. 2, Part III, sect. 3) But he would not be the first to speak more truly than he knew.

CHAPTER FIVE

Cognitive Psychology

Cognitive psychology cannot be defined simply in terms of content, that is, as being concerned with questions of knowing, as opposed to questions of feeling or willing; it represents also a particular approach to these questions. The point is that all the basic cognitive processes, perceiving, learning, remembering, thinking, imagining, etc., have been tackled at one time or another along strict associationist lines which sought to minimise the role of central mediating mechanisms in the organisation of behaviour and treated the brain as little more than a glorified switchboard which permitted the formation of stimulus-response connections. Historically, the cognitive approach in psychology represented the antithesis of the associationist-peripheralist approach. The opposition between a conditioning model and a cognitive model in present day psychology has its roots in the bifurcation of European philosophy during the 17th century into the Empiricist and Rationalist Schools. When, in the 19th century, experimental psychology got going under the leadership of Wundt and his followers, they simply took over the Empiricist outlook ready-made although, from the start, they faced an undercurrent of opposition from the act-psychologists who followed Brentano. Behaviourism in due course discarded the subjectivism of the Wundtian approach, but not its associationism. It was the Gestalt school which, in the epoch between the Wars, came to represent the cognitive approach in experimental psychology.

The Gestalt tradition, however, embodied two distinct strands: the one, from which it derived its name, was concerned to stress the essentially holistic nature of mental processes; the other, which was more truly the precursor of current cognitive theory, emphasised the creative aspect of mind in the cognitive process. The former culminated in Köhler's doctrine of 'isomorphism' which sought to replace the switchboard model of the brain with a field-theory model but remained, in other respects, as deterministic as the associationist model. The latter revolved around such key concepts as 'insight', 'restructuring', 'set', and so on, and is to be found pre-eminently in the work of Duncker in Berlin during the 1930s and among such German expatriates in America as Scheerer and Lewin. [cf. Humphrey (1951) Chap. 6] Sometimes, however, both strands of Gestaltism are to be found in the work of the same psychologist: thus both Köhler and Wertheimer are preoccupied with the holistic issue when they discuss perception, but Köhler, in his famous study of problem-solving in apes [Köhler (1957)], and Wertheimer, when he discusses the educational implications of Gestalt principles [Wertheimer (1961)], represent a straightforward cognitive approach. In the field of learning theory, especially as developed by the influential American school of animal experimentation from Thorndike to Hull, the associationist tradition remained supreme but a rival cognitive school held its ground and included such names as Tolman, Krechevsky, Maier and, to some extent, Lashley, all of whom came under Gestalt influence.

A new chapter in cognitive psychology opened with the advent of the computer age following the Second World War and with the galaxy of attendant sciences that emerged in its wake: cybernetics, information and communication theory, statistical decision theory, game theory, and so forth.[1] The main implication of these new sciences so far as psychology was concerned is that, for the first time, a whole range of concepts pertaining to the higher mental processes could be expressed in objective terminology and mathematical language. The appeal of stimulus-response theory was that it alone seemed capable of providing the rigorous concepts and quantitative measures which an experimental science seemed to demand. The weakness of the Gestalt challenge was that it had to rely on concepts which were inherently vague and qualitative. The introduction of computer analogies meant that thinking could now be discussed in terms which did not carry with them the suggestion of anything ineffably mentalistic. Whole sectors of psychology which had virtually lain dormant since the decline of introspectionism now once again came to the fore. For example, during the 1950s Broadbent, Cherry and others developed the 'split-span' technique for studying attention and immediate memory storage. A message is fed to one ear and a different message is simultaneously fed to the other ear. It is remarkable how fertile this simple methodology proved to be in opening up whole new areas to experimental attack. [see Broadbent (1958), Cherry (1957), Moray (1969)] Concurrently, a new attack on some of the classic problems of perception, such as the problem of the visual illusions, was undertaken by Gregory, MacKay and other scientists who adopted what may loosely be described as an engineering approach to perception, wherein the brain is conceived as perpetually formulating models of external reality and testing them against the information picked up by the sense organs. [see Gregory (1966) and (1970)]

It has been said that we have not understood something properly until we can construct something like it. At all events, model building has always been one of the ways in which scientists have attempted to come to grips with the complexities of nature. The advent of computers meant that behaviour could now be simulated symbolically and theories of behaviour translated into computer programmes. The consequences proved to be of particular importance for the study of thinking, which, of all topics in psychology, was perhaps the most impervious to conventional psychological methods both observational and introspective. The foremost pioneers of the new computer-simulation approach to thinking were a trio of American scientists: Newell, Shaw and Simon. They studied the heuristic strategies which human subjects use when confronted by a problem in the conventional way and then translated these into programmed instructions for a computer. They could then compare directly the performance of the computer with the performance of human subjects, with respect to both the successes and failures of the one and the other, and in this way test the adequacy of their theory as to what was critical in human thinking in this context. [cf. Newell, Shaw and Simon (1961)] They also devised along these lines a chess-playing programme which enabled a computer to compete directly, and usually successfully, with a human player.[2] Today a science of automata or of 'artificial' or 'machine' intelligence has become a discipline in its own right. One might say that it runs parallel with cognitive psychology and that there is a certain amount of cross-fertilisation between the two, but it is not restricted to problems of simulation.[3] In a sense one could say that its terms of reference have become wider than those of psychology inasmuch as it is concerned with the concept of behaviour in general, not just of behaviour as found in living organisms.

Skills

Perhaps the most fundamental notion in cognitive psychology is the notion of a skill. As with all concepts of very great generality, it is not easy to define. Taken in its very broadest connotation it is applicable to any form of flexible and adaptive, as opposed to rigid and stereotyped, behaviour. In this sense we can speak of the skills of birds or insects even though we know them to be mainly dependent on inborn or maturational factors. Human skills, however, always refer to complex activities which have had to be specially learned and cultivated and, typically, to locomotor or manipulatory activities. Psychologists use the expression 'perceptuo-motor' skills, emphasising that there can be no coordinated motor activity which is not intimately dependent on perception. One could compare these with, on the one hand, the primarily perceptual skills, as exemplified at its highest level in the expertise of the wine-taster, the art connoisseur or the medical diagnostician, and, on the other, with the primarily intellectual skills which embrace problem-solving in all its innumerable guises. In this section, however, we shall concentrate on the perceptuo-motor skills where the test of the skill lies in some overt motor performance.

What the concept of the reflex was for behaviouristics, the concept of skill has become for cognitive psychology. Yet it is only recently that this has become apparent. In the early days the topic of skills was treated as a kind of extension of the reaction-time experiment while, later on, it came more and more to be subsumed under the rubric of trial-and-error learning. In either case most academic psychologists, apart from a few prescient exceptions such as Woodworth[4] and Bartlett,[5] tended to look upon it as tangential to the main theoretical issues in psychology, and it was left mainly to applied psychologists working in an industrial context to study its peculiarities. Some of the classic studies of skills, that still figure in the textbooks, belong to this practical approach. Such, for example, was Bryan and Harter's study of 1899 on the training of subjects to send and receive signals in Morse code, or Book's study of 1908 on the acquisition of proficiency in touch-typing; but it is only lately that the full theoretical implication of such investigations has begun to be appreciated. Much of the literature on skills is still to be found in the byways of the psychological literature under headings such as 'engineering psychology', 'human performance', 'ergonomics', etc.

After the Second World War, however, in the wake of the cybernetic revolution about which we have spoken, a new approach to the whole topic came into being. A new conception emerged of man as essentially an information-processing system and of his behaviour as a continuous cyclical flow of information between input and output. One of the pioneers of this new approach who was among the first to appreciate the significance of cybernetic ideas for experimental psychology was Kenneth Craik. [see Craik (1943) and (1966)] Welford, another Cambridge psychologist and a notable authority on skills, has this to say about Craik, that he insisted 'that the brain should not be conceived either as a vast telephone exchange of reflex arcs or as a vaguely defined field of interacting forces. Rather, he urged, it must be thought of as a computer receiving inputs from many sources and combining them to produce an output which is unique to each particular occasion although nevertheless lawful.' [Welford (1968) p. 13]

Because of a superficial resemblance between the acquisition of a skill and the acquisition of a set of conditioned responses it is worth comparing the two cases in order to distinguish clearly between them. Logically speaking, there are, we may say, three different ways in which a given sequence of responses may be assembled: (a) each response may be completely independent of every other response; or (b) each response may be made contingent in some way upon the preceding response or responses; or (c) each response may be related to some overall plan or directive and thus only indirectly related to other responses in the sequence. The first case we may ignore since a succession of wholly independent responses would never normally occur in real life. The second case is exemplified by a fixed-order chaining of responses where each item is triggered off by the preceding item in a simple cause-effect sequence. For we must remember that every response is also, potentially, a stimulus or cue: threading a path through a maze or reciting a list of nonsense syllables approximates to this scheme. The third case is the one which characterises a skill. For the point about a true skill is that the individual responses cannot be explained except in relation to the ends which they are produced to serve. A skilled performance, unlike a series of conditioned responses, is inherently goal-directed. It can be explained only if we suppose that it is governed throughout by a perceived discrepancy between the existing state and some goal-state symbolically represented in the brain of the operator.

No doubt this must always have been intuitively obvious if only because, in nature, no two specimens of behaviour are ever likely to be identical since the exact stimulus situation which produces them is unlikely ever to recur. Hence any sequential principle of action in which each move was dependent on its predecessor would be far too inflexible. However, for a long time, psychologists, labouring under the influence of a narrow behaviourism which denied them the use of any teleological concepts in their theorising, failed to notice that they had become stuck in a logical impasse. But with the advent of cybernetics, as the science of self-regulating ('servo-') mechanisms, it became apparent that their scruples were unnecessary. If one could speak of a homing missile as exhibiting purpose it was pointless to deny the property to the behaviour of living organisms. Teleology and Mechanism could be reconciled after all.

But, while every skilled action will differ, however subtly, from every other, if we subdivide the action into its components we find that the smaller the unit the more frequently it is likely to recur. The obvious case in point is speech itself as we descend from sentence to phrase, to word, to morpheme, to phoneme, but a similar analysis could be made with respect to the playing of a musical composition or to any other complex performance. Thus, while the overall performance must retain a high degree of freedom and flexibility with respect to the ordering of its parts, the component responses can afford to be roughly constant and inflexible. Indeed we may expect that the more the specific responses can be made automatic and routine the smoother and more effective the whole performance will tend to become. Hence the strong emphasis in the teaching of most skills on sheer repetitive drill; every skill would seem to have the equivalent of its five-finger exercises. Hence, also, a certain convergence between the units of a skill and the units of conditioning; both represent a highly stereotyped form of response although drill is a deliberate, conscious process which the subject imposes on himself, while in conditioning the subject is being manipulated by external forces.

This polarity between a high-level flexibility and a low-level rigidity is one of the salient characteristics of a true skill. It represents yet another example of the hierarchical principle which crops up in so many places alike in biology, in engineering and in society. Arthur Koestler, who has written extensively on hierarchical systems,[6] has pointed out that they have two special advantages over other forms of organisation: first, they can come into being gradually by assimilating more and more elements into a unified whole (one may compare this with a structure such as the arch which is only stable when it is complete). Secondly, once such a system has evolved it is in a much better position to withstand damage since, in an emergency, the units have sufficient autonomy to keep going of their own accord without direction from above.[7] But there is also a further point to consider in the case of a skill. Since the decision-making processes will here correspond to the upper echelons of the hierarchy, the arrangement insures that a minimum of decision-making will be necessary relative to routine activities. The situation may be compared with that of a social hierarchy where power is concentrated in a few hands.

Thus we see that a number of important consequences follow from the fact that a skill is organised hierarchically: (1) it can be built up step by step from semi-autonomous habits or routines; (2) it can resist a high degree of stress and distraction without disintegrating altogether; and (3) it can minimise the amount of conscious attention that will be needed. To this latter point, which we may call the principle of mental economy or least effort, we may now add a further principle (4) of constant effort whereby the system permits the attainment of ever greater complexity without increasing the cognitive strain involved. This is achieved by virtue of the fact that a skill represents what Koestler would call an 'open hierarchical system' without a fixed apex or a fixed base. As the subject progresses in proficiency, what had previously been a matter for decision-making can now be downgraded as yet another automatic subroutine. Thus, by this continual downward funnelling of strategies, as these are successively perfected, the amount of mental effort or cognitive load involved remains roughly constant.

Another fundamental distinction between a typical motor skill and the ordinary conditioned response lies in the critical role which the time factor plays in the former case. In a skilled performance it is never just a question of making the right responses or even of making the right responses in the right order, it is rather a question of timing the entire sequence so that each movement occurs at the right moment. Sometimes this timing may be dictated by events in the outside world beyond the control of the subject, as when catching a ball or shooting at moving targets; at other times the subject may have more autonomy; for example, in serving at tennis or playing a stroke at golf the subject decides when to initiate the relevant sequence. But, in every case, the movements must follow each other in a very precise temporal order or rhythmic flow. This is seen in its purest form in the rhythmic arts of music and dancing, but even in a strictly practical skill it is never enough just to know what is to be done next, one must be able to do it deftly and fluently.

It is in this connection that the concept of 'feedback' becomes all-important, a concept which psychologists took over from the engineers.[8] In motor activity feedback is provided either by the distance receptors (that is, one can normally see or hear what one is doing), or by the proprioceptors situated in the muscles and joints which supply a kind of running commentary on the disposition of one's limbs from moment to moment. The former has been called 'extrinsic feedback', the latter 'intrinsic feedback'. It can be shown experimentally that any interference with either form of feedback is liable to have drastic effects on performance. For example, it is very difficult to control the volume of one's voice when one can no longer hear oneself speak. Sometimes, however, the one kind of feedback can at least partially compensate for the lack of the other. Thus, those who are forced to rely on artificial limbs and are thus deprived of proprioceptive feedback can to some extent manage by watching the movements that they make. Conversely, the blind who are deprived of the most important source of extrinsic feedback can fall back on intrinsic feedback; similarly, the touch-typist learns to rely mainly on the feel of her fingers rather than on looking at them.

Ever since the introduction of mirror-drawing into a psychological laboratory a large amount of work has been done to study the consequences of tampering with the perceptual input while the subject is engaged on some skilled activity. The most drastic types of transformation used in this connection involve the subject wearing spectacles which invert the up-down dimension of the visual field or reverse the left-right dimension, or both. The surprising finding from such studies has been the extent to which the subject can learn to adapt to such optical transformations after prolonged exposure to such conditions.[9] Indeed, once a new coordination between hand and eye has taken place the transformed field will no longer appear strange and bewildering and it is only with the removal of the spectacles that difficulties again arise. The advent of closed-circuit television and video-tape recording has now also made it possible to study the effect of delaying visual feedback. In this case the subject cannot see directly the movements of his hand but watches it on a monitoring screen, and the interval of delay can be varied by the experimenter. It is apparently much harder to adapt to such temporal interference in feedback. [see Smith and Smith (1962)] The same is true when the subject's voice is fed back to him through earphones after a brief interval of delay.

However, the concept of feedback is not adequate to explain certain facts about skilled performance. The point is that there are a large number of skills, of which playing the piano is one example, where the pace is too fast for the performer to be able to rely on feedback. It was the physiological psychologist Lashley who first drew attention to this point and to its implications; the minimal reaction-time would impose an insuperable limit to the speed with which one could hope to execute a particular sequence of movements, and yet the observed speeds far exceeded this theoretical limit.[10] The inescapable implication of this fact is that such sequences must be pre-programmed and then simply run off following a single initial decision. Such movements which do not depend on continuous correction are now known technically as 'ballistic' movements or actions.[11] At the same time the pre-programming of such sequences must take into account the requirements of the situation in which they are to occur; they cannot be pre-programmed too far in advance. Thus, in a broader sense, there is still a vital interplay between the activity and the overall perceptual input from the environment. That is why, in many situations, it is possible to make one's response coincide with some external signal without any time-lag at all; there is sufficient information available to make it possible to anticipate the arrival of the signal in question. Even in a task like that of steering a vehicle, where there is continuous correction, accuracy depends in part upon anticipating such correction on the basis of the visual information available at any given instant. [*cf.* Welford (1968) p. 14]

One of the striking changes that can be observed as a subject becomes more proficient in a given skill is that he will start making the necessary adjustments well ahead of the critical stimulus. An illustration of this change is provided by another laboratory task in which the subject has to join a succession of points on a table using a stylus to do so. The beginner can be observed to move in straight lines from one point to the next. The practised subject, however, will describe a curve with his stylus which encompasses all the points in a single smooth sweep of the arm. [*cf.* Montpelier (1935)] It is clear that the latter is able to anticipate the total configuration of points and is no longer bound by the next point alone: by trial and error he has found the path which allows for the most rapid traversal with the smallest amount of effort. This capacity to anticipate one's responses is particularly important in connection with any form of 'decoding' skill: typing, translating, sight-reading in music, and so on. The novice has to react immediately to each successive signal, whereas the expert can tolerate a considerable interval of delay between the taking in of the information and the giving of it out in the appropriate form. This gives the expert a much better chance to adjust in good time to signals requiring special attention, such as an unfamiliar word or phrase, etc. In this way, while the input may vary markedly in degree of difficulty, the output can continue to function with more or less uniform speed and efficiency.

There is one final aspect of skills which I want to mention: this concerns their unconscious or inarticulate basis. A motor skill is the prime example of a 'knowing-how' as opposed to a 'knowing-that'. Once we have mastered a given skill it is as if we no longer needed to think about what we are doing; our body, as it were, does our thinking for us.[12] This is what we mean by calling something a habit, and the process of automatisation, whereby as much as possible in a skill is relegated to the domain of habit, is part of that mental economics about which we spoke earlier. This process is never normally completed, there is always a residue which persists in engaging our conscious faculties, apart from the anomalous case of sleep-walking or the occasional report of persons who have carried out some complex task while asleep or in a trance. But the contrast between the practical knowledge implied in the display of a skill and the theoretical ignorance that usually goes with it can be very striking. The fable of the centipede who walked without any bother until he was asked in which order he moved his legs seems in general to be borne out in the study of skills, although it is relevant more to the initial stages of a skill than to its final stages. The real virtuoso is unlikely to be embarrassed by having to describe what he does or to analyse what is involved; that is why a first-rate musician will often make a first-rate teacher. Nevertheless, this gap between explicit knowledge and implicit ability shows itself in many ways. Polanyi, the eminent philosopher of science, has this to say about the humble skill of riding a bicycle:

> From my interrogation of physicists, engineers and bicycle manufacturers, I have come to the conclusion that the principle by which the cyclist keeps his balance is not generally known. The rule observed by the cyclist is this. When he starts falling to the right he turns his handlebars to the right, so that the course of the bicycle is deflected along a curve to the right. This results in a centrifugal force pushing the cyclist to the left and offsets the gravitational force dragging him down to the right. This manoeuvre presently throws the cyclist out of balance to the left, which he counteracts by turning his handlebars to the left; and so he continues to keep himself in balance along a series of appropriate curvatures. A simple analysis shows that for a given angle of unbalance the curvature of each winding is inversely proportional to the square of the speed at which the cyclist is proceeding.
> But does this tell us exactly how to ride a bicycle? No. You obviously cannot adjust the curvature of your bicycle's path in proportion to the ratio of your unbalance over the square of your speed; and if you could you would fall off the machine for there are a number of other factors to be taken into account in practice which are left out in the formulation of this rule. Rules of art can be useful, but they do not determine the practice of an art; they are maxims, which can serve as a guide to an art only if they can be integrated into the practical knowledge of the art. They cannot replace this knowledge. [Polanyi (1958) pp. 49-50][13]

In this delightful passage the paradox of the cyclist, who follows the correct rule without knowing what it is, is developed to the full. Actually, it is no more paradoxical than the bird which flies while being ignorant of the aerodynamics of flight. Obviously the correct mathematical formulation of the mechanics involved in maintaining equilibrium on a bicycle, which Polanyi obligingly supplies, belongs to an entirely different order of activity from actually riding the bicycle. What does demand an explanation is how, precisely, the cyclist discovers the rule about turning the handlebars and how he succeeds in learning this without ever becoming aware that he has done so. In a typical complex skill we usually start with a number of formal instructions which we then have to try and realise in practice—this would, for example, be the usual way of learning to drive a car; the case of the cyclist is closer to that of swimming or even walking. There is, in fact, a class of very primitive skills which we do seem able to acquire of our own accord without necessarily having any formal instruction whatever and without necessarily ever being able to articulate what rules we have followed. At this level we are again confronted by the parallel with operant conditioning, the distinction being only that here it is a *rule* that is being learned on a trial-and-error basis rather than some specific response. It is by virtue of this fact that a skill is immediately transferable to any situation to which the rule is applicable and, operationally speaking, it is the *fact* that a response can be thus generalised that shows it to be the manifestation of a skill.

Language

Language is the great divide which separates man as animal from man as human being; man in a state of nature from man in society. It is the human skill *par excellence*; with it, no defect is so gross that it can rob us of our essential humanity; without it, we can be no more than the simulacrum of a human being. Were we, as in a fairy-tale, to encounter a talking frog, we should at once recognise a fellow human in animal guise. Likewise, if, as no longer seems quite so fanciful, we were to rear a breed of non-human primates with whom we could converse, we would find it impossible to treat them as mere animals; inevitably our moral attitude towards such creatures would no longer be that which we now take towards a totally alien species but rather that which we now take towards, say, a mentally defective child. That, as matters stand, we can restrict the term 'human' to a single species is due to an accident of evolution whereby all the intervening species of hominids have perished, leaving a vast mental chasm separating man from his nearest relatives among the anthropoid apes.

The significance of language for our mental life is twofold: it is at once our natural means of communication and the vehicle for our thoughts. All animals communicate with their kind, but only man communicates through that system of conventional symbols which we call a language and without which society could not have come into being. The origins of language must remain forever a topic for conjecture but it has been suggested that it was the needs of communication when the higher apes took to hunting in packs that put a premium on the development of language. But, once in being, the potentialities of language for the development of thinking and reasoning was exploited, we may presume, to insure for man that intellectual superiority over his competitors to which his large brain entitled him. We need not go so far as some modern philosophers in equating language and thought, although this idea has been an intriguing one ever since Plato described thinking as a dialogue of the soul with itself. Much of what goes to make up our thought processes is not even conscious, let alone verbal, but, undoubtedly, conceptual thought would never have been possible but for the availability of words in which to embody our concepts and of sentences in which to combine them.

Like most things that are of cardinal importance in human life, language has never been the preserve of any one discipline. The philosopher and logician no less than the philologist, the grammarian and the pedagogue live by language. Linguistics, the study of language for its own sake, is a very ancient and respected branch of scholarship and linguists can count among their number such intellectual giants as Wilhelm von Humboldt in early 19th century Germany, or the Swiss, Ferdinand de Saussure, in the early 20th century. It is convenient to subdivide linguistics into a number of specialist sciences among which we may include (a) *phonetics*, which deals with the acoustic or phonological aspects of speech; (b) *grammar*, which deals with the rules governing syntax and word changes; and (c) *semantics*, which concerns itself with problems of meaning and definition. When we come to the psychology of language, or 'psycholinguistics' as it is now usually called, it is necessary to start by distinguishing the genuinely psychological problems from the purely linguistic ones. For example, the classification of the known languages into their separate families is clearly a problem for comparative linguistics, not for psychology, although the fact of their diversity may in itself have psychological significance. At the other extreme, pathological disorders of language are clearly the concern of psychology, not of linguistics. But what about the analysis of ordinary language? Here linguistics and psychology converge. If we regard linguistic behaviour as a special sort of skill or a special case of information-processing, then, clearly, it forms part of cognitive psychology. Likewise, the problem of verbal acquisition in childhood or of second-language learning in maturity is clearly part of learning theory.[14]

The term 'psycholinguistics', which epitomises this marriage between linguistics and cognitive psychology, became current only during the late 1950s (it is thus roughly of the same vintage as the expression 'behaviour therapy'). In this instance, a terminological innovation signalised a genuine change in the whole character of this field which had come about as the result of the work of one individual, Noam Chomsky of the Massachusetts Institute of Technology, whose first major publication, *Syntactic Structures*, appeared in 1957. Not, perhaps, since Freud invented psycho-analysis has any psychological science revolved so much around the work of one man. Chomsky, himself, could be described as a theoretical linguist or grammarian with a special interest in symbolic logic and the logical foundations of mathematics; he is not a psychologist. To his followers he is the undisputed genius of the linguistic revolution; to his critics he is a brilliant but essentially mediæval mind, somehow strayed into the computer age.

To understand the impact which he has had on psychology certain facts should be borne in mind. Prior to this time there was very little in common between linguists and psychologists. The dominant school of linguistics in America was that known as 'Structural Linguistics', whose foremost exponents were Leonard Bloomfield and Chomsky's own teacher, Zellig Harris. This school adopted a basically behaviourist philosophy of language but was in general little concerned with the psychological aspects of language and was intent mainly on making linguistics a rigorous and autonomous discipline. The fact is that most of the experimental work on language behaviour and language acquisition up to that time was too crude and too naïve to interest the linguist. For example, Skinner's attempt to bring language learning and performance under the principles of operant conditioning [Skinner (1957)], words being regarded as just so many operant responses, was amongst the earliest victims of Chomsky's radical new approach. [Chomsky (1959)]

Nor did the advent of information theory and the statistical approach as exemplified by Miller [1951] before he fell under the influence of Chomsky [Miller (1964)] do much to bridge the gap. On the other hand, the computer approach, linked as it was with the practical problems of machine translation, did help to pave the way for the Chomskian revolution if only by highlighting the extraordinary complications involved in the decoding and encoding of sentences.[15] But, in the end, perhaps the main reason for the enthusiastic reception which Chomsky's theories have enjoyed among a section of psychologists is that the time was ripe for a reaction against the orthodoxies of behaviourism and stimulus-response psychology, and Chomsky represented that reaction in its most sophisticated and extreme form. For, not only did Chomsky demolish some of the more obvious absurdities of behaviourism, he called into question the entire empiricist tradition of Western science and philosophy and openly embraced a form of Rationalism that goes back past Kant to Descartes and even to Plato.[16] In psychology it is never easy to say something that will invite sheer incredulity. Freud did so, of course, with memorable effect, and Chomsky succeeded on a lesser scale in creating something of the same sort of *éclat* by challenging a number of ideas that had long been taken for granted and had acquired the sanction of common-sense.

In what follows I shall try to expound as briefly as possible what I take to be the distinctive features of the Chomskian approach. In doing so I shall rely especially on his *Language and Mind* of 1968, which is the clearest general statement of his current position so far.[17] There are, however, certain aspects of his work to which I must first draw attention. Chomsky is not an experimentalist and, indeed, rarely alludes to the empirical findings of his psycho-linguistic followers or to the experiments which they perform on adults or on children concerned with the learning or comprehension of linguistic material.[18] Like Freud, his contribution to psychology is of a theoretical nature but, whereas Freud's data were such things as the case-history material or dream-protocols of his patients, Chomsky's data are specimen sentences selected to illustrate some point of grammar and, in particular, to bring out the critical distinction between acceptable and non-acceptable constructions. It has also to be said that most of Chomsky's writings are of a highly abstruse nature and presuppose an expert knowledge of linguistic technicalities. Here I can only consider the wider implications of what he is saying without going into the detailed arguments on which it is based, but the task is rather like trying to expound Einstein without the mathematics.

There are three ideas, in particular, that I want to discuss which I take to be both fundamental to and characteristic of the Chomskian doctrine. The first, which I shall call the 'nativistic hypothesis', states that every human being is born with a ready-made knowledge of language. Obviously this knowledge can only be of a very general and abstract kind; we still have to learn the particular language of our community, but this learning takes place against a pre-existing cognitive structure, we do not have to start with a blank slate. The second, which I shall call the 'discontinuity hypothesis', states that language capacity is exclusively a property of the human brain, is distinct from any other skill and, in particular, owes nothing to any more primitive form of animal communication. The third, which is closely related to the other two, is the view that beneath the superficial variety of different languages there is an underlying unity which pervades them all and which reflects this innate and unique property of the brain. I shall now elaborate on each of these three points and then attempt a critical assessment of them.

(1) The 'Nativistic Hypothesis'

The point of departure for the whole of Chomskian psycholinguistics seems to be an observation which at first may seem rather too obvious to be of much significance, until we remember that many profound insights come to seem obvious once they are pointed out. It is this: we continually utter sentences which we have never spoken before and understand sentences which we have never heard before. Hence, so far as sentences are concerned, as opposed to individual words, no theory which presupposes any kind of rote-learning could possibly explain this 'productive' aspect of speech communication. It follows that we must have at our disposal a certain finite set of rules which when applied to a certain finite vocabulary is sufficient to generate an infinite set of possible sentences. But how do we learn these rules in the first instance? Obviously not in the sort of way we learn our Latin at school. 'We observe,' says Chomsky, 'that knowledge of language is acquired on the basis of degenerate and restricted data and that it is to a large extent independent of intelligence and of wide variations in individual experience.' It is thus impossible, Chomsky thinks, that the child could derive the necessary rules by any sort of inductive process: 'If a scientist were faced with the problem of determining the nature of a device of unknown properties that operates on data of the sort available to a child and gives as "output" ... a particular grammar of the sort that it is necessary to attribute to the person who knows a language, he would naturally search for *inherent principles of organization* that determine the form of the output on the basis of the limited data available' (my italics). It is these 'inherent principles of organization' that constitute Chomsky's innate ideas: 'The child cannot know at birth which language he is to learn, but he must know that its grammar must be of a predetermined form that excludes many imaginable languages. Having selected a permissible hypothesis, he can use inductive evidence for corrective action, confirming or disconfirming his choice.'

(2) The 'Discontinuity Hypothesis'

Like Descartes, Chomsky is impressed by the fact that, when it comes to language, even the most intelligent ape seems to be incapable of achieving what even the dimmest of human imbeciles seems able to take in his stride, even though the ape may be far superior in a great many other skills. 'So far as we know,' says Chomsky, 'possession of human language is associated with a specific type of mental organization not simply a high degree of intelligence.' 'There seems to be no substance', he goes on to say, 'to the view that human language is simply a more complex instance of something to be found elsewhere in the animal world'; and, finally, 'There seems to be little useful analogy between the *theory of grammar that a person has internalized* and that provides the basis for his normal creative use of language and *any other cognitive system* that has so far been isolated and described' (my italics).

(3) The 'Universal Grammar' Concept

To understand Chomsky's concept of a 'universal grammar', it is necessary first to consider certain prior concepts which he has introduced into psycholinguistics. The first of these is the distinction he makes between 'performance' and 'competence'. It is a distinction which, in one form or another, permeates the whole of cognitive psychology; the point is that our performance, on any given occasion, is is always liable to be affected by all kinds of extraneous factors which have nothing to do with the knowledge on which the performance is based. The fact, for example, that all of us make slips from time to time in our numerical calculations does not demonstrate that none of us *knows* the rules of arithmetic! In language this distinction is specially vital inasmuch as our ordinary speech is notoriously slipshod and defective. All talk, one could say, is careless talk; perfect grammatical correctness is seldom found outside the written text.[19] Chomsky is therefore on safe ground, surely, when he insists that it would be futile for the psycholinguist to pay attention indiscriminately to every utterance, no matter how deviant it may be; the critical problem is to explain how every native speaker can at once discriminate between an admissible sentence in his language and an inadmissible one. Since the speaker himself cannot tell us how he does this, any more than our cyclist could tell us how he rides a bicycle, it is up to the psycholinguist to make explicit for us the nature of this 'competence'. If he can do that it is a relatively simple matter to explain the occasional vagaries of 'performance'.

A competence, then, is the internalised set of rules or 'grammar' governing any given activity. It is important, in this context, to distinguish between this special use of the word 'grammar' and its more familiar traditional use to refer to the codification of the various conventions which regulate correct usage in a particular language. Chomsky's use of the term always has definite psychological implications and not only is there a 'grammar' governing the syntax of sentences but another 'grammar' governing their phonological structures, and yet another governing its semantic interpretation. This generalised concept of grammar is one that has since caught on in other areas of cognitive psychology. Granted, then, that it is the business of psycholinguistics to make explicit the grammar underlying our competences, what sort of a grammar do we find when we consider the competence of an ideal 'speaker-listener'? Chomsky's first attempt to answer this question was in terms of what is known technically as a 'phase-structure' grammar. If one takes a given sentence one can carry out a phrase structure analysis by using a 'tree diagram' to express a hierarchy of generality. The bottom layer would then consist of the actual words spoken. The parts of speech to which these words correspond, their parsing, would then constitute the next layer above. Above this would come the type of phrase, whether noun phrase or verb phrase, to which these parts of speech belong and, finally, crowning the top of the tree or apex of the hierarchy, we arrive at the symbol S standing for the class of all admissible sentences of the language. Proceeding downwards, one then moves from one level to the next by substituting the particular for the general case, applying the appropriate 're-write rules' of the language until one reaches the specific sentence in question.

Formally, the procedure is reminiscent of the way in which, in logic or mathematics, one proceeds from the axioms and definitions of the system down to the specific theorem which is to be proved, using only the accepted operations of substitution or transformation. Chomsky's grammar, however, is *not* a formal system but is intended to symbolise a real process such as is involved in the actual production or interpretation of a sentence (at any rate on the syntactical level). Thus, in opposition to the earlier naïve view that we construct our sentences on a left-to-right basis, such that each word we utter becomes the cue for the next word in the sentence, the phrase-structure grammar suggests that, on the contrary, we proceed on a top-to-bottom basis whereby we decide on the phrase structuring of a sentence before we decide on the specific words we are going to emit. Similarly, in the case of the listener, although acoustically speaking the sentence is of course received on a left-to-right basis, it is assumed that the sentence as a whole can be held long enough in acoustic storage for it to be analysed on a top-to-bottom basis. As Miller has pointed out [Miller (1968) p. 74], it is still a matter of argument among psycholinguists 'whether speaking and listening are two separate entities, coordinate but distinct, or whether they are different manifestations of a single linguistic faculty'. One theory, that of 'analysis-by-synthesis', suggests that we understand a sentence by generating an equivalent sentence internally to match the input sentence.

It soon transpired, however, that a phrase-structure grammar on its own would quickly lead to an impasse. Thus, two sentences might have the same phrase-structure and yet require radically different interpretations. To take Chomsky's own stock example, consider 'John is eager to please' and 'John is easy to please'. If we transpose the latter sentence it can be seen to be identical in meaning to the sentence 'It is easy to please John', where 'John' now functions as the object of the verb phrase 'easy to please', whereas there is no equivalent transposition in the case of 'John is eager to please'. At all events, already by 1957 Chomsky had reached the conclusion that a phrase-structure grammar could never deal adequately either with the semantic ambiguities that may arise or with the fact that the same basic sentence can be expressed in a variety of forms: passive as well as active, interrogative or imperative as well as declarative, negative as well as affirmative. Accordingly, Chomsky set out to formulate the rules of a grammar that would cover the relationships between a given *class* of sentences and would not be restricted to the analysis of of individual sentences. These rules included such operations as 'substitution', 'deletion', 'addition', 'permutation', etc., operations which allow the speaker to shift gear, as it were, from active to passive, from declarative to interrogative, from affirmative to negative, etc., in a way which preserves the 'deep structure' of the sentence while altering its 'surface structure'. Much of subsequent psycholinguistic theory has, in fact, been occupied with exploring the properties and implications of this 'transformational' or 'generative' grammar, as it is now called, and the nature of the 'deep structure' on which it is based. [*cf.* Herriot (1970) Chap. 3] Chomsky's own views on the topic have undergone certain developments and revisions which it is not necessary to pursue here.

With the concept of 'deep structure' we reach the heart of Chomskian doctrine. It plays, in fact, much the same role there as does the concept of the Unconscious in depth psychology. For it is on the basis of this 'deep structure' that Chomsky comes in the end to posit his 'universal grammar', hidden beneath the bewildering array of actual languages each with its different 'surface structure', much in the way that Jung came to posit his innate archetypes beneath the endless variety of symbols, myths, dreams, rituals and suchlike creations of the human mind. 'The most challenging theoretical problem in linguistics,' he tells us, 'is that of discovering the principles of universal grammar that interweave with the rules of particular grammar to provide explanation of phenomena that appear arbitrary and chaotic. To study the principles of universal grammar is to study the very nature of human intellectual capacity.'

Whether Chomsky's neo-Nativist, neo-Rationalist conception of the human mind will supplant the strongly entrenched empiricist and behaviourist conceptions remains to be seen. It will depend, in the first instance, on whether he succeeds in convincing his fellow psycholinguists that nothing less radical is adequate to meet the phenomenon of language.[20] Meanwhile, until the experts are agreed, it is not impertinent to consider how the system at issue stands up when called before the bar of commonsense. I should now like to examine Chomsky's central theses from the standpoint of his critics and in the light of certain general objections.

Let us start with the problem of language acquisition. Here the 'naïve' view would be that the child learns to talk in much the same piecemeal fashion, by imitation and trial-and-error, as he learns anything else. That he starts with the odd single words, that he proceeds to short simple phrases until, eventually, he is ready to put together long and complicated sentences. The fact that, when this final stage is reached, he may be producing new sentences never before uttered is important; but novelty, as we have seen, enters into everything we do, it is not just confined to language, and, even if we do not yet fully understand such operations as 'transfer', 'extrapolation', 'analogical thinking', etc., it seems rash to disregard these explanatory concepts which have served us so well in connection with all our other cognitive activities. Chomsky, however, as we have seen, will have none of this. Nothing less than an inborn grammar will serve his turn. What, then, are we to say to this solution of the problem of language acquisition? Certainly, we can no longer rule it out on any *a priori* biological grounds.[21] Psychology today is much more receptive to nativistic theories than it was a generation ago. It would now be generally conceded that we would never learn anything at all if we had to start with nothing more than a totally unstructured potentiality for learning. There is now evidence, for example, that we inherit certain perceptual skills, notably those concerned with depth and movement perception which were formerly thought to be acquired in early infancy. [*cf.* Bower (1971)] Moreover, when we consider the rapidity and facility with which young children learn to talk and compare this with their tardiness in mastering even the rudiments of arithmetic (in striking contrast to man-made computers, which are ideally suited to doing arithmetic but are apt to defeat even the most ingenious attempts to get them to cope with a natural language), we must be tempted to agree with Chomsky that we are all born linguists. And yet there are also children, however exceptional, who show an astonishing natural aptitude for handling numbers, or for music, or even for playing chess. Are we in such cases forced to attribute to them an innate knowledge of number theory, or of harmony and counterpoint, or of chess strategy? Perhaps so; perhaps Plato was right after all in thinking that all learning is merely making explicit what we already know.[22] However, it will clearly require more than the recherché arguments which Chomsky has so far advanced in defence of his nativistic hypothesis to convince his empiricist critics in psychology that no other option is open to them.

Of the three tenets of the Chomskian system that we have chosen to discuss, the 'discontinuity hypothesis' seems to lend itself most readily to the possibility of disconfirmation. Since doubt has been expressed as to whether the Chomskian view is a testable theory at all, in the sense of being falsifiable, this is an important consideration. For, if Chomsky is right in holding that language capacity did not evolve from any simpler cognitive ability or from any known form of animal communication, but emerged suddenly full blown with the human race, then it should follow that it is impossible to train any infra-human primate in the use of language.[23] Conversely, if we did succeed in producing a real live counter-example, then the theory needs reconsideration. It would be naïve to suppose that this could lead to a conclusive refutation of the theory. In the first place there is too much latitude at present in defining the limits of what we are going to regard as a case of genuine language and, in the second place, it could still be argued that the animal was using a quite different cognitive mechanism from the human language user. However, those who insist that the Chomskian view is a testable scientific theory and not just a metaphysical schema would welcome all such empirical attempts to overthrow it. Now, it might be thought that such an attempt had been made and failed. In a classic study by the Kelloggs, an ape was reared in the nursery alongside their own child and, as far as possible, given the same treatment. Yet, despite all its cleverness and precocity, it never managed to master more than a few ineffectual vocalisations.[24] Was this due to inherent limitations in its brain? Two recent researches cast serious doubt on this conclusion; both suggest that the reason may have been due to the more superficial limitation imposed by the structure of the ape mouth which is unsuitable for producing human speech sounds. In the first of these researches the Gardners taught their chimpanzee 'Washoe' to make the gestures of American Sign Language, a language specially designed for communication with the deaf. An intensive training schedule was continued for some years, by the end of which 'Washoe' had acquired a fair-sized vocabulary and a large number of two-sign combinations by means of which she was able to make simple requests or answer simple questions to an extent that was at least comparable with that of a two-year-old child. Psycholinguists are still arguing as to whether anything corresponding to a syntax can be discerned in the chimpanzee sentences, but there can be no doubt that an effective two-way linguistic type of communication was established with a non-human subject.[25]

We come now, lastly, to the problem of a universal grammar. If we grant the two preceding theses then we may assume that it is the innate grammar with which each of us is born that constitutes the hidden unity behind the diversification of actual languages. We might argue, however, that even without adopting any Chomskian assumptions some degree of uniformity could be expected, if only because of certain universal features in the human situation. Language, for example, is concerned with actions and an action may consist either in a person acting on his environment or, alternatively, in the environment acting on him. If every language, therefore, were to make provision for both an active and a passive form of sentence this would be readily understandable without recourse to innate ideas. This, however, is not what Chomsky has in mind when he talks about a universal grammar. His account stresses mainly its negative aspects, that is to say the constraints it places on what is admissible or inadmissible in any natural language: 'The principles of universal grammar provide a highly restrictive schema to which any human language must conform, as well as specific conditions determining how the grammar of any such language can be used.' An example which Chomsky gives is that while many languages, like English, transform a declarative into an interrogative sentence by reversing the order of subject and verb (e.g. 'John is taking off his overcoat' becomes 'Is John taking off his overcoat?'), it would be quite unthinkable for a language to have a rule for the interrogative transformation which simply reversed the order of the first and last words of the sentence ('overcoat is taking off his John'). In technical parlance a transformation is said to be necessarily 'structure-dependent', never 'structure-independent'. No doubt one could easily think up dozens of bizarre rules about which one could confidently say that they would not be found in any known language, just as one could think up dozens of bizarre customs that would never be found in any known society, but does this mean that we are forced to postulate inborn universals? Once again the extravagance of the conclusion seems to have outstripped the grounds on which it is based.

In this connection, George Steiner has recently made a telling plea not to ignore what he calls the 'Tower of Babel' phenomenon. Some four thousand distinct languages, he points out, are still extant, leaving aside an indefinite number that have vanished. Why so many? 'Why, by a factor of a thousand, more languages than, say, there are human races or blood groups?' he asks. Admittedly this diversification does not invalidate the concept of language as a biological property of the species but it certainly does not support it. Hence, 'the key feature of the Chomskian language revolution appears to go against the situation in which the human race finds itself and in which it has existed as far as history and conjecture can reach back'. [Steiner (1969)]

Chomsky began with a penetrating question and one that still demands an answer: how, in effect, are we able to put our thoughts into words and, at the same time, arrange these words into meaningful and grammatical sentences? He ends, as we have seen, by propounding a doctrine that to the layman and to many of his critics seems to offend against the canons alike of good sense and scientific caution. How did this come about? An eminent contemporary linguist, Charles Hockett, believes that the root of the fallacy which vitiates the entire Chomskian superstructure is the assumption that language constitutes a 'well-defined' system, in the technical sense in which the game of chess or 'the set of all formulae for hydrocarbons of the methane series' is a well-defined system. Hockett argues that only conventional systems like games or ideal systems of notation are ever 'well-defined'; all natural systems are more or less 'ill-defined'. In particular, natural languages which, like human societies, developed organically and were never planned are decidedly not a well-defined system. [*see* Hockett (1968) esp. Chaps 3 and 5] Once we recognise this fact we no longer need to equip ourselves with Chomsky's fantastic computing machinery inside our heads in order to explain how we ever contrive to speak at all. Chomsky's infant is innately provided with, in his own words, 'an algorithm for determining the structural description of an arbitrary sentence given an arbitrary grammar'. For Hockett, on the other hand, algorithms belong to the world of well-defined mathematical systems. 'There is,' he says, 'no algorithm for the discovery of *any fact about the real world*. There are, at best, *discovery procedures*: more or less systematised and channelled methods of trial-and-error not guaranteed to be successful, but the best we have and, by virtue of the fundamental nature of the real world, the best we can hope to have' (author's italics), and adds, 'In this regard language is exactly on a par with all other phenomena.' [Hockett (1968) p. 41]

Creativity

We come next to a topic which, in the course of not much more than a decade, has become one of the more vigorous growing points of psychological research and has already produced a large specialist literature of its own. Why this should have been so is not so easy to say. Unlike similar spurts in other sciences, it does not appear to stem from any critical new discovery or new technique. The conception of creativity is one that was always familiar to psychologists even if, in the older literature, it is usually discussed under such headings as 'the faculty of imagination', 'productive thinking', 'the psychology of invention and discovery', etc.[26] In default, therefore, of any obvious scientific reasons for this development one may be forgiven for speculating about possible sociological reasons. Some authorities have suggested that it was the space race which first made America self-conscious about its technological leadership and worried about the supply of scientific manpower and this, in turn, sparked off a reappraisal of its whole educational policy.[27] At all events, by the late 1950s a wave of heart-searching can be discerned among leaders of opinion in the United States regarding the fundamental aims and methods of education, as a result of which more emphasis was given to encouraging originality and initiative in children even at the expense of some sacrifice in docility and conformity. During the 1960s there was a further swing towards anti-authoritarianism and the old American Protestant ethic of hard work and worldly success lost its appeal. It was then that creativity seemed to promise a more inspiring set of values. Within psychology itself, moreover, a reaction was due against the narrow preoccupations of behaviourism and, as in the case of language, psychologists found it refreshing to be able to concentrate once again, and with a good conscience, on aspects of behaviour that are pre-eminently human. Man alone, after all, has used his creative powers to transform his own existence. Thus, for many reasons, despite the amorphous nature of the problem and the difficulty of agreeing on any exact definition of its central concept, once the new movement was launched it rapidly gained momentum.

In this area there are two main problems to be distinguished: the one being that of the 'creative process', the other being that of the 'creative person'. The former, no doubt, is the more fundamental of the two, it alone is strictly a problem for cognitive psychology; the latter embraces differential psychology, psychodynamics and much else besides. As it happens, however, it is on the latter problem that psychologists have had most to say in recent times. Perhaps there is an inherent contradiction between the spontaneity and unpredictability of the creative act and the controlled artificiality of the laboratory but, at any rate, experimental research has so far contributed little to our understanding of the creative process. At all events, once one goes beyond the study of problem-solving, where there is of course a large experimental literature,[28] one is forced back upon the introspective reports of scientists, inventors, artists and suchlike creative individuals [cf. Ghiselin (1952)] or upon biographical studies by historians of science, art historians, literary critics and other scholars. Some of the most illuminating as well as copious contributions to the problem in recent years have come, not from a professional psychologist, but from a well-known writer and polymath, Arthur

Koestler.[29] Koestler has explored in greater depth than any previous writer the common basis of creativity in the sciences and the arts; he is also perhaps the first to realise the significance of the fact that the creative process—the process, that is, whereby something new is brought into being—is, in the first instance, a universal process in nature even though when it occurs in nature we refer to it as evolution.[30] But these are questions that must for the time being be relegated to the sphere of speculative inquiry and are some degrees removed from the preoccupations of the researcher;[31] here it is the more amenable problem of the creative person that will concern us.

Creativity, conceived as a trait, comprises two distinct though related notions; one is that of high achievement, the other is that of originality. A person may have a highly original mind and yet, for one reason or another, be incapable of creating anything of lasting value. Where originality is combined with achievement we speak of genius. Galton, the first empirical psychologist to discuss the topic of genius [Galton (1892)], assumed that what distinguished the genius from the generality of mankind was that he was endowed with an innately superior intellect. Essentially the same assumption still pervades the pioneer work of Terman in the 1920s. Terman undertook what remains to date the only large scale follow-up study of the superior child. His 'gifted children' whose careers he pursues through successive volumes of his *Genetic Studies of Genius*[32] represent, in point of fact, the top ½ per cent of the California School System for the year 1922, the year in which his project was launched. Now, although these children by and large lived up to their early promise, as reckoned later by various criteria of success in life, few made any permanent impact on their times and there was no evidence that those with the highest IQ were those who achieved most. On evidence such as this it would be hard to equate genius and high IQ.

Terman also tackled the problem from the other end, as it were. Basing themselves on the extant juvenilia of 300 of the most famous men of history, he and Catherine Cox attempted to estimate retrospectively their probable IQs.[33] Not surprisingly, they tended to lie well within the upper reaches of the normal distribution but not a few would have failed to qualify for Terman's Californian sample and, in general, no particular advantage was discernible once the IQ exceeded 140. Beyond that other considerations, sometimes having little to do with intellectual superiority, assumed more importance. Some contemporary authorities would now place the minimum level of IQ necessary for outstanding achievement in most walks of life as low as 120 points of IQ.

But, even without the empirical evidence, it is clear that neither the concept of general intelligence nor that of the special abilities could, of itself, cover everything that is required of the concept of creativity. For the former refers essentially to a capacity of some sort while the latter implies that the person has the will or resolution to make good that capacity in the attainment of certain ends. Thus a person could, conceivably, possess the brain of a perfect computer and solve any problem presented to him and yet never in his life produce a single new idea. The conventional IQ test is, primarily, a test of the subject's efficiency in thinking or reasoning; it was not designed to test, for example, the productivity or originality of his thinking. Psychometrists, it is true, had experimented with other types of cognitive tests, notably tests of fluency, both for words and for ideas, but they were never regarded as more than of minor interest until Guilford began systematically to extend the scope of cognitive testing. On the basis of his extensive factor-analytic studies and of a comprehensive theoretical schema of the intellect[34] he arrived at certain conclusions which have since played a crucial part in creativity research.

In particular, Guilford distinguished two types of operation which he called respectively 'convergent thinking' and 'divergent thinking'. Both kinds of thinking would be relevant in solving a given problem but, while convergent thinking is directed towards finding the one correct solution, divergent thinking is directed towards extending the range of possible solutions by producing as wide as possible a variety of different associations to the stimulus situation. Now, the conventional intelligence test, Guilford pointed out, consisted of items which were, in effect, measures of convergent thinking ability. Such items have one and only one correct answer and, since the alternatives are normally set out for inspection, the subject has only to identify which of them is correct. Guilford therefore set about devising items that would, he hoped, assess divergent thinking ability. Thus the subject might be required to suggest as many unusual uses as he could think of for some common object such as a brick or a paper-clip, or he might be told the plot of some story and asked to suggest plausible titles for it. Such tests are known as 'open-ended tests'; there are no right or wrong answers but some answers will be rated better than others. In some cases one can simply count the total number of different responses produced. This, however, would be primarily a measure of fluency so if one wanted to tap something closer to what we mean by creativity the responses would have to be scored by suitable judges, for such qualities as 'wit', 'imaginativeness', 'resourcefulness', 'ingenuity', and so on. Naturally, such tests are more trouble to score than multiple choice items, an important consideration if mass testing is involved, but the extra trouble is considered worthwhile if it enables one to detect abilities that would elude the conventional test.

Guilford never went so far as to identify divergent thinking with creativity, a confusion which not all his followers were so careful to avoid, but he did insist that divergent thinking was an important ingredient of creativity.[35] The educational implications of Guilford's message were not lost and soon a growing band of enthusiasts were applying batteries of open-ended tests in classrooms all over America. The most influential of the studies which followed in Guilford's wake was that which Getzels and Jackson carried out at the University of Chicago 'Laboratory School'.[36] What they did was to compare two groups of adolescents: one consisting of those who were very intelligent, judged by their performance on a standard test of IQ, but were relatively uncreative, as judged by their performance on a specially designed battery of open-ended tests; the other consisting of those who were less intelligent but were rated as highly creative. An intensive investigation of the personality, home background and school performance of these two different groups was then undertaken. The creative group, they found, revealed an intellectual adventurousness that was lacking in the non-creative group despite the latter's superiority in IQ. They appeared to enjoy 'the risk and uncertainty of the unknown' in marked contrast to the other group who tended to 'seek out the safety and security of the known'. This contrast, moreover, showed up in general behaviour and social activity, not just in cognitive performance. An interesting sidelight of this study was that although the creative group actually did better in their school work they were not nearly as popular with the teachers as the 'high IQ' group. The inference which the authors draw from this is that the creative child is inevitably going to be more troublesome. He is less prone simply to do as he is told, he is not content just to accept adult standards and models and to become the sort of person that he is expected to be, he is more inquisitive and less willing to take things for granted. In short, the creative child requires more effort and imagination on the part of the teacher who cannot in his case fall back upon well tried and stereotyped methods of teaching.

Getzels and Jackson used only a small sample of children from one highly selective school (for example even their 'less intelligent group' had an average IQ of 127, while their 'high IQ group' averaged 150!). However, E. P. Torrance, working at the University of Minnesota Bureau of Educational Research on large samples of representative children, arrived at very similar conclusions. [Torrance (1962)] Indeed, Torrance went even further and claimed that if one were to cream off the top 20 per cent of the population on the basis of IQ alone one might lose 70 per cent of its most creative and hence potentially most able members! Torrance further urged teachers to encourage pupils to learn creatively. He pointed out that even though the high IQ child may appear to be the more studious, the creative child may well be learning things even when he appears to be just fooling around. The whole problem of stimulating creativity became a key issue among educationists during the 1960s and Torrance's views were widely influential.

When the vogue for the open-ended tests had run its course for a few years, Wallach and Kogan [1965] decided to consider how far such tests were in fact measuring the same thing as was implied by calling them tests of creativity. To everyone's surprise they found that such tests correlated among themselves no better than they correlated with conventional tests of IQ. At this point the entire concept of creativity seemed in imminent danger of collapse. However, Wallach and Kogan suggested that these findings need not necessarily be interpreted as exploding the idea of a general creativity factor, they could be due to an artefact of the way in which the tests were administered. They pointed out that the tests were usually given in the classroom setting with its competitive atmosphere, that the subjects were expected to perform within certain time limits and that they would be aware that the tests were being used for purposes of evaluation. Accordingly, using a large number of eleven-year-olds as subjects, they took a number of open-ended tests and presented them individually, in an atmosphere of play, without time limits and without suggesting that they would be used as a means for assessing the child's ability. The tests were scored both in terms of the number of different responses produced and for the originality or unusualness of the responses. Under these conditions they duly found that while their creativity measures intercorrelated to the extent of 0.4 and their IQ measures intercorrelated to the extent of 0.5, the creativity measures correlated with the intelligence measures only to the extent of 0.1. From these results they concluded that, provided creativity was measured in the proper way, free from the taint of competition, then, in spite of the apparent overlap in the cognitive processes involved, it could be legitimately regarded as a separate dimension independent of general intelligence.

Wallach and Kogan then followed up their findings by comparing not just two groups of children, as Getzels and Jackson had done, but all the four groups that could be selected by combining high and low creativity with either high or low intelligence. They noted that children high on creativity were much more prone to attention-seeking and disruptive behaviour in the classroom than the others but that there was an important difference between those who were also high on IQ and those with low IQ. The disruptive behaviour of the former group suggested to them a 'brimming over with eagerness' to try out their own ideas and an impatience 'in the face of boredom with the customary classroom routines', whereas the disruptive behaviour of the latter suggested to them rather 'an incoherent protest against their plight'. In fact the high-creativity-low-intelligence group was worse off both socially and academically and less self-confident than the group which was low on both factors. It follows, as the authors point out, that any discussion of creativity in children must specify whether it occurs in conjunction with high or low intelligence.

Concurrently with these attempts to validate the concept of creativity among children or among the general population, attempts were also being made to do so in relation to men and women whose actual achievements had earned them a reputation of being exceptionally creative. Perhaps the two most ambitious undertakings in this direction were, first, Ann Roe's investigation of sixty-four of the most eminent American men of science whose cooperation she could obtain [Roe (1952) and (1952a)] and, secondly, the investigation carried out at the Institute of Personality Assess-

ment of the University of California, Berkeley, under the directorship of D. W. MacKinnon, of the most eminent living authors,
architects and mathematicians who could be persuaded to spend a
living-in weekend undergoing intensive examination. [MacKinnon
(1962) and Barron (1965)] The Roe study showed that it is dangerous
to generalise about creativity without specifying the particular field
in which the creative impulse finds its outlet. For example, she
found a marked contrast in personality between biologists and
physicists on the one hand and the social scientists (which included
psychologists) on the other. Among the former, 'the characteristic
pattern', says Roe, 'is that of the shy, lonely, over-intellectualised
boy', whereas the latter were, characteristically, extraverts who, from
a young age, were prominent in social activities and showed a
lively interest in the opposite sex. Of course, there were exceptions
on both sides. Roe's study is full of fascinating sidelights and
important case-material for students of the scientific mind but, as
far as any generally valid conclusions are concerned, there was
only one thing she could find in common between all her sixty-four
eminent scientists and that was a 'driving absorption in their work',
often to the virtual exclusion of vacations or leisure pursuits. Some
of them acknowledged that it was the intense satisfaction they
discovered early in their career from doing research which determined the subsequent course of their lives. This is an important
point to bear in mind, I believe, when we consider what it takes
for a person to graduate to the calibre of Nobel Prize Winner.

MacKinnon's study covers a wider range of creative activities,
comprising, as it did, literature, architecture and mathematics. His
study also makes use of strict control groups by adopting the
expedient of dividing the eminent in each of these fields into those
who, on a poll of their co-professionals, were rated as being out-
standingly creative with those who, though successful, were not
so regarded. MacKinnon and his associates were particularly
interested in the personality correlates of creativity and their subjects
were required to complete a wide variety of personality questionnaires. One of these was the 'MF Scale', a test which purports to
measure a person's masculinity or femininity according to his or her
interests and attitudes. [see Terman and Miles (1936) or Tyler
(1965)] Speaking about his 'creative architects', the group he studied
most intensively, MacKinnon comments on their surprisingly high
femininity rating: 'The more creative the architect, the more he

reveals an openness to his own feelings and emotions, a sensitive intellect and understanding self-awareness and wide ranging interests including many which, in the American culture, are thought of as feminine ...' 'In the realm of sexual identification and interests,' he concludes, 'our creative subjects appear to give more expression to the feminine side of their nature than do the less creative persons.' When Terman was originally attempting to validate his MF scale he found that architects, like engineers, were, as a group, well up towards the masculinity end of the continuum so that it is all the more striking that MacKinnon's creative group should form an exception in this respect. His creative writers, incidentally, were even higher on femininity than his architects. Even among his female mathematicians, the more creative scored higher on femininity than the less creative, although both were relatively masculine for their sex in general. The question of sex difference in creativity is an intriguing one that presents certain paradoxes. On the one hand there can be few real-life variables that differentiate so sharply between the sexes as creativity if we reckon this in terms of achievement. Even in this era of emancipation one has to search hard to find a woman's name in any list of top people outside the world of entertainment. Moreover, the traits that so often seem to go with high achievement, egoism, ambition, ruthlessness, are notably masculine traits. Perhaps that is also the reason why criminality no less than creativity discriminates between the sexes. Yet, as judged by the appropriate open-ended tests, females are not found to do worse than males and when it comes to creative achievement a certain leavening with those characteristics usually regarded as *par excellence* feminine (sensibility, intuitiveness, etc.) is, as MacKinnon showed, a positive asset.

Some fresh light has also been shed, by the researches of MacKinnon and others in recent years, on the age-old question of the relation between genius and madness. Using the MMPI test, designed to detect various psychopathological tendencies, MacKinnon and his associates reported that 'the creative groups consistently emerge as having more psychopathology than do the representative members of the profession'. On the other hand, in marked contrast to most mental patients, the creative individuals had notably strong and secure egos. 'They are almost as superior to the general population in ego-strength as they are deviant on such pathological dispositions as Schizophrenia, Depression,

Hysteria and Psychopathic Deviation.' In short, if it does not help to be too well balanced and well adjusted if you are going to be creative, neither is it an advantage to be either 'crazy' or neurotic. Ann Roe comments with respect to her scientists that, contrary to much popular misconception, 'freedom from neurosis is more likely to liberate than inhibit creativity'. It is not hard to understand why the truly original mind should often appear to contemporary opinion as possessing a certain streak of madness, nor is it hard to find plenty of examples from history of men of genius who at some time in their lives were afflicted with genuine mental disorders. But even if it should prove to be the case that such disorders were specially prevalent among such persons this would prove no more than that fame is not easy to bear and that possessing great gifts carries a heavy responsibility. At all events, there seems to be no empirical justification for the romantic notion of the great artist as necessarily an outsider and an outcast living precariously on the verge of insanity.

The work of the California School raises the wider question of whether creativity should be regarded as primarily a function of personality or primarily a function of intellect. Barron, for example, points to the 'independence of judgment' and 'freedom of expression' that he sees as typical of the creative person, often going along with such negative characteristics as 'rebelliousness, disorderliness and exhibitionism'. [Barron (1955)] Both, he suggests, spring from an initial resistance to acculturation which demands of the individual the surrender of his individuality or otherwise inhibits his spontaneity. In like vein, Rogers points to the 'openness to experience', the readiness to expose oneself to a wide variety of experiences and ideas, which one finds in creative people along with an ability to tolerate ambiguous or conflicting information without immediately trying to impose upon it one's own preconceived interpretations. [Rogers (1954)] Most of these authorities have drawn attention to the importance of providing the right kind of background, at home or at school, in which creative spontaneity can flourish free from authoritarian restraints. MacKinnon mentions the high proportion of his creative architects who enjoyed a secure and supportive home environment where their autonomy was respected from an early age. On the other hand, some critics have also expressed concern that a too permissive upbringing might lack that stimulus and challenge that also seems to figure in the background of successful persons. It is perhaps no accident that out of the 100 most famous men of history studied by Cox and Terman, whose childhood had been sufficiently documented, no less than 20 attained their true vocation in the teeth of stiff parental opposition! [Terman (1947)]

Should we conclude, then, that great achievement depends upon having the right kind of personality rather than upon the right kind of abilities? Such a conclusion, I believe, would be premature. It is important, at this point, to separate the idea of originality from the idea of achievement. It could be that while personality factors were paramount with respect to the former, cognitive factors were what counted with respect to the latter. My own suspicion is that when we consider specifically the psychology of genius what ultimately matters is a certain aptitude for the task in question, not any peculiarities of temperament or character.[37] That this is so in certain cases, notably with respect to the great composers or the great mathematicians, or the great chess players, would be hard to deny. Their vocation usually reveals itself at an early age when in all other respects they appear no different from the ordinary child of that age. Unless, therefore, we are prepared to write off music, mathematics and chess as altogether different from other fields of creative endeavour, the obvious place to look for the sources of genius is in the individual's natural aptitudes. Of course, in most fields, a lengthy apprenticeship is necessary before anyone can make an important original contribution, but it could still be the case that those who do eventually succeed in doing so are precisely those who from the start possessed just the right combination of talents. Such, at any rate, would seem to be the implication of what we mean when we say about someone that he has a 'flair' for something. This 'flair' may be some aspect of our cognitive processes that is too subtle or elusive to show itself on any standard test of intelligence or primary abilities, but it may be real for all that. Certainly, it does not follow that, because conventional tests of IQ are known to be poor predictors of achievement, achievement is not based primarily on cognitive factors. On this view, then, genius becomes rather like the Grace of God: one is either born one of the elect or one is not.[38]

It remains only to explain why, on this view, highly creative individuals should differ at all in personality from the rest of us, as they appear to do. The answer would have to be that once a person has discovered his power to create this takes precedence over everything else in life. The boldness, the singlemindedness, the heroic self-discipline, and so on, that one associates with genius and which in a lesser being would be taken for recklessness, egoism and ruthlessness could well be no more than a reflection of the high aspirations engendered by the knowledge that one has the capacity to do great deeds. Nor should it be difficult, on this view, to account for that streak of pathological deviance which MacKinnon observed in his creative groups. Anyone possessed of exceptional powers, and hence the object of exceptional expectations, will inevitably be exposed to all sorts of psychological pressures and stresses which the undistinguished do not have to endure. On top of this the genius is, almost by definition, an innovator and hence a disturber of the existing order. How can he be expected to preserve the harmony of his inner life if his activities bring him into constant conflict with society? But these are no more than conjectures. If we are ever to settle the question of the relative priority of personality or intellect in the genesis of genius we should need another longitudinal study *à la* Terman which would enable rival predictions to be made and tested.

But, if we do adopt a predominantly hereditarian approach, does it follow that there is nothing we can do to boost the creative potential in our midst? Not necessarily. There may indeed be nothing we can do to increase the number of potential geniuses in the population, but creativity is not an all-or-nothing concept and there may well be many ways of cultivating originality, ingenuity, imagination and other manifestations of creativity short of genius. Moreover, even in the case of genius there is much that society can do to provide adequate outlets. As we know from history, some cultures and some epochs of civilisation were conspicuously creative, others were notoriously sterile. Yet it seems unlikely that there have been in historic times any large biological fluctuations in different populations or generations. It is much more plausible to suppose that at some periods and in some places conditions were such as to promote the flowering of the human spirit while at other times and in other places the creative spirit lay dormant.

*   *   *

In this chapter we have discussed three topics which have each in its own way served as rallying points for the new cognitive psychology. We could equally have selected other topics to illustrate our point, from the study of perception or memory, areas that have traditionally been central to cognitive theory, or we could have turned our attention to developmental psychology, especially as it concerns the thought processes of the child, which has been undergoing an astonishing resurgence during the past decade. But, in whichever direction we look, the implication would seem to me to be clear, that cognitive psychology has now established itself as the current growing point of academic psychology and, in doing so, has ousted behaviouristics from this dominant position. The latter can still, I think, claim to have more to offer in terms of its practical implications and social utility, but the whole conditioning model on which it is based, which once looked so seductive to the experimentalist, is now exposed as threadbare when confronted with any of the more interesting problems of behaviour, more especially of behaviour that we would recognise as distinctively human. With this shift in priorities, the human subject has once again come into his own in the psychological laboratory where for so long the white rat reigned supreme. For many reasons that we mentioned in our discussion of comparative psychology, animal experimentation is unlikely ever to lose its fascination or its devotees, but, in the future, it can no longer be considered the *sine qua non* of a scientific psychology. Perhaps the present vogue for cognitive psychology is no more than a belated recognition by psychologists of the fact that man has a brain and that this brain is more than a switchboard for coupling receptors and effectors. What exactly that something is forms the real point of departure for the cognitive psychologist.

Summary

Skills

In its most general sense the word 'skill' may be applied to any form of behaviour that is adaptive, purposeful and flexible, from the most elementary locomotor and manipulatory activities at the one end to the most highly developed intellectual, linguistic and aesthetic activities at the other. But, historically, it is the 'perceptuo-motor' skills, especially those involving rapid hand-eye coordination, which have provided psychologists with their main testing ground and have become the paradigm case of a skill. These include: ballistic skills (as in ball games), tracking skills (as in driving a vehicle) and various coding-decoding skills (e.g. typing, signalling, sight-reading in music). Certain features common to all such skills are (a) their intimate dependence on feedback, (b) their hierarchical organisation whereby the part is subordinated to the whole, the tactical move to the overall strategy, (c) their progressive automatisation with practice, (d) the progressive extension of the interval between input and output as practice proceeds, and (e) their tacit nature. With respect to this last item, skills provide us with the prime example of a 'knowing how' that is not necessarily accompanied by a 'knowing what' or a 'knowing why'.

Language

Linguistics, an ancient discipline in its own right, covers many sub-disciplines such as (a) phonetics, (b) semantics, and (c) grammar. 'Psycholinguistics' is a product of the 1960s and was inspired by the work of Chomsky, a theoretical grammarian and logician. Chomsky defended three controversial theses with respect to human language ability: (1) the nativist thesis, that human infants are born with a general abstract knowledge of how language functions which they then only have to adapt to the particular language of their community rather than having to acquire it *ab initio*; (2) the discontinuity thesis, that language is an exclusively human attainment which owes nothing to any more primitive forms of communication found among animals and is quite unlike any other non-linguistic human skills; and (3) a universalist thesis which posits the existence of a universal grammar underlying the grammars of all particular languages. Arguments for and against these three theses are discussed, in particular Hockett's contention that Chomsky commits the fallacy of treating natural language as if it were a 'well-defined system', as the term would be applied in mathematics and logic. In conclusion, it is suggested that despite Chomsky there is as yet no compelling reason why language should not be regarded as just another high-level skill, even if the most important of all when it comes to distinguishing what it is that makes us human.

Creativity

The problem of creativity which has received so much attention in recent years falls into two parts: (a) the problem of the creative process, and (b) the problem of the creative person. Though it is the former which is of more direct concern to cognitive psychology, it is the latter which has attracted more research since it clearly lends itself to a more empirical approach. The concept of creativity as a trait distinct from IQ stems largely from the work of Guilford in the early 1950s. It embraces two main aspects: (i) that of originality, and (ii) that of high achievement potential. With respect to (i), Guilford introduced his influential distinction between 'convergent' and 'divergent' thinkers and devised the open-ended test item as a means of identifying the latter. Through the work of Torrance, Getzels and Jackson and others during the 1960s these ideas began to percolate the approach to education. Some attempts were also made during the 1960s to provide some validation for the concept of creativity by investigating directly the personalities of individuals of known creative achievement in different walks of life. In spite of these studies, however, it remains problematical as to how far we can regard creativity as a product of personality and upbringing and how far it is a function of certain inborn aptitudes of a rather special kind which, for want of a more technical term, one might just call 'flair'. Certainly the old idea that geniuses (and poets) are born rather than made is one that cannot lightly be discarded.

Notes

1 The presiding genius of the new movement was the American mathematician, Norbert Wiener, and the book which launched it was his *Cybernetics: or Control and Communication in the Animal and the Machine*, of 1948. [*see* Wiener (1961)] Other landmarks of the movement include: C. Shannon and W. Weaver, *The Mathematical Theory of Communication*, 1949, which introduced information theory; J. von Neumann and O. Morgenstern, *Theory of Games and Economic Behaviour*, 1944, which inaugurated game theory; A. Wald, *Statistical Decision Theory*, 1950, which extended

the game-theory approach to the general problem of decision-making. [*see* Edwards and Tversky (eds) (1967)] Dr M. V. Wilkes, FRS, of the Cambridge Mathematical Laboratory reckons that the computer age may be said to have commenced in 1944 when the first digital computer went into operation at Harvard University.

2 *See* A. Newell, J. Shaw and H. Simon, 'Chess Playing Programs and the Problem of Complexity', in *IBM Jl Res. Dev.* 2, 1958, 320-35. Many other chess programs have been devised since then and though computers are not yet ready to compete in the world championship the fact that they can already present a serious challenge to the experienced players is, in itself, a triumph for proponents of artificial intelligence.

3 A Department of Machine Intelligence and Perception was set up some years ago at the University of Edinburgh. Those who possess the necessary mathematical sophistication to follow the progress of this new science may be referred to their annual publication *Machine Intelligence* (University of Edinburgh Press) which has appeared since 1967 under the general editorship of Professor Donald Michie, the head of the department.

4 R. S. Woodworth ranks among the founding fathers of American psychology. His earliest contribution to experimental research, in a productive career lasting more than half a century, was an article on 'The Accuracy of Voluntary Movement' in *Psychol. Rev.* Monograph Supplement 3, 1899 [reprinted in Legge (1970)]; his last, which also has implications for the study of skill, was his book *Dynamics of Behavior* [Woodworth (1958)].

5 Sir Frederick Bartlett, who was head of the Cambridge Psychological Laboratory 1922-1952, was a key figure in British psychology. Hearnshaw [1964] has estimated that in 1960 more than half the chairs of psychology in Britain were held by Cambridge graduates trained by Bartlett. His interest in the problem of skills led to the establishment of the Applied Psychology Research Unit at Cambridge after the Second World War, now under the direction of D. E. Broadbent.

6 Notably in his *The Act of Creation* [Koestler (1964)], esp. Bk. 2

'Habit and Originality', and in his *The Ghost in the Machine* [Koestler (1967)]. Koestler discusses the problem of skill in terms of 'matrix' and 'code', the matrix being roughly a 'frame of reference', an 'associative context', a 'universe of discourse', the code being the rules governing particular moves within the matrix. In Koestler [1967] Chap. 3, we are introduced to yet another Koestlerian neologism, the 'holon'. This is the functional unit at any given level of the matrix or hierarchy. The term carries with it something of the same connotation as 'gestalt' but with the special implication that its wholeness is always strictly relative: it is a whole in relation to the lower levels of the hierarchy but a part in relation to the higher levels. It is, in Koestler's words, 'Janus-faced'.

7 *See* Koestler [1967] p. 47. Koestler goes on to remark: 'We do not know what forms of life have evolved on other planets in the universe, but we can safely assume that *wherever there is life, it must be hierarchically organised*' (author's italics). [*see also* 'Beyond Atomism and Holism—The Concept of the Holon' (Koestler (1969))]

8 Feedback is the general concept which has been used to cover both 'knowledge of results', as the term is used in human learning experiments, and 'reinforcement', as the term is used in operant conditioning. The expression 'negative feedback' is applied to situations where information is used to correct deviations from some set norm, as in the case of tracking tasks. Any self-regulating engineering system such as a heating system controlled by a thermostat is said to display negative feedback. For a recent short survey of the concept of feedback in psychology, *see* Annett [1969].

9 The original experiments involving inverted vision were those of George Stratton published in the *Psychological Review* for 1896-97. [*see* Dodwell (1970) excerpt 17] An intensive attack on this problem was carried out during the late 1940s by Erismann and Ivo Köhler at the University of Innsbruck, Austria, with continuous exposure periods lasting in some instances for several weeks. [*see* Köhler, I. (1951) or Dodwell (1970) excerpt 18] A more recent discussion of these and related findings may be found in Harris [1965] and in Rock [1966], esp. Chap. 4.

10   *See* K. S. Lashley (1951), 'The Problem of Serial Order in Behavior', reprinted in Legge [1970]. This highly influential paper did much to demonstrate the inadequacy of an S-R chain theory of skills and the need for a cognitive approach.

11   The term 'ballistic movement' appears to have originated with Craik, in his article 'The Operator as an Engineering System', *Brit. J. Psych.*, 1947, reprinted in Legge [1970], excerpt 10.

12   This absence of self-consciousness is the special aim of the Zen devotee who seeks 'enlightenment' through the cultivation of some practical skill or art, *cf.* the following passage: 'If one really wishes to be master of an art, technical knowledge is not enough. One has to transcend technique so that the art becomes an "artless art" growing out of the unconscious. In the case of archery, the hitter and the hit are no longer two opposing objects, but are one reality. The archer ceases to be conscious of himself as the one who is engaged in hitting the bull's-eye which confronts him. This state of unconsciousness is realized only when, completely empty and rid of the self, he becomes one with the perfecting of his technical skill ...' D. T. Suzuki in his foreword to Herigel [1953].

13   Polanyi has developed what amounts almost to a complete epistemology based on his key distinction between 'focal' and 'subsidiary' awareness. The following passage is typical of his approach: 'The unique character of our body lies in the fact that it is the only collection of things which we know almost exclusively by relying on our awareness of them for attending to something else. All parts of our body serve us as tools for observing objects outside us and for manipulating these for purposes of our own. Every time we make sense of the world, we rely on our tacit knowledge of impacts which the world makes on our body and of responses of our body to these impacts.' 'Tacit Knowing', *Reviews of Modern Physics* **34**, 1962, reprinted in Polanyi [1969].

14   Lyons [1968] introduces four dichotomies into the field of linguistic studies: (i) theoretical vs. applied; (ii) general vs. descriptive (i.e. concerned with particular languages); (iii) synchronic vs. diachronic (i.e. concerned with the way a language changes over time); and (iv) micro- or structural linguistics, which treats

language as an abstract formal system, vs. macrolinguistics, which deals with language as a functioning system of communication in a definite socio-psychological context. Psycholinguistics, as discussed here, is theoretical, general, synchronic and structural. [*see also* Lyons (1970) and Lyons (ed.) (1970)]

15 *Cf.* J. P. Thorne, 'Translation and question-answering are complex human functions: the best way to get a computer to perform them must surely be to investigate the processes involved in these forms of human behaviour with a view to constructing models which can be realized on a computer. Admittedly this makes the possibility of attaining the goals of machine translation and mechanical information retrieval from natural language data seem very remote, but it seems to be the only course worth following. There is no possibility that a computer will ever analyze sentences better than human beings do in the course of ordinary verbal communication—in the sense in which computers might eventually play chess or chequers better than human beings do.' 'Grammars and Machines', *Trans. Philol. Soc.*, 1964, reprinted in Oldfield and Marshall (eds) [1968] excerpt 21.

16 *Cf.* N. Chomsky, 'Linguistics and Philosophy' in Hook (ed.) [1969] and the various criticisms of his position by a number of prominent American philosophers at this symposium organised by the NYU Institute for Philosophy in 1968.

17 This work consists of three short chapters headed respectively 'Past', 'Present' and 'Future' and based on the Beckmann Lectures he delivered at the University of California, Berkeley, 1967. It has since been published in an enlarged edition. [*see* Chomsky (1972)] The quotations in this section are from the 1968 edition.

18 For a survey of such studies *see* Herriot [1970], Oldfield and Marshall (eds) [1968], Greene [1972].

19 *Cf.* the late Professor R. C. Oldfield (until recently head of the Speech and Communication Unit of the University of Edinburgh): 'I suspect that syntax ... represents a kind of superstructure on language functions generally and one as yet incompletely evolved. Elaborate grammatical structure tends to assume practical import-

ance with the development of prolonged one-way communication in replacement of two-way interchange. I suggest that its use and the need for it is tied up with the development of procedures of formal educational instruction, and the use of written language as an adjunct to and replacement for spoken language, and with the spread of ... propositional speech, of logic, of scientific knowledge and abstract thinking. Viewed in terms of the history of language these are relatively recent developments' [in Lyons and Wales (eds) (1966]. Incidentally this remark strikes me as having profoundly anti-Chomskian implications, which the distinction between competence and performance cannot easily erase.

20 Not even so sympathetic a commentator as Professor Lyons [see Lyons (1970)] would claim that there is anything like a consensus of views even among the linguists. For the reaction of one eminent psychologist see Broadbent [1970], who considers that the kind of approach advocated by Chomsky inevitably leads to dogmatism.

21 Chomsky draws support from the work of the biologist E. H. Lenneberg [(1964) and (1967)] who, however, while supporting a discontinuity hypothesis, admits that it does create problems for evolutionary theory in view of the relative suddenness with which man evolved.

22 The Platonic doctrine is set out in the *Meno*. Socrates demonstrates that a slave boy can be made to recognise the truths of certain propositions in geometry though he had no previous knowledge of them in this life at least.

23 One linguist who strongly supports the discontinuity hypothesis is John Marshall, see his 'The Biology Communications in Man and Animals' [Lyons (ed.) (1970) Chap. 12], but he does not develop there this particular implication.

24 *Cf.* Kellogg and Kellogg [1967]. An even more concerted attempt to teach a primate to talk, using sophisticated psychological methods, was made by Dr and Mrs Hayes with their 'adopted' chimpanzee 'Viki'. Yet in six years Viki learned only four sounds that approximated to English words. This case is cited by Gardner and Gardner [1969], *see* note 25.

25 *See* Gardner and Gardner [1969]. When I last heard, the experiment was still in progress and Washoe was being used to facilitate learning in other chimpanzees. In some ways an even more ambitious project was that of Premack [1970] who likewise used a chimpanzee, 'Sarah'. His method was to introduce into her cage small plastic objects that could serve as word-symbols from which sentences could then be made by stringing them into a sequence. Sarah also learnt to use the 'yes' and 'no' symbols to answer questions about the sameness or difference of two objects.

26 For example, Binet's studies of creative thinking during the 1890s included investigations of the thought processes of 'lightning' calculators, of chess masters and of French dramatists. [*see* Reeves (1969) pp. 198-232] Whether the thinking of either lightning calculators or chess masters would now be regarded as typical of 'creative' thinking is another matter, but the tradition which Binet started of interrogating exceptional thinkers about their thought processes has continued down the years. It is exemplified by Wertheimer, who interviewed Einstein in 1916 [*see* Wertheimer (1961) Chap. 10], and, more recently, by my predecessor at Edinburgh, Dr Ian Hunter, who interviewed his colleague, the late Professor A. C. Aitken, a mathematician with an extraordinary talent for mental arithmetic. [*see* Hunter (1962)]

27 The critical event in this connection was, of course, the launching of Russia's Sputnik in 1957. However, by then the new-found interest in creativity in the United States was already well under way. Golovin, who was at the time technical adviser on Space Science at the White House, warned his countrymen that 'it is probably dangerous folly to discount the creativeness of Iron Curtain physical scientists and engineers on the presumed grounds that their abilities have been stunted by authoritarian political indoctrination'. [Taylor and Barron (eds) (1963) p. 21]

28 *Cf.* Bolton [1972], Ray (ed.) [1967] or Wason and Johnson-Laird (eds) [1968]. There is, of course, no clear-cut distinction between the kind of thinking required to solve difficult problems and the kind of thinking which qualifies as 'creative', although the creative thinker is sometimes taken to be someone

who can not merely solve problems but discover new problems or, at least, see old problems in a new light.

29   *See* Koestler [1964]. In Book 1 of this volume Koestler develops an idea which he first adumbrated in his earlier book *Insight and Outlook* (London: 1949), namely that laughter and humour depend upon similar psychological processes to those which underlie the creative insights of artists and scientists. Both involve what he calls 'bisociation', the bringing together into a new synthesis of two unrelated universes of discourse. In Book 2, 'Habit and Originality', he goes on to construct a psychological and biological framework into which his theory of the creative process can be fitted.

30   *See* Koestler [1967] Chaps 10 and 12, also his article 'The Wings of Analogy', Koestler [1968] pp. 261-74. The analogy in question is that between the evolutionary phenomenon of 'paedomorphis' (the first appearance of some evolutionary novelty in the larval or embryonic stage) and the psychological phenomenon of *'reculer-pour-mieux-sauter'* (progress through regress) which he sees as a prerequisite of all important advances whether biological or mental.

31   When confronted with broad synoptic systems like that of Koestler, the research scientist is apt to display impatience because, however rich and illustrative they may be, they are usually meagre in testable hypotheses, *cf.* Medawar's review of the *Act of Creation* and the subsequent exchange between him and Koestler as reproduced in Medawar [1967] pp. 85-96. As I see it, while spotting the weakness of Koestler's position, Medawar fails to appreciate how far this is inherent in the nature of the topic. The fact is that one cannot as yet devise a theory of the creative process which is precise enough for experimental testing without its being trivial. Perhaps this is why Koestler is at his most interesting, in my view, when discussing the lives of the great scientists. [*see* Koestler (1964) App. 2, or Koestler (1959), esp. for its biography of Kepler]

32   These volumes, under the general editorship of Lewis M. Terman, were published by the Stanford University Press. They comprise: Vol. I *Mental and Physical Traits of a Thousand Gifted*

Children (1926); Vol. II (with Catherine Cox) *The Early Mental Traits of 300 Geniuses* (1926); Vol. III *The Promise of Youth* (1930); Vol. IV *The Gifted Child Grows Up* (1947); Vol. V (the final volume) *The Gifted Child at Mid-Life* (1959). The initial population was 1,444 children of different ages whose IQ, as measured by the tests then available, was not less than 140. A summary of this investigation is given in Vernon (ed.) [1970] excerpt 2.

33　See note 32 (Vol. II).

34　*See* Guilford [1959] or [1967]. Guilford's presidential address to the American Psychological Association in 1950 is often taken as the first blast which awakened interest in this whole field of research. [*see* Guilford (1950)]

35　Guilford's distinction has certain obvious affinities with Koestler's distinction between 'bisosciation' and 'association', and with de Bono's distinction between 'lateral' (or paralogical) and 'vertical' (or logical) thinking. [*see* de Bono (1969)] In Britain, Hudson [1966] and [1968] applied the Guilfordian dichotomy to the problem of distinguishing those destined for a career in the sciences or technologies and those embarking on a career involving a degree in Arts or Social Sciences. On the question of creativity as manifested respectively in scientific or aesthetic outlets, *see also* my own article, Beloff [1970].

36　*See* Getzels and Jackson [1962] or the summary of their findings in Taylor and Barron (eds) [1963], reprinted in Vernon [1970] excerpt 16. *See also* the review of Getzels and Jackson [1962] by C. L. Burt in *Brit. J. Educ. Psych.*, 1962, reprinted as excerpt 17 of Vernon [1970]. A partially successful confirmation of the Getzels and Jackson findings with Scottish schoolchildren was reported by Hasan and Butcher [1966].

37　The same idea has been expressed by R. B. MacLeod in his summing up of the 1958 Colorado Symposium on creativity [MacLeod (1964a) p. 194], where he asks: 'Is there such a thing as a creative person? If so, is he born or bred? There are those who believe he is born, and I don't think this idea should be discarded too lightly. It has been said that "genius will out". This is obviously untrue, because genius can be throttled literally or figuratively; but we should not overlook the possibility that whatever underlies creativity may be lodged in the genes.'

38   One must, however, always be on one's guard against accepting a too naïvely hereditarian view of genius. It is entirely feasible to suppose that most of the eminent men of history, given precisely the same innate capacities, would never have emerged from obscurity had they lived at another time or place or had circumstances been other than they were.

CHAPTER SIX

Social Psychology

Social psychology is an acknowledgment of the fact that for man the social environment is no less important, in some senses more important, than the physical environment. The very concept of being human implies a social form of life, not only in the sense that we are dependent on others for all our vital needs, but because language which permeates all our thinking is itself a social product. Since, however, all the social sciences purport to deal with social phenomena of one sort or another we must begin by trying to distinguish the aims of social psychology from those of such other allied disciplines as sociology and social anthropology. Allport [(1968) p. 3] defines social psychology as 'an attempt to explain how the thought, feeling and behaviour of individuals are influenced by the actual, imagined or implied presence of others'. On this definition there is much to be said for the view expressed by Wundt, the founding father of experimental psychology, that, in psychology, whatever is not strictly physiological psychology is social psychology.[1] Undoubtedly, once one goes beyond the basic psychophysiological processes of the organism, it becomes impossible to ignore the 'actual, imagined or implied presence of others'. Perception involves person-perception and speech-perception; learning embraces socialisation, acculturation and the acquisition of social skills; the study of motivation has to take account of the fact that social motives are the preponderant ones in human life. Yet despite these obvious facts, opinion has always been divided as to whether it is necessary to have a separate science of social psychology rather than simply applying the laws and concepts of general psychology to the social situation. In this chapter we will look first at the enduring controversy between individualism and collectivism in the explanation of social phenomena and then, in the next section, we will consider two specific social phenomena and see how they have been handled by those calling themselves social psychologists.

The Individual and the Group

Historically there have been two main schools of thought on the question of the priority of the individual or the group in the understanding of social behaviour. On the one side there were those whom we may here call 'individualists' who argued that there could be nothing in social life which could not ultimately be reduced to the actions of individual human beings. John Stuart Mill, the most influential spokesman of this point of view during the 19th century, insisted that we were not to be led away, in this instance, by the analogy of chemistry. A chemical compound, he admitted, exhibits true emergent properties that cannot be predicted from the properties of its constituent atoms; 'human beings in society', on the other hand, 'have no properties but those which are derived from and may be resolved into the laws of the nature of individual man'.[2] On the other side we have those we shall call 'collectivists', who argued that the social whole was more than the sum of its parts, more even than the predictable resultant of their joint interactions. Hegel, who may here be taken as representing the opposite extreme from Mill, believed that the State had a reality greater than and transcending the reality of its individual members. The controversy was further complicated by the respective ideological commitment of the two parties: by and large, the reductionists stood for political liberalism, the holists for one or another brand of totalitarianism.[3]

It was this connection between collectivism and totalitarianism which, in our own day, inspired Karl Popper to launch his celebrated counter-offensive against its philosophical foundations.[4] Yet, despite Popper's important, indeed admirable, contribution to the ongoing debate, the problem of the emergent properties of social groups and institutions is one that, like any other problem in science, must ultimately be decided on its own merits free from any ideological partisanship. Indeed, Popper's own struggles to find a defensible position somewhere between Mill and Marx show how complex the issue is and how unlikely one is to find any simple obvious solution. Thus, at one point Popper appears to be agreeing with Mill when he writes: 'The "behaviour" and "action" of collectives, such as states or social groups, must be reduced to the behaviour and action of human individuals', and yet in the very same chapter he also says, as if endorsing Marx: 'If a reduction is to be attempted at all, it would therefore be more hopeful to attempt a reduction to, or an interpretation of, psychology in terms of sociology than the other way round.' [see Popper (1962) Vol. II Chap. 14] The paradox arises because Popper identifies 'psychologism', the doctrine he attributes to Mill, as the view that whatever properties reside in the collective they must be the outcome of individual intentions, and Popper has no difficulty in showing that such cannot be the case. On the contrary, every individual action normally has many different consequences that may be neither intended, foreseen nor welcome. To take a topical example, not only is it in no one's interest to have inflation but we even seem powerless to get rid of it! Furthermore, psychologism cannot account for the origin of society, it is driven to postulate mythical founders and mythical social contracts which are self-contradictory since the individuals involved would themselves have to be social beings. It follows that the relationship between society and the individual is always a two-way affair; history may be seen as the sum total of individual human actions but none of those actions would have any meaning outside the historical context in which they occurred.

In place of 'psychologism', therefore, Popper offers what he calls 'methodological individualism'. According to this formulation we no longer needed to invoke a universal human nature which was simply overlaid by different social influences; instead we could recognise that human nature is what it is because of the institutional structure of society. At the same time we must still insist that such collectivist concepts as the 'group mind', the 'general will', the 'collective unconscious', the 'zeitgeist', the 'spirit, genius or destiny of the nation', etc., be exposed as fictions and explicated in terms of individuals acting in a social framework. There can thus be no emergent properties at the level of the collective; there will of course be some properties which, logically, can be predicated only of groups, properties pertaining to their size, composition or their relationships with other groups (it is Britain that enters the Common Market, not Britons); but it is a dangerous fallacy to attribute to a group or an institution a will and a purpose of its own that is not that of its individual members.

But is it a fallacy? J. O. Wisdom has recently challenged Popper's 'Methodological Individualism' and has advocated in its place his own doctrine of 'Transindividualism'.[5] He suggests, for example, that a correct diagnosis of what is wrong with Britain today may well require that we identify a particular syndrome that is true of Britain but not necessarily of any individual Britons. If so, then we would have to reckon with a genuine emergent property of a group that was more than just a shorthand convention for certain statistical facts about its members. Now, whatever we may think about the particular example which Wisdom presents, I shall proceed to show that there can be no *a priori* argument against it. The first point to note is that what one calls an 'individual' and what one calls a 'collective' depends entirely upon the particular level of discourse at which the terms are being used. There are, in science, no natural individuals; whether, therefore, a particular entity or concept is treated as analysable or not depends on whether it is regarded as indispensable, as a theoretical construct, or dispensable. And this is not something one can tell in advance. Take, for example, the concept of the nervous system. This, as we know, consists of nerve cells and nothing but nerve cells in a particular configuration. Every time a given nervous system is activated, certain nerve cells fire and, conversely, every time a given sequence of nerve cells fires, the nervous system functions in a certain determinate way. Finally, if all the constituent nerve cells were destroyed and not replaced, the nervous system would cease to exist. From this account we may correctly deduce that a nervous system has no ontological existence apart from the nerve cells of which it is composed. But we would be quite wrong if we were to infer that the nervous system can have no functional properties that are not also properties of its cells. In point of fact a cell has only one functional property: it can either fire or not fire; a brain, on the other hand, can, among other things, solve problems. We can say accordingly that, for physiology, the nervous system is an indispensable, irreducible, theoretical entity.

The situation is, logically, no different when we come to the social sciences. The relationship between the individual and the social system is, in all relevant respects, analogous to the relationship between the nerve cell and the nervous system. The fact that the human individual is a much more complex kind of unit and the fact that people are not related to one another by biophysical bonds in no way affects the argument. Furthermore, just as the firing of a cell will depend on the state of the nervous system as a whole and where that cell is situated within it, so we may say that the action of an individual will depend on the state of the social system and what position that individual occupies within it. It follows that there can be no *a priori* reason why some organisation, be it a bank or an industrial corporation, an army or a political party, should not be treated as an entity in its own right governed by its own laws and logic, and not just as a set of interrelated individuals. Whether we are in fact justified in treating them so in any given case is another matter; in the last resort it is for sociologists to decide. But it is worth noting that the most advanced of the social sciences, economics, seems long since to have outgrown the stage where it was thought necessary to base its theoretical postulates on the hypothetical behaviour of 'economic man' or on any simple-minded psychological principles of utility as invoked by the early pioneers of this science.

Although 19th century collectivism took its stand on Idealist philosophy or its offshoots, the case for collectivism or for trans-individualism does not depend on such support. Indeed, one of the more curious consequences of the cybernetic revolution of the 20th century is that it has given a new plausibility to the notion of a group mind.[6] For mind itself, from the cybernetic point of view, is conceived as an information processing system and this conception applies equally to any organised social group. But can we not go further and recognise not merely the possibility of a collective intelligence but also of collective aims, aspirations, motives, etc.? There are, I suggest, two reasons why we may wish to recoil from doing so. First, we may consider that a particular corporate body lacks the degree of cohesion, coherence or rationality which we associate with the use of mentalistic expressions. Secondly, and this, I think, is the more profound reason, a corporate body has no centre of consciousness, for consciousness, at any rate, is uniquely associated with the individual organism. This, incidentally, would also explain our reluctance to credit computers with minds even when they exhibit a high degree of coherence and rationality.

We are now in a position to distinguish social psychology from the other sciences. The crux of the distinction devolves on what to take as the appropriate unit of analysis. In the case of social psychology this is always the individual human being, even though he may be studied in a social setting; in the case of other social sciences the object of inquiry is the collective, in anthropology this may be an entire society or culture, in sociology it is more often some institution or some group or sub-culture within society. Not that there is any objection to calling social psychology a social science as well as a psychological one; historically the two are inter-dependent, moreover one cannot say that the psychological approach is necessarily the more fundamental. Whether we choose to explain social phenomena in terms of human nature or human nature in terms of social phenomena is arbitrary and depends upon our interests.

Initially, social psychology came into being largely to provide an infra-structure for the social sciences, but at the present time the two pursue separate but parallel courses. Insofar as social psychology owes its origins to any single individual, credit is probably due to Auguste Comte, the acknowledged father of sociology.[7] Comte, the positivist, had no use for psychology as the term was understood in his own day, that is, as an introspective science of experience. At the same time, he foresaw the necessity of a science that would combine both the biological and the sociological approach to man. This hypothetical science he called 'la morale positive', it may be compared with Mill's 'Ethology', or science of national differences,[8] but it would not be straining his meaning to see it as the forerunner of social psychology. Writing in the 1850s, Comte found a quasi-biological basis for his new science in the theory of the faculties as expounded by the brain anatomist Gall (a theory which, in the hands of Gall's disciple Spurzheim gave rise to the popular cult of phrenology). In similar vein, McDougall [1908] drew upon the theory of instincts and their attendant sentiments. At various times various mechanisms have been canvassed as providing the psychological foundation for social phenomena including 'sympathy', 'imitation', 'contagion', 'suggestion', 'identification' and, of course, the ubiquitous 'pleasure principle'. In general there have been two main categories of theories used in social psychology:

irrationalist theories, which see social behaviour as governed largely by instinctive or automatic forces, and rationalist theories that give precedence to the rational motives that operate in society. But, for a long time, social psychology was mainly a hunting ground for sociologists and one of the first volumes to bear the title of *Social Psychology* was written by the American sociologist E. A. Ross. It appeared in 1908 in the same year as McDougall brought out his book and it dealt with such social phenomena as the spread of fads and crazes. It thus belongs to the same tradition as Le Bon's classic study of 1895 of crowd psychology.[9]

The critical development that was eventually to secure for social psychology recognition as an independent psychological discipline was the advent of the experimental method. One of the earliest applications of experiment in this area was in connection with the problem of 'social facilitation'. The problem was to ascertain to what extent the subject's output on a given task could be boosted as a result of getting him to perform in a competitive setting. Although some of this work goes back to the experiments in America in the 1890s[10] and to the work of a number of investigators before the First World War, it was not until the 1920s that it attracted much attention. F. H. Allport's *Social Psychology* of 1924, one of the first textbooks to survey the experimental work in this area, introduces a distinction between 'co-acting' groups and mere 'face-to-face' groups.[11] By the time that Murphy and Murphy published their *Experimental Social Psychology* of 1931[12] the volume of experimental literature had expanded to respectable dimensions and this expansion was to continue with increasing vigour during the 1930s, especially after the publication of Kurt Lewin's selected papers, *A Dynamic Theory of Personality*, of 1935, and Muzafer Sherif's book, *The Psychology of Social Norms*, of 1936.[13] Lewin's arrival in America from Germany, where he was identified with the Gestalt School, was a turning point in social psychology. His experiments on 'social climates' where boys' clubs were run in three comparative ways, designated respectively as 'authoritarian', 'democratic' and 'laissez-faire', are still regarded as classics of their kind.[14] Lewin further provided a theoretical framework for his experiments in terms of his 'field theory' which conceives of the subject as operating in a 'life-space' where he is exposed to various competing valences.[15]

The discovery that experimentation was possible in social psycho-

logy tended to sharpen and clarify its terms of reference. It began
to concentrate on those problems that it could make peculiarly its
own and which could yield to the experimental approach and, as
it did so, it began to develop its own specialised terminology and
concepts. Among the phenomena that figure prominently in modern
social psychology are: competition, cooperation, hostility, aggression, prejudice, conformity, obedience, deviance, alienation, affiliation, socialisation, role-playing, dominance, leadership and conflict.
Typical of the basic concepts of this science are: attitude, norm,
value, model, stereotype, role, power, status, interaction. [*cf.*
Kelvin (1970)]

In the remainder of this section I want to discuss certain distinctive features of the socio-psychological experiment. The first fact
that emerges is somewhat alarming. The typical experiment in
social psychology is a hoax, if not indeed a conspiracy! An ordinary
psychological experiment involves two key persons: the subject and
the experimenter. The socio-psychological experiment usually
involves three key persons: the subject, the experimenter and the
experimenter's confederate or 'stooge'. If this fact was ever to
become too widely known it would become practically impossible
for anyone who was known as a social psychologist to conduct an
experiment! In other words, the subject has to be made to think that
the experiment is concerned with one sort of an effect when in fact
it is concerned with something quite different.

By way of illustration let us consider the classic experiment in
conformity by Solomon Asch. Ostensibly the task, in this instance,
was a straightforward psychophysical discrimination. For each trial
the subject is shown a set of three lines of different length and a
standard line which he is asked to match with one of the three
comparative lines. On some pretext he is put in with three other
persons whom he believes to be subjects like himself but who in
fact are in league with the experimenter and have been briefed as
to what response to make on each trial. The task is such that if
the subject had simply to make his calls in isolation he would have
little difficulty in doing so without error. However, on certain
critical trials the confederates have been briefed to call out a
particular answer which is in fact incorrect. In these circumstances
will the subject stick to his guns and give the right answer (the
seating arrangement is such that he calls last) or will the pressure
to conform triumph over the evidence of his own senses? Asch

found that only about 25 per cent of his subjects gave the correct answer on all critical trials, 75 per cent deferred to the majority verdict on at least one trial. Asch, who belonged to the 'rationalist' school of social psychology, interpreted these results as showing that, unless we have overwhelming evidence to the contrary, we quite naturally and sensibly give due weight to the general consensus.[16] This interpretation has, however, been challenged in recent years. In one of the modifications of the Asch experiment in which the subject was instructed to write down his answer instead of calling it aloud it was shown that very little conformity ensued. This suggests that fear of ridicule is probably a large factor behind the 'Asch effect'. However, it is the methodology rather than the theoretical implications of the experiment that I wish to emphasise. The point is that, whatever the effect we are trying to demonstrate, it is essential that the subject should remain unaware of it, otherwise it is impossible to say what part he played in bringing about the result. Indeed, ideally, even the immediate experimenter who runs the test should not be in the know, but this is seldom practicable.

Being a subject for a social psychology experiment may be no 'picnic'; even the Asch experiment can be very upsetting—you start to wonder whether it is you who are peculiar or whether it is the others who have taken leave of their senses! It is necessary therefore for the experimenter to exercise great care in selecting his 'victims' and to make sure that when all is revealed they do not bear him a grudge. Usually the experimenter ends with a special 'de-hoaxing' session for the subject. In addition to laboratory experiments, like the Asch experiment, social psychologists also make use from time to time of what is called 'natural experiments'. In a natural experiment you have to wait on events and find a situation in real life which affords a suitable test of your hypothesis.[17] We shall next take a look at one such experiment. To take full advantage of such a situation usually calls for a planned operation involving many observers, but when it is feasible it can hopefully help in bridging the gap between laboratory and life that is a specially acute problem for the social psychologist. Akin to the natural experiment is the so-called 'cross-cultural study'. If we are fortunate enough to find two societies that are alike in most relevant respects except for some critical variable, then conditions exist for investigating the social effects of that variable. This approach has proved specially valuable for the study of child-rearing practices; for example, in some societies it was customary to swaddle infants whereas this custom was lacking in other similar societies. In general, the whole concept of cultural relativism which has played so much part in the thinking of social psychologists has been tied up with cross-cultural studies.[18] [*cf.* Hunt, R. (ed.) 1967]

Dissonance and Obedience

In this section I shall concentrate on two specimen problems in social psychology. The first belongs to the psychology of self-deception and provides one answer to the question of how it is possible for otherwise intelligent people to believe in absurdities. The second concerns the phenomenon of obedience and whether it is possible to induce otherwise humane people to do cruel things merely by ordering them to do so. Let us start with the first of these.

There can be few theories in the whole of social psychology that have stimulated so much experimental research as Festinger's theory of 'Cognitive Dissonance'.[19] Leon Festinger, a disciple of Kurt Lewin, was specially interested in the determinants of people's attitudes and beliefs. Essentially, and in non-technical language, what his theory states is that when you are confronted by evidence that appears to conflict with certain strongly held attitudes or beliefs you will either (a) discount or ignore such information, (b) reinterpret or reappraise it so as to bring it closer in line with your preconceptions or, should neither (a) nor (b) be feasible, then you will (c) seek out other consonant information that will strengthen your preconceptions. Certain additional corollaries are necessary before the theory as stated could be used to make predictions in particular cases, but the gist of what Festinger proposes is contained in the statement we have given.

It will be clear that we are here dealing with a type of theory that comes under that large class of what, in our last section, we called 'irrationalist' theories. That is to say, rationally, it always pays to profit from experience. If you discover that things turn out differently from what you expect or that your beliefs are mistaken then, no matter how disappointing this may be, no matter how much your feelings may be hurt, you are well advised to acknowledge the fact and revise your ideas accordingly. Unfortunately, the completely rational man who can remain objective about himself under all circumstances is a shining exception if indeed such a person exists. Most of us strongly resent anything that impugns our judgment and strive for as long as possible to dig in our heels. Obviously a point may come when even the most complacent among us are forced to admit defeat on pain of losing our sanity—a bankrupt cannot indefinitely continue to believe in his solvency—but, before that point is reached, it is astonishing to what lengths people will go and what postures and contortions they will adopt rather than relinquish their fonder illusions.

Exposed as we all are on all sides to so many different sources of information and opinion, there is ample scope for dissonance to arise. Whatever opinion we may espouse, we are bound to run into those who champion the opposite point of view. Whatever decision we take we are bound to reckon with the 'cons' as well as with the 'pros'. Whatever success we achieve something always falls short of our hopes. In all cases we find ourselves in a quandary from which we seek an escape. According to the Festinger theory this state of dissonance is itself the motivating factor in such situations. By comparing it with the state of hunger he implies that, just as we cannot help seeking to appease our hunger, so we cannot help seeking to reduce our dissonance and, just as the more hungry we are the more actively we seek food, so the greater the dissonance the more intently we strive to reduce it. It is the dynamic of 'drive reduction' translated onto the cognitive plane.

An everyday example of a dissonance in modern life is provided by the practice of smoking. A smoker today has to reconcile his indulgence with the knowledge that smoking is a definite hazard to health. What is likely to be his reaction to this knowledge supposing he finds himself too strongly addicted to abandon the habit altogether? Dissonance theory would predict that he will belittle the alleged danger, perhaps dwelling as he does so on the much greater dangers connected with alcohol, overeating or other health hazards to which he does not happen to be addicted, and finally, that he will seek the company of other, perhaps heavier smokers whose imperviousness to anti-smoking propaganda provides him with the necessary moral support. Fortunately, the Minnesota Poll of 1954 which was taken soon after the publication of the first official report to publicise the relationship between smoking and lung cancer enabled Festinger to test one such hypothesis. Respondents were asked whether they considered that the connection between smoking and lung cancer had in fact been demonstrated or not. Festinger predicted that the more respondents were already addicted to smoking the more they would tend to deny the alleged relationship. At that time scepticism was still widespread, for as many as 55 per cent of non-smokers were not satisfied that the connection had been proved. On the other hand, no less than 86 per cent of the category designated 'heavy smokers' denied the connection, while the 'medium smokers' and 'light smokers' fell at positions intermediate between these two extremes. What was providential about this situation was that the revelations about the hazards of smoking could not yet have influenced people's smoking habits. It follows that their beliefs in this instance could only have been influenced by their prior commitment. [see Festinger (1957) pp. 153-56]

One reason why dissonance theory attracted so much attention from social psychologists is that it was eminently testable provided only one had the wit to think up suitable test situations. Of the many laboratory experiments that were specifically designed to test the Festinger hypotheses one of the more ingenious was that by Aronson and Mills [1959]. They reasoned, on the basis of the theory, that someone who has had to undergo some ordeal in order to attain some objective ought subsequently to value that objective more than another person who secures it without the same trouble. In their experiment the subjects were a group of women students (63 in all) and the goal was to be membership of a discussion group which, it was announced, would be holding a series of discussions on the psychology of sex. Each subject who had expressed a desire to be accepted as a member was told that she would first have to pass an 'embarrassment test' to make sure that she really was sufficiently sophisticated for the discussion group. Two versions of this 'embarrassment test' were used, one for the 'severe initiation condition', the other for the 'mild initiation condition'. The women were randomly assigned to the one or the other. For the former the test involved reading out loud, in the presence of a male experimenter, a list of obscene words and some very frank descriptions of sexual activities taken from contemporary novels. For the latter the test involved merely reading aloud a number of words (e.g. 'virgin', 'petting', etc.) which had sexual connotations but were not obscene. The one subject who refused to undergo the test was eliminated from the experiment, the rest were all told afterwards that their behaviour had been satisfactory and that they were to be admitted as members. In addition a control group of subjects were admitted outright as members and no mention of an embarrassment test was made.

For the next stage, the subject was told that before she participated in the discussion group it would be advisable for her to listen in on a session without herself taking part and she was given a pair of headphones for this purpose. What she then heard was in fact the recording of a bogus session that had been deliberately designed to be as dry, boring and banal as possible (it dealt with the secondary sex-activities of the lower animals!). Apparently only one subject expressed any suspicions about this set-up and so her results were not included in the final reckoning. The rest were all convinced that they were in fact listening to a live discussion. In this situation how did the subjects, especially those of the 'severe initiation condition', react to this let-down? Were they enraged with the experimenters for having been put upon? The authors, on the basis of dissonance theory, predicted that, on the contrary, the more severe the initiation the more favourably disposed the subjects would be both towards the content of the discussion and towards those who were participating in it. Accordingly, after the conclusion of the mock session, each subject was asked to make various ratings concerning the discussion she had just heard and the different women who had contributed to it. It was then found that the ratings of the 'severe initiation' subjects were significantly more favourable on all counts to those of the other subjects although there was no significant difference between the 'mild initiation' category and the controls. One is relieved to learn that when, at the end of the experiment, a de-hoaxing session was held for the benefit of the subjects the experimenters were not lynched but that, on the contrary, 'none of the subjects expressed any resentment or annoyance at being misled'. Was this, one wonders, another case of dissonance reduction?

The experiment has been criticised on the grounds that other hypotheses besides those of dissonance theory might account for the results. It might be, for example, that the 'severe initiation' subjects were so relieved to find that the actual discussion was quite innocuous after the shock of the embarrassment test that they naturally felt well disposed towards it. However, it could be said about virtually all experiments that other interpretations than the ones given are possible. That is why no hypothesis can ever be conclusively proved although it may take only one experiment to disprove one conclusively! Of course, by no means all the experiments carried out to test dissonance theory gave a positive result like that of Aronson and Mills. Indeed one can say that, in general, the effects that have been demonstrated are relatively slight considering the enormous amount of ingenuity that has gone into devising plausible procedures.[20]

Undoubtedly the most dramatic demonstration of cognitive dissonance is an investigation which Festinger himself, together with two of his associates, undertook during the formative period of dissonance theory. This was a 'natural experiment' based on the study of a small apocalyptic sect whose activities were then about to come to a head.[21] Millennial and messianic sects have, of course, been a recurrent feature of the social scene right from the beginnings of the Christian era.[22] Each in turn comes forward with some stupendous message proclaiming the end of the world as then known and the beginnings of a new dispensation, each attracts adherents who take up the cry, oblivious of the fiascos which all previous doomsday enthusiasts had to face, and each eventually dissolves and lets the world carry on as before until some new prophet comes along. There can be no doubting the sincerity of the believers, often they give the most tangible proof of their commitment by selling or giving away all their worldly possessions in anticipation of imminent supernatural compensation. What becomes of such people when the fateful day arrives and nothing happens? Do they curse themselves for their folly and wreak vengeance on the false prophet who deluded them? Or, in the proper Festinger manner, do they become even more fervent than before and either postpone the apocalypse for a little longer or insist that it has taken place after all only in some Pickwickian sense not immediately apparent to the eyes of the uninitiated?

The particular sect which Festinger elected to study centred around the figure of a certain middle-aged suburban housewife whom we shall call simply the 'prophetess'. She appears to have had some mediumistic propensities and one day found herself producing automatic scripts purporting to emanate from her late father. Before long, however, the scripts began to convey messages from beings of another planet. The prophetess had been an enthusiast for flying saucers as well as a student of the more traditional occult lore and her ideas reveal the imprint of spiritualism and theosophy as well as contemporary science fiction. After attracting a number of followers who called themselves the 'Seekers' her messages eventually began to take on a more and more apocalyptic slant until she was confidently proclaiming that, on a certain specific date, only a few months hence, the entire American continent would be overwhelmed by a cataclysmic flood in which everyone would perish; everyone, that is, except her followers who would, in the nick of time, be rescued by a flying saucer specially sent to Earth for that purpose by her extra-terrestrial 'Guardians'. The only consolation she could offer unbelievers was that although their bodies would be destroyed their souls would be transported to another planet to commence there a new incarnation. This, then, was the gist of the messages which, for a short time, became the gospel of some two dozen or so apparently normal Americans, old and young.

In order to obtain first-hand evidence about the activities of the sect and the beliefs and attitudes of its members, Festinger planted a small number of trained observers among them who posed as followers. He was specially interested to find out as much as possible about how the individual members of the sect would react to the disconfirmation of the prophecy. As time drew near, the local press took up the story. This created an ideal situation from the standpoint of dissonance theory since it meant that commitments had to be made and sustained in the full glare of publicity and in the face of public derision. Festinger predicted that, in these conditions, only the marginal supporters would fall away following the disconfirmation; those who were more deeply committed, especially any who had given away all their possessions, would not only persist in their faith but would actively strive to make converts. This last point was of particular importance because from a merely commonsense point of view we would expect just the contrary, we would imagine that they would be feeling far too shamefaced about the whole affair to go out of their way to attract further attention to themselves. On the other hand, from the standpoint of dissonance theory, it is just at such a time that one has most need of converts; in other words, the less the objective evidence in a given case, the more one looks for support to others and the more one seeks to increase the number of like-minded persons.

What actually happened on the critical 21st December was, briefly, as follows: when it became apparent that there would be no cosmic disaster and no miraculous delivery the reaction of the faithful was at first one of stunned dismay; the prophetess herself, we are told, broke down and wept. However, this reaction did not last long. By Christmas Eve the Seekers had rallied sufficiently to hold a carol service outside the house of the prophetess, undismayed by some two hundred jeering spectators and still hoping that a visitation of some kind might yet materialise. The chief spokesman for the group was a local physician, let us call him the 'doctor'. After the carol service he was interviewed by a reporter. He denied that the group had been expecting any rescue operation but, at the same time, he put out the rumour that 'space men' had actually been present at the service but had gone unrecognised by the crowd. On the Christmas Day Festinger sent a new observer to seek admission to the group. To his surprise he got a rapturous welcome and it soon became apparent that he was being regarded as an extra-terrestrial visitor in disguise! But this *élan* was short-lived; soon the hostility of the neighbourhood forced the prophetess to flee her home, her followers deserted her except, significantly, the doctor who continued to travel and to preach the message of the 'Guardians'. Festinger claimed, on the basis of a detailed analysis of each of the participants, that his hypotheses were fulfilled. The lukewarm and the sceptical severed their relations straight after the débâcle but those who by their previous actions were most exposed to the effects of dissonance persisted to the bitter end and even tried to make converts.

Festinger published his book on the case in 1956. It was not long, however, before another apocalyptic group surfaced in America and were spotted by two social psychologists who saw in it an excellent opportunity to try and corroborate Festinger's findings. [*see* Hardyck and Braden (1962)] The sect in question was the 'Church of the True Word', a much more imposing body than the Seekers. On 4th July 1960, 29 families of the faithful, comprising 135 men, women and children, went down into their bomb-proof shelters in response to a prophecy that the United States would be destroyed in a nuclear attack, and there they stayed in considerable discomfort for no less than 42 days. Once again, there can be no question of their sincerity or commitment. What, then, happened when eventually they emerged and found the world to be the same as when they left? First, despite (or should I say 'because of'?) their ordeal, they were less disconcerted than the Seekers had been. A prayer meeting was convened and their leaders explained that God's message to them had been misinterpreted; it now appeared that there had been no mention of an imminent attack. But all was not wasted, God had been testing their faith while, at the same time, using them to warn an unregenerate world. Having shown themselves worthy of His trust, they now more than ever deserved to be among His elect! With arguments such as these consonance was restored in the minds of the faithful. However, with respect to Festinger's other critical hypothesis, namely that they would now increase their proselytising, no evidence at all was forthcoming. As the authors point out, the prayer meeting of 16th August, attended as it was by newsmen, cameramen and TV representatives, afforded a golden opportunity had they wished to appeal for supporters, but apparently they made no effort to do so.[23]

Discussing this discrepancy the authors suggest that perhaps the greater size and solidarity of the Church of the True Word, as compared with the Seekers, made it a matter of much less urgency to try to increase their numbers. They also point out that they were subject to much less ridicule and abuse than the Seekers, indeed they were even given an award by the local civil defence organisation for performing a public service! Meanwhile, however, the discrepancy remains and points to the need for dissonance theory to be more specific about the range within which its predicted effects should operate. Otherwise it exposes itself to the charge of itself seeking to avoid dissonance!

In the light of such researches it is instructive to take a fresh look at some of the historic religions, creeds and ideologies of mankind. The one thing we then find that they all have in common is that they have made themselves proof against disconfirmation. Although Paul appears to have expected the Second Coming to fall within the lifetime of those to whom he preached, Christianity soon learnt to trim its eschatology to a Kingdom that was not of this world. Similarly, Judaism allowed the Jewish people to preserve down the centuries a belief in its special relationship with the deity no matter how many individual Jews might perish in successive holocausts. Indeed, as dissonance theory would predict, the more they suffered persecution the more reluctant they were to abandon their traditions or their ethnic identity. But perhaps no other movement has provided more striking exemplifications both of dissonance avoidance and dissonance reduction than that of Marxism. Marx inherited the

Millennial aspirations of Christianity and Judaism and translated them into secular terms. But the strength of his 'inexorable laws of history' lay precisely in their elasticity. World Revolution was assured but, since no timetable was ever set down, no one need ever feel cheated. Or, consider the Communist Party, surely the most cannibalistic organisation known to history. By what strange magnetism was it able to count on the allegiance of certain Western intellectuals throughout all the outrages of the Stalin era? The answer which dissonance theory suggests is that, once such a person could be got to commit himself by word or deed to the movement, perhaps by playing upon his moral revulsion from the injustices he could observe in his own society, dissonance reduction could be relied upon to do the rest: nothing after that could shake his faith in the infallibility of the Party.[24] As for those who found themselves willy-nilly under Communist dictatorship, the imposition of an iron curtain made it very much easier to persuade them that the capitalist grapes were sour anyway!

Let us turn now to our other topic, that of obedience. At first it may seem that this is not really a psychological problem so much as an institutional one. Every state has at its disposal for good or ill a more or less elaborate apparatus of coercion by means of which it can enforce obedience; in the army disobedience may even be punishable with death. The question I want to consider here is: in the absence of any sanctions whatever to apply against those who refuse to obey, how much obedience can we count upon? Until recently it was tacitly assumed that it would not be possible to induce anyone to harm either himself or another person except, possibly, under hypnosis.[25] We now know, thanks to Stanley Milgram of Yale University whose work I shall describe, that such a view is far too optimistic. Milgram asked himself the question why so many Germans under Hitler were willing to be a party to atrocities? Was it, perhaps, some fatal flaw in the German character which makes them unable to resist the demands of authority? Or is blind obedience a universal human failing? To find out whether it existed among his fellow Americans (America was once thought to be the home of rugged individualism) he very cunningly devised the following set-up. [see Milgram (1963)]

The subject is told that his help is needed in connection with a learning experiment. He is then introduced to another subject and they are told that one of them—it does not matter which—is to be the 'learner', the other the 'teacher'. Lots are drawn as the result of which the first subject finds himself cast in the role of 'teacher'. In fact, of course, the lottery was rigged—both slips of paper bore the word 'teacher'—and the other subject was not really a subject at all but a confederate of the experimenter.[26] The real subject is then told of his duties as 'teacher'. He is shown a list of paired words and told that the 'learner' has to memorise them; each time he calls out the first word of a pair, the 'learner' is to respond by calling out its paired associate. If he fails to do so or if he makes no answer he is to get an electric shock. He is then shown a bank of thirty switches ranging from one marked 'Mild Shock: 15 volts' up to one marked 'Danger Severe Shock: 450 volts'. They are graded in intervals of 15 volts. To enhance verisimilitude, the subject is given a sample shock of 45 volts and is told: 'although the shocks can be extremely painful they cause no permanent damage'. He also watches while the 'learner' is strapped to a chair from which he cannot escape and while electrodes are attached to his wrist. His instructions are to start at the lowest level of shock for the first error and then to work his way up by one interval for every subsequent error. Since, by pre-arrangement, the 'learner' keeps on making mistakes, the supposed level of shock keeps on increasing. By the time the 75 volt level is reached the 'learner' has to start grunting; by the time the 100 volt is reached he has to start expostulating; at 150 volts he has to insist on being released. He has then to go on complaining and yelling until the 285 volt mark is reached, whereupon he is to let out a piercing scream and refuse to give any further answers. Meanwhile, the experimenter keeps insisting that the 'teacher' must persevere regardless right up to the 450 volt limit. Should the subject hesitate, the experimenter must say: 'Please continue'; should he still demur, he must say: 'The experiment requires that you go on'; if that is still not enough: 'It is absolutely essential that you go on'; and, finally, 'You have no choice but to go on'.

For his original experiment Milgram's subjects were forty men drawn from a wide range of different occupations and varying in age from 20 to 50 years. They were contacted through advertising and direct mail solicitation and were each given $4.50 as remuneration, which they received as soon as they arrived; it was made plain that the money was theirs whatever they did. Under these conditions how many of them went all the way up to the 450 volt limit? Forty prominent psychiatrists who were asked to make a prediction, after being given a full account of the situation, estimated that most subjects would not go beyond the 150 volt switch ('strong shock') and that no more than one tenth of one per cent would go to the limit.[27] In fact, twenty-six out of the forty subjects (65 per cent) went all the way and not one subject desisted before he had reached the 300 volt switch. So much for those who say that psychological experiments never demonstrate anything we do not know already! Milgram himself was astonished at the results he obtained and indeed the facts are so incredible that at first they were met with blank incredulity.[28] Could it be that subjects realised all the time, at least at one deep level of awareness, that it was all a put-up job? That no self-respecting experimenter could possibly ask him to do anything as mischievous on such a flimsy pretext?

Perhaps this possibility, which is now thought to invalidate the earlier hypnotic experiments on obedience, can never be completely ruled out but, in this case, all the evidence is against this conjecture. Both from their demeanour and from the post-experimental interview it seems that the subjects were labouring under real and acute distress.[29] Some of them even gave way to long and uncontrollable fits of nervous laughter. Why then did they do it? Obviously there can be no such thing as pure obedience, only a complete zombie would obey without any motivation to do so. In this instance it is not hard to find a number of plausible motives if we look for them: a sense of obligation in fulfilling a paid assignment, a reluctance to become embroiled with the experimenter in a face-to-face confrontation, and so forth. Yet, even so, such motives seem inadequate to account for the extent of the observed compliance.

Could it be that the subjects were simply overawed by the ambience of an illustrious university? Milgram considered this possibility and, to test it, he hired some rooms in a run-down office block in downtown Bridgeport. No hint was given that the set-up had any connection with Yale, and the fictitious title 'Research Associates' was used as an inscription on the door. Yet, even so, there was no significant decrease in the percentage of subjects who obeyed up to the limit. [Milgram (1965)] Milgram next considered the possibility that it was because the subject could not see the 'victim' but only hear him that he was so compliant. In another experiment, therefore, Milgram varied the feedback available to the subject according to four different degrees of 'immediacy'. These were: (1) *remote feedback*, subjects neither heard nor saw the 'victim'; (2) *voice feed-*

back, subjects heard but did not see the 'victim' (as in the original experiment); (3) *proximity*, the subject sat a few feet away from the 'victim' whom he thus saw and heard; and (4) *touch proximity*, the subject was required to hold the 'victim's' hand forcibly against a metal plate from which the shock was supposed to come. Forty different subjects were randomly assigned to each condition of immediacy. Not surprisingly, there was a steady decline in the percentage of maximally obedient subjects in each successive condition and in the mean level of shock reached. Yet, even so, as many as 30 per cent never defied the experimenter even under the harrowing conditions of 'touch proximity'! [Milgram (1965)]

Finally, can we really be quite sure that Milgram's subjects were truly representative? Certainly they were a miscellaneous enough set of men in age occupation and background, but it is worth noting that in none of the variants of this experiment did he ever compel a whole group of subjects, say students, to act as subjects; in all cases he relied on volunteers. Were they perhaps more acquiescent to start with?[30] After all, the really 'bloody-minded' type does not volunteer for scientific experiments even for 4½ dollars! But even if we exclude the really negativistic individual as unlikely ever to have got as far as the laboratory door, the evidence Milgram has amassed remains disquieting and still calls for an explanation. How, then, are we to conceptualise what took place? Are we really all sadists at heart even if we do not know it? It does not seem so; with rare exceptions the subjects hated their assignment and were deeply disturbed by it. What seems more likely is that because they were obeying orders the subjects absolved themselves from the consequences. Although in private life they might never dream of doing anything so cruel, the fact that they were now doing it at someone else's instigation made all the difference. One subject, when asked afterwards why he did not stop before the end, explained that he wanted badly to do so and pleaded with the experimenter to let him but, he said, *'He would not let me'*! (my italics). [Milgram (1965a) p. 128]

Perhaps, also, cognitive dissonance plays some part in this phenomenon as in so many other situations. Accepting payment may be seen as the first step towards commitment, after that every shock meted out makes it that much harder to refuse the next shock and the easier to persuade oneself that a few more volts won't make all that difference! (As every seducer knows, the further you can get a girl to go the harder it is for her to draw back!) The dissonance effect comes in again when the hoax is laid bare. Milgram faced a barrage of censure from colleagues on the grounds that the moral harm he was doing to his subjects was hardly less reprehensible than the harm which the subjects thought they were doing to the 'victim'. Milgram countered by pointing out that all his subjects were interviewed some time after the experiment by psychiatrists who could discover no traces of any residual disturbances. He further pointed out that less than 2 per cent of subjects expressed the wish that they had never taken part in the experiment, while 84 per cent expressed positive satisfaction that they had done so. [Milgram (1965) p. 58 n. 3] Like the women students in the Aronson and Mills experiment, Milgram's subjects apparently bore him no grudge for playing this trick on them. But was this perhaps another case of a 'severe initiation' effect?

To sum up: it may be that from the standpoint of social psychology in general, the Milgram investigation, however dramatic, represents something of a side-show; it clinches no outstanding theoretical issue and it has not so far led to any important new research. Even as a comment on Nazism it tells us nothing about the dynamics of prejudice or the roots of anti-semitism, without which the policy of genocide would not have been conceivable. If anything, it provides a more fitting comment on the Great Purges where it was, for the most part, completely unpredictable who would and who would not be selected as the next victim. No doubt terror, once unleashed, has a momentum and a logic of its own, yet the fact that Stalin could get so many men to do his bidding far beyond the confines of his own country is a fact worth pondering. But what Milgram did succeed in showing, with devastating effect, is that simple obedience, without which no community could long survive, can on occasion override the dictates of conscience.[31] As such, it helps us to understand what Hannah Arendt, discussing the case of Adolf Eichmann, has called 'the banality of evil'.[32]

* * *

In view of all the complications, practical and ethical, involved in carrying out experiments in social psychology and in view of the doubts about their validity that inevitably arise, critics may feel that at best they can be no more than a methodological *tour de force*. In the face of such criticisms two lines of defence are open. First, it may be argued that it is only by means of experiments, however ludicrous, artificial or even scandalous they may appear to onlookers, that we can ever get any firm and rigorous evidence on the strength of which we can test our theorising about cause-effect relationships. To abandon them would be either to return to the era of armchair social psychology or to leave the field to the purely observational and survey methods of the anthropologist and sociologist. [cf. Mills (1969)] The second line of defence looks upon the socio-psychological experiment as having a certain intrinsic interest irrespective of any theoretical implications that may be drawn from it. Their virtue, it is claimed, is that they demonstrate, in a more or less pure and distilled form, certain striking facts about the variation and limits of human behaviour under fully controlled conditions. Even if such experiments *explain* nothing, they add something to our knowledge of what human beings are like.

Summary

The Individual and the Group

There have been two schools of thought with respect to the explanation of social phenomena: the 'individualists', or reductionists, who believe that social phenomena are to be explained in terms of individual behaviour or by reference to the interaction between individuals; and the 'collectivists', or holists, who insist that social phenomena can be explained only in terms of certain autonomous social laws and that, so far from being reducible to individual behaviour, the latter can be understood only by reference to the social context in which it occurs. Here it is pointed out that, whatever unfortunate political overtones 'collectivism' may have acquired, there can be no logical reasons why there should not be laws pertaining to social collectives that are not reducible to laws pertaining to individuals. In science, there can be no natural individuals; what entity or concept we treat as fundamental depends upon the level of discourse with which we are concerned. Social psychology, as distinct from sociology or other similar social sciences, focuses on the individual person and treats the social environment as one essential determinant of behaviour.

Social psychology came of age as an independent discipline only during the 1930s with the acceptance of the experimental method in this field. Some of the special problems which this created, both practical and ethical, are here discussed, and the reasons why experimenters are driven to hoaxing their subjects. The use of the 'natural' experiment is also discussed.

Dissonance and Obedience

Two particular problems of social psychology are considered in this section. The first concerns the effect on a person's attitudes and behaviour of being confronted with evidence which goes contrary to his beliefs, expectations, preconceptions, etc. Festinger's theory of cognitive dissonance, which predicts that whenever possible evidence will be distorted to make it conform to expectation, is discussed at some length and some attempts to test the theory, both in the laboratory and in the field, are described. Of the latter mention is made of one particular apocalyptic sect whose behaviour was studied at the point when it became apparent that their doomsday prophecy would not be fulfilled.

The second problem arises out of the fact that, all through history, those in positions of authority have been able to rely on the blind obedience of their underlings. The recent work of Milgram,[33] who tried to see how far he could go in commanding the obedience of his subjects in a controlled laboratory situation where they thought they were administering electric shocks to another subject, is then described in some detail. Their behaviour was found to be less a release of latent sadistic tendencies than a manifestation of sheer passive acquiescence. Some of the wider political implications of both these phenomena are also considered.

Notes

1   Although Wundt's fame rests on the work of his laboratory, he wrote at length on social and cultural topics especially in his later years. Between 1910 and 1920, the year before his death at the age of 89, he brought out the ten volumes of his *Völkerpsychologie* (the first three volumes were translated into English and published by

Macmillan, New York, under the title *Elements of Folk Psychology*). There he covers such diverse topics as language, custom, myth, forms of art, religious practices, legal systems, and so on, but his approach is that of the older speculative tradition and contrasts strongly with his experimental studies. The point is that Wundt regarded thinking, along with all the higher mental processes, as essentially socially conditioned phenomena and so beyond the scope of the experimental methodology applicable to physiologically conditioned phenomena.

2 *See* Mill [1875] Bk 6, Chap. 7, Sect. 1, 'Of the Chemical or Experimental Method in the Social Science'. It is noteworthy that Mill used the same chemical analogy in a positive sense to argue against reductionism as applied to the laws of mental experience, *see* note 2 to Chap. 1 of this volume.

3 I say 'by and large' advisedly. Thus the British School of Idealists, though holistic in their metaphysics, were less prone to political collectivism than their German counterparts. In particular, T. H. Green was a man of liberal principles. [*cf*. Milne (1962) Chap. 4, 'T. H. Green's political philosophy'] It is somewhat harder to think of an exception of the other side; however, Hobbes, a reductionist in metaphysics, was an absolutist in his political philosophy.

4 First in his *Open Society and its Enemies* of 1945 [Popper (1962)], which has been described as Sir Karl's contribution to our war effort, and later in his *Poverty of Historicism* [Popper (1957)], which he dedicated to 'the countless men and women of all creeds or nations or races who fell victim to the fascist and communist belief in the Inexorable Laws of Historical Destiny'.

5 *See* his 'Situational Individualism and Emergent Group Properties' in Wisdom [1970] where he analyses the strength and weakness of the Popperian position with much skill. *See also* J. Agassi's article 'Methodological Individualism' [Agassi (1960)], but whereas Agassi seeks to salvage Popper's doctrine, Wisdom seeks to go beyond it in order to justify a neo-collectivism. Against both these philosophers and against Popper himself, the sociologist G. C. Homans refuses to abandon psychologism, arguing that Popper's methodological individualism entails psychologism. While

not denying that actions may have unforeseen consequences, Homans [1970] maintains that either social phenomena cannot be explained at all or they can be explained on strictly psychological principles, e.g. by reinforcement theory, etc.

6 It was William McDougall who tried to introduce the concept of the group mind in psychology, in his *The Group Mind* of 1920. It was strongly attacked by the contemporary social psychologists led by F. H. Allport but, in fact, in his introductory chapter 'The Province of Collective Psychology', McDougall makes out a plausible case for it, even if the rest of his book is mainly speculative social theorising of the now discredited armchair variety.

7 *Cf.* Allport [1968] p. 7. 'If it were possible to designate a single "founder" of social psychology as a science, we should have to nominate Comte for this honour.' Note that the term 'sociology' was Comte's own coinage.

8 *See* Mill [1875] Bk 6, Chap. 5, 'Of Ethology or the Science of the Formation of Character'. Mill argues that even if human nature is not the same in all societies, there must, nevertheless, be certain universal laws to account for these differences. For him, of course, these could be none other than the laws of association which he called 'the laws of mind'.

9 Gustave Le Bon's *Psychologie des Foules* (Paris: 1895, transl. as *The Crowd: A Study of the Popular Mind*, London: 1896) enjoyed a great vogue in its day and went through many reprintings. Essentially, it is a lengthy essay on the characteristics of mobs as manifested in history, with the example of the great French Revolution very much to the fore. Le Bon stressed especially the moral deterioration which comes about when individuals submerge their individuality into that of the mob.

10 Notably those of Norman Triplett, a professor of psychology at Indiana University. An account of his work is to be found in Wheeler [1970] Chap. 1, 'The Early Years 1900-1935'.

11 In his *Social Psychology* (1924) Chap. 11, 'Response to Social Stimulation in the Group', Allport describes some of the pioneer

German studies of social facilitation.

12 *See* Murphy and Murphy [1937], which was eventually superseded by Newcomb [1950]. Newcomb is Professor of Sociology and Psychology at the University of Michigan.

13 Lewin [1935] consists of translations of his various articles in the German periodicals. Sherif [1963] describes his work using the so-called 'autokinetic phenomenon', an ambiguous perceptual stimulus consisting of a pin-point of light in a darkened room which appears to move around in an irregular way. Sherif was able to demonstrate that, when groups of subjects are tested together, they tend to establish their own norms with respect to the extent of the perceived movement.

14 *See* Lewin, Lippitt and White [1939] or any of the many standard textbooks on social psychology where this work has been described, e.g. Wheeler [1970] Chap. 3.

15 His theoretical ideas are to be found in Lewin [1967], a posthumous collection of papers covering the period 1940 to the author's death in 1947. Lewin was founder and director of the Research Center for Group Dynamics at MIT. For a recent evaluation of the place of field theories in social psychology *see* Shaw and Costanzo [1970] Chap. 6.

16 *See* Asch [1952] or the summary given by Wheeler [1970] Chap. 8. A recent modification of the Asch experiment which dispenses with the need for confederates was devised by C. Marino, who gave his subjects printed booklets, which they naturally assumed to be identical, but, in fact, the booklet given to the real subject differed from the rest on the critical items. [*see* Marino and Parkin (1969)]

17 It is interesting to note that Mill took it for granted that the natural experiment was the only one possible in the social sciences; thus he writes: 'The first difficulty that meets us in the attempt to apply experimental method to the laws of social phenomena is that we are without the means of making artificial experiments ... we can only watch those which nature produces or which are pro-

duced for other reasons ... if the spontaneous instances found by contemporary events and by the succession of phenomena recorded in history afford a sufficient variation of circumstances, an induction from specific experience is attainable; otherwise not.' [Mill (1875) Bk 6, Chap. 7, sect. 2] We do not know what Mill would have thought of the 'artificial experiments' of our modern social psychologists.

18   *Cf.* Whiting and Child [1953]. On the specific question of swaddling *see* Benedict [1967] and Gorer and Rickman [1959] esp. App. I 'The Development of the Swaddling Hypothesis'. This latter volume created something of a furore in literary circles when it was first published. Critics were scandalised by the idea that such a trivial cause should have such far-reaching consequences, i.e. in moulding the Russian character. The book is dedicated to the memory of Ruth Benedict, the great cultural anthropologist, who died in 1948.

19   *See* Festinger [1957] and its sequel Festinger *et al.* [1964]. Festinger is Professor of Psychology at Stanford University, California. His theory, however, was only the best known of a number of 'consistency' theories in social psychology, the first of which, perhaps, was that of Fritz Heider as set out in his article 'Attitudes and Cognitive Organization' *J. Psych.* 51, 1944, 358-74. [*see* Shaw and Costanzo (1970) Chap. 8] Zajonc [(1968) p. 359] says of Festinger's theory: 'No theory in social psychology has stimulated more research than the theory of cognitive dissonance. Articles in this area constitute the model category in journals publishing results of social-psychological research.'

20   For a critical assessment of the theory *see* Chapanis and Chapanis [1964], Weick [1965] or Rosenberg [1965]. Such critical counterattacks are, however, the fate of all important psychological theories and they have not by any means put paid to Festinger.

21   *See* Festinger, Riecken and Schachter, *When Prophecy Fails* [1956]. An entertaining fictional account of this episode has been written by the American novelist Alison Lurie, *see* her *Imaginary Friends* (Heinemann: London 1967).

22   Norman Cohn has written a fascinating history of such move-

ments, *see* his *The Pursuit of the Millennium* (Secker and Warburg: London 1957: Mercury Books PB 1962).

23 Hardyck and Braden also cite the case of a Dutch sect who, in the words of a Dutch psychologist who visited them: 'gathered together near the top of Mont Blanc in expectation of a flood which would destroy the world on July 14th 1960. They had existed as a group for four years and many members had lived in the lodge on Mont Blanc for several months separated from the other people living in that area. They had one prophet, one body of beliefs and ... a feeling of community and fellowship. When their prediction was disconfirmed the leader announced to the waiting reporters: you should be happy that we made that error. Our faith does not waver ... Amen.' Yet they too made no attempt to proselytise. [Hardyck and Braden (1962) p. 140]

24 *Cf.* David Caute, *The Fellow-Travellers.* Weidenfeld & Nicolson: London 1973. Yet even communists have their breaking-point and it is instructive to study the rapid disintegration of the monolithic party image which followed Krushchev's secret speech to the 20th Congress of 1956.

25 The sinister possibilities of hypnosis have long been a talking-point but were first subjected to experimental testing by Rowland [1939] and subsequently by Young [1948]. The task in this instance was (a) to pick up a venomous snake and (b) to throw acid in the face of the experimenter. Actually, an invisible curved sheet of plate glass protected the subject from the snake and the experimenter from the acid but these investigators claimed that their subjects believed in the reality of what they were about to do and yet were helpless to desist. However, Orne and Evans [1965], in a replication of this experiment, on the basis of a post-experimental interview, report that their subjects 'were quite convinced that they would not be harmed because the context was an experimental one, presumably conducted by responsible experimenters'. Orne and Evans also used waking subjects who proved to be not much less compliant than the hypnotised ones. *See also* Barber [(1969)] Chap. 12: Barber cites the Milgram experiments (*see* below) as proof that, if the suggestions are made emphatically enough, hypnosis is not necessary to elicit anti-social behaviour.

26 Milgram's 'stooge' is described by him as 'a 47-year-old account-
ant, trained for the role; he was of Irish American stock whom most
observers found mild-mannered and likable'. [Milgram (1963) p.
373]

27 Similar forecasts were made by Milgram's own colleagues and
graduate students who were sure that no more than an insignificant
minority of subjects would obey right to the bitter end. [see Milgram
(1965), esp. p. 72 and Fig. 3]

28 Cf. Wheeler [1970] p. 91. 'When I first heard of this research,
I dismissed it as unbelievable and assumed that the subjects somehow knew that they weren't really shocking anyone. But having
seen auxiliary data and films of experimental sessions, I must accept
the data as being perfectly valid.'

29 One independent observer reported as follows: 'I observed a
mature and initially poised businessman enter the laboratory smiling
and confident. Within twenty minutes he was reduced to a twitch-
ing, stuttering wreck, who was rapidly approaching a point of
nervous collapse ... and yet he continued to respond to every word
of the experimenter, and obeyed to the end.' [Milgram (1963) p. 377]

30 I owe this suggestion to my wife, Dr Halla Beloff, herself a
social psychologist, who put the point to Dr Milgram. In his reply
to her he pointed out that approximately 20 per cent of those who
received a direct mail solicitation turned up at the laboratory (private
communication 28th Feb. 1967), a large return for such a request.
Even so, we cannot tell whether they represented the more acquiescent 20 per cent of the population. This, however, is a reservation
which applies very widely in social psychology wherever we are
forced to rely on the services of volunteers.

31 Cf. Milgram [1965] p. 75. 'The results as seen and felt in the
laboratory are to this author disturbing. They raise the possibility
that human nature, or—more specifically—the kind of character
produced in American democratic society, cannot be counted on to
insulate its citizens from brutality and inhumane treatment at the
direction of malevolent authority.' The My Lai massacre a few
years later showed all too well that Milgram's fears were not ex-

aggerated. The work earned him the Socio-psychological Prize of the American Association for the Advancement of Science in 1964.

32 *See* Hannah Arendt, *Eichmann in Jerusalem: A Report on the Banality of Evil* (Faber: London 1963), based on the series of articles which Miss Arendt contributed to the *New Yorker* on the Eichmann trial then in progress. Eichmann is the obvious prototype of Milgramian man. It is specially noteworthy that, despite his hero-worship of Hitler, he was, of all the Nazis, the least anti-semitic. His motives were no more than those of the zealous functionary anxious to carry out his instructions to the last letter. As he told his Israeli captors (against whom he bore no grudge and with whom he dutifully cooperated) he would have sent his own father to the death-camps had those been his orders!

33 Milgram has since published a comprehensive account of his experiments in book form, *see* Stanley Milgram, *Obedience to Authority* (Harper & Row: New York, Tavistock: London, 1974).

CHAPTER SEVEN

Depth Psychology

One's first reaction may be to ask whether we really need to burden psychology with something as opaque and enigmatic as unconscious states of mind. It has, of course, always been a matter of common knowledge that much of our behaviour is mediated by activities of the nervous system which never, at any point, figure in consciousness. We would not even be able to lift a finger if it were necessary for us to be conscious of the neural processes which successively intervene between the decision to lift a finger and that finger being raised. Similarly, when it comes to perception, we are at last beginning to realise what an astonishing amount of information processing must go on in the brain to make possible even the basic awareness of one's surroundings. The question is: between those experiences which are conscious and those neural events that are not conscious do we also need to posit certain entities which can neither be observed nor yet introspected but which must, nevertheless, in some important sense, be designated as 'mental'?

Since the late 19th century, when the idea first began to impinge on academic psychology, there has never been any lack of sceptics to say 'No'. They have argued that all the phenomena which are cited as evidence for an unconscious mind, notably behaviour which ordinarily we associate with consciousness but which, exceptionally, is to be found in the absence of consciousness, can, more plausibly and more economically, be explained either by reference to the autonomous functioning of the nervous system or by reference to such concepts as 'marginal awareness', 'diminished attention', 'sub-threshold sensitivity', and so on.[1] Had this view prevailed there would, of course, never have been any such thing as depth psychology, which I here take to mean that science to which the unconscious is an indispensable concept. Yet, even as late as 1925, Freud could still write, with some justification, that 'the overwhelming majority of philosophers regard as mental only the phenomena of consciousness. For them the world of consciousness coincides with the sphere of what is mental.'[2]

The fact is that the entire weight of the mechanistic tradition in science, from Galileo onwards, which placed the whole of nature into the category of the physical, all except the secondary or sensual qualities which could be relegated to the inferior category of mind, militated against any *tertium quid* which was neither physical nor sensuous. And clearly if one insists upon defining mind according to the Empiricist tradition as that which is given in experience or that which is known without inference then any talk of unconscious mental events or entities can only be a flagrant contradiction in terms.[3] But the simplicities of Cartesian metaphysics and the certainties of Empiricist epistemology have lost much of their authority and such a definition of mind has come to appear increasingly arbitrary and unwarranted. Consciousness is, no doubt, the most salient and distinctive manifestation of mind, but to equate the two would be like equating motion and energy or any theoretical entity in science with any of its possible manifestations. A more promising and less question-begging approach, I suggest, is to regard both conscious experience and 'mind-like' behaviour as, equally, manifestations of mind. Mind may then be defined, provisionally at least, as 'the critical factor in mind-like behaviour' where the expression 'mind-like' can be explicated without circularity in terms of such manifest characteristics as those of being purposive or adaptive or intelligent or rational or the like. On this definition, be it noted, nothing whatever is implied about the role of consciousness in mind-like behaviour even if, as a contingent fact, consciousness always supervenes whenever such behaviour occurs. As to the ontological status or mode of existence of our hypothetical mind-factor, that is another problem to which we shall be returning in our concluding chapter. But, even if we should decide to opt in favour of a materialist solution which identifies mind with brain on the *ontological* plane, this would still not be an argument for prematurely conflating the two on the *conceptual* plane. For, even in the physical sciences, we need concepts belonging to different levels of analysis or different logical categories. In the case of the psychological sciences the question is whether we can get by with only a two-tiered structure where the upper tier is occupied either by behavioural or introspectible data and the lower tier is occupied by physiological data, or whether we also need an intermediate tier on which to place certain theoretical entities and dispositional properties.

We have already seen, in our chapter on cognitive psychology, that any adequate account of human cognitive performance requires concepts such as skills, competences, rules, grammars, plans, strategies, and so forth. None of these are reducible to physiological facts, even though they are all dependent, causally speaking, on physiological processes, but neither are they observable or introspectible. Yet, as some philosophers have been assuring us, it is precisely with such constructs as these that any genuine psychological science is crucially concerned, that nothing beyond positivistic dogma has all this while obscured this from us. If that is so then we can see that we are no more justified in refusing to explain individual behaviour by reference to unconscious forces than we are in refusing to explain social behaviour by reference to social forces and group properties and, of the two, the concept of the unconscious has so far proved itself incomparably the more fruitful. It is possible, however, that we may also have been misled in this matter by certain logical features of the situation for, as Dixon [1968] has pointed out, 'since the only stimuli which we are aware of responding to are stimuli of which we are aware, it is only too easy to draw the false conclusion that awareness always mediates between stimulus and response'; whereas, as his own work on subliminal perception amply demonstrates, not only discrimination but even the semantic processing of verbal stimuli can be shown to occur in the absence of awareness provided a suitably subtle and ingenious design of experiment is used.[4]

The Unconscious

Viewed historically, depth psychology owes its origin to three distinct, though interwoven, developments in 19th century science: the practice of hypnotism, the study of pathological behaviour and symptomatology and, to a lesser but by no means negligible extent, to psychical research. Before we can discuss these developments, however, it is necessary to take account of certain profound changes in European culture which prepared the ground for them. For the idea of the unconscious was, in the first instance, a legacy of the Romantic movement both as this found expression in the imaginative and critical literature of the period and in the anti-rational, anti-intellectualist trends of post-Enlightenment philosophy. Poetic inspiration was in fact one of the earliest topics to give currency to the idea of the unconscious. The Romantic writer and artist, freed from the conventions and restraints of the classical tradition, was driven inwards to reflect upon the nature of his own creative processes. Inspiration, one could say, was as necessary to give authenticity to the Romantic work of art as the voice of conscience had been to the religious innovators of the Reformation, and both inspiration and conscience pointed to aspects of mind that transcended consciousness. At the same time, the philosopher of the Romantic epoch was no longer content to look on Nature as the soulless machine of Newtonian cosmology, not even when natural theology coupled this with a remote deity to act as designer and prime mover. On the contrary, with the decline of revealed religion, Nature more and more took on the attributes of divinity to be revered as the font of life and source of all true wisdom. Hence the vogue of *Naturphilosophie* emanating from Germany, the rightful home of the Romantic movement.[5] Hence the new-found interest in Spinoza, in whose metaphysics God and Nature become one and whose doctrine of the 'Conatus' has been regarded by some as one of the sources of depth psychology.[6] Hence, too, the appeal of mystical, esoteric and oriental beliefs of the sort that have once again found favour with the neo-romantic radicals of our own so-called youth culture. The effect of all these influences, then as now, was to depreciate our ordinary waking consciousness as being responsible for alienating us from Nature and, correspondingly, to extol intuition, instinct, feeling and sentiment as a means of restoring the balance.

The story of hypnotism, one of the most extraordinary in the history of science, has been told many times and here I shall confine myself to a few of the more salient incidents that have a direct bearing on our theme.[7] Franz Anton Mesmer, with whom the story begins, was, like Freud, a Viennese physician of somewhat unorthodox propensities. With Mesmer one is hard put to decide whether one is dealing with a latter-day successor of the great sorcerers and faith-healers of a bygone age, purveying his own new-fangled magic, or with the real precursor of modern psychotherapy and psychosomatic medicine. There is no doubt that Mesmer regarded himself as a scientist and as a man of the Enlightenment. Indeed, his insistence that his treatment was based on a purely natural physical force, albeit of an unusual kind, may well have been a defence against the suspicion that it was either supernatural or else a mere matter of suggestion. At the same time he was never averse to using any trick of showmanship that might impress the gullible; for example, the playing of suitable music was a regular feature of the treatment. There is some question, however, as to whether Mesmer can be considered the discoverer of hypnotism. The aim of the treatment, with its hocus-pocus, was to bring the patient to a state of emotional crisis, or even to precipitate a convulsion, following which he would find his symptoms alleviated. It was Mesmer's principal lay disciple, the Marquis de Puységur, who, while going through the usual routine, induced in his patient, a local peasant boy, the condition that came to be known as the state of 'somnambulism' or, as we should now say, of deep hypnosis. From then on it was this trance state that was the principal focus of interest among practitioners even though it is only a minority of subjects that are capable of any deep level of hypnosis.

Largely as a result of opposition from his medical colleagues, Mesmer left Vienna to seek his fortune in Paris. There, in collaboration with a French physician, Charles d'Eslon, he soon attracted an enthusiastic following both among the rich and fashionable and among the poor whom he treated without fees. In marked contrast to Freud, he was not an original thinker; his own writings are singularly lacking in coherence. He belongs, in fact, to that special class of innovators in the history of science who contrive to misunderstand the significance of what it is they are doing but whose work nevertheless has prodigious consequences. Although the idea of the magnetic fluid[8] was not such an implausible one at a time when the marvels of magnetism and electricity were so little understood, it was, as events turned out, a most unfortunate one which queered the pitch of the new movement for the best part of a century. For, when the idea was discredited, following the Royal Commissions of 1784,[9] mesmerism was outlawed by the medical establishment and d'Eslon, together with a few other physicians who refused to renounce the practice, was expelled from the Faculty. Official disapproval, however, could not prevent the rapid spread of mesmerism as a popular new cult over the whole of Europe and America.[10] Theories, moreover, are easier to dispose of than facts and a few intrepid doctors, impressed by demonstrations which they happened to witness, put the welfare of their patients first and risked using the forbidden art despite the consequences.

One such person was John Elliotson, an outstanding figure in British Medicine in the early 19th century, a professor at University College, London, and a founder of University College Hospital. His championship of the movement cost him his job and he was ostracised and vilified by his colleagues. Undeterred, he founded in 1843 *The Zoist*, which at once became the organ of mesmerism in Britain until it ceased publication in 1856. Another fearless champion was the Scottish surgeon James Esdaile, who realised the possibilities of the mesmeric trance for use in surgery at a time when chloroform had not yet been introduced. He worked mainly in India where, with the help of Indian assistants whom he trained in his technique, he carried out innumerable major operations. His painless surgery enabled him to attempt far more drastic operations than other surgeons then dared and, at the same time, to claim a much lower mortality rate. All this, however, did not save him from official condemnation.[11] Another Scot who was attracted to hypnotism was James Braid, who practised in Manchester as a specialist in eye diseases. He was more fortunate in avoiding a breach with the profession, partly because he at once discarded the older physicalist hypothesis to which both Elliotson and Esdale had clung. In its place he substituted his own psychological explanation which stressed the suggestibility of the patient in the somnolent state following the induction of the hypnosis. It was, in fact, Braid who coined the word 'hypnotism' (from the Greek *hypnos* = sleep) although, to many of his contemporaries, his new style of mesmerism was better known as 'Braidism'.[12] Actually, Braid was by no means the first to surmise that mesmerism was in fact based on suggestion; the Royal Commissions which had rejected the theory of animal magnetism acknowledged the power of the

imagination and a number of the early French mesmerists anticipated Braid's theories.[13] After Braid, this became the accepted
interpretation of hypnosis, although belief in some kind of a vital
fluid died hard.[14]

Braid's work, however, attracted little attention in Britain and
it was the French, taking their cue this time from Braid rather
than Mesmer, who once again became the leaders in the field. The
first of these French pioneers was a Dr Azam, a Bordeaux surgeon,
an account of whose experiments appears in the *Archives de
Médecine* for 1860. Soon after, Liébault, a humble and much
beloved country doctor who, in 1864, settled at Nancy, began
using hypnotism as an aid in general practice. Then in 1882 he
was joined by Bernheim, a professor of the Medical School at
Nancy, who, though at first sceptical and incredulous, was won
round when Liébault cured a patient of his who suffered from a
specially recalcitrant case of sciatica. As a result, the clinic at Nancy
soon became the acknowledged centre for hypnotic therapy in
Europe. At roughly the same time, Charcot, perhaps the most
powerful figure in French medicine at that period,[15] began using
hypnotism in connection with his researches on hysteria at the
Salpêtrière. There is a certain irony in the fact that although
Charcot, thanks to his enormous prestige, did more than any one
before him to reconcile the medical profession to the practice of
hypnotism, he quite misunderstood its nature. Finding that he
could produce in the hypnotised person the various symptoms which
he had observed in his hysterics, he developed a theory according
to which hypnosis was to be regarded as a kind of artificial hysteria
or, alternatively, hysteria was to be thought of as a kind of natural
hypnosis.[16] Although the school of Nancy, with its vastly greater
experience of applying hypnotism, had no difficulty demolishing
this theory, Charcot's name insured for it a wide currency. Charcot
was no less mistaken about the nature of hysteria itself, which he
attributed primarily to an inherited weakness in the patient's nervous system. Historically, however, he was of the first importance.
Both Janet and Binet were trained under him and it was to him
that Freud went, in 1885, at a critical moment in his career.

Psychoanalysis, the first psychological system in which the unconscious plays a central role, began, one can say, when Freud, finding
that some of his patients were resistant to hypnosis, decided to
abandon hypnotism, as a means for recovering their buried

memories, in favour of 'free association'. But Freud always acknowledged the importance of hypnotism in revealing those unconscious forces which he believed to lurk within each individual. He was specially impressed with Bernheim's demonstrations of the phenomenon of 'post-hypnotic suggestion' which he witnessed when, to improve his own hypnotic technique, he made the pilgrimage to Nancy in 1889.[17] In fact he often mentions post-hypnotic suggestion as the paradigm case of an idea that is at once dynamic and unconscious, for the subject, following suggested amnesia, can no longer recall in the waking state what the hypnotist suggested to him during the trance state; when, therefore, at some pre-arranged signal, he finds himself carrying out some pointless action, he cannot know the real reason and, if challenged, will invent some more or less plausible pretext or 'rationalisation'. Freud thought that the typical hysteric behaves very much like the victim of a post-hypnotic suggestion inasmuch as he too remains unaware of his true motive. The distinction is that, in the case of the hysteric, the true motive is repressed because it is too subversive or embarrassing to admit to consciousness.

It was as a contribution to medical psychology that depth psychology first took shape and, but for the genius of Freud, it might never have gone beyond this; but gradually out of the welter of assorted hypnotic and pathological phenomena that came to light in the course of the 19th century in the wake of mesmerism, a new conception of human personality began to emerge. The classic Cartesian picture of an indivisible conscious self or soul, executing its will by manipulating the machinery of the nervous system, began to give way to the less flattering picture of a person as the more or less precarious resolution of a multitude of conflicting thoughts and impulses, most of which never enter consciousness at all. A whole new range of phenomena from automatic writing to full-blown secondary personalities gave substance to the idea of an active underground mental life. The relationship between hypnotism and the unconscious is one that must not be misunderstood. When a person is hypnotised he does not thereby become unconscious. What happens is that his consciousness or, more specifically, his attention becomes abnormally restricted and selective. It is as if his whole mind had become rigidly compartmentalised so that his cognitive processes function without access to their normal sources of information. Hence the singular lack of critical intelligence which, in the normal waking state, serves as a counter-poise to external suggestions. In hypnosis, the hypnotist's words are immediately translated into a subjective reality.[18] In this condition it becomes comparatively easy to produce phenomena such as automatic writing, where the subject watches his hand as it writes meaningful messages while remaining ignorant of their content, or to produce negative hallucinations with respect to some designated object or person. The paradox of the negative hallucination, like that of 'perceptual defence' in subliminal perception, is that there must be unconscious recognition in order for there to be conscious non-recognition![19]

It took some time, however, before the implications of these abnormal phenomena began to penetrate academic psychology. This is well illustrated in the case of William James who, more than most thinkers of his generation, was open to ideas from the most varied sources. Thus, when he was writing his great textbook *The Principles* of 1890, he deployed all his literary skill to pour ridicule on the idea of unconscious mental states which he castigates as 'the sovereign means for believing what one likes in psychology and of turning what might become a science into a tumbling-ground for whimsies'. [James (1890) Vol. I, p. 163] After listing ten so-called proofs for the existence of unconscious ideas together with his own rebuttal to each one, he concludes: 'None of these facts appealed to so confidently in proof of the existence of ideas in an unconscious state prove anything of the sort. They prove either that conscious ideas were present which next instant were forgotten; or they prove that certain results, similar to the results of reasoning, may be wrought out by brain processes to which ideation is attached.' James remained unmoved by the writings of von Hartmann, that encyclopedic German protagonist of the unconscious;[20] 'Hartmann', he roundly declares, 'fairly boxes the compass of the universe with the principle of unconscious thought. For him there is no nameable thing that does not exemplify it. But his logic is so lax and his failure to consider the most obvious alternative so complete that it would, on the whole, be a waste of time to look at his argument in detail. The same is true of Schopenhauer in whom the mythology reaches its climax.' [*idem* p. 169]

And yet, barely ten years later, when he comes to deliver his celebrated Gifford lectures at Edinburgh on 'Varieties of Religious

Experience' he performs a complete *volte-face* on this question. He now declares that the conception of 'an underground mental life' is the most important advance in psychology since he was a student; that, moreover, unlike previous advances, it has 'revealed an entirely unsuspected peculiarity in the constitution of human nature'. 'Hereafter,' he resolves, 'whenever we meet with the phenomenon of automatism, be it motor impulse or obsessive idea or unaccountable caprice or delusion or hallucination, we are bound, first of all, to make search whether it be an explosion into the fields of ordinary consciousness of ideas elaborated outside those fields in subliminal regions of the mind. We should look, therefore, for its source in the subject's subconscious life.' [James (1960) Lect. 10] What, one may ask, had brought about this change of outlook during the intervening years that put James, too, among the prophets? For it is abundantly clear from the *Principles* that James had followed closely the developments in hypnotism and was fully *au fait* with the work of Charcot and of Janet on hysteria. I suggest that, after completing the *Principles*, James, who was always as much philosopher as psychologist, began to lose interest in straightforward experimental, physiological psychology and was all agog to explore some of the more mysterious and imponderable aspects of the human psyche. He was impressed when Breuer and Freud published their *Studies in Hysteria* in 1895, and during the 1890s his long-standing interest in psychical research intensified.[21]

His friendship with Frederick Myers, the foremost pioneer of psychical research in Britain, contributed to this enthusiasm. Since about 1892 Myers had been putting forward his own theories on what he called the 'Subliminal Self'. He uses this somewhat nebulous concept to try and make intelligible a range of phenomena from the pathological to the supernormal, from hypnosis and hysteria to mediumship, ecstasy and the manifestations of genius.[22] James was also in close touch with the Swiss psychologist Theodore Flournoy who, in 1891, had been appointed to a Chair of Experimental Psychology at the University of Geneva. Flournoy was interested in a medium known to the literature as 'Hélène Smith' who, in the trance state, would produce vivid reincarnationist fantasies about her previous lives. Her material, unlike that of Mrs Piper, the celebrated Boston medium whom James himself first investigated in 1885, is of dubious value as evidence of paranormal knowledge but it provided a graphic illustration of the astonishing inventiveness of the unconscious mind.[23] Thus it was not, after all, surprising that, by the time he came to write his 'Varieties of Religious Experience', James was a firm believer in unconscious mental life.

Yet, by no means all his contemporaries agreed with James. Hugo Münsterberg, James's colleague at Harvard whom he had himself brought over from Germany in 1892 to run the laboratory for him, distinguishes three interpretations of so-called 'subconscious phenomena' then current[24]: (1) that they are the manifestations of a complete mind existing in parallel below the mind of the primary self or personality; (2) that they are fragments of the primary personality split off or 'dissociated' from the main stream of thought and persisting in a sort of artificial limbo; and (3) that, in common with the processes underlying normal psychological functions, e.g. memory, attention, etc., they are not mental at all but purely physical. Each of these alternatives, Münsterberg suggested, appealed to a different approach: the first to the 'emotional demands of the mystic' (no doubt he had Myers here in mind); the second to 'the practical demands of the physician' (here, presumably, he was thinking of Janet who taught that hysteria was the disintegration of the personality in an organism too feeble to maintain its psychic unity);[25] the third was more consonant with the 'theoretical demands of the psychologist'. On the whole, Münsterberg himself preferred this last interpretation to the others.

The intriguing possibility implied by the first and second of these three interpretations, namely that the subconscious might not be unconscious at all in the literal sense, but merely inaccessible to the primary consciousness, was one explicitly advocated by the American psychiatrist Boris Sidis who saw nothing amiss in the concept of a 'subconscious consciousness' or 'co-consciousness'. On such a view our unconscious thoughts would exist rather like dreams that are never subsequently recalled, except that they would run parallel with our conscious thoughts whereas dreams occur when the mind is not otherwise engaged. The bizarre cases of multiple personality that were being brought to the attention of the medical world at that time lent substance to this conception, especially when one personality would claim knowledge of the other's thoughts but not *vice versa*![26] To Freud, however, the whole idea of a consciousness that did not belong to any identifiable individual seemed even more far-fetched than the idea of unconscious mental events which it was designed to eliminate.[27] In the end, most students of the unconscious have sided with Freud on this point. Ironically, Münsterberg omitted the one interpretation which, thanks to Freud, eventually prevailed: that of a subconscious which was neither 'psychical' (conscious) nor 'physical', but a pure theoretical construct of psychological science.

The Impact of Freud

If one could feed into a computer the entire output of world literature for this century and get it to count every occasion where a psychological scientist, of whatever kind, received a mention it would, I am convinced, count more references to Freud than to all the other names put together. The first difficulty one has in discussing Freud is that virtually nothing has been left unsaid. He looms so large in the cultural history of our time, his work has generated such a superabundance of commentary and controversy, one is at a loss to know where to start. Moreover, Freud was himself a fluent and prolific expositor of his own ideas[28] and, in his disciple Jones, he was fortunate in having a dedicated and painstaking biographer. [see Jones (1953/55)] Accordingly, I shall make no attempt to present even a condensed account of Freud's theories, I shall take for granted some degree of familiarity and, for the rest, I must refer the reader to the many excellent brief introductions that are currently available.[29] Instead I propose to consider the question of what *kind* of a science it was which Freud created and to which he gave the name 'psychoanalysis'.

Perhaps the first thing to be said in this connection is that an evaluation of the man does not, in this instance, rest upon an evaluation of his work. By this I mean that Freud's greatness—and it was such that he would have to be considered for a place in any list of the hundred most eminent men of history—does not depend upon the truth or falsity of what he taught. In this respect he differs from the other key figures of the history of science with whom he is sometimes compared. For, in science, however much a man's discoveries may be superseded or his theories rendered obsolete, his importance is bound up with the claim that he was instrumental in enlarging the boundaries of knowledge. In philosophy or religion, on the other hand, where mutually contradictory systems of thought of equal historical importance can flourish alongside one another, an individual's importance is assessed rather by the extent or depth of his influence. For example, no serious historian of philosophy could dismiss Hegel on the grounds that Hegel's doctrines were fallacious. From this point of view Freud can more readily be compared with Hegel than with Darwin, however often he may have been acclaimed by his admirers as the Darwin of modern psychology. With Freud there can be no doubt that one is confronted with a thinker of the first magnitude, original, profound, imaginative, daring; but, equally, there appears to be no prospect of arriving at any consensus as to how much truth there is in what he had to say.[30]

Yet that this should be so is ironic since, to his followers, what distinguished Freud from earlier thinkers who likewise proposed radically new conceptions of human nature, like Schopenhauer, Kierkegaard, Nietzsche, and so on, was, precisely, that Freud's views were securely based on scientific observation. For Freud, we must remember, spent his entire working life within the ambit of medicine, as the inventor and practitioner of a particular technique of psychotherapy. One might suppose, therefore, that his theories would no longer be a matter of philosophical debate but would by now have proved themselves in practice. Of course, the success of psychoanalysis as a therapy could not guarantee its validity as a theory, any more than the very real successes obtained by the mesmerists guaranteed the truth of the fluidic theory. But it would at any rate have been a beginning; the pragmatic test is not one that can be lightly set aside in science. Unfortunately, all attempts so far to validate the therapeutic efficacy of psychoanalysis have failed. Freud, himself, never even realised that any such validation was required. He took it for granted that the physician was in the best position to know whether the patient benefited from his treatment or not. In this, he was no different from any other medical man of his day; it is only recently that we have become sophisticated about such matters. We now accept it as axiomatic that one and the same person cannot both apply the treatment and be the judge of its success and that success itself can be assessed only in relation to some control group who have *not* undergone the treatment, and that this holds good whether the treatment in question is physical or psychological. And yet we still find psychoanalysts even now echoing Freud's plea that only the trained analyst operat-

ing in the therapeutic situation is competent to decide the validity
of psychoanalysis either as a theory or as a therapy.[31]

When eventually objective methods of assessment *were* applied
to psychoanalysis and to psychotherapy generally the results were
shattering. Surveys carried out in the United States following the
Second World War enabled comparisons to be made between the
rate of recovery for patients undergoing psychoanalysis, for patients
undergoing psychotherapy of an eclectic kind and for patients
receiving no form of psychotherapy at all. The latter, consisting
of persons diagnosed as severely neurotic and as such eligible for
sickness benefits, provided the necessary baseline control; apart
from visits to their GP for drugs, sedatives, etc., they received no
therapy. From these surveys it transpired that for *each* of these
three categories the recovery rate, after about two years, was around
two in three while, after five years, some 90 per cent of the control
group had recovered sufficiently, without benefit of therapy, to be
able to resume work.[32]

Now, obviously, there was plenty of scope here for argument
about the adequacy of the criteria used either for the diagnosis of
the patient or for the assessment of his recovery. The point is, however, that as the first objective evidence of its kind it presented
a challenge which could only be met by appropriate counter-
evidence. Yet, so far as I have been able to ascertain, no such
counter-evidence has been forthcoming. Indeed, when the American
Psychoanalytic Association undertook their own survey, presumably
with this object in mind, their findings were so unfavourable that
the facts were withheld from publication.[33] What happened next
can best be described as a strategic retreat. The whole concept of
what we mean by a 'cure' in this context was called into question
by the advocates of psychotherapy. It now appeared that we were
mistaken all along in thinking that psychoanalysis was concerned
with anything as crude as the mere removal of symptoms. That
was in any case better left to such newer techniques as behaviour
therapy, psychosurgery or psychopharmacology. What psychoanalysis should be doing was helping the patient gain a better
understanding of himself, or of his situation, so that he might lead
a fuller, more satisfying life. Indeed, as Storr [1966] reminds us,
those who visit a psychoanalyst are not necessarily ill, in any
definable sense, they are just ordinary people who happen to be
going through a period of emotional distress. But, if they are not

sick to start with, in what sense can they be cured?[34]

Now I think it would be wrong to regard such a view of psychoanalysis as nothing more than a desperate last-ditch stand. It is not, of course, the original Freudian view. Freud was certainly cautious not to claim too much, he even declared once that he was content if he could convert a case of hysterical misery into one of common unhappiness,[35] but his patients came to him because they were suffering from bizarre and often incapacitating disabilities. Nevertheless, self-knowledge is itself a laudable ideal and has always been one of the principal goals of practical philosophy, so if psychoanalysis can contribute something towards it, that would be an achievement deserving of our respect and gratitude. The point I want to make here, however, is that once we drop the question of a 'cure' in any objective sense we remove one of the main props upon which psychoanalysis has rested its claim to be a testable scientific theory; especially as the self-knowledge or insight which the analysand is reputed to acquire as the result of analysis tends, in practice, to be equated with his acceptance of the interpretations of his troubles suggested to him by his analyst.

Even if we cannot expect to validate psychoanalysis in terms of its therapeutic effects, it has, fortunately, implications that extend far beyond the clinic. From the very beginning, Freud was groping towards a general model of the mind and a general theory of personality development. Indeed, had this not been so, had he not come to view the neurotic as displaying in exaggerated form what is latent in all of us, his theories would be of no greater interest to us now than those of any other psychiatrist. But, in the end, Freud came to attach more importance to psychoanalysis as a contribution to general psychology than as a clinical technique. Eventually, from the late 1930s, attempts were made, mainly on the initiative of academic psychologists, to bring about a rapprochement between psychoanalysis, which up to that time had developed in isolation, and mainstream psychology.[36] Experimentalists in search of hypotheses began to discover in the Freudian corpus a veritable mine of inspiration. Three aspects of the theory were seized upon as specially suited to empirical investigation: (1) its assumptions about child behaviour at certain critical ages; (2) its postulation of certain peculiar syndromes such as the so-called 'oral character' and 'anal character'; and (3) its hypotheses about the ways in which we deal with unwelcome information by means of such mental mechanisms as 'repression', 'projection', 'reaction-formation' and so on. In addition, experimental analogues of the various psycho-analytic concepts were devised so as to enable tests to be carried out on animals.

The outcome of all this work was, however, inconclusive.[37] With respect to (1) above, systematic observations on representative samples of young children failed to uphold some of the generalisa-tions to which Freud was heavily committed on the basis of his own clinical experience. No evidence, for example, was forthcoming in either children or adults of a preference for the parent of the opposite sex, as would seem to be implied in the concept of the 'Oedipus complex'. Nor was there any sign of the supposed 'penis envy' in small girls. With respect to (2), some evidence was indeed forthcoming, based on statistical analysis of personality test data, that the 'oral' and 'anal' character did correspond to identifiable constellations of traits but it was much more dubious whether these bore any causal relationship to, respectively, breast feeding and toilet training experiences in infancy.[38] Evidence on (3), the defence mechanisms, was mixed. Some positive claims were put forward but were not always corroborated by later workers, but, at any rate with regard to repression—the most vital of them from the psycho-analytic point of view—a fair amount of data was amassed which appeared to demonstrate the reality of the phenomenon, especially in connection with the 'perceptual defence' hypothesis.[39] Finally, the animal studies showed that there were points of contact between psychoanalysis and behaviourism.

Now the fact that this evidence was inconclusive did not detract from the importance of the theory; it is indeed just what one would have expected, given its speculative nature and intuitive origins. What did, however, begin to raise serious doubts about its scientific status was the indifference with which the evidence was greeted. When the findings were positive they were sometimes mentioned by psychoanalysts intent on showing that Freud had been right all along; where the findings were negative they were dismissed as based on a misunderstanding of the theory. And, of course, it was easy to see that the possibility of psychoanalytic con-cepts or hypotheses being misconstrued was, in the nature of the case, a very real one, especially where these were extended to the field of animal behaviour. Nevertheless this was objective evidence of a sort, and to dismiss it all as irrelevant without offering more suitable hypotheses was tantamount to admitting that no external validation of the theory was possible.

The consequence of this refusal to submit to the normal canons of scientific criticism was to render psychoanalysis defenceless in the face of the schisms and secessions which in due course assailed it. Ultimately, Freud could deal with heretics in the only way that is open to proponents of doctrinaire beliefs: by excommunication. It is not, as has sometimes been insinuated, that Freud was by nature authoritarian, or that his disciples were a band of peculiarly quarrelsome, vain or egotistical individuals. Freud could, with some justification, claim that psychoanalysis was never intended to be a 'system' in the sense in which he feared that both Adler and Jung were trying to make it one. Nor was he being disingenuous when he maintained that his theory was 'incomplete and subject to constant alteration'.[40] His polemics are, for the most part, restrained; at any rate he never descends to the level of denunciation and vulgar abuse to which both Marx and Lenin habitually resorted whenever they were confronted with a deviationist. Nevertheless, the logic of his situation was no different from theirs; he too wanted to maintain the purity of his doctrine even if this meant splitting the movement.[41] The doctrine was, after all, his brain-child and his alone. He had brought it into being during the lonely years between the time that he broke with Breuer in 1894 and the time he began to gather around himself a small following in about 1901 or 1902. When he published his *Interpretation of Dreams* in 1900, which he thereafter regarded as his most important book, all the main principles of psychoanalysis were already in evidence.[42] Yet neither Freud's authority as founder nor his acknowledged intellectual pre-eminence sufficed to prevent the emergence of rival doctrines.

The first serious breach occurred, it would seem, over the position which Freud assigned to sex in his psychology. His obsession with the sexual motive to the virtual exclusion of all other motives is one of the more puzzling aspects of Freud's thought. Various explanations have been suggested. It has been pointed out that, in his time at least, sex was the principal target for repressions and was thus bound to figure prominently in the aetiology of the neuroses. Or, adopting a more *ad hominem* approach, it has been seen as a reflection of Freud's inverted puritanism[43] or as an example of an almost Marxian glee in exposing our illusions and unmasking our hypocrisies. For my part, I think it is best understood as a case of 19th century 'scientism'. Freud sincerely believed that by insisting on the sexual motive he was making psychology scientific in just the same way as Marx believed that by insisting on the economic motive he was making socialism scientific. We must remember that, as a pupil of Brücke, Freud was reared in the strictest mechanistic school of biology associated with Helmholtz. This influence is very noticeable in his earliest theorising with its psychic determinism, its conservation of excitation, its dynamics of cathexis and discharge, etc. But, once having cut himself adrift and invented a new science and, indeed, a new way of doing science, he was apprehensive that he might lose all contact with reality. By continually stressing the sexual basis of behaviour he felt that he could still retain a firm foothold in biology.[44] And, in the event, his apprehensions were not so ill-founded. The first schismatics, having jettisoned the 'dogma of sex',[45] took psychoanalysis even further from the realm of science and into the realms of ideology and of a new secular religion: a move utterly abhorrent to someone of Freud's austere intellect and temperament.

The first to rebel was Alfred Adler, whose defection occurred shortly after the founding of the International Psychoanalytic Association in 1910. He saw life as a struggle for power rather than a search for sensuous gratification and had little use either for instinct theory or even for the unconscious. He brought psycho-analysis closer to commonsense and to that extent widened its appeal but, as a theorist, he was lightweight as compared with Jung and he never acquired the same following or prestige. By the time he died in 1937 (two years before Freud) his school of 'Individual Psychology' had virtually ceased to exist. Yet in the long run his influence on the movement as a whole was greater than that of Jung, perhaps because he never diverged quite as far from the master. The rise of 'ego theory' in modern psychoanalysis [cf. Hartmann (1959)], with its emphasis on the role of the active self as opposed to the unconscious forces of the 'id', has been traced to the challenge presented in the first instance by Adlerianism.

By the time the Fourth International Congress met in Munich in 1913, Jung, the first president of the International Association, had reached the point of no return. Jung, more of a visionary and less of a scientist than Freud, was never as much concerned about the scientific status of psychoanalysis. What fascinated him in

Freud's teachings was the capacity they had demonstrated for the mind to express itself through symbols. In the end he came to regard the unconscious as a great reservoir of all the myths and 'archetypes' of the human race. What he resented in Freud was the latter's preoccupation with man's animal nature. The system which he himself developed as its antithesis has been described as a sort of sublimated Freudianism in which spiritual entities and processes do duty for erotic ones. At any rate it is concerned less with repressed conflicts than with the patient's outlook on life. The ultimate aim of therapy, as Jung saw it, was to help the patient find a faith by which to live.[46] If it was necessary for this faith to express itself in traditional religious form it was no business of the analyst to disabuse him of it. Jung's own writings, of which the most important is his book *Psychological Types* of 1921, are replete with recondite allusions to literature and history and have had a very powerful appeal to many who prefer to approach psychology through the humanities rather than through the sciences.

Further rifts in the movement started appearing soon after the First World War and since then innumerable variations on the theme of psychoanalysis have competed for attention.[47] However, one can say, in broad terms, adapting political terminology, that the movement has had two main wings: a right wing typified by the Jungians and a left wing exemplified first by Adler[48] and then culminating in the neo-Freudians of America. While the right wing endeavoured to relate the patient's problems to certain eternal aspects of the human psyche, the left wing sought to relate them to his life situation and to society generally. This left wing approach became specially prominent after the centre of gravity of the psycho-analytic movement had shifted to the United States following the rise of Hitler.[49] Lately a 'New Left' deviation has emerged in the 'existentialist' school of 'anti-psychiatry' associated with R. D. Laing, with its outspoken attack on the family as an institution.

In addition to the two main wings there was also a small centre party of what might be called 'ultra-Freudians'. It flourished mainly in Britain under the leadership of Melanie Klein, a pioneer of child analysis. Unlike the neo-Freudians, who saw neurosis as a social problem, the Kleinians insisted on going even further back into the patient's past than Freud has done: to the very first few months of life, or rather, to be more accurate, to the fantasies which the patient was presumed to have suffered from during that phase of his existence. Yet in spite of these inherently divisive trends in psychoanalysis, there are signs, latterly, that some degree of ecumenicism is gaining ground over sectarianism. Most practising analysts these days, it would be safe to say, are more or less eclectic. The pure Freudian has become something of a rarity and the neo-Freudian has never been as exclusive.

Such, then, very briefly, has been the history of the psychoanalytic movement; what now of its prospects? From all that has been said so far these must seem uncertain. We have seen the variety of theories that have sprung up in its wake, all, it would seem, equally arbitrary and untestable, and we have seen the even greater variety of practical techniques to which they have given rise, not one of which is definitely known to be effective. We have seen, moreover, how attempts to integrate these findings into the main body of scientific knowledge have so far proved abortive and how the movement developed encapsulated in its own ideas, which it expressed in its own luxuriant and esoteric jargon, to an extent far exceeding that of any other school of psychology. I want now, however, in fairness, to suggest that it did nevertheless produce at least three ideas of great power and generality which are likely to retain a permanent place in any future psychological science. These ideas, to which we have already alluded in passing, are: (1) the idea of behaviour as something requiring interpretation; (2) the idea, to borrow the stock Wordsworthian cliché, of the 'child as father of the man'; and (3) the idea of sexuality as an all-pervasive factor in human life. The fact that for Freud all three ideas belonged together within a coherent structure does not mean that we cannot ask whether they possess a validity that transcends the use to which he put them. Let us now, therefore, examine each of them in turn.

The first of them is, I believe, at once the most distinctive and the most valuable. That we do, on occasion, express more in our behaviour than we intend is something which no doubt was always common knowledge to shrewd observers of the human scene. Freud, however, carried the logic of interpretation further than anyone previously had ever ventured to go and, in so doing, revealed a whole new symbolism through which we contrive to express, in word, in thought or in deed, wishes, beliefs, attitudes which, though our own, we do not recognise as such. In particular, Freud extended the application of this logic to activities which would otherwise be deemed accidental, involuntary or meaningless: to dreams, to unguarded slips of the tongue and lapses of memory, and, of course, to symptoms of all sorts. It is, indeed, impossible to read Freud's own works, especially his early case studies, his *Interpretation of Dreams* of 1900 or his *Psychopathology of Everyday Life* of 1901, without recognising that he was himself a virtuoso at this art of interpretation even if, like so many virtuosi, he at times appears to overdo it, finding meanings within meanings and piling one cryptic allusion upon another.

It is now no longer necessary to accept Freud's rash generalisation to the effect that *all* dreams, when suitably interpreted, turn out to be wish-fulfilments in disguise in order to acknowledge that *some* dreams, properly decoded, tell us something important about the individual's state of mind. Thanks to the new physiological techniques now available for monitoring sleep, sleep research has, over the past two decades, become one of the most flourishing areas of psychophysiological research. As a result, the topic of dreams has once again come to the fore in current psychological controversy, but no longer as the preserve of clinical psychologists and psychoanalysts. For the first time we now have available representative samples of dreams reported immediately on waking and these have shown how selective were the dreams discussed by analysts and others intent upon proving a theory. On the general question, however, as to whether dreams are meaningful or meaningless, two schools of thought are to be found in the literature. The one, which adopts a more physiological orientation, regards dreaming as nothing more than the mental concomitant of that special brain-state which researchers call 'paradoxical sleep' and denies that dreams, as such, have any ulterior significance in their own right. The other, which takes a more psychological stance, argues that dreaming provides, as Freud believed, a safety valve or outlet through which we can express our current anxieties in an innocuous form and work through the emotional problems that are worrying us. Which of these schools will ultimately prevail, or whether some compromise formula will be found, remains to be seen.[50]

To some among Freud's latter-day followers, especially to those who have come under the influence of Existentialist philosophy, interpretation has survived as the be-all and end-all of analysis. They regard Freud's attempt to construct a quasi-mechanical model of the mind as misconceived and hold that psychoanalysis is better understood as a semantic rather than a causal theory of behaviour. On this view the function of the analyst is to act as an interpreter so that the patient can make sense of what he himself is unconsciously trying to say.[51] One attraction of this new approach is that it gets round the vexed problem of validation. One interpretation of behaviour is accepted as more convincing than another, just as one interpretation of an historical event or of a literary text may be accepted in preference to another even though there can be no question of proving that one is right and another wrong. Psychoanalysis then becomes an activity closer to that of the historian or the literary critic than to that of the experimental psychologist and it is perhaps significant that its greatest impact has, on the whole, been among philosophers and students of the humanities and the social sciences. [cf. Miller, J. (ed.) (1972)]

This is, however, only one view and perhaps an extreme one. To Freud himself, interpretation, however necessary, was never more than the first step towards explanation. And it was in pursuit of such explanation that he turned repeatedly to the events of early childhood. Previously, it would have seemed paradoxical to try and explain adult behaviour by reference to events belonging to a period of life of which we no longer retain any conscious recollection, but it is one of the achievements of depth psychology that this idea no longer seems to us far-fetched. Freud, at any rate, came to the conclusion that all through life we go on echoing or recapitulating the experiences and situations of the first critical years in various forms. In particular, in our choice of a love object, in our relationships with others, even in our choice of a career, we constantly hark back without realising it to our nursery and to the way we interacted there with parents or siblings. And of all the many facets of Freudianism this is perhaps the one that has received the most empirical support. Some of this has come from studies of children, some of it from the primate laboratory. In particular, the long-term effects of maternal deprivation has received a great deal of attention since 1951 following publication of the report which the English psychiatrist John Bowlby prepared for the World Health Organisation.[52] Of the animal studies, by far the best known and most impressive are the experiments of Harlow on the effects of maternal and social deprivation in infancy on the Rhesus monkey.[53]

In the course of reverting to the patient's childhood, Freud at first was puzzled as to why so often this disclosed a scene of seduction or sexual assault by some older person, usually, in the case of his female patients, by their father. In the end it dawned on him that these were not recollections of any actual events at all but rather the resuscitation of childhood fantasies.[54] From this he concluded that children no less than adults must be capable of sexual emotions and appetites. In his *Three Essays on Sexuality* of 1905 (the only one of his books, apart from the *Interpretation of Dreams*, to which he attached sufficient importance to revise through several successive editions) he expounds his theory of the development of the sex instinct from birth to maturity and introduces to the world such concepts as the 'erogenous zones' of the body and coins such expressions as 'polymorphous pervert' to describe the sexual behaviour of the infant. No other theory of his, one may add, earned him so much notoriety!

Few aspects of social life can have changed so radically since Freud's day as our attitude to sex—it is even hard for us to grasp why his contemporaries were so surprised and shocked. But, if so, this is in no small measure due to Freud himself. There had, of course, been other medical men before him—Krafft-Ebing, Magnus Hirschfield, Havelock Ellis—who, through their encyclopedic sexology, had promoted a more objective approach to sexual behaviour, but no one had ever before elevated sex to such a position of prominence and centrality in human affairs. Indeed, in spite of his repudiation of the charge of 'pan-sexualism', there were in fact very few mental processes or behavioural activities to which Freud did not at some time or another succeed in attaching some kind of a sexual connotation. It was in this respect that his theory of human motivation differs so strikingly from all earlier doctrines of hedonism. Ironically, he was ill-suited to the role of sexual liberator in which history had cast him. He was scrupulously conventional in his own private life and was much more interested in sex as a source of pathological fixations and deviations than in its life-enhancing properties. There is little in common between him and such prophets of the sexual revolution as D. H. Lawrence or his own eccentric erstwhile disciple Wilhelm Reich, both of whom openly took the side of the instincts against the forces of repression represented by the super-ego or by society.[55] Freud, on the contrary, believed that a certain amount of sexual renunciation was the price we had to pay for civilisation. [*see* Freud (1930)]

*   *   *

To many thoughtful contemporary scientists, the defects of psycho-analysis or of any other equivalent system of depth psychology are so gross from the scientific standpoint that they have already consigned it to the scrap-heap of history as an intellectual aber-ration of monumental proportions.[56] For my part, I consider such an outright rejection unwarranted. The day may come when we can pronounce the epitaph on depth psychology but that day will dawn only when we have something much superior to put in its place. At present I know of no approach which can cover the same range of phenomena with anything like the same conviction. In particular, when we come across some grossly irrational, absurd, self-destructive or self-defeating behaviour (James's 'unaccountable caprice or delusion') on the part of someone whom we would other-wise regard as normal and rational (and this is not uncommon), I still find it far more plausible and profitable to think in terms of some depth-dynamic explanation than to appeal to 'faulty con-ditioning' or 'maladaptive learning', as the behaviour therapists would now have us do.

Summary

The Unconscious

Does psychology require us to postulate 'unconscious states of mind'? The entire Empiricist tradition in European philosophy from Descartes to Russell militated against it on the grounds that while a state of the brain could be unconscious, a state of mind was, by definition, conscious. The rise of the concept was part of the legacy of the Romantic movement with its strong anti-rational, anti-intellectual bias. The eventual emergence of a depth psycho-logy at the end of the 19th century, i.e. of a psychology centred upon the concept of the unconscious, was due to three closely interwoven developments: (a) the progress of hypnotism which Charcot had at last made respectable in medical quarters, (b) the growing rapprochement between medical and academic psychology, and (c) the advent of psychical research with its studies of mediumship. The history of hypnotism is here outlined from Mesmer to Freud and its contribution to the overthrow of the Cartesian conception of man as a self-conscious, rational being is here discussed. Finally it is argued that there are no *a priori* grounds for rejecting the unconscious as a theoretical construct in science, though its continued usefulness is likely to remain bound up with the future of Freudian and kindred ideas.

The Impact of Freud

Psychoanalysis is the brain-child of a single man of genius. The cornerstones of the doctrine are (1) the supremacy of unconscious thoughts and wishes in the determination of behaviour, (2) the prepotency of the sex instinct in mental life, (3) the primacy of early infantile experiences in the formation of the mature personality, and (4) the sexual aetiology of the neuroses and psychoses. Apart from its obvious influence on clinical psychology, which provided the primary testing ground and field of application for the theory, its influence on Western culture generally was extensive. However, a science, unlike a philosophical system, a religion or an ideology, cannot rest solely on the insights of its founder no matter how great he may be, and the trouble with psychoanalysis was its failure to submit its propositions to the arbitrament of statistical and experimental validation. Consequently when faced with schismatics Freud was powerless to prevent the limitless proliferation of rival systems and had only his own authority to fall back on. Attempts by independent researchers to test Freudian hypotheses yielded at most equivocal results. Hence, although many contemporary psychologists believe that there is much truth in psychoanalytic ideas generally, the question whether psychoanalysis qualifies as a science or a pesudo-science is one that has never been resolved.

Notes

1   Consider the following statement by the eminent physiologist Arturo Rosenblueth (with whom Norbert Wiener once collabo-

rated and to whom he dedicated his *Cybernetics* of 1948): 'Since I define "mental processes" as the conscious experiences of which someone is aware, the concept of "unconscious mental processes" is, in my opinion, an unacceptable contradiction in terms. This contradiction might be eliminated by adopting a different *ad hoc* definition for mental processes. I personally think, however, that it is not possible to formulate any definition of the unconscious that will be operationally meaningful and I do not believe that the concept of the unconscious explains or clarifies any of the problems in which it has been used.' [Rosenblueth (1970) p. 92] Rosenblueth takes as a case in point the use of the unconscious to explain the sudden insights of the problem solver but decides that even here it is better to appeal to 'the physical determinism which holds for nervous aggregates' than invoke the 'cumbersome and spurious ghost or demon of the unconscious mind'.

This is a view that has been repeatedly urged, at least since the physiologist W. B. Carpenter, in 1853, coined the expression 'unconscious cerebration'. The following passage, written by Galton in 1879, is quoted by Reeves [1969]: 'The more I have examined the workings of my own mind ... the less respect I feel for the part played by consciousness. The unconscious operations of the mind frequently far transcend the conscious ones in intellectual importance. Sudden inspirations and those flashings out of results which cost a great deal of conscious effort to ordinary people, but are the natural outcome of what is known as genius, are undoubted products of *unconscious cerebration* ... Consciousness seems to do little more than attest the fact that the various organs of the brain do not work with perfect ease or cooperation. Its position seems to be that of a spectator of but a minute fraction of *automatic brain work*' (my italics).

2 The remark is quoted by L. L. Whyte in his useful treatise *The Unconscious Before Freud*. [Whyte (1960) p. 169] Whyte takes Freud to task for exaggerating his own originality: 'It cannot be disputed that, by 1870-1880, the general conception of the unconscious mind was a European commonplace and that many applications of this general idea had been vigorously discussed for several decades.' I suspect that Whyte has here let himself be carried away by his many enticing *trouvailles* among the pre-Freudians of the 19th century. No doubt the word 'unconscious' crops up in many

different places, but either it is used in some quite vague sense or else it was used as Galton or Carpenter used it to refer to activities of the nervous system which do not, though they conceivably could, become conscious. It was only after Freud abandoned the attempt to physiologise his theory of mind, as represented by his abortive 'Project for a Scientific Psychology' of 1895, that he, and psychology with him, was forced to come to grips with the unconscious as a necessary postulate.

3 Russell, the last great representative of classical Empiricism, defined the 'mental' as that with which we are directly or non-inferentially acquainted, see his 'Mind and Matter'. [Russell (1948) Part II, Chap. 7]

4 See Dixon [1971]. Dixon was able to show, among other effects, that when subjects were required to guess at words presented well below recognition threshold they tended to respond with associated words more often than could be attributed to chance. The response words were semantically rather than structurally related to the stimulus words and they frequently involved symbolism of a distinctly Freudian character.

5 Whyte [1960] traces the origins of *Naturphilosophie* to such German writers of the late 18th-early 19th centuries as Hamann, Herder, Goethe and Schelling. Sir Isaiah Berlin, in his broadcast lecture series 'Some Sources of Romanticism', suggests a possible political reason why Romanticism flourished on German soil: in reacting against the political domination of France, as represented by Napoleon, the Germans rejected also the philosophy of the Enlightenment which they associated with the hated French.

6 It was Spinoza, as romanticised by Goethe, who was influential during this period rather than the original austere metaphysician. The 'conatus' was Spinoza's term for the tendency of each individual to persist in its own being (its instinct of self-preservation, as it were), which Spinoza took to be the essence of all individuality.

7 The best contemporary source for 19th century hypnotism is J. M. Bramwell's *Hypnotism* of 1903 which has an extensive bibliography [see Bramwell (1956)], but also worth consulting is Binet

and Féré's *Animal Magnetism* [Binet and Féré (1887)]. *See also* Part I, 'Historic', of Shor and Orne (eds) [1965] and the Appendix which gives a selected bibliography on the history of hypnotism. Zilboorg and Henry [1941] also cover the history of this topic, and there is a short, readable biography of Mesmer himself by Walmsley [1967].

8   Although Mesmer began his career as a healer using real magnets, he soon discovered that he could get results without them. However, as explained in his 'Propositions' of 1779, he thought the body had properties analogous with those of the magnet and he therefore coined the vague expression 'animal magnetism' or 'magnetic fluid'.

9   In that year Louis XVI authorised two commissions to report on the work of Mesmer and d'Eslon, one representing the Academy of Sciences, the other the Royal Medical Society of Paris. The former was the more prestigeful, being presided over by no less a person than Benjamin Franklin, then in his 78th year and living in retirement at Passy, its active chairman being the astronomer J-S. Bailly. Among the signatories of its report was Dr Guillotin (who did not, in fact, invent the guillotine but merely recommended it as a more humane form of execution) and also the young Lavoisier. The commission claimed to 'have demonstrated by decisive experiments that imagination apart from magnetism produces convulsions, and that magnetism without imagination produces nothing', and concluded that the treatment 'must, in the end, be productive of evil results'. In a 'secret report' they further stressed the possible danger to morality from the fact that most magnetisers are men and most patients are women! [*see* Binet and Féré (1887) pp. 13-25] The medical commission reported only five days later to, essentially, the same effect—all, that is, except the botanist de Jussieu who, as a result of his own experiments with a blind woman, was not satisfied that everything could be laid to the door of 'imagination' and duly entered a minority report. It is hard not to sympathise with d'Eslon who commented on these reports: 'If the medicine of the imagination is the most efficient, why should we not make use of it?'

10   In 1785, de Puységur founded the first 'Société d'Harmonie' at Strasbourg which became a training school for mesmerism. There-

after most of the missionary work was done by travelling French mesmerists who gave lecture tours and public demonstrations. Both Elliotson and Braid (*see* below) first encountered mesmerism in this way. Its introduction to the United States came early. The Marquis de Lafayette was an enthusiast and, despite Franklin and the Royal Commission, wrote in 1784 to George Washington commending Mesmer. In 1815 a certain Dr du Commun went to the United States and started a society of magnetisers in New York. Everywhere mesmerism became a meeting ground for two distinct interests, the one medical, the other parapsychological, since it was widely believed that the somnambulist attains clairvoyant powers. In America its healing potentialities were developed especially by Phineas Quimby, best remembered perhaps for his more famous patient, Mary Baker Eddy, the founder of Christian Science. The supernatural aspects of mesmerism were developed by Andrew Jackson Davis, one of the founders of Spiritualism, who claimed to have clairvoyant powers himself while in the trance state and delivered many public lectures while entranced. One could say that America imported mesmerism and then later exported both Spiritualism and Christian Science. [*see* Angoff (1968) and Podmore (1963) and (1963a)]

11 Esdaile obtained an appointment with the East India Company after graduating from Edinburgh in 1830. His first mesmeric operation was performed in 1845 when he knew nothing more about mesmerism than what he had read in Elliotson. Encouraged by his success, he persevered and was fortunate enough to gain the support of the Deputy Governor of Bengal who, in 1846, placed at his disposal a small hospital in Calcutta. He stayed on in India until 1851 by which time, according to Bramwell [1956] he had performed 'nearly 300 capital operations and many thousand minor ones'. On his return to Scotland he introduced the practice at the Perth Infirmary until medical opposition put a stop to it. In 1852 he published a pamphlet on 'The Introduction of Mesmerism as an Anaesthetic and Curative Agent into the Hospitals of India', and complained bitterly of the suppression of all mention of his work by the British medical press. Esdaile's work represents the high-water-mark of hypnosis used as an analgesic; already before Esdaile left India chloroform (the discovery of a fellow Scot, Simpson) was being used in surgery. The detailed accounts that have

come down to us of Esdaile's operations make incredible reading. At the present time perhaps only acupuncture provides a similar medical enigma.

12 In 1843, Braid published his first tract: *Neurhypnology: or the Rationale of Nervous Sleep*. At first he spoke of 'neuro-hypnotism' but later, dropping the prefix, he begins to use the term hypnotism (together with its derivatives: hypnotic, hypnotise, hypnotist) as substitutes for the older mesmeric terminology.

13 Among them the physician, A. Bertrand, who, in 1823, published his *Traité du Somnambulisme*, and the Abbé Faria, a Portuguese priest in Paris who had visited India and may well have known something of yoga. Faria demonstrated the subjective nature of the phenomenon by dispensing with the customary magnetic 'passes' and putting his subjects into a trance merely by gazing into their eyes and commanding: *'Dormez!'*.

14 Thus Esdaile, even after he had learnt of Braid's theories, persisted in explaining his own practice in quasi-physical terms. He pointed out very logically that his patients were mostly poor ignorant Indians who knew nothing of what was expected of them and could not even understand English. They were prepared for their operation in a darkened room with their eyes shut so that even visual cues were at a minimum, the mesmerist simply passing his hands over the patient's body sometimes for hours on end. 'It is a nonsequitur to maintain that because many of the mesmeric phenomena can be produced by suggestion *therefore* there is no such thing as an independent mesmeric power in Nature', writes Esdaile, and concludes: 'From all that has come under my observation I am convinced that mesmerism, as practised by me, is a physical power exerted by one animal over another under certain conditions and circumstances of their respective systems.' Aldous Huxley, in his last novel *Island* (London, 1962), has given a vivid but authentic description of an Esdaile-type operation, see pp. 123-28.

15 *Cf.* Jones [1953/55] Vol. I, p. 227. 'No one before or since has so dominated the world of neurology and to have been a pupil of his was a permanent passport to distinction. The Salpêtrière could be called the Mecca of neurologists.' *See also* the recent biography of Charcot by Owen [1971].

16 Charcot, it would appear, made one of those classic blunders to which even the very eminent are not immune. Supposing his hypnotised subjects to be oblivious of anything he might say to others, he would cheerfully expound his theories to the assembled audience not realising that they were all the time picking up cues on how they were expected to behave!

17 Freud translated into German Bernheim's *Hypnotism and Suggestion in Psychotherapy* of 1884/86 as, some years before, he had translated Charcot's lectures into German.

18 I have tried to give here what I hoped might be considered a fairly unexceptionable modern view of hypnosis but, like nearly everything else in psychology, it is still very controversial. [*cf.* Sutcliffe (1965)] Sarbin [1962] believes that hypnotism is best conceived as a form of 'role-playing', and Barber [1969] adopts an even more radically sceptical approach which denies the very existence of the hypnotic trance and admits only different degrees of suggestibility. Barber's views are in keeping with the behaviourist approach to hypnotism as pioneered by Hull [1933]. His main justification for refusing to recognise a trance state is that, unlike sleep, there are no known physiological indices which can be taken as unequivocal evidence of hypnosis, and, of course, introspection is inadmissible. The behaviourist approach, be it noted, has no use for the concept of the unconscious either, whether in the hypnotic or the waking state.

19 The long-drawn-out controversy over 'perceptual defence' began with an article by McGinnies [1949] in which he reported that his subjects were giving an enhanced GSR response to certain 'taboo' words (relative to neutral words) before there was any conscious recognition of them and that, moreover, a longer interval of tachistoscopic exposure was necessary to reach the recognition threshold with such words. Repeated attempts were made by sceptical critics to show that this effect could be explained without postulating unconscious mechanisms [*cf.* Brown (1961)], but the latest work would appear to vindicate a depth-psychological interpretation. [*see* Dixon (1971) Chap. 7]

20 Edouard von Hartmann published his *magnum opus, Philo-*

sophy of the Unconscious, in 1868. By 1882, according to Whyte [1960], it had gone into nine editions in Germany. It was translated into French in 1877 and into English in 1884 and was extensively reviewed and discussed in all three countries.

21 *See* Murphy and Ballou (eds) [1960], a compilation of James's articles on psychical research between 1886 and 1909. James was a corresponding member of the Society for Psychical Research of London from 1884 to 1889 and, in 1886, he helped to found the American SPR, at first a branch of the London Society. He was vice-president of the London SPR from 1890 to 1910 except when he was president in 1894 and 1895.

22 *See* Gauld [1968] Chap. 12, 'Myers's Theory of the Subliminal Self'. Myers developed this theory in his posthumous 2-vol. work, *Human Personality and its Survival of Bodily Death*, of 1903, which James reviewed for the *Proceedings of the SPR* for 1903. [*see* Murphy and Ballou (1960)]

23 *See* Flournoy [1963]. Her previous lives included being the wife of a 15th century Hindu prince, an inhabitant of Mars (samples of the Martian script and language were obligingly supplied) and Marie Antoinette (always a popular figure with mediums!). After receiving a copy of his friend's book, James wrote a fulsome letter of congratulations (Jan. 1st 1900): 'My reading was interrupted with loud exclamations of joy. Upon my word, dear Flournoy, you have done a bigger thing here than you know; and I think your volume has made a decisive step in converting psychical research into a respectable science.' [le Clair (ed.) (1966) p. 90] Then, two years later, James again mentions the case in a letter after reading a supplementary investigation of this medium which Flournoy had just published: 'What a wonderful extension the case gives to our notion of subconscious activities and to cryptomnesic activities ...' [*idem* p. 127]

24 *See* H. Münsterberg *et al. Subconscious Phenomena: A Symposium* (London: No Date, but not earlier than 1909, date of latest reference, or later than 1916 when Münsterberg died). Although Freud gets a mention, the tone of the symposium is definitely pre-Freudian. *See also* J. Jastrow, *The Subconscious* (Boston: 1905),

which has no reference to Freud but does contain a lengthy discussion of Flournoy's Mlle Smith.

25 Janet propounded these ideas in his *L'Automatisme Psychologique* of 1889, and at greater length in his 2-vol. work *Névroses et Idées Fixes* of 1898. [*see* Ey (1968)] As Ey points out, Janet and Freud never knew one another personally and worked in ignorance of each other's work. Although both were exponents of unconscious mental life they differed radically as to its nature. 'For Janet', writes Ey, 'the essential thing about neuroses is loss of information; for Freud, neurosis gives one information which one must know how to decode.' Although Ey pleads that there is room in modern psychiatry for the insights of Janet as well as those of Freud, it would probably be true to say that Freud gradually supplanted and finally eclipsed Janet.

26 Morton Prince, a disciple of Janet, became renowned for his studies of split personality, a rare form of hysteria, especially in connection with Sally Beauchamp, a classic case often cited in philosophical discussions of personal identity. (*see* M. Prince, *The Dissociation of a Personality* (New York: 1906))

27 The two opposing views are represented side by side in the *Proc. S.P.R.* 26, 1912 (Special Medical Part), where Freud contributes 'A Note on the Unconscious in Psychoanalysis' (his first article to be published in Britain) pp. 312-19, and Boris Sidis expounds his own ideas in 'The Theory of the Subconscious' pp. 319-44.

28 A chronological list of all Freud's publications is given in Fine [(1963) Appendix]. His complete works in English have been assembled in *The Standard Edition*. [Freud (1955/64)] While much that he wrote is of purely technical interest, much was directed at a wider audience and remains eminently readable. A good entry point is his *An Autobiographical Study* of 1925 and his very brief *Outline of Psychoanalysis* written in 1938 and published posthumously.

29 Three such books which attempt to convey the gist of Freud from the standpoint of modern clinical psychology are Fine [1963],

Holzman [1970] and Stafford-Clark [1967]. For a more profound philosophical study of Freud's ideas *see* Wollheim [1971].

30 *Cf.* Stafford-Clark [1967] p. 16. 'This was a man whose name will always rank with those of Darwin, Copernicus, Newton, Marx and Einstein; someone who really made a difference to the way the rest of us can begin to think about the meaning of human life and society'; or Wollheim [1971] p. 9: 'It would be hard to find in the history of ideas, even in the history of religion, someone whose influence was so immediate, so broad and so deep.'

The comparison with Einstein, that so readily comes to mind, is of special historical interest. Sir Karl Popper recounts how, as a student in Vienna after the First World War, three topics were constantly coming up for discussion: the theory of Relativity, the Marxist theory of history, and psychoanalysis of both the Freudian and Adlerian varieties (Popper knew Adler personally). It was the contrast between Relativity theory on the one hand and Marxism and Psychoanalysis on the other which posed for Popper the question that dominated his philosophy of science for the rest of his life, namely: when can a theory be considered scientific? Both Marxism and psychoanalysis claimed to be able to explain everything that came within their purview and took each new fact to be a confirmation of the theory. The trouble was that, in complete contrast to Relativity, they never committed themselves to a prediction so that their explanations were always retrospective. It was in this way that Popper arrived at his celebrated criterion of 'falsifiability' as affording the crucial distinction between genuine and spurious science. [*see* Popper (1967a)] Similar criticisms have been made more recently by other philosophers, notably Hook [1960] and Cioffi [1970].

After that it is of some interest to learn what Einstein himself thought of Freud. In an interview he gave to Max Eastman in 1937 he describes Freud as 'a very great man' but then adds this telling remark: 'I think he invented some wonderful ideas but whether they are true or not we in our lifetime will probably never know ... the trouble is that in psychiatry verification is impossible. The fault, I think, is in the subject rather than in Freud.' [Eastman (1959) p. 29] Finally, we may note that, in one of his rare flashes of self-denigration, Freud himself seems to have anticipated the verdict of his own critics: 'You often estimate me too highly. For I am not really a man of science, not an observer, not a thinker. I am nothing but by temperament a conquistador—an adventurer, if you want to translate the word—with the curiosity, the boldness and the tenacity that belongs to that type of being. Such people are treasured if they succeed, if they have really discovered something; otherwise they are thrown aside.' [Jones (1953/55) Vol. I, p. 382] The passage is dated Feb. 1st 1900, but Jones does not say whom Freud was addressing.

31 *Cf.* Freud [1920] preface. 'None but physicians who practise psychoanalysis can have any access whatever to this sphere of knowledge or any possibility of forming a judgment that is uninfluenced by their own dislikes and prejudices.' This must surely be one of Freud's most unfortunate pronouncements. It is exactly as if the Marxist were to say that only the active revolutionary can judge the correctness of Marxism uninfluenced by bourgeois dislikes and prejudices!

32 The evidence was first collated and publicised by Eysenck [1953] Chap. 10. He refrained from claiming that this demonstrated the futility of psychotherapy but he presented it as a challenge. Twenty years later he is still waiting for the challenge to be met. [*see* Eysenck (1972)]

33 We owe this candid disclosure to an analyst, Dr Anthony Storr [*see* Storr (1966) p. 59], who in turn quotes it on the authority of London [1964].

34 The first full-scale attack on the conception of psychoanalysis or psychotherapy as a branch of medicine was made by the American psychiatrist, T. S. Szasz. [*see* Szasz (1962)] He argued that it was a mistake ever to have regarded neurosis as a psychiatric category, neurotics were just ordinary people who needed help and advice with their problems of living.

35 The remark occurs early in his career in his *Studies in Hysteria* which he and Breuer published in 1895. [Jones (1953/55) Vol. I, p. 269]

36 One of the earliest attempts was that of R. R. Sears. [*see* Sears

(1951) and Sears (1944)] E. R. Hilgard, a distinguished experimental psychologist, wrote: 'It is a tribute to Freud and his psychoanalytic followers that the problems faced by psychologists in their laboratories have been enormously enriched by the questions the analysts have taught us to ask.' [Hilgard (1952)] Ten years later he was still writing hopefully: 'A great many pertinent investigations are now under way in these fields and we have every reason to expect a reconstruction of psychoanalysis to emerge from them. It will be a reconstruction rather than a validation, for the very act of validation requires reconstruction.' [Hilgard (1970)]

37 Two recent publications which have attempted to survey this literature are Lee and Herbert (eds) [1970] and, more especially, Kline [1972]; both have a basically pro-Freudian orientation.

38 *Cf.* Beloff, H. [1957]. 'From our data we may conclude that although the anal character is a meaningful dimension of variation for the description of our subjects' attitudes and behaviour, it is not related to toilet training experiences, but strongly to the degree of anal character exhibited by the mother.'

39 *See* note 19 above. For the experimental evidence on repression, *see* MacKinnon and Dukes [1962].

40 The phrase occurs in his contribution to the 1926 Edition of the *Encyclopaedia Britannica, see* 'Psychoanalysis', which has been reprinted almost in its entirety in the current 1969 Edition. The complete sentence reads: 'Psychoanalysis is founded securely on the facts of mental life, and for that very reason, its theoretical superstructure is still incomplete and subject to constant alteration.' The trouble is that Freud never made clear the distinction between 'facts' and his 'theoretical superstructure'; what he called facts, most people would call inferences. There is no question that he himself went on modifying his doctrines all his life but this was largely in response to his own inner promptings and cannot be taken as proof that he was really a good empiricist all along.

41 It was in defence of his brain-child and to justify the expulsion or Adler and Jung that he wrote his 'History of the Psychoanalytic Movement'. [Freud (1914)] *See also* Rieff's introduction to this tract in Chap. 4 of Rieff [1966].

42 For a close study of the development of Freud's ideas in the early years, *see* Stewart [1969]. The most important primary source for this period is Freud [1954].

43 *Cf.* Rieff [1959] p. 154. 'Freud was no celebrant of the senses; there is not a trace of the lyrical in his analysis of the sexual instinct and its satisfactions. He hardly claimed or—from what we know of his life—himself desired to be rid of the civilizing aversions. While urging, for the sake of our mental health, that we dispense with such childish fantasies of purity as are epitomized in the belief that Mother (or Father) was too nice to have done those nasty things, Freud at the same time comes to the tacit understanding that sex really is nasty, an ignoble slavery to nature.' And, elsewhere in this chapter, Rieff attributes to Freud a deep-seated misogyny based on his belief that in women sexuality takes precedence over intellect. In like vein, Eastman [1959] suggests that it was 'the astonishment of a natural born puritan at finding out how much frank and raw sexuality there is in the world' that led Freud to exaggerate this aspect of life.

44 Freud's first published paper of 1877 was about work he had done under Brücke at the Institute of Physiology in Vienna on the histology of the nerve cells of a certain species of fish. Freud himself called Brücke 'the greatest authority who affected me more than any other in my whole life'. [Jones (1953/55) Vol. I, p. 31] 'Brücke's Institute,' says Jones, 'was an important part indeed of that far-reaching movement best known as Helmholtz's School of Medicine ... In 1842, Du Bois-Reymond wrote: "Brücke and I pledged a solemn oath to put into effect this truth: no other forces than the common physical and chemical ones are active within the organism".' [*idem*, p. 45] *See also* Stewart [1969]: 'From a historical point of view, Freud's application of the principle of the conservation of energy to psychoanalysis was probably due to the consequences of his working under Brücke, who in turn had been influenced by Helmholtz, who had given a lecture on his principle of the conservation of energy to a group that included Brücke.'

45 In the autobiography which he began dictating to his disciple and amanuensis, Aniela Jaffé, in the Spring of 1957, during his 81st year, Jung tells the following story about his first encounter with

Freud which seems to shed some light on both of them even if its literal accuracy cannot be vouched for [see Jung (1963) Chap. 5]: 'I can still recall vividly how Freud said to me: "My dear Jung, promise me never to abandon the sexual theory, that is the most essential thing of all. You see we must make a dogma of it, an unshakeable bulwark." He said that to me with great emotion, in the tone of a father saying "and promise me this one thing, dear son: that you will go to church every Sunday". (Jung was the son of a Swiss pastor—*J.B.*) In some astonishment I asked him, "A bulwark against what?" to which he replied, "Against the black tide of mud" —and here he hesitated for a moment and then added "of occultism"'. Later in the chapter Jung writes: 'Freud never asked himself why he was compelled to talk continually of sex, why this idea had taken such possession of him. He remained unaware that this "monotony of interpretation" expressed a flight from himself, or from the other side of him which might perhaps be called mystical ... he remained the victim of that one aspect he could recognize, and for that reason I see him as a tragic figure; for he was a great man, and what is more a man in the grip of his daemon.' Freud, for his part, saw Jung's reluctance to accept the sexual interpretation as a species of moral cowardice: 'All the changes that Jung has wrought in psychoanalysis,' he remarks [Freud (1914)], 'flow from an ambition to eliminate all that is disagreeable in the family complexes so that it may not evidence itself again in ethics and religion. For sexual libido an abstract term has been substituted of which one may safely say that it remains incomprehensible to fools and wise men alike.'

46 Rieff comments as follows: 'Accepting as the leading premise of his psychology the failure of established religions in the West, Jung looked back on his entire life as the fortunate unfolding of a countermyth ... It was his task to communicate, through his matured psychology, not the God of the Bible or church but the dark, subterranean God of each man's secret life.' ['The Therapeutic as Theologian: Jung's Psychology as a Language of Faith', Chap. 5 of Rieff (1966)]

47 One recent authority has described no less than 36 distinct schools of psychotherapy all of which can be regarded as off-shoots of the original movement. [see Harper (1959)]

48 *Cf.* Freud [1914]. 'The importance of theological tradition in the former history of so many Swiss is no less significant for their attitude to psychoanalysis than is the socialistic element in that of Adler for the line of development taken by his psychology.' Adler's commitment to socialism was well known; Rieff's remarks on this score are worth quoting: 'Some modern psychologies are themselves the surrogates of political theory, as others are surrogates of theology. The feeling of "organ inferiority" which Adler so easily discovered as the core of neurotic behaviour, may be interpreted as his trans-literation into psychological terms of the class war. The weak, ugly, misshapen, crippled, miserable—these were Adler's own, privately designated proletariat, whom he set out to cure of their inferiority complex.' [Rieff (1966) pp. 95-96]

49 Karen Horney and Erich Fromm, both Berlin trained analysts, played the role of missionaries in this connection. For a time they worked together with the American analyst, Harry Stack Sullivan. Both were impressed with the fact that neurosis in the New World did not necessarily mean the same thing as neurosis in the Old World. Both regarded Freud's orientation as too narrowly biological and both sought to rectify this by stressing cultural and sociological factors. In the case of Fromm this was further accentuated by his strong Marxist affiliations, *cf.* Brown, J. [1967] Chaps 7 and 8. According to Gorer [1966] p. 46: 'Even before Hitler annexed Austria and drove Freud and his followers into exile, the theory and practice of psychoanalysis were more widely spread and widely accepted in America than in any other country.' The origin of psychoanalysis in the States goes back to the invitation extended to Freud in 1909 by the psychologist G. Stanley Hall, then president of Clark University, to deliver a course of lectures there. Jung and Ferenczi were also among the speakers on that occasion.

50 Dr Ian Oswald, head of the Sleep Laboratory of the University of Edinburgh, adopts a physiological approach to dreams [*see* Oswald (1966)] as compared, say, with Dr David Foulkes, an American sleep-researcher, who takes a more psychological view-point. [*see* Foulkes (1966)] For a further discussion of these issues *see also* Webb (ed.) [1968].

51 *Cf.* Rycroft [1966] also MacIntyre [1958] Chap. 4, 'Describing and Explaining'.

52 *See* Bowlby [1953]. For the most recent reassessment of this issue, *see* Rutter [1972] who gives qualified support to Bowlby's claims.

53 *See* Harlow and Zimmermann [1959], Harlow [1961] and Harlow and Harlow [1969]. Harlow has acknowledged the initial inspiration of Bowlby for his work. For a recent analysis of the mother-child relationship, *see* Schaffer [1971] esp. Chap. 7, 'Formation of the Bond'.

54 Already by the Spring of 1897 Freud realised that he had blundered. Jones blames the influence of Charcot, which had stressed the importance of traumatic experiences in the genesis of a neurosis, and regards the abandonment of the seduction theory as the turning point of Freud's career: 'Now he had to prove whether his psychological method on which he had founded everything was trustworthy or not.' [Jones (1953/55) Vol. I, p. 292] Jones, of course, had no doubts that Freud did succeed in vindicating his method; critics would say that it was inherently subjective and untrustworthy.

55 Reich represents a highly idiosyncratic amalgam of Marxist and psychoanalytic ideas all equally unorthodox which it would be useless to try and reduce to any coherent system. This, however, has not prevented him from becoming a posthumous hero and martyr of the New Left and he seems to have anticipated Laing in his contempt for the family, *cf*. Rieff [1966] p. 160: 'Sex education becomes the main weapon in an ideological war against the family; its aim is to divest the parents of their moral authority.' D. H. Lawrence took issue with Freud in his book *Psychoanalysis and the Unconscious* of 1923. Rieff [1966] remarks, p. 194, that what Lawrence disliked in Freud was the latter's attempt to rationalise the erotic life, whereas Lawrence was the advocate of 'a religious mood that was specifically irrational and erotic'.

56 Sir Peter Medawar, biologist and Nobel Prize Winner, in the course of a polemical exchange with Dr Anthony Storr, writes as follows: 'There is some truth in psychoanalysis ... as there is in mesmerism and phrenology ... but, considered in its entirety, psychoanalysis won't do. It is an end-product, moreover, like a dinosaur or a Zeppelin; no better theory can ever be constructed on

its ruins, which will remain forever one of the saddest and strangest of all landmarks in the history of 20th century thought' (*Encounter* 33, 1969, p. 94). Dr Henry Miller, formerly Professor of Neurology and now Vice-Chancellor of Newcastle University, is even more brusque. In response to a letter from Dr J. H. Tizard, the psychiatrist, he writes: 'The whole of psychoanalytic doctrine seems to me a monstrous imaginative fabrication based on no more than a few grains of anecdotal data.' (*Encounter* 35, 1970, p. 93)

CHAPTER EIGHT

Parapsychology

It should be clear from the preceding chapters that a salient characteristic of all the psychological sciences that we have discussed is that
opinion is deeply divided even on fundamental issues. Nor is this
surprising when we recall how the very idea of a psychological
science has itself been a source of endless controversy. But, in the
cases we previously considered, argument tended to devolve on the
interpretation of the facts rather than on the facts themselves. For
example, that certain patients suffered from certain symptoms was
not a cause for dispute, it was only when it came to the interpretation of those symptoms that argument began. In the case of parapsychology, which I shall here define as the scientific study of
paranormal phenomena, controversy starts with the facts themselves.
Right at the outset of our inquiry we have to ask whether there are
indeed any paranormal facts; facts, that is to say, which contravene
one or more widely-held and well-entrenched assumptions about the
limits of the physically possible, or whether there are only facts that
appear to transcend these limits.[1]

It is strange as well as lamentable that, after all this while, it is
still not possible in all honesty to give a straightforward answer to
this primary question. It is strange because parapsychology has been
going for at least as long as conventional experimental psychology
and because, even if its progress has been on a much smaller scale,
it has, one way or another, managed to amass a quite formidable

body of evidence. However, this evidence, when closely scrutinised, invariably falls short of being definitive; hence the doubt remains. Now, if all that were at stake were just a few marginal phenomena, let us say some minor statistical anomalies in the guessing performances of a few individuals, this uncertainty would not be a matter of grave concern. But what in fact is at stake is, in the last resort, whether there are any properties of mind that go beyond anything which conventional psychology and physiology would lead us to expect or, more far-reaching still, whether there are any properties of the universe that go beyond anything which modern physics would allow us to infer.[2] We can surely all agree that whatever the truth should turn out to be we stand only to gain by knowing it. Should the answer be 'no', it would at least be a relief to find that assumptions we have come to hold about ourselves and about the world after four centuries of science have not proved seriously misleading. Parapsychology would then have to be redefined as the study of the *ostensibly* paranormal, but it could still make a useful if modest contribution to psychological knowledge by treating its phenomena as belonging, along with similar fallacies, delusions and superstitions, with the pathology of belief. Indeed, relieved of the onus of having to reckon with the veridicality of its phenomena, it could profitably concentrate on explaining why they are so widespread. But if, on the contrary, the answer should turn out to be 'yes', then it goes without saying that the phenomena should be receiving far more attention than they have so far been getting.

The State of the Evidence

It is not my intention here to try and answer the question as to whether the evidence justifies belief in the paranormal or not. To do this properly would, in any case, require an intensive examination of concrete cases and that would take up more space than the rest of the book. What I shall do instead is to offer some suggestions about the sort of considerations that are relevant to reaching a decision on this question. In particular, I shall discuss (a) what sort of evidence has so far been forthcoming, (b) why it is inconclusive, and (c) what prospects there are of coming to any definite conclusion either of outright acceptance or outright rejection. I shall defer until later in the chapter any consideration of the secondary question, namely what the existence of paranormal phenomena might imply, assuming that they do exist.

In default of any decisive answer one way or the other, the present situation with respect to parapsychology is one that can adequately be described only in terms of paradox. Consider the following statement: 'The trouble with parapsychology is that it is nearly impossible to believe it is true and nearly impossible to believe it is false.' [Rushton (1971) p. 186] I shall call this 'Rushton's Dilemma'. It has been one of the more serious defects of most previous discussions of this issue that they have failed to take account of this dilemma. On the one side there have been those who, priding themselves on their robust commonsense, have seen no reason to dissent from the Humean view that there are some things that no rational man can be expected to believe and therefore anyone who says he can prove such things, no matter who he is or what his credentials, stands self-condemned as a liar or a fool.[3] In a more moderate vein, they may content themselves with pointing out that the mere fact that these claims have been heard for so long to so little effect is itself strong grounds for treating each new case with suspicion. Or they may go further and question the good faith of those who make such claims which they construe as a surreptitious attack on science and an invitation to indulge in mystification. For some reason this militant opposition is commoner among the psychological than among the physical scientists. On the other side of the fence there are those who, being completely convinced themselves, find it unreasonable of others to doubt. They insist that such proof as it is possible, in the nature of the case, to provide has been provided and that those who are still not satisfied are those who would never be satisfied because their incredulity is obsessional and unappeasable. Accordingly they resent as futile any further attempt to wear down the sceptic and ask only to be left alone to get on with the job of discovering more about the nature of the phenomena.

In what follows I shall not feign a neutrality to which I am not entitled since I have made no secret of the fact that, all in all, I consider it more likely than unlikely that paranormal phenomena do exist. Nevertheless I regard both extreme positions as, alike, dangerous and misguided. The dangers of dogmatic scepticism are well known. One can find plenty of historical examples of science being kept back because of a refusal to come to terms with awkward new facts; hypnotic phenomena, as we saw earlier, are a case in point. But the dangers of excessive credulity are even more serious. Science would never progress at all if it allowed itself to be diverted by the clamour of every crank, charlatan or bungler who claimed to speak in its name. For nothing is more seductive than to erect vast edifices of belief on the basis of a few ill-founded observations. We saw something of this process at work in the history of the psychoanalytic movement, and scores of pseudo-sciences stand witness to its ravages.[4] If science did not take steps to protect itself from those who abuse it, we would quickly revert to the Dark Ages and all distinction between fact and fantasy would be lost. This is a point that specially needs to be stressed at the present time. When parapsychology first got going in the 1880s, science had reached an apogee of optimism and self-confidence. Today, even if its achievements are unsurpassed, the seeds of doubt and defeatism have been sown and the scientific outlook is being widely blamed for all the ills of modern society. In such circumstances parapsychology has a special duty not to lend its authority to those who seek to destroy alike both science and Western civilisation.

But there is a more immediate practical reason why it is to the advantage of the believer to maintain a dialogue with the sceptic. For the fact is that parapsychology can at present count upon no more than a tiny fraction of the money, manpower and creative talent available to conventional psychological research which is itself, I may add, something of a beggar among the sciences. No government agency or major grant-giving foundation, so far as I know, subsidises parapsychology, which has only kept going at all thanks to private benefactions and to the work of dedicated amateurs. Moreover, parapsychology is still deprived of that wider forum which the other sciences can take for granted. It is extremely rare for the editor of any of the main organs of science or of the main psychological journals to accept a paper which presents findings of a paranormal nature. It is true that parapsychology has its own specialist journals[5] but these are not easily accessible and not many university libraries consider it necessary to subscribe to them. Yet, until the primary evidential question has been settled, there seems little prospect that this state of affairs will change and that the isolation and neglect which parapsychology has had to endure will be ended.[6] In the meantime, it makes it exceedingly difficult for parapsychologists to persuade the rest of the scientific community that they are 'onto something' and that they deserve recognition and support. It is in their own interests, therefore, to break through this vicious circle and produce the kind of evidence that will force the sceptic to take notice.

There is, however, one school of thought which would deny that our primary and secondary question can be separated in this way. Facts, they point out, never make any impact in science until they can be fitted into some kind of a theoretical framework. What tells against parapsychology in the last resort is not so much the inadequacy of its evidence as the lack of an intelligible conceptual framework. Accordingly, rather than spending any more time vainly arguing with their critics, parapsychologists would do better to look for those lawful relationships among their data that will provide them with the bases for future theories and models. This view has received a powerful impetus in recent years from the writings of an influential historian of science, Thomas Kuhn. According to Kuhn [1970], the history of science does not consist in a steady expansion of knowledge but rather in a series of revolutions or 'paradigm-shifts', in the course of which one world view is replaced by another more successful world view. These revolutions are always preceded by a period of crisis brought on by the failure of the prevailing paradigm to cope with certain outstanding problems and difficulties. But one paradigm is never simply discarded, no matter how many contradictions it may have engendered, until another paradigm is ready to take its place. Kuhn, who is mainly concerned with such historic paradigm-shifts as the transition from Newtonian to Einsteinian physics, does not discuss the case of parapsychology, but the relevance of his ideas has been pointed out by McConnell [1966]. Certainly, it is tempting to see in the current state of parapsychology, with its intense individualism, its lack of common working assumptions and its disorderly plethora of ill-assorted and undigested observations, all the signs we have learnt to associate with a pre-paradigmic science. One may further agree with McConnell that the mistrust which most contemporary scientists show towards parapsychology is strongly reminiscent of the resistance we have come to expect from the upholders of one paradigm as soon as they see it being threatened. Nevertheless, the prospect of parapsychology duly achieving paradigm status is at present barely more than a pious hope and, in the meantime, the basic problem of evidence remains.

There are, I suggest, three logically distinct categories of evidence which have to be taken into consideration. The first is that which pertains to specific *events*. These may range from the odd experience —a telepathic signal of distress, a dream that comes true, etc., such as many people claim to have had once or twice in their lives—to the unexplained movement of objects such as is reported during a so-called 'poltergeist outbreak'. The second is that which centres on particular *individuals* who, over a period of years, have given evidence of possessing some paranormal ability, whether it be a knack of guessing cards or influencing dice, or some fully fledged mediumistic power of either the mental or physical variety. The third has to do with the *phenomena* as such, their conditions of occurrence, their peculiar characteristics, their relationships with other known phenomena. This last category presupposes that there are phenomena of a sufficiently regular and recurrent kind to be amenable to the experimental approach.

Each of these three categories of evidence poses its own special problems and is beset with its own characteristic weaknesses. Where we are dealing with unique events, as in our first category, we are faced with the problem of reconstructing the past on the basis of documentary records or the testimony of witnesses, much in the same way as the historian and the lawyer who likewise are interested in unique events. This is never in principle insoluble, or there could be no history and no law, but the pitfalls are obvious. It was one of the crowning achievements of early experimental psychology to have demonstrated just how unreliable human testimony can be even under optimal conditions. When there is any element of the marvellous or mysterious involved, the tendency to exaggerate and embroider is well-nigh irresistible. It is this category that is the most vulnerable to the Humean critique.

Where we are dealing with special individuals, the hazards involved are of a rather different sort. Often their reputation or even their livelihood depends on their being able to produce phenomena to order and, even if they are genuine in the first instance, they are unlikely to have much control over their abilities. In these circumstances the temptation to cheat must be very strong and, with so much opportunity to practise, it should not be too difficult for them to devise ways of doing so. All this would not matter much if the investigator were in a position to dictate the exact conditions under which they had to perform. In practice, however, the conditions are nearly always a compromise between what the experimenter wants and what he can get his subject to agree to. Should the experimenter refuse to compromise, the subject can simply threaten to withdraw his services. Since promising subjects are rarer than would-be investigators, the subject usually has the whip-hand in this contest of wills. In these circumstances it is not surprising that many persons who were credited with paranormal powers later turned out to be merely clever tricksters; even experienced investigators have been taken in. But, even if one finds the perfect docile subject who will try anything one asks of him, his performance is likely to be wildly idiosyncratic with respect to the sort of things he can or cannot do. Consequently, each investigation is apt to become a separate, self-contained episode in parapsychological history rather than another step in a progressive series of discoveries.

It is largely because of the notorious difficulties associated with these first two categories that so much stress has been laid in the more recent period on the experimental evidence of our third category. Unfortunately, this approach in turn is exposed to a variety of criticisms as well as running into certain additional difficulties of its own. The trouble is not merely that the evidence is of a purely statistical nature but that the rate of scoring, in the vast majority of cases, is so close to chance that a statistically significant effect in the overall score can be demonstrated only by dint of using a very large number of trials. In these circumstances the slightest flaw in the experimental set-up—a bias in the checking or recording of responses, unsuspected subliminal cues, and so on—would suffice to produce a spurious overall deviation. This is inevitable where one is trying to detect an effect that has a very low signal-to-noise ratio and, in the long run, it would not matter providing other workers could rely on replicating results using whatever refinements of methodology they deemed fit; but, in the absence of such replication, the importance of every putative flaw becomes magnified. The truth is that an unrepeatable experiment is no more cogent as evidence than any other unique event.[7]

Some critics have denied that it is necessary to take account of every kind of evidence before pronouncing judgment on parapsychology. It is sufficient, they claim, to fasten attention on certain experiments only which are most widely regarded as affording the strongest scientific evidence for one or another paranormal phenomenon. If these outstanding experiments can then be shown to have been faulty in some particular, there is no need to go further since no amount of weak or defective evidence will ever add up to an impregnable case. Their strategy, accordingly, is to subject a number of these 'exemplary' experiments to a minute scrutiny for possible flaws. Since there is probably no such thing as the perfect experiment it is usually just a matter of time and patience before such a flaw is found. Indeed, if the critic is willing to go to any lengths, including imputing deliberate fraud to the experimenters, this becomes a game in which he can scarcely lose. It requires only some ingenuity to think up some way in which the results *might* have been faked and, with any luck, suspicious features of the data can be found to substantiate these conjectures.

This strategy has proved very effective in the hands of an adept[8] but it belongs more properly to the court of law and the conduct of a cross examination. It is quite alien to science, which relies upon a more gradual process of sifting whereby untenable ideas fall by the wayside and valid ideas ultimately gain acceptance. It is too soon to say whether parapsychology belongs with the former or with the latter but we shall not find out by resorting to these inquisitorial techniques. Rushton's dilemma cannot be solved by any impatient short-cuts. The most we can ask for in present circumstances is a responsible judgment on whether a case has been made out which justifies further research. Such a judgment cannot be based on the analysis of a few isolated experiments nor even, if it comes to that, on a reading of the published literature, for it is also a question of judging the integrity and competence of those who carry out the experiments.

It is, however, highly symptomatic of the state of the evidence that the ugly question of experimenter-fraud should figure in this field to an extent unknown in any of the other sciences.[9] It is ironic that one of the most highly regarded investigations in the whole of the experimental literature which was deliberately designed to safeguard the experimenters from subsequent suspicions of duplicity, by having outside observers present at every session, failed miserably in this objective. I refer to the Soal-Goldney experiments of 1941-43 with the card-guessing subject Basil Shackleton.[10] Eventually Soal became the victim not merely of insinuations but even of outright accusations of fraud! The one lesson we can learn from all this is that no experiment, however carefully designed, will ever indefinitely be regarded as impeccable if it stands on its own.[11]

The parapsychologists, themselves, are by no means agreed on the relative weighting one should assign to the different types of evidence. J. B. Rhine, for example, regards the experimental evidence as alone worthy of scientific attention. On this point, at least, he seems to be at one with his critics. Spontaneous cases, in his view, have at best an heuristic value inasmuch as they can suggest hypotheses for experimental testing. Even the study of special subjects does not come high in his order of priorities, since ESP is regarded as a universal ability so that we are all of us potential subjects to some degree. Now, if parapsychology were anywhere near to being what Kuhn calls 'normal science', there could be no question that Rhine would be right. Just as the study of natural history was largely superseded by the advent of experimental biology so, it can be argued, the study of the paranormal in its spontaneous manifestations has been largely superseded, except as a kind of auxiliary field-work, by the advent of experimental parapsychology. But how far is this analogy valid?

Rhine himself occupies a unique position in the history of parapsychology precisely because it was his work, at the Duke University Parapsychology Laboratory, that came closest to providing parapsychology, if not with a strict paradigm, at any rate with some of the attributes of normal science. Thus, the terminology now in general use, including the word 'parapsychology' itself as a substitute for the older expression 'psychical research',[12] is his coinage along with such now familiar terms as 'ESP' (Extra-sensory perception, to cover all forms of paranormal cognition) and 'PK' (Psychokinesis, to cover all forms of paranormal physical effects). He further standardised the techniques of testing for ESP, using his special pack of 'ESP cards' with their five 'Zener symbols', and even imposed on parapsychology the nearest thing to an orthodoxy, in the sense that certain tenets about the nature of ESP and PK (for example, that they functioned independently of the physical parameters of space, time and matter) could not be questioned by anyone who wanted to remain in his entourage. When he published his research findings in his first monograph *Extra-Sensory Perception* in 1934 and followed this up with *New Frontiers of the Mind* in 1937 the impact which this made in psychological circles was greater than with any other development in parapsychology before or since. Eventually, however, interest waned when it became clear that the overwhelming majority of attempts to replicate these findings yielded nothing but chance scores. Nor were these failures confined to the sceptics. One early enthusiast, J. C. Crumbaugh, carried out a massive number of guessing tests adhering closely to Rhine's recommended procedures but all to no avail (unless it be to reaffirm the laws of chance!)[13]

Meanwhile, at the Duke Laboratory itself, interest had shifted away from demonstrating the existence of a non-chance factor in the overall scores to subsidiary aspects of the scoring patterns, for example, the so-called 'decline effect' or the 'differential effects' obtained when different kinds of targets are used or different categories of subjects. These minor effects were no doubt of great interest to parapsychologists, but they cut little ice with psychologists who were not as yet convinced that any *psi* factor was involved. Whether because they ceased to exist once conditions were made stricter, as the sceptics suggested, or because they were no longer needed, as Rhine maintains, the fact is that steady scorers capable of sustaining an above chance score for any length of time were somehow no longer around[14] and, without them, all parapsychology could show for itself were these small quantitative side-effects of a more or less *recherché* kind. The Rhine revolution, in short, proved abortive. Rhine succeeded in giving parapsychology everything it needed to become an accredited experimental science except the one essential: the know-how to produce positive results when and where required. Without that the rest could never amount to more than the trappings of a science. The full significance of this failure is partly disguised in the literature because only the successful experiments ordinarily get published. The *Journal of Parapsychology* (Rhine's own mouthpiece) makes no secret of the fact that it will accept for publication only results that are significant at the 1 per cent level of confidence. But far more effective than any editorial selectivity is the self-censorship that operates. Most parapsychologists that I know are just too disheartened and abashed when they fail to get results to have the necessary determination to write up a report on their experiment and submit it for publication. I sometimes wonder how many young hopefuls are drawn each year to parapsychology by the exciting reports they read in the journals, oblivious of this huge silent majority of negative instances.

In such a situation, any too exclusive preoccupation with the quantitative aspects of *psi* can only end by trivialising the whole enterprise. For the fact remains that the real-life phenomena are so immeasurably richer in content and in psychological interest that some authorities have even queried whether there is much connection between these and the small statistical anomalies we find in the laboratory. At all events, there has been a very noticeable reaction among the new generation of parapsychologists against any arbitrary restrictions and a readiness to explore a wide range of qualitative phenomena that had been virtually confined to the lumber-room during the ascendancy of the Rhine regime. Dreams, hypnosis, 'out-of-the-body' experiences, mediumship, poltergeists and many other such topics are once again claiming a place on the parapsychological agenda. Even such hoary topics as Survival or Reincarnation are receiving serious attention and a fresh approach. If this trend sounds reactionary to the scientific purist it is perhaps because we have not yet reached a stage in parapsychology where we can ignore our history in favour of the latest experimental report. To me, at any rate, the records of the great sensitives of the past still offer the best assurance we have that *psi* is not just a mirage or an artefact, even if, in every case, the authenticity of such evidence is less than absolute.

Rhine freely admits that in the present state of our knowledge the demand for repeatability, except in some very weak sense, cannot be met.[15] At best we can try and produce the sort of conditions which past experience has shown to be conducive to *psi*, but we can never count on its showing up. The trouble is that if it does not, it is all too easy to find reasons after the event; anything from the personality of the experimenter to the mood of the subject can be invoked. Now, it is true that replication has been a stumbling-block with all the psychological sciences and if this has created less of a scandal in conventional psychology it is only because less was at stake. The more far-fetched the claim, the more imperative the need for replication. Curiously, Rhine does not appear to appreciate that his repudiation of this criterion is incompatible with a whole-hearted commitment to an experimental approach. But how far must we resign ourselves to this defeatist position? I now want to consider very briefly two recent developments in experimental parapsychology which could, if they continue, rapidly transform the whole situation by giving us the repeatability which alone can enable us to consummate the revolution which Rhine began.

The first of these developments arises from a purely technological advance. The fact is that testing procedures have become infinitely simpler and more fool-proof as a consequence of the introduction of automated electronic equipment. For the first time it has now become technically feasible to leave a subject alone with a machine which he can operate at his own leisure and in the intimacy of his home surroundings, as the mood takes him. Such a machine acts both as tester and scorer, it randomly selects a target, the subject registers his guess by pressing an appropriate button and the trial-by-trial sequence of target-guess pairs can be recorded onto punched tape ready for computer analysis. If the experimenter wishes to test his subject's precognitive ability he can instruct him to register his guess on each trial *before* the machine has made its random selection. In all cases instantaneous knowledge of results can be made available to the subject by having the appropriate target-lamp light up as soon as the subject has registered his guess. By these means thousands of trials can quickly be got through in a relatively painless fashion for all concerned. Dr Helmut Schmidt, an enterprising and resourceful young physicist, who, in 1969, took over from Rhine the directorship of the FRNM Institute (the successor organisation to the Duke Laboratory) has already demonstrated the efficacy of this new technique. Working with pre-selected subjects on a special machine of his own design he was able to attain astronomical odds-against chance even though his subjects scored at a rate only a few per cent above the chance baseline. [Schmidt (1969) (1969a) and (1969b)] This work still remains to be corroborated by other laboratories but, in the meantime, the fact that parapsychology has surmounted the challenge of automation against the forebodings of sceptics augurs well for the future.[16]

My second example is the product of combining animal experimentation with automated testing equipment. Despite persisting anecdotal accounts of the paranormal abilities of pets, animals have figured very little in experimental parapsychology. [*cf.* Morris (1970)] Perhaps the fact that parapsychology was anti-behaviourist in its philosophy impelled it towards the humanistic camp. However, a few years ago an eminent French authority on animal behaviour with a long-standing interest in parapsychology decided to test for ESP in mice. A mouse was placed in a special cage where, at intervals, a shock could be delivered to the floor-grille either on the right half of the cage or on the left half depending on a random number generator which governed the current. Under these conditions the mouse could avoid being shocked only by being on the safe side of the cage at the right time. But, since no sensory cues were available to tell it where the shock was coming next, it could do this better than 50 per cent of the trials only to the extent to which it could use its precognitive ESP! An analysis of the results duly revealed that the mice escaped shocking to a significant extent. The odds involved were not of the astronomical order, but the beauty of this experiment was that it was fully automated so that there was no human intervention at any point in the run. [see Duval and Montredon (1968)] Since these findings were published, this experiment has been successfully replicated with further refinements in the automated set-up at the FRNM Institute under the supervision of Dr Schmidt. [see Levy et al. (1971)][37] It is much too soon to jump to any conclusions on the basis of these very small-scale experiments, especially as the replication succeeded at a very reduced level of significance, but should it prove possible to demonstrate a *psi*-effect in a relatively lowly organism using a standard procedure, the prospects of achieving strict repeatability become very hopeful. For, the lower down we go in the phylogenetic scale the less likely we are to be bothered by intra-specific variability and, even if such individual differences were to emerge, there should be no great difficulty in breeding a special strain of high-ESP animals!

Whether repeatability will emerge in the near future either from these developments or from any of the other new directions that are currently being explored, such as training human subjects to control their own brain-rhythms—whether, indeed, it will ever emerge at all, remains to be seen. Perhaps *psi* is so inherently anarchic and unstable that it will elude for ever our attempts to run it to ground and bring it under control. In that case, I see no escape from Rushton's dilemma. Belief in the paranormal, like belief in God, will remain forever a matter of faith or of metaphysical proclivity.

The Nature of the Phenomena

Since there is still no consensus among those best qualified to judge as to whether there are any paranormal phenomena, it may seem premature to be asking what they mean. Since, however, one of the main reasons for denying their existence has been precisely their apparent lack of meaning, it may be worth stopping to consider what creates this impression and how far it is justified. To those who have already made up their mind that parapsychology is nothing more than an updated version of the age-old belief in magic, such speculations can only appear a waste of time. This section is addressed rather to those who are not quite so sure that they know what kind of a world it is that they inhabit. To them I hope to show that parapsychologists are not simply interested in anomalies for their own sake, or for the sake of puncturing other people's complacency, but are as much concerned to understand man and his world as any other kind of scientist.

My task, unfortunately, is complicated from the outset by the fact that when one turns to the authorities one finds no general agreement as to which phenomena deserve to be taken seriously. Each parapsychologist draws the map in his own way. Thus, those who regard as authentic only such phenomena as have been demonstrated in the laboratory by means of quantitative experiments, present a very different picture from others who attach greater weight to studies of mediumship or to accounts of real-life phenomena. As usually happens in any controversial field, a wide spectrum of belief opens out between the 'maximalists' at the one extreme and the 'minimalists' at the other. In the history of parapsychology the maximalist position was represented mainly by the Spiritualist wing of the movement. Spiritualism is, of course, a religious creed, not a science, but it is almost unique among religions in holding that its central tenets can be made a matter of proof rather than of faith. At all events, there can be no doubt that the origins of psychical research are closely interwoven with its bizarre and, it must be admitted, unedifying history.[17] For it was, after all, the mediums, the priesthood, as it were, of this new church, who furnished the researchers with their staple phenomena. Furthermore several of the most ardent among the early pioneers, men like Crookes or Myers or Lodge, shared with the Spiritualists the hope that it would be possible to prove personal survival. The question of survival, the question, that is, as to whether any part of the personality survives the dissolution of the organism at death, is an empirical question and its answer does not commit us to any religious faith. Belief in an after-life is entirely compatible with atheism even if not, presumably, with materialism. Nevertheless, the religious motive in parapsychology, that is the idea that scientific method can be used in order to vindicate an essentially religious outlook on life, has never been far beneath the surface and in Victorian times, at least, psychical research could well have been described as the Spiritualism of the intellectual.

In due course, however, the problem of survival which had so dominated early research receded even further into the background while attention shifted to other topics that seemed more amenable to solution. This shift may have been expedited by an increasing scarcity of good mediums or it may have been due to the realisation that, in the absence of any known limits to paranormal cognition, there was no straightforward way of deciding whether a given communication was inspired by a discarnate communicator or whether it should be attributed to the extrasensory powers of the medium herself. At all events, the issue of survival, though it remains an open one, now occupies a position on the periphery of parapsychology, not at its centre.[18] Evidence in its favour has impressed a number of eminent philosophers[19] but a definitive solution seems as far off as ever.

Although Spiritualism concerned itself mainly with verbal messages it also sought evidence of the spirit world in various physical manifestations. Loud raps signifying the answer to a question, table-tiltings and levitations, the moving around of small objects and other such wonders were all part of its stock-in-trade during its heyday. The most dramatic of these seance-room phenomena was that known as 'materialisation'. This referred to the appearance of ghostly forms and faces supposed to be composed of a mysterious substance, known as 'ectoplasm', emanating from the medium's own body. This physical aspect of Spiritualism soon attracted an unsavoury crew of charlatans who profited from the credulity of bereaved clients and, despite repeated exposures and scandals, fraudulent mediumship continued to flourish. There would be no need to dwell on these sordid swindles had it not been that a few of these so-called physical mediums were of such brilliance (or such audacity) that they cannot be glossed over. The most spectacular, as well as the earliest, of these was the American medium D. D. Home whose performances quickly made him an international star. But he died in 1886, somewhat before psychical research had really got going or investigators had yet had much opportunity to become sophisticated in their methods. Accordingly, the crux of the case for the reality of physical mediumship came, in the end, to rest on the claims of an Italian woman, Eusapia Palladino. She was investigated *ad nauseam* by a host of scientists or experts in Italy, France, England, Poland and, finally, the United States. But opinion was divided about her during her lifetime and she has remained an enigma to this day.[20] There have, of course, been other physical mediums since she died in 1918 but none as notable as she, and today the species is virtually extinct, at any rate the kind who are willing to submit to investigation.

The minimalist position is the one best calculated to appeal to scientists or to science fiction enthusiasts. Rather than regarding paranormal phenomena as intimations of some supernatural order, it prefers to look on them as pointers to the science of tomorrow. By an appropriate modification of existing physical theory, it is hoped that the findings of parapsychology may before too long be brought into line with the scientific outlook without, at any point, having to appeal to dualistic assumptions about unique properties of mind.[21] Indeed, some proponents of this approach prefer the term 'paraphysics' to 'parapsychology' to express what they are trying to do. Their position has received some encouragement from Soviet sources, now that parapsychology is no longer taboo in the Soviet Union.[22] Russian parapsychologists are, of course, understandably anxious not to be associated with any movement that might be thought of as having religious or 'Idealistic' overtones. To this school of thought, telepathy represents the *psi* phenomenon *par excellence*, inviting, as it does, analogies with radio and general systems of telecommunication. It has been suggested that, in telepathy, it is the brain itself, or some specialised part of it, that functions as the sense organ and both receives and transmits the appropriate signals. It is, however, admitted that these signals could not be mediated by the very feeble electrical activity which is picked up on the EEG and that it would be necessary to assume some as yet unknown form of radiation as the carrier. Theorising is still further complicated by the fact that it is very difficult to divorce the evidence for telepathy from evidence for precognitive telepathy, which means that any viable theory is more or less bound to incorporate one or more unorthodox postulates concerning the nature of time and/or causation. This, in itself, raises vast philosophical problems which we cannot enter into here but it can at least be said that modern physics, unlike its classical counterpart, provides ample precedent for introducing counter-intuitive notions of time and causation.[23]

Even more bothersome, however, for the 'paraphysicist' than

these time-displacements is the clairvoyance evidence. By definition, clairvoyance involves a paranormal acquisition of information about external physical events that are not necessarily known to any other person. In a typical clairvoyance experiment, the subject may be required to guess his way through a shuffled stack of cards where no-one, at least until the test is scored, knows the order of the target symbols. If the clairvoyant test is scored by machine, no-one need ever know the correct order, merely the overall number of hits which the subject scores. It is exceedingly hard to comprehend how one could even begin to explain clairvoyance (if it exists) in terms of any radiation theory. Of course, every theorist is entitled to select from among phenomena only those that lend themselves to his explanation and to ignore the rest. No-one holds it against Newton that his laws of motion do not explain electromagnetic phenomena. A workable theory of telepathy and/or precognition would, in itself, represent such an enormous step forward that we would not condemn it on the grounds that it could not also explain clairvoyance. Indeed, since all paranormal phenomena are still suspect we are surely entitled to disregard those that do not fit in with our theory.

Nevertheless, it must be clearly understood that there is no warrant for making such distinctions within the evidence itself. Clairvoyance is not any less well established than telepathy, if anything the reverse: its much greater methodological simplicity has made it a more widely used technique among modern researchers. Indeed, an experiment in pure telepathy, i.e. one which excludes any other interpretation *but* telepathy, is virtually impossible to design since there has to be a physical target of some description. In practice, the distinction is usually made on methodological grounds; a telepathic design of experiment is one where there is a second person or 'agent', a clairvoyant design is one where there is no 'agent'. The point of using such neutral expressions as 'ESP' or even 'GESP' ('General ESP'), is to avoid having to distinguish between these different manifestations of *psi* cognition. The stark truth is that parapsychology is a slippery slope to tread; the more 'absurd' phenomena do not appear any less well supported than the less 'absurd' phenomena. Those whose credulity is too easily strained are better advised not to set foot on the slope in the first place!

Perhaps the most serious criticism of all the physicalist and quasiphysicalist theories to date is, not that they cannot yet explain everything, but rather that they have not as yet explained anything. Not one, to my knowledge, has yet issued in any empirical discovery or gone beyond a purely abstract speculative level. We have been offered plenty of new-fangled concepts—'*psi*-energy', '*psi*-fields', even '*psi*-particles'—but not one critical experiment or falsifiable hypothesis. I am not, let it be clear, objecting to such speculations. So long as there are facts that lie outside the present boundaries of science it is right and proper that scientists should continue to speculate in this vein. My point is that we have no right to take for granted that physicalistic explanations must be all-embracing, least of all where human beings are concerned. [*cf*. Beloff (1973)] Moreover, what stands out most conspicuously from the parapsychological evidence is how little the various physical parameters of the experimental situation seem to influence the results. Thus, no lawful relation has so far been found between the magnitude of the spatial or temporal distance separating target from subject and the level of scoring.[24] Similarly, neither the size nor intensity of the target considered as a physical stimulus seems to have any bearing on the subject's performance, nor the extent to which the target is physically screened from the subject. Of course, it may be that the evidence is still so scanty that no conclusions can yet be drawn, either positive or negative. Alternatively, it may be that physical parameters really *are* irrelevant to the *psi* process and that what alone counts are the purely mental variables. Thus, distance as such may be irrelevant, but not the feelings of remoteness which distance may induce; opaque screens as such may not be relevant but the subject's belief that they are may be. I shall now pursue this frankly dualistic line of thought and consider the consequences of assuming that while *psi* transcends physical limitations it remains acutely sensitive to prevailing psychological conditions.

Suppose, therefore, that instead of asking how information is transmitted in ESP we start with the admittedly wild assumption that somehow, at some level of awareness, all information throughout time and space, no matter in what form it may be encoded, is potentially accessible. The question, then, is no longer the familiar one, i.e. 'How does ESP work?', but rather, 'Why, if this is the case, is ESP so rare, so unstable and unreliable, so inaccurate and, for the most part, so trivial in content?' In other words, it is the negative rather than the positive aspects of ESP that now demand an explanation. For, considering the immense advantages that might be thought to accrue to any individual or species which gained control over its extrasensory powers, how is it that natural selection has failed to exploit them? Every conceivable *modus vivendi* seems to have its own ecological niche; how comes it that, even if *psi* has played some part in evolution, this appears at best marginal and exceptional?[25] The suggestion one sometimes hears that ESP is an archaic mode of communication which was once highly developed among our ancestors, but which we lost in the process of becoming civilised, rests upon little more than a few shreds of anecdotal anthropology (which is not to say, of course, that there might not be considerable variations in the incidence of ESP as between widely different cultures with their different outlooks and belief-systems).[26] Ultimately we have got to explain why nature should have gone through all the long-drawn-out process necessary to equip us with our complex perceptual apparatus, if another and more powerful method of obtaining information existed which did not depend on this elaborate biological machinery.

Not only is it difficult to reconcile the existence of ESP with current evolutionary theory, it seems no less difficult to reconcile it with current learning theory. For, if there is one safe generalisation in all psychology it is surely that every ability or skill can be improved to some extent by applying certain elementary principles of feedback. ESP alone, it seems, is impervious to the universal laws of learning. Indeed, one of the most salient features of the parapsychological data is an absence of learning curves and a prevalence of decline effects. The nearest anyone seems able to get to controlling his ESP is to put himself into a frame of mind which he has found to be favourable to its manifestation. There may be an analogy here with the process of falling asleep. We cannot will ourselves to fall asleep but we can so compose our body and our thoughts that we can facilitate the onset of sleep.

What all such considerations point to, I submit, is that there must be some very powerful forces at work in nature which counteract the *psi* process wherever this threatens to intrude or erupt. We must assume that whatever potential benefits ESP might confer they are outweighed by their potential dangers. But what are these dangers? The main danger would seem to be an overloading of our cognitive capacities with an excess of information. The following illustration may help to explain my meaning. Suppose there was someone who was so hard of hearing that he was incapable of catching anything that was said more than a foot away from his ear. Such a person would obviously be severely handicapped in his daily life. But would such a person be more handicapped in the long run than another whose hearing was so acute that every conversation was audible to him within a mile radius (assuming such a thing were physically possible)? It is this latter kind of handicap that would correspond to the free play of ESP.

The analogy, admittedly is not very exact. The man with hyperacuity of hearing would not necessarily be handicapped at all provided he retained the power of focusing on the one conversation which he wanted to listen to and of treating all the others as just so much background noise, as we all can do to some extent when listening to a conversation in a crowded room. One is not necessarily overwhelmed with information simply because one is being bombarded with acoustic stimuli. Similarly, with ESP, if the subject did not possess some power of attending to the target and ignoring all other objects he would never score a hit. And yet, if there were no constraints at all on the exercise of his ESP, he would be faced with an environment whose information content was infinite. It would be like finding oneself endowed with a memory having an infinite store and infinite powers of retrieval. Now, while such omniscience might be compatible with certain conceptions of godhood, it would scarcely be compatible with our continued existence as separate and finite individuals each intent on his own business. Hence, insofar as evolution works through discrete and competing organisms, we can expect sensory communication to be the rule and ESP as far as possible to be excluded. The sacrifice of its paranormal powers is, so to speak, the price which mind had to pay for entering into a union with physical nature. Where we still do find traces of ESP, despite all this, we may look for some temporary disturbance in the balance of forces which regulate normal mental life.[27]

If this analysis is right, then the outstanding sensitive or 'paragnost' (to use the convenient expression popular among Dutch parapsychologists) may be regarded not so much as a genius endowed with gifts beyond those of the ordinary run of mankind but rather as a defective or 'leaky' vessel. His brain, on our analogy, could be likened to a semi-permeable membrane through which information is absorbed by osmosis, as compared with our brain which acts like an impermeable membrane and prevents any flow of information. ESP is not, however, just a matter of individual differences. The decline effects I spoke about could be interpreted from this point of view as a rallying of the brain against an alien intrusion, comparable to the immunological reaction of the body to alien tissues or alien organisms. Pursuing further this line of thought may also help us to understand the phenomenon known to parapsychologists as '*psi*-missing'. This refers to the tendency on the part of a subject to score *below* chance expectation, a tendency which seems to be specially noticeable when the task is an uncongenial one or where the conditions are for some reasons inhibiting. [*cf.* Rao (1965) and (1966) Chap. 5 or Rhine (1969)] It may be compared with the phenomenon of repression or of perceptual defence in depth psychology. Not content with screening out *psi* influences, the brain, as it were, actively strives to negate them. At the conscious level this sometimes shows itself in a fear of the paranormal. I have heard of many cases where, following some dramatic initial success in an ESP experiment, the subject has taken fright and refused ever to participate in such an experiment again. But far more often the fear seems to operate at an unconscious level. It may well be that the secret of mediumship lies in the fact that the medium is taught to attribute her ESP to some external agency (her 'spirit guide' or the 'deceased communicator'), and thus overcomes her natural unconscious inhibitions, in much the same sort of way as a stammerer often overcomes his disability if he takes part in a play which enables him to speak through an assumed character.

The practical implication of adopting this view is that research is directed more towards cultivating *psi*-favourable states of mind than attempting to condition *psi*-hitting behaviour. At one time it was thought that hypnosis held the key to this problem but, although hypnotism still has its advocates among contemporary parapsychologists, it cannot be said that it has stood up well to attempts to confirm the claims that have been made for it.[28] Nor, for that matter, has much come of the hopes aroused when the psychedelic drugs started to come into use.[29] Of much greater importance have been the attempts to utilise the techniques of modern sleep research for parapsychological ends, in particular those of the Maimonides team in New York who use pictorial targets in a bid to influence the content of their subjects' dreams.[30] Yet another line of attack, also pioneered by the Maimonides team, has been to train the subject to regulate his own EEG activity, the idea being that a high incidence of alpha-rhythm, indicating a relaxed state of mind, would enhance ESP scoring.[31] What is common alike to all these approaches is the implicit recognition that one has to circumvent the brain's normal defence mechanisms if *psi* is to be given a chance to show itself.

In discussing the nature of ESP it is necessary to distinguish at least four distinct levels of performance. At the lowest level we have the typical guessing-subject who, though he can score consistently beyond chance, has no more insight into his own mental processes than the onlooker and cannot discriminate subjectively between his hits and his misses. The fact that the great bulk of the experimental evidence for ESP rests on just this sort of performance should not blind us to the fact that it is, after all, a very degenerate form of ESP. It bears, in fact, much the same relation to full-blown ESP experiences as subliminal perception bears to normal perceptual experience. The next level is exemplified by unconscious *psi* performances, as in trance mediumship or in automatic writing, etc., where the communications appear to be conveyed *through* the subject rather than *by* him. At a higher level still, the level at which the medium or paragnost operates in a conscious state, a train of images and free associations, often of a disguised or symbolic nature, is triggered off by the sitter or by some 'token-object' which is connected with the target person and the subject has to interpret the information appropriately in order to arrive at a meaningful message.[32] Finally, at the highest level of all, a level attained by only a small number of subjects in the history of parapsychology, it appears possible to achieve a completely accurate ascertainment of the target object, picture or event. Such achievements would seem to demand an almost superhuman power of concentration and a unique state of mind compounded of extreme passivity towards incoming impressions with an ardent striving to know the answer.[33]

Our speculations so far point, then, to there being two alternative and antagonistic modes of knowing: the familiar sensory mode, about which science has already told us a great deal, and this other utterly baffling extrasensory mode, about which science remains silent but which parapsychology insists upon exploring and which appears to have some affinity with mystical modes of knowing. [*cf.* LeShan (1974) or Hardy (1966)] Most of us, of course, for most of the time, appear to rely exclusively on the normal mode, but once in a while, perhaps in some acute emergency or when all other channels are blocked for us, we suddenly find ourselves using this other paranormal mode. We can also try using it intentionally, as when we participate as subjects in an ESP experiment, but the amount of information we can obtain in this way is, in all but the rarest cases, absolutely minimal.

I have discussed the position with respect to ESP, since this is the better known aspect of parapsychology, but a very similar analysis could be made with respect to PK. In the latter case the dichotomy would have to be between the two modes of controlling environment: the normal mode corresponding to the exercise of muscular force, augmented by whatever mechanical extensions of it human ingenuity can provide, and this other, antagonistic, extra-muscular force. As in the case of ESP, various levels of performance could be distinguished starting with the experimental PK using dice or, as in more recent research, electronic randomisers, and graduating to the stronger manifestations of PK associated with physical mediumship, poltergeist disturbances, paranormal healing, psychic photography or *psi* influences on plant growth.[34] What seems crucial to an understanding of PK is that it represents a quasi-intelligent application of force, not just that its source of energy is mysterious. The action of PK, moreover, seems to represent an instance of pure teleology since the subject concentrates exclusively on the end-state that he wishes to bring about and the events leading up to this state then seem to follow automatically.[35] Superficially, the process is not unlike that which we associate with the ordinary voluntary movement of a limb where we also think only of the effect we are trying to achieve and ignore the physiological processes which make that movement possible. The reason why we do not call the latter 'paranormal' is, of course, that we assume a deterministic chain of neural impulses between the excitation of the relevant centres of the motor cortex and the innervation of the appropriate muscle groups, whereas, in the former case, there is an obvious hiatus in the causal sequence.

*   *   *

I may have given the impression, in this final chapter, that parapsychology is a science without any firm foundations in fact and without any prospect of achieving the kind of theory which alone might make its facts acceptable. What justification, then, can we offer for including it among the accredited psychological sciences? It would certainly be hard to justify its inclusion on practical grounds. Until (or unless) a far greater degree of control over the phenomena becomes possible than is at present foreseeable, its practical applications could be no more than marginal. For the present, its justification is likely to remain primarily philosophical. The point is that, alone among the sciences, it provides us with empirical evidence bearing on the traditional mind-body problem. All the other psychological sciences we have surveyed were entirely compatible with the assumption that man is, in the first instance, a physical system, even if they did not *require* any such assumption. Even those psychologies of an holistic or teleological complexion, which deny the possibility of establishing any sort of a one-to-one correspondence between mental states and physical states, appeal to logical or semantic considerations and stop short of positing any kind of ontological dualism. And yet, it is surely still worthwhile considering the alternative view, namely that 'mind' (of which consciousness is merely the subjective aspect) exists for a purpose, i.e. because it enables us to do things which, as purely physical systems, we ought not to be able to do. But the long-standing issue between epiphenomenalism and interactionism can never be settled on the basis of *a priori* arguments. If there are paranormal powers this would suggest that we are more than just physical systems (unless we persist in using the term 'physical' in some quite unspecified sense). Conversely, if parapsychology fails to reveal the existence of any such inexplicable powers this suggests that the monistic view of man is the correct one. It is this which gives parapsychology its critical importance.[36]

Summary

The State of the Evidence[38]

Parapsychology is here defined as the scientific study of the paranormal, but there is still no consensus among those best qualified to judge whether there exist any genuine paranormal phenomena or not. The two main categories of paranormal phenomena of interest to parapsychologists are (a) *ESP* (*Extrasensory Perception*, which covers all instances of paranormal cognition, i.e. telepathy, clairvoyance and precognition), and (b) *PK* (*Psychokinesis*, which covers all instances of paranormal action, i.e. on random events, in physical mediumship, in poltergeist manifestations, in psychic photography, paranormal healing, etc.). The evidence that has been amassed on these two categories of phenomena can be divided into three classes: (1) spontaneous cases pertaining to certain unique events, (2) systematic investigations of particular individuals who appear to possess paranormal abilities, and (3) experimental studies of a quantitative or statistical nature designed to test hypotheses about particular effects. Here we have argued that none of these three classes of evidence can, given our present state of ignorance, be ignored or neglected and that to concentrate exclusively on the laboratory findings would be to impoverish the whole field. No general acceptance of parapsychology can be expected, however, until or unless at least one repeatable *psi*-effect can be unequivocally demonstrated. Two recent developments are finally discussed which have brought this goal somewhat nearer: (a) the introduction of automated electronic testing equipment, and (b) the discovery of an ESP effect in animals using an automated set-up.

The Nature of the Phenomena

Can *psi*-phenomena be accounted for by a further extension of the laws of physics or must we regard them as intimations of an entirely different order of reality beyond the physical domain? While scientists should be encouraged to attempt a physicalistic explanation we should bear in mind that the most striking aspect of *psi*-phenomena that has so far come to light is their relative independence of physical parameters in contrast to their extreme sensitivity to psychological conditions. The suggestion made here is that perhaps the question we should be asking is not 'How does ESP work?' but, starting from the assumption that all information, past, present and future, no matter how it may be encoded, is potentially accessible to us, 'Why is ESP in fact so scanty, so weak and so limited?' The answer which then suggests itself is that there must be powerful counteracting forces in nature working to prevent the individual mind from being swamped with an excess of biologically useless information to which it would otherwise be exposed. The implications of this admittedly speculative train of thought are then discussed, pointing to the importance of attempting to by-pass the brain's normal defence mechanisms by testing the subject during certain special states of consciousness, e.g. dreaming, meditation, etc. In conclusion, the present significance of parapsychology appears to be not so much scientific or practical as philosophical since, alone among the sciences, it can offer the kind of empirical evidence that is critical to a solution of the traditional mind-body problem.

Notes

1   The concept of the paranormal is not one which can be defined with any exactitude since, clearly, what is thought possible or impossible changes as science itself changes. It is a concept which belongs more properly to the commonsense of science than to its formal logic. However, Broad [1949] has attempted to make explicit the 'limiting principles' that serve to define the domain of the paranormal. [see also his Introduction to Broad (1962)] Of course, from the definition nothing follows about the nature of the phenomena in question: whether, in particular, they will eventually be subsumed under an expanded conception of physical reality or whether they will remain forever outside it. Meanwhile, in practice, apart from a few borderline cases, there is rarely much dispute as to what would qualify as paranormal, the dispute is only as to whether anything actually does so.

Paranormal phenomena assumed to be brought about by human (or animal) agency are variously referred to as 'parapsychical', 'psychical', 'psychic' or, in the current technical literature, as *'psi* phenomena'. The term *'psi'* (ψ) was introduced by Dr R. H. Thouless in 1947 to cover the two main categories of such phenomena: paranormal cognition, which he designated *psi-gamma* (ψ_γ), and paranormal action, which he designated *psi-kappa* (ψ_κ). However, J. B. Rhine's term 'ESP' (extrasensory perception), despite its question-begging implications, has remained the standard generic term for all manifestations of paranormal cognition which include, in particular, telepathy (extrasensory communication between individual), clairvoyance (direct extrasensory perception by an individual of external objects or events), and precognition (direct extrasensory knowledge of future information). Similarly, it was Rhine's term PK which became the standard generic term for every kind of paranormal physical effect assumed to be produced by purely mental influences.

2 The universality of physics is one of the tacit assumptions of the philosophy of science. The eminent American physicist Richard Feynman, recently said that he knew of no phenomena which could not be explained with reference to physical laws. After mentioning 'super-conductivity' as a case of a phenomenon which at first seemed incapable of being explained by known laws but later was seen to be fully explicable, he went on to say: 'There are other phenomena such as extrasensory perception which cannot be explained by our knowledge of physics. However, that phenomenon has not been well established and we cannot guarantee that it is there. If it could be demonstrated, of course, that would prove that physics was incomplete and *it is therefore extremely interesting to physicists* whether it is right or wrong' (my italics). [Feynman (1965) p. 121]

3 To be fair to Hume I must point out that, in his famous essay on miracles, he does not deny that miracles *might* occur but only that we would never be justified in believing that they had occurred since this would imply that the falsity of the testimony would be even more miraculous than the truth of the miracle to which it testified! However, he showed himself to be keenly alive to 'Rushton's Dilemma', especially when discussing, in a lengthy footnote to his essay, the miraculous cures alleged to have taken place some years previously at the tomb of the Abbé François Paris (a much venerated Jansenist priest) at the cemetery of St Médard on the outskirts of Paris. 'Where shall we find such a number of circumstances agreeing to the corroboration of one fact?' he asks, 'and what have we to oppose to such a cloud of witnesses but the absolute impossibility or miraculous nature of the events which they relate?' (*Enquiry Concerning Human Understanding* of 1748, sect. 10)

4 There is an entertaining account of a mixed bag of such pseudo-

sciences in Gardner [1957]. It is significant that Gardner, a well-known science journalist, should see fit to include parapsychology among his pseudo-sciences (*see* Chap. 23). While apologising for including someone as obviously sincere as J. B. Rhine among his gallery of charlatans, he explains that he did so 'because he is an excellent example of a borderline scientist whose work cannot be called crank yet who is far on the outskirts of orthodox science'.

5 The three principal learned journals in English are:
   The Journal/Proceedings of the Society for Psychical Research,
      London 1882-
   *The Journal/Proceedings of the American Society for Psychical
      Research*, New York 1907-
   Journal of Parapsychology, Durham, N. Carolina 1937-
This last is the organ of the FRNM (Foundation for Research into the Nature of Man), the successor organisation of the Duke University Parapsychology Laboratory, now an independent research foundation. It was always the most experimentally oriented of the three English language journals.

6 There was much jubilation in parapsychological circles when, in 1969, the PA (Parapsychological Association) was admitted as an affiliated society to the AAAS (American Association for the Advancement of Science). Whether this betokens a thaw it is still too early to say. The PA is the only professional organisation of parapsychologists, with a membership of around 200; it is international but is in fact predominantly American.

7 A useful recent survey of the criticisms which are levelled at the parapsychological evidence has been made by Ransom [1971]; he cites lack of repeatability as the most common complaint. *See also* Crumbaugh [1966] and Dommeyer [1966], both sympathetic critics who constantly revert to the question of repeatability. Dommeyer, a philosopher, makes the point that it is not so much sheer repetition that is important as control, i.e. being able 'to specify the causal conditions that, when present, are generally productive of ESP or PK'. West [1971] makes the point that 'the strongest reason for continued doubt is not, as many critics imply, that experimenters may be thought to be fraudulent or incompetent. It is the tendency of the results to dwindle away with continued investi-

gation that makes the phenomenon so uncertain'. I have myself discussed the whole problem of scepticism in Beloff [1972].

8 The outstanding exponent of this approach is C. E. M. Hansel, Professor of Psychology at the University College of Wales, Swansea, whose book [Hansel (1966)] was extravagantly acclaimed by those who knew little about parapsychology but who hoped that Hansel had delivered its *coup de grâce*! [*see* esp. Stevens (1967), Slater (1968) and Gardner (1966)] In fact, for all its undoubted cleverness, the book was not, as its title proclaimed, a scientific evaluation of ESP, but a very one-sided polemic with far too many serious omissions and inaccuracies; *see* McConnell [1968], Stevenson [1967], Gauld [1968] App. B, and the correspondence in the *Brit. J. Psychiatry* for 1968 between Slater and Hansel on the one side and Eysenck, West, Beloff and Stevenson on the other.

9 I am not saying, of course, that the question of fraud never arises in other sciences; the classic case of the Piltdown skull is of special interest in this connection because it was an almost unmotivated piece of devilry. Recently Koestler [1971] has disinterred the baffling case of the Austrian biologist, Paul Kammerer, whose experiments purported to demonstrate the inheritance of acquired characteristics but who committed suicide in 1926 after coming under suspicion of faking his results. Koestler does his best to clear Kammerer but here too only a successful replication of the experiments could finally clear his name.

10 This investigation was so highly regarded in academic quarters that S. G. Soal, then a lecturer in mathematics at London University, was awarded a Doctorate of Science, a unique honour, I believe, in parapsychology. For a full account of this series of experiments *see* Soal and Goldney [1943] or, for a more general account, Soal and Bateman [1954] Chaps 8-11.

11 The first critic to suggest fraud as a possible counter-explanation was G. R. Price, an American research chemist, *see* Price [1955] and Soal's reply to Price in *Science* 123, 1956, 9-11. Price's suggestions were then taken up and elaborated by Hansel in Hansel [1966] Chap. 9. The one actual accusation of fraud came from a certain Mrs G. Albert who had been asked to act

as 'agent' in certain of the sessions and insisted that, on one occasion, she had seen Soal altering '1s' into '4s' and '5s' on the record-sheet! Nearly thirty years later the late Dr R. G. Medhurst, who had himself been a witness in some of the sessions, thought he could clear Soal of this accusation by using a computer to recon-struct the original target sequence of random digits on the basis of the precise instructions which Soal had specified for generating these from log tables. To his intense chagrin, the computer analysis revealed instead (a) that Soal had not obtained his random numbers in the way he said he had and, worse still, (b) on the critical session there was indeed a deficit of target '1s' and an excess of hits on target '4s' and '5s'! [*see* Medhurst (1971)]

The question was further pursued by C. Scott and P. Haskell in *Nature*, **245**, 1973, 52-54. A fuller version of this article together with rejoinders by others including myself in defence of Soal is due (1974) to appear in *Proceedings of the Society for Psychical Research*.

12 In the 1966 edition of the *Encyclopaedia Britannica* 'para-psychology' and 'psychical research' are given separate headings. The former article deals only with the post-Rhine developments and is written by two American psychologists, P. E. Mechl and E. Girden; the latter article is written by R. H. Thouless, an English parapsychologist (as well as psychologist). In this chapter we are using the one word parapsychology to cover the entire field of the paranormal. The Germans have always used the expression 'para-psychologie'; the French equivalent of 'psychical research' is 'la metapsychique' but I gather that 'la parapsychologie' is now catching on.

13 *Cf.* Crumbaugh [1966] p. 524. 'I entered the parapsycho-logical scene in 1938 with a Master's Thesis on extrasensory per-ception. At the time of performing the experiments involved I fully expected that they would yield easily all the final answers. I did not imagine that, after 28 years, I would still be as much in doubt as when I had begun. I repeated a number of the then current Duke techniques, but the results of 3,024 runs (1 run = 25 guesses) of the ESP cards—as much work as Rhine reported in his first book—were all negative. In 1940 I utilized further Duke methods with high-school students, again with negative findings.'

My own story is very similar. I recently completed a seven-year programme of parapsychological research with the help of one full-time research assistant. No-one would have been more delighted to obtain positive results than we but for all the success we achieved ESP might just as well not have existed. While this confession may prove nothing more interesting than my incompetence as an investigator I have not found on comparing notes with other parapsychologists, in this country at least, that my experience is in any way out of the ordinary.

14   The only 'steady scorer' around during the 1960s, if that is the correct term for someone whose performance changed in various unpredictable ways over the years, was a Czech, Pavel Stepanek, the discovery of a Czech parapsychologist, Dr Milan Ryzl, who was, in fact, financed by Rhine. Stepanek has by now had the longest career of any card-guessing subject and has performed for the greatest number of different investigators. At one point he seemed on the point of petering out like all previous card-guessers (at about the time when I was in Prague in 1964) but he has since been kept afloat largely as a result of the unremitting efforts of Dr J. G. Pratt, who took charge of the investigation in 1965, made regular visits to Prague and twice even managed to bring Stepanek over to stay at the University of Virginia. However, the fact that Pratt could find no better subject nearer home, but had to go to Prague, of all places, to meet one, speaks for itself. *See* Ryzl [1970] pp. 15-21 for an account of the first phase of the Stepanek story and, for later developments, *see* the regular reports of Pratt and his collaborators in the *J. Amer. Soc. Psychic. Res.* from 1967 onwards. I have myself given a brief popular account of this episode in *New Scientist* 40, 1968, 76-77, after it had achieved what, for parapsychology, is the rare distinction of making the columns of *Nature*. [*see* Pratt *et al.* (1968)]

15   *Cf.* Rhine [1959], where he states his reasons for declining to take up Crumbaugh's challenge to provide psychologists with at least one experimental design which could be repeated enough times to satisfy a duly appointed committee of scientists.

16   From this point of view Hansel [1966] was not wholly destructive. His final paragraph read as follows: 'An acceptable model

of future research with which the argument could rapidly be settled one way or the other has now been made available by the investigators of the US Airforce Research Laboratories. If 12 months' research on VERITAC can establish the existence of ESP, the past research will not have been in vain. If ESP is not established, much further effort could be spared and the energies of many young scientists directed to more worthwhile research.' The statement was quoted with approval by Gardner [1966] in his laudatory review of Hansel's book. I doubt if either of them realised how soon their challenge would be met, for in December 1967 Schmidt read a paper to the FRNM review meeting announcing the highly significant results of his own tests using a machine every bit as sophisticated as VERITAC. We have still to hear from Messrs Hansel and Gardner whether they now agree that ESP *has* been established and whether past research has *not* been in vain.

17   The classic work in this connection is Podmore's 2-vol. *Modern Spiritualism* of 1902 [Podmore (1963a)]. Frank Podmore, one of the founders of psychical research in England, began his career as a convinced spiritualist but became progressively disillusioned. By the time he came to write this book he had rejected, as most probably fraudulent, all of the physical phenomena and, as unproven, almost all of the mental phenomena except, perhaps, in the case of the incomparable Mrs Piper. For an authoritative recent treatment of the interplay between Spiritualism and psychical research *see* Gauld [1968]. A useful brief guide to the beliefs, practices and history of Spiritualism from a critical standpoint is provided by Edmunds [1966].

18   A symposium on the theme 'What Next in Survival Research?' was organised by W. G. Roll, director of the Psychical Research Foundation Inc., Durham, N. Carolina, the proceedings of which were issued as a bound set of reprints from the *J. Amer. Soc. Psychic. Res.* 1965/66 *passim*. Among the contributors were a number of parapsychologists and philosophers of widely differing views.

19   Notably the American philosopher C. J. Ducasse and the English philosophers H. H. Price and C. D. Broad. [*see* Ducasse (1961), Price (1965) and Broad (1962)] This last concludes with the words: 'For my part, I should be slightly more annoyed than

surprised if I should find myself in some sense persisting immediately after the death of my body. One can only wait and see or,
alternatively (which is no less likely) wait and not see.' (p. 430)

20 The key document in this case is the report of the so-called
'Naples Committee' on eleven sittings with Eusapia Palladino held
in Naples Nov.-Dec. 1908. [see Proc. Soc. Psychic. Res. 23,
1909, 306-570, reproduced in Fielding (1963)] The committee was
backed by the SPR who, in this instance, departed from their
custom of not having any further dealings with mediums who had
been detected in fraud. Eusapia was, of course, notorious for cheating at the slightest opportunity (a favourite dodge was to make
her sitters think they were holding both her arms when in fact the
two on either side of her were holding the same arm!). Nevertheless, on the basis of intensive tests carried out during the late 1890s,
Charles Richet, the French physiologist and Nobel Laureate, convinced himself that Eusapia could produce genuine phenomena
when the possibility of cheating was excluded. Both Frederic
Myers and Oliver Lodge, who had attended some of Richet's sittings, became likewise convinced of this and, in due course,
persuaded the SPR to reopen her case. The upshot was the Naples
Committee, headed by E. E. Fielding, for the SPR, with two
American investigators: W. W. Baggally and H. Carrington. All
three men were expert conjurors in their own right, all three had
built up a reputation for exposing fraudulent mediums, indeed
Carrington had just published a book *The Physical Phenomena
of Spiritualism* which was in fact an *exposé* of the various fraudulent practices then current. Yet, after the Naples sittings, all three,
jointly and individually, stated that they had witnessed phenomena
for which they could offer no normal explanation and, from the
blow-by-blow account they provide, it is hard indeed to see what
normal explanation there could be. Electric light was used at the
sittings and the report is emphatic that some of the most evidential
observations were made when the light was strongest (i.e. where
the intensity is described as being sufficient to read small print)
and where, in general, the precautions were at their most stringent.
Yet the phenomena mentioned include not just the numerous table
levitations and miscellaneous noise-effects but even the appearance
of 'materialised' hands and heads and the sensations of being
touched or grasped by invisible fingers!

Emboldened by these findings, Carrington obtained financial backing to enable him to bring Eusapia to the United States. In due course, three sittings were held at the Physical Laboratory of Columbia University in the presence of an assorted team of academics and professional magicians. The result was a fiasco; Eusapia was repeatedly caught in the most flagrant trickery (*see* D. S. Miller *et al. Science* **31**, 1910, 776-80, or the account in J. Jastrow, *The Psychology of Conviction*, Boston 1918) and she returned home to Naples a defeated woman. When, a year later, Fielding again visited her there and held a few more sittings he could obtain no worthwhile phenomena.

Not the least of the questions which her case poses for us is whether fraud and paranormality can coexist alongside one another. Writing to his friend, Andrew Lang, Sir Oliver Lodge had this to say on the topic: 'It may be asked why on earth does she do the cheating when it has been so often discovered? For the woman, though uneducated, is not a fool. The thing puzzled me for some time but I think I have seen the truth of it for the last few years. The fact is her organism has got into such a condition that it responds to all kinds of stimuli and is not fully amenable to her conscious control like that of ordinary people. It must be remembered that what we call "cheating" is the production of an effect by normal means. I am convinced that she does not always distinguish between them but gets things done somehow, or as near as she can manage it, by whatever channels are left open. It is the business of the sitter to prevent the operation of normal methods ...' (Letter to Andrew Lang dated 22nd Dec. 1909, *Archives of the S.P.R.*, Lodge Collection Envelope: 1803). I am indebted to Mrs K. M. Goldney for drawing my attention to this document. Casuistry or commonsense?

21   *Cf.* the following pronouncement by the late Norbert Wiener: 'With an ever increasing understanding of memory and its mechanisms, psychology, which has been largely a phenomenological science, is going to become more and more tied up with neurophysiology. Many other considerations which have, up to the present, been situated in a somewhat shameful background, such as the study of the direct communication at a distance between nervous systems, possibly by some sort of radiative phenomena, are going to be subjected to a real trend in scientific examination which

will not be corrupted by the unscientific assumption that we are dealing with phenomena with no physical correlates. I am looking forward with some confidence either to seeing physical correlates discovered for these phenomena if they do exist, which I regard as quite possible, or to their being finally pushed out of consideration.' [Wiener (1964)]

22 The regime has never been able to make up its mind whether to encourage parapsychology, for fear the West might gain some material advantage over the Soviet Union if it lags behind, or whether to discourage it, for fear of it stirring up superstitious and magical beliefs! The idea that the Russians are rapidly outstripping the rest of us in this field seems to me to be without foundation, though it has become extraordinarily widespread in the West and is kept alive by mercenary journalists who know how to exploit it. There is no Soviet journal devoted to parapsychology and it is very difficult even for those who know Russian or who travel in Russia to find out what exactly is going on. There appear to be some very exceptional subjects in that part of the world but, in general, I would say that Soviet parapsychologists are still as much at sea as their Western colleagues, only they have to contend with even more hostility and suspicion than we do in our more tolerant society. Some inkling of developments there can be had from the special issue on Soviet parapsychology in the *Internat. J. Parapsych.* 7, 1965, No. 4, or from Ebon [1971].

23 *Cf.* Arthur Koestler, 'The Perversity of Physics', Chap. 2 of Koestler [1972], or the late Adrian Dobbs, 'The Feasibility of a Physical Theory of ESP' in Smythies (ed.) [1967].

24 Some parapsychologists would contest this statement. Thus, Osis [1965] claims that the available data do point to a falling off of scoring with increasing distance, even if this is not indicative of an inverse square relationship. However, the evidence is by no means unequivocal and would certainly not preclude a psychological interpretation. Moreover he has himself reported some very significant scoring with the subject in Australia and the experimenter in America!

25 One eminent zoologist, Sir Alister Hardy, FRS, has suggested

tentatively that telepathic communication might help to explain how animals of the same species developed and stabilised certain common behavioural patterns. [*see* Hardy (1965) p. 255] Some recent speculations about a possible evolutionary role for '*psi*' have been put forward by Randall [1971].

26 A few enterprising parapsychologists have recognised the importance of testing pre-literate peoples before Western influences have completely destroyed their traditional way of life [*cf.* Rose (1952) and (1955)], but their data are too slight to support any firm conclusions.

27 I claim no originality whatever for this particular speculation. It was first put forward by the French philosopher, Henri Bergson [*see* Bergson (1929) and (1913)], where he develops the idea that the primary function of the brain is to act as a screening device designed by nature to restrict our attention to what is of direct biological relevance to us. A similar view was recently put forward by the physiologist W. A. H. Rushton, FRS, (also, as it happens, in the course of a presidential address to the SPR [*see* Rushton (1971)] which concludes with the following words: 'Perhaps our personal integrity rests as delicately upon the *information* we take in from the outside as upon the proteins. We filter information with our sense organs and build our mentality in our own way from these elements of experience. Information seeking entry by extrasensory paths is almost completely kept out, and any successful entry quickly builds immunity against the like occurring again. We should therefore praise, not blame, our marvellous imperviousness to extrasensory perception. It is bad enough for you to hear my words; be thankful you are screened from my thoughts' (author's italics).

28 *Cf.* Honorton and Krippner [1969]. Although these authors cite positive evidence from the recent literature, one feels that it is more a case of *faute de mieux* when they conclude their survey by saying: 'It would appear that hypnosis provides one of the few presently available techniques for affecting the level of *psi* test performance.' The most far-reaching claims for hypnosis in this connection of recent times were those put forward by Dr Milan Ryzl, the Czech parapsychologist, but, although he repeats these

claims in his latest book [Ryzl (1970)], he offers no evidence to substantiate them, and others, including myself, who have tried his technique have not found it efficacious. [*see* Beloff (1967)]

29 The most ingenious attempt so far to use a psychedelic drug to enhance ESP performance is that of Cavanna and Servadio [1964] who got some positive indications, but a Dutch team of psychologists and physicians were wholly negative in their efforts. [*see* van Asperen de Boer, Barkema and Kappers (1966)]

30 The 'Dream Laboratory' of the Maimonides Hospital, Brooklyn, New York, was founded in 1962 by the psychiatrist, Dr Montague Ullman, but the formal series of experiments date from 1964 when he was joined by an experimental psychologist, Dr Stanley Krippner. Though their findings have not been dramatic in statistical terms, their initiative represents, in my view, one of the most hopeful developments in parapsychology during the past decade. Its sustained purpose and high level of professional competence has produced an impact on scientific opinion not normally receptive to parapsychological research. [*see* Ullman, Krippner and Feldstein (1966), Ullman and Krippner (1970) or, for a more popular account of their work, Ullman, Krippner and Vaughan (1973)]

31 *See* Honorton [1969], Stanford and Lovin [1970], Stanford [1971]. One of the first to suggest such a relationship was an English parapsychologist, McCreary [1967].

32 For the role of imagery and symbolism in the thought processes of the professional 'psychic' *see* pp. 100-04 of Drage [1960]. The book presents an intimate portrait of a fashionable London clairvoyant, since deceased, by the writer who was himself one of his regular clients. The most celebrated exponent of token-object reading (or 'psychometry') is the Dutch paragnost, Gerard Croiset, who was extensively studied and written up by his discoverer and investigator, Professor W. Tenhaeff, who, until his recent retirement, held a chair of parapsychology at the University of Utrecht. Much of this literature is in Dutch but bulletins in English were occasionally issued by the Institute at Utrecht. [*see also* Tenhaeff (1966), which deals not only with Croiset but with other Dutch paragnosts]

33 Perhaps the most articulate witness in this connection is the late Mary Craig Sinclair, wife of the American novelist Upton Sinclair, who acted as his subject for the epoch-making series of telepathy experiments which he has described in his book *Mental Radio* of 1930, *see* Sinclair [1962], Chap. 21, where Mrs Sinclair gives a detailed account of her state of mind while in the throes of attempting an ascertainment of the target drawing which her husband, as agent, had drawn. [*see also* White (1964)] Perhaps the greatest sensitive of all time at this level of performance was the Pole, Stefan Ossowiecki; an account of some of the experiments in which he took part is given in Borzymowski [1965].

34 A useful popular survey of the experimental literature on PK is to be found in Rhine, L. [1970]. For a discussion of the polter-geist evidence *see* Owen [1964] and the account of some recent cases in Germany by Bender [1968]. For the special case of psychic photography, *see* the spectacular but controversial story of Ted Serios as related in Eisenbud [1967], Eisenbud *et al.* [1967], and Stevenson and Pratt [1968].

35 In an article describing a highly significant PK effect using an electronic randomiser, Dr Helmut Schmidt concludes on the following thought-provoking note: 'The fact that the electronic generator was such a complicated system, which none of the subjects fully understood, and the fact that the subjects directed their attention only to the display panel, may suggest that PK works teleologically. It may be goal-oriented in the sense that the psycho-logical appeal of the display is more relevant to the occurrence of PK than the detailed structure of the random generator used.' [Schmidt (1971)]

36 I have argued the point elsewhere, in Beloff [1962] and [1965]. My contention has been explicitly challenged by the psychiatrist Dr Stephen Black who, while rejecting the mechanistic view of mind, argues in favour of a neo-Aristotelian teleology mainly on the basis of evidence from the field of psychosomatic medicine, including some fascinating hypnosis experiments of his own in which he succeeded in inhibiting the subject's normal allergic reaction to an innoculation while under deep hypnosis. [*see* Black (1969)] I cannot follow Black's philosophical conclusions but I see

his experiments as belonging to the borderline of parapsychology, inasmuch as they appear to represent the special case of a PK influence directed to one's own organism.

My own position on the meaning of parapsychology coincides with that of the Australian philosopher, David Armstrong, despite the fact that Armstrong is a leading proponent of the materialist theory of mind: 'I consider that the claims of psychical research are the small black cloud on the horizon of a materialist theory of mind. If there was no question of paranormal phenomena to consider, there would seem to be little serious obstacle to the complete identification of mental states with physico-chemical states of the nervous system ... the identification would be as certain as the identification of the gene and the DNA molecule.' [Armstrong (1968) p. 364] I only wish that all philosophers were as conscientious as he when he adds: 'The upholder of any doctrine has a duty to consider very carefully the evidence that seems most likely to undermine his view. So the Central State Materialist has an intellectual duty to consider very carefully the alleged results of psychical research.'

37 Since this book was first published a major scandal has come to light affecting the credibility of these findings. The senior author, Dr Walter J. Levy, a young medical graduate whom Rhine had recently promoted to research director of the FRNM Institute in succession to Dr Helmut Schmidt, was detected by his co-workers engaging in fraudulent manipulation of the data. He confessed and resigned. How much of the small rodent work will have to be rejected must now await the outcome of the replication being undertaken by the staff of the Institute. For details of this unhappy affair, *see* J. B. Rhine, 'A New Case of Experimenter Unreliability', *J. Parapsych.* **38**, 1974, 215-26.

38 As a supplement to this chapter *see New Directions in Parapsychology*, Elek: London, 1974, a volume edited by John Beloff and consisting of invited articles by seven leading researchers, which has appeared since this book was first published. *See also* White, Rhea and Dale, Laura, *Parapsychology: Sources of Information*, Scarecrow: Metuchen, N.J., 1973, for a comprehensive annotated bibliography of the field.

Chronology of key figures mentioned in the text, in order of birth

MESMER, Franz Anton (1733-1815)
BRAID, James (1795-1860)
COMTE, Auguste (1798-1857)
FECHNER, Gustav T. (1801-1887)
MILL, John Stuart (1806-1873)
DARWIN, Charles (1809-1882)
HELMHOLTZ, Hermann von (1821-1894)
GALTON, Francis (1822-1911)
CHARCOT, Jean-Martin (1825-1893)
SECHENOV, Ivan M. (1829-1905)
WUNDT, Wilhelm (1832-1920)
BERNHEIM, Hippolyte (1837-1919)
BRENTANO, Franz (1838-1917)
JAMES, William (1842-1910)
MYERS, Frederic W. H. (1843-1901)
PAVLOV, Ivan P. (1849-1936)
EBBINGHAUS, Hermann (1850-1909)
MORGAN, C. Lloyd (1852-1936)
BINET, Alfred (1857-1911)
FREUD, Sigmund (1856-1939)
BEKHTEREV, V. M. (1857-1927)
JANET, Pierre (1859-1947)
KÜLPE, Oswald (1862-1915)

SPEARMAN, Charles (1863-1945)
TITCHENER, Edward B. (1867-1927)
WOODWORTH, Robert S. (1869-1962)
ADLER, Alfred (1870-1937)
JUNG, Carl Gustav (1870-1961)
MCDOUGALL, William (1871-1938)
THORNDIKE, Edward Lee (1874-1949)
YERKES, Robert M. (1876-1956)
TERMAN, Lewis M. (1877-1956)
WATSON, John B. (1878-1958)
WERTHEIMER, Max (1880-1943)
MICHOTTE, Albert (1881-1965)
BURT, Cyril L. (1883-1971)
HULL, Clark H. (1884-1952)
KOFFKA, Kurt (1886-1941)
TOLMAN, Edward C. (1886-1961)
BARTLETT, Frederic (1886-1969)
THURSTONE, L. L. (1887-1955)
KÖHLER, Wolfgang (1887-1967)
LEWIN, Kurt (1890-1947)
WIENER, Norbert (1894-1964)
RHINE, J. B. (1895-)
GUILFORD, J. P. (1897-)
POPPER, Karl R. (1902-)
LORENZ, Konrad (1903-)
HEBB, D. O. (1904-)
SKINNER, B. F. (1904-)
CATTELL, R. B. (1905-)
HARLOW, Harry (1905-)
MOWRER, O. H. (1907-)
EYSENCK, Hans J. (1916-)
FESTINGER, Leon (1919-)
CHOMSKY, Noam (1928-)

Bibliography and References

Agassi, J. (1960) 'Methodological Individualism'. *Brit. P. Sociol.*, II, 244-70

Allen, G. W. (1967) *William James*. Viking Press: New York

Allport, G. W. (1961) *Patterns and Growth in Personality*. Holt, Rhinehart & Winston: New York

Allport, G. W. (1968) 'The Historical Background of Modern Social Psychology'. *See* Vol. I of Lindzey and Aronson (eds) (1968)

Angoff, Alan (1968) 'Hypnotism in the United States of America 1800-1900'. *See* Vol. IV of Dingwall (ed.) (1968)

Annett, John (1969) *Feedback and Human Behaviour*. Penguin

Anokhin, P. K. (1968) 'Ivan P. Pavlov and Psychology'. *See* Wolman (ed.) (1968)

Ardrey, Robert (1967) *The Territorial Imperative*. Collins: London

Ardrey, Robert (1970) *The Social Contract*. Athenaeum: New York

Armstrong, D. M. (1968) *A Materialist Theory of Mind*. Routledge: London

Aronson, E. and Mills, J. (1959) The Effect of Severity of Initiation on Liking for a Group. *J. Abn. & Soc. Psych.*, 59, 177-81

Asch, S. (1952) *Social Psychology*. Prentice Hall: New York

van Asperen de Boer, S., Barkem, P. and Kappers, J. (1966) 'Is it Possible to Induce ESP with Psilocybin?' *Internat. J. Neuropsychiatry* (Special ESP Issue) 2, 447-73

Ayllon, T. and Azrin, N. (1968) *The Token Economy*. Appleton Century Crofts: New York

Banks, Charlotte and Broadhurst, P. L. (eds) (1965) *Stephanos: Studies in Psychology*. Univ. of London Press

Barber, T. X. (1969) *Hypnosis: A Scientific Approach*. Van Nostrand PB. New York/London

Barber, T. X. and Silver, M. J. (1968) 'Fact, Fiction and the Experimenter Effect'. *Psychol. Bull. 70 Monograph Suppl.*, 1-29. (*See also* comment by R. Rosenthal 30-47 and reply by Barber and Silver 48-62)

Barron, F. (1955) 'The Disposition towards Originality'. *J. Abn. & Soc. Psych.*, **51**, 478-85. (Reprinted in Vernon (ed.) 1970)

Barron, F. (1965) 'The Psychology of Creativity'. *See* Holt, Rhinehart and Winston (eds) (1965)

Bass, B. and Berg, I. (eds) (1959) *Objective Approaches to Personality*. Van Nostrand: New York/London

Beach, Frank (1955) 'The Descent of Instinct'. *Psychol. Rev.*, **62**, 401-10. (Reprinted in Haber (ed.) (1966) and in Birney and Teevan (eds) (1961)

Beech, H. R. (1969) *Changing Man's Behaviour*. Penguin

Beloff, Halla (1957) The Structure and Origin of the Anal Character. *Genet. Psych. Monogr.*, **55**, 145-72. (Reprinted in Lee and Herbert (eds) (1970)

Beloff, John (1962) *The Existence of Mind*. MacGibbon & Kee: London. (Citadel Press PB: New York, 1964)

Beloff, John (1965) 'The Identity Hypothesis: A Critique'. *See* Smythies (ed.) (1965)

Beloff, John (1967) 'Can Paranormal Abilities be Learned?' *J. Amer. Soc. Psychic. Res.*, **61**, 120-29

Beloff, John (1970) 'Creative Thinking in Art and in Science'. *Brit. J. Aesthet.*, **10**, 58-70

Beloff, John (1972) 'Belief and Doubt'. (Presidential Address) *Proceedings of The Parapsychological Assoc.*, **9**, Scarecrow: Metuchen, N.J.

Beloff, John (1973) 'The Place of Theory in Parapsychology'. *See* Van Over (ed.) (1973)

Bender, Hans (1969) 'New Developments in Poltergeist Research' (Presidential Address). *Proc. Parapsychol. Assoc.*, **6**, 81-102

Benedict, Ruth (1967) 'Child Rearing in Eastern European Countries'. *See* Hunt, R. (ed.) (1967)

Bergson, Henri (1913) Presidential Address (in French). *Proc. Soc. Psychic. Res.*, **26**, 462-79

Bergson, Henri (1929) *Matter and Memory*. Allen & Unwin: London. (7th Impression 1962. Transl. from French Edition of 1908; First Edit. 1896)

Berlyne, D. E. (1960) *Conflict, Arousal and Curiosity*. McGraw-Hill: New York

Bindra, D. and Stewart, Jane (eds) (1966) *Motivation*. Penguin

Binet, A. and Féré, C. (1887) *Animal Magnetism*. Kegan Paul: London. (Transl. from French of 1886)

Binet, A. and Simon, T. (1905) 'Methodes Nouvelles pour le Diagnostic du Niveau Intellectuel des Anormeaux'. *L'Anneé Psychologique*, **11**, 191-244. (Reprinted, in transl., in Jenkins and Paterson (eds) (1961))

Birney, R. and Teevan, R. (eds) (1961) *Instinct: An Enduring Problem*. Van Nostrand PB: New York

Black, Stephen (1969) *Mind and Body*. Kimber: London

Bolton, N. (1972) *The Psychology of Thinking*. Methuen: London

Bono, Edward de (1969) *The Mechanism of Mind*. Cape: London

Borger, R. and Cioffi, F. (eds) (1970) *Explanation in the Behavioural Sciences*. Cambridge University Press

Boring, E. G. (1950) *A History of Experimental Psychology*. (Second Edition) Appleton Century Crofts: New York

Borzymowski, A. (1965) Experiments with Ossowiecki. *Internat. J. Parapsych.*, **7**, 259-84

Bower, T. G. (1971) 'The Object in the World of the Infant'. *Scientific American*, **225**, 30-48

Bowlby, John (1953) *Child Care and the Growth of Love* (ed. Margery Fry). Penguin

Bramwell, J. M. (1956) *Hypnotism: Its History, Practice and Theory*. Julian Press: New York (1st Edit., London, 1903)

Breger, L. and McGaugh, J. (1965) 'Critique and Reformulation of "Learning Theory" Approaches to Psychotherapy and Neurosis'. *Psychol. Bull.*, **63**, 338-58. (See also reply by S. Rachman and H. J. Eysenck, *idem* **65**, 65-69, and counter-reply by Breger and McGaugh, *idem* **65**, 160-73)

Broad, C. D. (1949) 'The Relevance of Psychical Research to Philosophy'. *Philosophy*, **24**, 291-309. (Reprinted in Broad (1953))

Broad, C. D. (1953) *Religion, Philosophy and Psychical Research*. (Collected Papers) Routledge: London

Broad, C. D. (1962) *Lectures on Psychical Research*. Routledge: London

Broadbent, D. E. (1958) *Perception and Communication*. Pergammon: London

Broadbent, D. E. (1970) 'In Defence of Empirical Psychology'. *Bull. Brit. Psychol. Soc.*, **23**, 87-96

Broadhurst, P. L. (1967) *Psychology in its Natural Habitat*. (Inaugural Lecture) University of Birmingham Press

Brown, J. A. C. (1967) *Freud and the Post-Freudians*. (Rev. Edition) Penguin. (First Edit. 1961)

Brown, W. P. (1961) *Conceptions of Perceptual Defence. Brit. J. Psych. Monogr. Suppl.* No. 35

Burt, C. L. (1949) 'The Structure of Mind'. *Brit. J. Educ. Psych.*, **19**, 110-11 and 176-99. (Reprinted in Wiseman (ed.) (1967))

Burt, C. L. (1966) 'The Genetic Determination of Differences in Intelligence'. *Brit. J. Psych.*, **57**, 137-53. (Reprinted in Butcher and Lomax (eds) (1972))

Burt, C. L. (1968) 'Mental Capacity and its Critics'. *Bull. Brit. Psychol. Soc.*, **21**, 11-18

Butcher, H. J. (1968) *Human Intelligence: Its Nature and Assessment*. Methuen: London

Butcher, H. J. and Lomax, D. E. (eds) (1972) *Readings in Human Intelligence*. Methuen: London

Cattell, R. B. (1946) *Description and Measurement of Personality*. Harrap: London

Cattell, R. B. (1950) *Personality*. McGraw-Hill: New York

Cattell, R. B. (1957) *Personality and Motivation: Structure and Measurement*. Harrap: London

Cattell, R. B. (1965) *The Scientific Analysis of Personality*. Penguin

Cattell, R., Blewett, D. and Beloff, J. (1955) The Inheritance of Personality. *Amer. J. Human Genetics*, **7**, 122-46

Cattell, R. B. and Stice, G. (1949) *The Sixteen Personality Factor Questionnaire*. I.P.A.T.: Champaign, Ill.

Cavanna, R. and Servadio, E. (1964) *ESP Experiments with LSD. 25 and Psilocybin*. Parapsychol. Foundat. Monogr.: New York

Chapanis, N. and Chapanis, A. (1964) 'Cognitive Dissonance: Five Years Later'. *Psychol. Bull.*, **61**, 1-22

Chappell, V. C. (ed.) (1962) *The Philosophy of Mind*. Prentice Hall PB: Englewood Cliffs, N.J.

Cherry, E. C. (1957) *On Human Communication*. Chapman & Hall: London

Chomsky, Noam (1959) Review of *Verbal Behaviour* by B. F. Skinner. *Language*, **35**, 26-58. (Reprinted in Fodor and Katz (eds) (1964))

Chomsky, Noam (1969) 'Linguistics and Philosophy'. *See* Hook (ed.) (1969)

Chomsky, Noam (1971) 'The Case Against B. F. Skinner'. (Review of Skinner (1971)) *New York Review of Books*. Dec. Issue

Chomsky, Noam (1972) *Language and Mind*. (Enlarged Edition) Harcourt, Brace, Jovanovich: New York. (1st Edit. M.I.T. Press PB, 1968)

CIBA Foundation (1968) *The Role of Learning in Psychotherapy*. Symposium. Edited by Ruth Porter. Churchill: London

Cioffi, F. (1970) 'Freud and the Idea of a Pseudo-Science'. *See* Borger and Cioffi (1970)

le Clair, R. C. (ed.) (1966) *The Letters of William James and Theodore Flournoy*. Univ. of Wisconsin Press: Madison, Wisconsin

Collingwood, R. G. (1939) *An Autobiography*. Oxford University Press. (Penguin 1944/O.U.P. PB. 1969)

Craik, K. J. W. (1943) *The Nature of Explanation*. Cambridge University Press

Craik, K. J. W. (1966) *The Nature of Psychology*. (Posthumous Volume of Collected Papers, edited by S. L. Sherwood.) Cambridge University Press

le Cron (ed.) (1948) *Experimental Hypnosis*. Macmillan: New York

Crumbaugh, J. C. (1966) 'A Scientific Critique of Parapsychology'. *Internat. J. Neuropsychiatry*, (Special ESP Issue) **2**, 523-32

Dethier, V. G. (1964) 'Microscopic Brains'. *Science*, **143**, 1138-45. (Reprinted in Endler, Boulter and Osser (eds) (1968))

Deutsch, M., Katz, I. and Jensen, A. (eds) (1968) *Social Class, Race and Psychological Development*. Holt, Rhinehart & Winston: New York

Dingwall, E. J. (ed.) (1967/68) *Abnormal Hypnotic Phenomena: A Survey of 19th Century Cases*. (4 vols) J. & A. Churchill: London

Dixon, N. F. (1968) 'Perception without Awareness'. *Acta Psychologica*, **28**, 171-80

Dixon, N. F. (1971) *Subliminal Perception: The Nature of a Controversy*. McGraw-Hill: London

Dodwell, P. (ed.) (1970) *Perceptual Learning and Adaptation.* Penguin

Dommeyer, F. C. (1966) 'Parapsychology: Old Delusion or New Science?' *Internat. J. Neuropsychiatry,* (Special ESP Issue) **2,** 539-55

Drage, Charles (1960) *William King's Profession.* Blond: London

Dreger, R. and Miller, K. (1968) 'Comparative Psychological Studies of Negro and White in the United States'. *Psychol. Bull. Monogr. Suppl.,* **70,** No. 3, Part 2

Drever Sr., James (1917) *Instinct in Man.* Cambridge University Press

Drever Jr., James (1968) 'Some Early Associationists'. *See* Wolman (ed.) (1968)

Dreyfus, H. L. (1972) *What Computers Can't Do.* Harper & Row: New York

Ducasse, C. J. (1961) *The Belief in Life After Death.* C. C. Thomas: Springfield, Ill.

Duval, P. and Montredon, E. (Pseudonyms) (1968) 'ESP Experiments with Mice'. *J. Parapsych.,* **32,** 153-66

Eastman, Max (1959) *Great Companions.* Museum Press: London

Ebbinghaus, H. (1964) *Memory: A Contribution to Experimental Psychology.* Dover Publications PB: New York. (Transl. from his *Über das Gedächtnis,* Leipzig, 1885)

Ebon, M. (ed.) (1971) *Psychic Discoveries by the Russians.* New American Library PB: New York

Edmunds, Simeon (1966) *Spiritualism: A Critical Survey.* Aquarion Press: London

Edwards, A. L. (1959) Social Desirability and Personality Test Construction. Bass and Berg (eds) (1959). (Reprinted in Semeonoff (ed.) (1966))

Edwards, W. and Tversky, A. (eds) (1967) *Decision Making.* Penguin

Efron, R. (1966) 'The Conditioned Reflex: A Meaningless Concept'. *Perspectives in Biology and Medicine,* **9,** 488-514

Eisenbud, J. (1967) *The World of Ted Serios.* Morrow: New York

Eisenbud, J., *et al.* (1967) 'Some Unusual Data from a Session with Ted Serios'. *J. Amer. Soc. Psychic. Res.,* **61,** 241-54

Endler, N., Boulter, L. and Osser, H. (eds) (1968) *Contemporary Issues in Developmental Psychology.* Holt, Rhinehart & Winston: New York

Erlenmeyer-Kimling, L. and Jarvik, L. (1963) 'Genetics and Intelligence: A Review'. *Science*, 142, 1477-79. (Reprinted in Wiseman (ed.) (1967)

Estes, W. K., *et al.* (1954) *Modern Learning Theory*. Appleton-Century-Crofts: New York

Evans, R. M. (1948) *An Introduction to Color*. Wiley: New York

Ey, Henri (1968) 'Pierre Janet: The Man and The Work'. *See* Wolman (ed.) (1968)

Eysenck, H. J. (1941) 'Type Factors in Aesthetic Judgments'. *Brit. J. Psych.*, 31, 262-70

Eysenck, H. J. (1947) *Dimensions of Personality*. Routledge: London

Eysenck, H. J. (1952) *The Scientific Study of Personality*. Routledge: London

Eysenck, H. J. (1953) *The Uses and Abuses of Psychology*. Penguin

Eysenck, H. J. (1954) *The Psychology of Politics*. Routledge: London

Eysenck, H. J. (1957) *The Dynamics of Anxiety and Hysteria*. Routledge: London

Eysenck, H. J. (1964) *Crime and Personality*. Routledge: London

Eysenck, H. J. (1965) *Fact and Fiction in Psychology*. Penguin

Eysenck, H. J. (1967) *The Biological Basis of Personality*. C. C. Thomas: Springfield, Ill.

Eysenck, H. J. (1970) *The Structure of Human Personality*. (Third Edit.) Methuen: London (First Edit. 1953)

Eysenck, H. J. (1971) *Race, Intelligence and Education*. Temple Smith PB: London

Eysenck, H. J. (1972) *Psychology is about People*. Allen Lane, The Penguin Press: London

Eysenck, H. J. (ed.) (1964) *Experiments in Behaviour Therapy*. Pergamon Press: London

Eysenck, H. J. (ed.) (1970/71) *Readings in Extraversion-Introversion*. (3 vols) Staples Press: London

Fearing, F. (1964) *Reflex Action: A Study in the History of Physiological Psychology*. Hafner: New York, 1964. (1st. Edit. 1930)

Festinger, Leon (1957) *A Theory of Cognitive Dissonance*. Row Peterson: Evanston, Ill.

Festinger, L., *et al.* (1964) *Conflict, Decision and Dissonance*. Tavistock: London

Festinger, L., Riecken, H. and Schachter, S. (1956) *When Prophecy Fails*. University of Minnesota Press: Minneapolis. (Harper & Row PB: New York 1966)

Feynman, R. (1965) *The Character of Physical Law*. (Cornell University Lecture Series recorded for the B.B.C.) B.B.C. Publications: London

Fielding, E. E. (1963) *Sittings with Eusapia Palladino and Other Studies*. (Edited and Introduced by E. J. Dingwall) University Books: New Hyde Park, N.Y.

Fine, R. (1963) *Freud: A Critical Re-evaluation of his Theories*. Allen & Unwin: London

Fletcher, Ronald (1957) *Instinct in Man: In the Light of Recent Work in Comparative Psychology*. Allen & Unwin: London

Flournoy, T. (1963) *From India to the Planet Mars: A Study of a Case of Somnambulism with Glossolalia*. University Books: New Hyde Park, N.Y. (Transl. from the French Edit. of 1900)

Fodor, J. A. (1968) *Psychological Explanation: An Introduction to the Philosophy of Psychology*. Random House PB: New York

Fodor, J. and Katz, J. (eds) (1964) *The Structure of Language: Readings in the Philosophy of Language*. Prentice Hall: Englewood Cliffs, N.J.

Foss, B. M. (ed.) (1961/1969) *Determinants of Infant Behaviour*. (4 vols) (Proceedings of Tavistock Study Group Seminars.) Methuen: London

Foulkes, David (1966) *The Psychology of Sleep*. Scribner: New York

Fowler, Harry (ed.) (1965) *Curiosity and Exploratory Behaviour*. (Part I: Inquiry and Argument. Part II: Selected Readings.) Macmillan PB: New York

Freud, S. (1914) *History of the Psychoanalytic Movement*. See Freud (1955/64)

Freud, S. (1920) *Three Essays on Sexuality*. (4th Edit.) *See* Freud (1955/64)

Freud, S. (1930) *Civilization and its Discontents*. *See* Freud (1955/64)

Freud, S. (1954) *Origins of Psychoanalysis: Letters to Wilhelm Fliess. Drafts and Notes: 1887-1902*. (Edited by Marie Bonaparte, Anna Freud and E. Kris. Transl. by E. Mosbacher and J. Strachey.) Basic Books: New York

Freud, S. (1955/64) *The Standard Edition of the Complete Psycho-*

logical Work of Sigmund Freud. (Edited by James Strachey.) (23 vols) Hogarth and The Institute of Psychoanalysis: London

Galanter, E. (1962) 'Contemporary Psychophysics'. *See* Holt, Rhinehart and Winston (eds) (1962)

Galton, Francis (1892) *Hereditary Genius*. (2nd Edit.) Macmillan: London. (1st Edit. 1869)

Galton, Francis (1907) *Inquiries into Human Faculty*. Everyman: London. (1st Edit. 1893)

Gardner, Martin (1957) *Facts and Fallacies in the Name of Science*. (Rev. Edit.) Dover PB: New York. (1st Edit. 1952)

Gardner, Martin (1966) 'Funny Coincidence'. Review of Hansel (1966). *New York Review of Books*. (May Issue)

Gardner, R. A. and Gardner, Beatrice (1969) 'Teaching Sign Language to a Chimpanzee'. *Science*, **165**, 664-72

Garvey, C. R. (1929) 'List of American Psychological Laboratories'. *Psychol. Bull.*, **26**, 652-60

Gauld, Alan (1968) *The Founders of Psychical Research*. Routledge: London

Getzels, J. W. and Jackson, P. W. (1962) *Creativity and Intelligence*. Wiley: New York

Ghiselin, B. (1952) *The Creative Process*. New American Library PB: New York

Gibson, J. J. (1966) *The Senses Considered as Perceptual Systems*. Houghton Mifflin: Boston, Mass.

Gorer, G. (1966) 'Psychoanalysis in the World'. *See* Rycroft (ed.) (1966)

Gorer, G. and Rickman, J. (1959) *The People of Great Russia: A Psychological Study*. Cresset Press: London

Gottesman, I. (1968) 'Biogenetics of Race and Class'. *See* Deutsch, Katz and Jensen (eds) (1968)

Greene, Judith (1972) *Psycholinguistics: Chomsky and Psychology*. Penguin

Gregory, R. L. (1966) *Eye and Brain*. McGraw-Hill PB: New York

Gregory, R. L. (1970) *The Intelligent Eye*. Weidenfeld & Nicholson: London

Gruber, H., *et al.* (eds) (1964) *Contemporary Approaches to Creative Thinking*. Athlone: New York

Guilford, J. P. (1950) 'Creativity'. (Presidential Address) *Amer. Psychol.*, **5**, 444-54

Guilford, J. P. (1959) 'Three Faces of Intellect'. *Amer. Psychol.*, **14**, 469-70. (Reprinted in Wiseman (ed.) (1967))

Guilford, J. P. (1967) *The Nature of Human Intelligence.* McGraw-Hill: New York

Haber, N. (ed.) (1966) *Current Research in Motivation.* Holt, Rhinehart & Winston: New York.

Haber, N. (ed.) (1968) *Contemporary Theory and Research in Visual Perception.* Holt, Rhinehart & Winston: New York

Hamlyn, D. W. (1953) 'Behaviour'. *Philosophy*, **28**, 132-45. (Reprinted in Chappell (ed.) (1962))

Hansel, C. E. M. (1966) *ESP: A Scientific Evaluation.* Scribner: New York. (MacGibbon & Kee: London 1967)

Hardy, Alister (1965) *The Living Stream: Evolution and Man.* (The Gifford Lectures, Aberdeen, 1963/64.) Collins: London

Hardy, Alister (1966) *The Divine Flame.* (The Gifford Lectures, Aberdeen, 1964/65.) Collins: London

Hardyck, Jane and Braden, Marcia (1962) 'Prophecy Fails Again: A Report of a Failure to Replicate'. *J. Ab. & Soc. Psych.*, **65**, 136-41

Harlow, H. F. (1953) 'Mice, Monkeys, Men and Motives'. *Psych. Rev.*, **60**, 23-32. (Reprinted in Fowler (ed.) (1965))

Harlow, H. F. (1961) 'The Development of Affectional Patterns in Infant Monkeys'. *See* Vol. I of Foss (ed.) (1961/69)

Harlow, H. F. and Harlow, Margaret (1969) 'Effects of Various Mother-Infant Relationships on Rhesus Monkey Behaviours. *See* Vol. IV of Foss (ed.) (1961/69)

Harlow, H. F. and Zimmermann, R. R. (1959) 'Affectional Responses in the Infant Monkey'. *Science*, **130**, 421-32

Harper, R. A. (1959) *Psychoanalysis and Psychotherapy.* Prentice Hall PB: Englewood Cliffs, N.J.

Harris, C. S. (1965) 'Perceptual Adaptation to Inverted, Reversed and Displaced Vision'. *Psychol. Rev.*, **72**, 419-44. (Reprinted in Haber (ed.) (1968))

Hartmann, H. (1959) *Ego Psychology and the Problem of Adaptation.* Hogarth: London

Hasan, Parween and Butcher, H. J. (1966) 'Creativity and Intelligence: A Partial Replication with Scottish Children of Getzel's & Jackson's Study'. *Brit. J. Psych.*, **57**, 129-35

Hearnshaw, L. S. (1964) *A Short History of British Psychology, 1840-1940.* Methuen: London

Hebb, D. O. (1955) 'Drives and the C.N.S. (Conceptual Nervous System)'. (Presidential Address to the Amer. Psychol. Assoc., 1954) *Psychol. Rev.*, **62**, 243-54. (Reprinted in Bindra and Stewart (eds) (1966))

Herigel, E. (1953) *Zen in the Art of Archery*. Routledge: London

Herriot, P. (1970) *An Introduction to the Psychology of Language*. Methuen: London

Herrnstein, R. and Boring, E. (eds) (1965) *A Source Book in the History of Psychology*. Harvard University Press: Cambridge, Mass.

Hess, E. H. (1962) 'Ethology'. *See* Holt, Rhinehart and Winston (1962)

Hilgard, E. R. (1952) 'Experimental Approaches to Psychoanalysis'. *See* Pumpian-Mindlin (ed.) (1952)

Hilgard, E. R. (1970) 'The Scientific Status of Psychoanalysis'. (Paper to the International Congress of Logic, Methodology and Philosophy of Science, 1960) *See* Lee and Herbert (eds) (1970)

Hilgard, E. and Bower, G. (1966) *Theories of Learning*. (3rd Edit.) Appleton-Century-Crofts: New York. (1st Edit. 1948)

Hilgard, E. and Marquis, D. (1961) *Conditioning and Learning*. (Revised by G. A. Kimble) Appleton-Century-Crofts: New York/Methuen: London

Hochberg, J. (1962) 'Nativism and Empiricism in Perception'. *See* Postman (ed.) (1962)

Hockett, Charles (1968) *The State of the Art*. Mouton: The Hague

Holt, Rhinehart and Winston (eds.) (1962) *New Directions in Psychology I*. Holt, Rhinehart & Winston: New York

Holt, Rhinehart and Winston (eds) (1965) *New Directions in Psychology II*. Holt, Rhinehart & Winston: New York

Holzman, P. S. (1970) *Psychoanalysis and Psychopathology*. McGraw-Hill PB: New York

Homans, G. C. (1970) 'Psychology and Social Phenomena'. *See* Borger and Cioffi (eds) (1970)

Honorton, C. (1969) 'Relationship between EEG Alpha Activity and ESP in Card-guessing Performances'. *J. Amer. Soc. Psychic. Res.*, **63**, 365-75

Honorton, C. and Krippner, S. (1969) 'Hypnosis and ESP Performance: A Review of the Literature'. *J. Amer. Soc. Psychic. Res.*, **63**, 214-53

Hook, S. (1960) 'Science and Mythology in Psychoanalysis'. *See* Hook (ed.) (1960)

Hook, S. (ed.) (1960) *Psychoanalysis, Scientific Method and Philosophy.* (Symposium) Evergreen PB: New York. (New York University Press 1959)

Hook, S. (ed.) (1969) *Language and Philosophy.* (Symposium) New York Univ. Press/University of London Press

Hubel, D. H. and Wiesel, T. N. (1962) 'Receptive Fields in the Cat's Visual Cortex'. *J. Physiol.,* **160,** 106-54. (Reprinted in Spigel (ed.) (1965))

Hudson, Liam (1968) *Frames of Mind,* Methuen: London

Hudson, Liam (1966) *Contrary Imaginations.* Methuen: London. (Penguin: 1968)

Hull, Clark (1933) *Hypnosis and Suggestibility: An Experimental Approach.* Appleton-Century: New York

Hull, C. L. (1943) *Principles of Behavior.* Appleton-Century-Crofts: New York

Humphrey, G. (1951) *Thinking: An Introduction to its Experimental Psychology.* Methuen: London

Humphrey, G. (1968) 'Wundt: The Great Master'. *See* Wolman (ed.) (1968)

Hunt, J. McV. (ed.) (1944) *Personality and the Behaviour Disorders.* (2 vols) Ronald: New York

Hunt, J. McV. (1961) *Intelligence and Experience.* Ronald Press: New York. (Chaps. 8 and 9 are reprinted in Wiseman (ed.) (1967))

Hunt, J. McV. (1968) 'Environment, Development and Scholastic Achievement'. *See* Deutsch, Katz and Jensen (eds) (1968) (Reprinted in Butcher and Lomax (eds) (1972))

Hunt, R. (ed.) (1967) *Personality and Cultures: Readings in Psychological Anthropology.* Natural History Press: New York

Hunter, I. M. (1962) 'An Exceptional Talent for Calculative Thinking'. *Brit. J. Psych.,* **53,** 243-58. (Reprinted in Wason and Johnson-Laird (eds) (1968))

James, B. (1942) 'A Case of Homosexuality Treated by Aversion Therapy'. *Brit. Med. J.,* **1,** 768-70 (Reprinted in Eysenck (ed.) (1964))

James, William (1890) *The Principles of Psychology.* (2 vols) Holt: New York. (Macmillan: London 1908)

James, William (1960) *Varieties of Religious Experience: A Study of Human Nature.* Collins/Fontana PB: London. (1st Edit. London 1902)

Jaynes, J. (1969) 'The Historical Origins of Ethology and Comparative Psychology'. *Animal Behaviour*, **17**, 601-6

Jenkins, J. and Paterson, D. (eds) (1961) *Studies in Individual Differences.* Methuen: London

Jensen, A. R. (1969) 'How much can we Boost I.Q. and Scholastic Achievement?' *See* Jensen *et al.* (1969)

Jensen, A. R., *et al.* (1969) *Environment, Heredity and Intelligence.* Harvard Educ. Rev. Monogr.: Cambridge, Mass. (re-issued by Methuen: London 1972)

Jones, Ernest (1953/55) *The Life and Work of Sigmund Freud.* (3 vols) Hogarth: London. (1-vol. Edit. Edited by L. Trilling. Penguin: 1967)

Joynson, R. B. (1970) 'The Breakdown of Modern Psychology'. *Bull. Brit. Psychol. Soc.*, **23**, 261-69

Joynson, R. B. (1971) 'Michotte's Experimental Methods'. *Brit. J. Psych.*, **62**, 293-302

Joynson, R. B. (1974) *Psychology and Common Sense.* Routledge & Kegan Paul: London

Jung, C. G. (1963) *Memories, Dreams, Reflections.* Routledge: London

Kassorla, Irene (1969) 'A New Approach to Mental Illness'. *Science Journal*, **5**, 68-75

Katz, David (1935) *The World of Colour.* (Transl. from the German Edit. of 1930 by R. B. MacLeod) Kegan Paul: London. (1st Edit. 1911)

Kellogg, W. N. and L. A. (1967) *The Ape and the Child.* Hafner: New York (1st Edit. 1933)

Kelvin, Peter (1970) *The Bases of Social Psychology.* Holt, Rhinehart & Winston: New York

Kessel, N. and Walton, H. (1965) *Alcoholism.* Penguin

Kline, Paul (1972) *Fact and Fantasy in Freudian Theory.* Methuen: London

Koch, S. (1954) 'Clark L. Hull'. *See* Estes *et al.* (1954)

Koch, S. (ed.) (1959/1963) *Psychology: A Study of a Science.* (6 vols) McGraw-Hill: New York

Koch, S. (1974) 'Psychology as a Science'. Chap. 1 of S. C. Brown (ed.) *Philosophy of Psychology.* Macmillan: London

Koestler, Arthur (1959) *The Sleepwalkers: A Study of Man's Changing View of the Universe.* Hutchinson: London

Koestler, Arthur (1964) *The Act of Creation.* Hutchinson: London (Panther PB)

Koestler, Arthur (1967) *The Ghost in the Machine.* Hutchinson: London

Koestler, Arthur (1968) *Drinkers of Infinity.* (Collected Essays) Hutchinson: London

Koestler, Arthur (1969) *Beyond Atomism and Holism—The Concept of the Holon.* See Koestler and Smythies (eds) (1969)

Koestler, Arthur (1971) *The Case of the Midwife Toad.* Hutchinson: London

Koestler, Arthur (1972) *The Roots of Coincidence.* (With a Postscript by Renee Haynes) Hutchinson: London

Koestler, A. and Smythies, J. R. (eds) (1969) *Beyond Reductionism.* (Symposium) Hutchinson: London

Koffka, K. (1935) *Principles of Gestalt Psychology.* Harcourt, Brace & World: New York

Kohler, Ivo (1951) *The Formation and Transformation of the Visual World.* Psychological Issues 3, No. 4, Monogr. 12. New York

Köhler, W. (1929) *Gestalt Psychology.* Liveright: New York. (Mentor PB: New York 1947)

Köhler, W. (1938) *The Place of Value in a World of Fact.* (Gifford Lectures) Liveright: New York

Köhler, W. (1940) *Dynamics in Psychology.* Liveright: New York

Köhler, W. (1957) *The Mentality of Apes.* (Transl. from the German Edit. of 1925) Penguin. (1st edit. 1917)

Köhler, W. (1967) Gestalt Psychology. *Psychologische Forschung,* 31, xviii-xxx. (In English)

Köhler, W. (1969) *The Task of Gestalt Psychology.* Princeton Univ. Press: Princeton, N.J.

Kuhn, T. (1970) *The Structure of Scientific Revolutions.* (Enlarged Edit.) University of Chicago Press: Chicago. (1st Edit. 1962)

Lee, S. G. and Herbert, M. (eds) (1970) *Freud and Psychology.* (Selected Readings) Penguin

Legge, D. (ed.) (1970) *Skills.* (Selected Readings) Penguin

Lenneberg, E. H. (1964) 'A Biological Perspective of Language'. In E. H. Lenneberg (ed.) *New Directions in the Study of Lan-*

guage. (M.I.T. Press 1964) (Reprinted in Oldfield and Marshall (eds.) (1968)

Lenneberg, E. H. (1967) *Biological Foundations of Language*. Wiley: New York

LeShan, L. (1974) *The Medium, the Mystic and the Physicist*. Viking: New York

Levy, W. J. and McRae, Anita (1971) 'Precognition in Mice and Jirds', *J. Parapsych.*, **35**, 120-31

Lewin, K. (1935) *A Dynamic Theory of Personality*. (Collected Papers) McGraw-Hill: New York

Lewin, K. (1967) *Field Theory in Social Science*. (Edited by D. Cartwright) Tavistock PB: London. (Harper & Row: New York 1951)

Lewin, K., Lippitt, R. and White, R. (1939) 'Patterns of Aggressive Behaviour in Experimentally Created "Social Climates".' *J. Soc. Psych.*, **10**, 271-99

Lindzey, G. and Aronson, E. (eds) (1968) *The Handbook of Social Psychology* (2nd Edit.) (5 vols) Addison-Wesley: Reading, Mass.

London, P. (1964) *The Modes and Morals of Psychotherapy*. Holt, Rhinehart & Winston: New York

Lorenz, K. (1966) *On Aggression*. Methuen: London

Lowry, R. (1971) *The Evolution of Psychological Theory: 1650 to the Present*. Aldine: Chicago

Louch, A. R. (1966) *Explanation and Human Action*. Blackwell: Oxford

Lynn, R. (1959) 'Two Personality Characteristics related to Academic Achievement'. *Brit. J. Educ. Psych.*, **29**, 213-16. (Reprinted in Eysenck (ed.) (1970/71)

Lyons, J. (1968) *Introduction to Theoretical Linguistics*. Cambridge Univ. Press

Lyons, J. (1970) *Chomsky*. Fontana/Collins: London

Lyons, J. (ed.) (1970) *New Horizons in Linguistics*. Penguin

Lyons, J. and Wales, R. (eds) (1966) *Psycholinguistics Papers* (Symposium) Edinburgh University Press

McClelland, D. C., *et al.* (1953) *The Achievement Motive*. Appleton-Century-Crofts: New York

McConnell, R. A. (1966) 'ESP Research at Three Levels of Method'. *J. Parapsych.*, **30**, 195-207

McConnell, R. A. (1968) Letter to Editor re. Stevens (1967). *Contemp. Psych.*, **13**, 41

McCreary, Charles (1967) *Science, Philosophy and ESP.* Faber: London

McEwen, Peter (1958) *Figural After-Effects.* Brit. J. Psych. Monogr. Suppl. 31. Cambridge University Press

McGinnies, E. (1949) 'Emotionality and Perceptual Defense'. *Psychol. Rev.*, **56**, 244-51

MacIntyre, A. C. (1958) *The Unconscious: A Conceptual Study.* Routledge: London

MacKay, Donald M. (1960) 'On the Logical Indeterminacy of a Free Choice'. *Mind*, **69**, 31-40

Mackenzie, B. D. (1973) *The Origins of Behaviourism.* (Unpublished Ph.D. Thesis) University of Edinburgh

MacKinnon, D. W. (1962) 'The Nature and Nurture of Creative Talent'. *Amer. Psychol.*, **17**, 484-94. (Reprinted in Semeonoff (ed.) (1970))

MacKinnon, D. W. and Dukes, W. F. (1962) 'Repression'. *See* Postman (ed.) (1962)

MacLeod, R. B. (1964) 'Phenomenology: A Challenge to Experimental Psychology'. *See* Wann (ed.) (1964)

MacLeod, R. B. (1964a) 'Retrospect and Prospect'. *See* Gruber, *et al.* (eds) (1964)

McNemar, Q. (1964) 'Lost: Our Intelligence. Why?' (Presidential Address) *Amer. Psychologist*, **19**, 871-82. (Reprinted in Butcher and Lomax (eds) (1972))

McDougall, W. (1946) *An Introduction to Social Psychology.* (28th Edit.) Methuen: London. (1st Edit. 1908)

Marino, C. and Parkin, C. (1969) 'A Modification of the Asch Experiment'. *J. Soc. Psych.*, **77**, 91-95

Maslow, A. H. (1954) *Motivation and Personality.* Harper: New York

Masserman, J. H. (1943) *Behaviour and Neurosis.* Univ. of Chicago Press

Maxwell, J. (1949) *The Trend of Scottish Intelligence.* University of London Press. (*See* Jenkins and Paterson (eds) (1961))

Medawar, Peter (1967) *The Art of the Soluble.* Methuen: London

Medhurst, R. G. (1971) 'The Origin of the Prepared Random Numbers used in the Shackleton Experiments'. *J. Soc. Psychic. Res.*, **46**, 31-39

Michotte, A. (1963) *The Perception of Causality*. Methuen: London. (Transl. from the French Edit. Louvain, 1946)

Michotte, A., *et al.* (1962) *Causalité Permanence et Realité Phénomenales*. (Festschrift volume on the occasion of Michotte's 80th birthday) University of Louvain Press

Michotte, A., Thinés, G. and Crabbé, G. (1964) *Les Compléments Amodaux des Structures Perceptives*. University of Louvain Press

Milgram, S. (1963) 'Behavioural Study of Obedience'. *J. Ab. & Soc. Psych.*, **67**, 371-78

Milgram, S. (1965) 'Some Conditions of Obedience and Disobedience'. *Human Relations*, **18**, 57-76

Milgram, S. (1965a) 'Liberating Effect of Group Pressures'. *J. Personal. & Soc. Psych.*, **1**, 127-34

Mill, John Stuart (1875) *A System of Logic: Ratiocinative and Inductive*. (9th Edit.) Longmans, Green: London. (1st Edit. 1843)

Miller, G. A. (1951) *Language and Communication*. McGraw-Hill: New York

Miller, George (1964) *Psychology: The Science of Mental Life*. Hutchinson: London

Miller, G. A. (1964a) 'The Psycholinguists'. *Encounter*, **23**, 29-37. (Reprinted in Miller (1968))

Miller, G. A. (1968) *The Psychology of Communication: Seven Essays*. Allen Lane: Penguin Press, London

Miller, Jonathan (ed.) (1972) *Freud: The Man, his World, his Influence*. Weidenfeld & Nicolson: London

Miller, Neal (1948) 'Studies of Fear as an Acquired Drive'. *J. Exptl. Psych.*, **38**, 89-101

Miller, Neal (1969) 'Learning of Visceral and Glandular Responses'. *Science*, **163**, 434-45

Mills, J. (1969) 'The Experimental Method'. *See* Mills (ed.) (1969)

Mills, J. (ed.) (1969) *Experimental Social Psychology*. Macmillan: Toronto

Milne, A. J. M. (1962) *The Social Philosophy of English Idealism*. Allen & Unwin: London

Mischel, T. (1969) 'Scientific and Philosophical Psychology: A Historical Introduction'. *See* Mischel (ed.) (1969)

Mischel, T. (ed.) (1969) *Human Action: Conceptual and Empirical Issues*. Academic Press: New York/London

Montagu, M. F. Ashley (1968) 'The New Litany of "Innate Depravity" or Original Sin Revisited'. *See* Montagu (ed.) (1968)

Montagu, M. F. Ashley (ed.) (1968) *Man and Aggression.* Oxford University Press PB

Montpélier, G. de (1935) *Les Altérations Morphologiques des Mouvements Rapides.* University of Louvain Press

Moray, N. (1969) *Listening and Attention.* Penguin

Morris, Desmond (1967) *The Naked Ape.* Cape: London. (Panther PB)

Morris, R. L. (1970) 'Psi and Animal Behaviour: A Survey'. *J. Amer. Soc. Psychic. Res.*, **64**, 242-60

Mowrer, O. H. (1950) *Learning Theory and Personality Dynamics.* (Selected Papers) Ronald: New York

Mueller, C. and Schoenfeld, W. (1954) 'Edwin R. Guthrie'. *See* Estes, W. K., *et al.* (1954)

Murphy, Gardner and Murphy, Lois (1937) *Experimental Social Psychology.* (Rev. Edit. with T. Newcomb.) Harper & Bros: New York. (1st Edit. 1931)

Murphy, G. and Ballou, R. (eds) (1960) *William James on Psychical Research.* Chatto & Windus: London

Newcomb, T. (1950) *Social Psychology.* Dryden: New York

Newell, A., Shaw, J. and Simon, H. (1961) 'Computer Simulation of Human Thinking'. *Science*, **134**, 2011-17

Oldfield, R. and Marshall, J. C. (eds) *Language.* Penguin

Orne, M. T. and Evans, F. J. 'Antisocial Behaviour and Hypnosis'. *J. Personal. & Soc. Psych.*, **1**, 189-200

Osgood, C. E., Suci, G. J. and Tannenbaum, P. H. (1957) *The Measurement of Meaning.* University of Illinois Press: Urbana, Ill.

Osis, Karlis (1965) 'ESP over Distance: A Survey of Experiments published in English'. *J. Amer. Soc. Psychic. Res.*, **59**, 22-46

Oswald, Ian (1966) *Sleep.* Penguin

Owen, A. G. R. (1964) *Can We Explain the Poltergeist?* Garrett/Helix: New York

Owen, A. G. R. (1971) *Hysteria, Hypnosis and Healing: The Work of J-M Charcot.* Dobson: London

Parapsychology Foundation (1971) *A Century of Psychical Research: The Continuing Doubts and Affirmations.* (Symposium) (Edited by A. Angoff and Betty Shapin.) Parapsychology Foundation: New York

Pears, David (1971) *Wittgenstein*. Fontana/Collins PB: London

Pearson, Karl (1924) Vol. II of *The Life, Letters and Labours of Francis Galton*. (4 vols 1914/1930) Cambridge University Press

Peters, R. S. (1958) *The Concept of Motivation*. Routledge: London

Podmore, Frank (1963) *From Mesmer to Christian Science*. University Books: New Hyde Park, N.Y. (Re-issue. 1st Edit.: London 1909)

Podmore, Frank (1963a) *Mediums of the 19th Century*. University Books: New Hyde Park, N.Y. (originally published as *Modern Spiritualism*, 2 vols. Methuen: London, 1902)

Polanyi, Michael (1958) *Personal Knowledge*. Routledge: London

Polanyi, M. (1969) *Knowing and Being: Collected Essays*. Routledge: London

Popper, K. R. (1957) *The Poverty of Historicism*. Routledge: London

Popper, K. R. (1957a) 'Philosophy of Science: A Personal Report'. In C. A. Mace (ed.) *British Philosophy in Mid-Century*. (Reprinted in K. R. Popper *Conjectures and Refutations*. Routledge: London 1963. Chap. 1)

Popper, K. R. (1962) *The Open Society and Its Enemies*. (Rev. Edit.) (2 vols) Routledge: London. (1st Edit. 1945)

Postman, L. (ed.) (1962) *Psychology in the Making*. Knopf: New York

Pratt, J. G., et al. (1968) 'Identification of Concealed Randomized Objects through Acquired Response Habits of Stimulus and Word Associations'. *Nature*, 220, 89-91

Premack, D. (1970) 'A Functional Analysis of Language'. *J. Exptl. Anal. Behav.*, 14, 107-25. (A popular account of this work is given in *New Society*, Oct. 29, 1970)

Price, G. R. (1955) 'Science and the Supernatural'. *Science*, 122, 359-67

Price, H. H. 'Survival and the Idea of "Another World".' See J. R. Smythies (ed.) (1965)

Pumpian-Mindlin, E. (ed.) (1952) *Psychoanalysis as Science* (Hixon Symposium) Stanford University Press

Rachman, S. and Teasdale, J. (1969) *Aversion Therapy and Behaviour Disorders*. Routledge: London

Rancurello, A. C. (1968) *A Study of Franz Brentano: His Psycho-*

logical Standpoint and his Significance in the History of Psychology. Academic Press: New York & London

Randall, J. L. (1971) 'Psi Phenomena and Biological Theory'. *J. Soc. Psychic. Res.,* **46,** 151-66

Ransom, C. (1971) 'Recent Criticism of Parapsychology: A Review'. *J. Amer. Soc. Psychic. Res.,* **65,** 289-308

Rao, K. R. (1965) 'The Bidirectionality of Psi'. (Presidential Address) *Proceedings of the Parapsychological Association,* **2,** 37-59

Rao, K. R. (1966) *Experimental Parapsychology. A Review and Interpretation.* C. C. Thomas: Springfield, Ill.

Ray, W. S. (ed.) (1967) *The Experimental Psychology of Original Thinking.* (Part I: Inquiry and Argument. Part II: Selective Readings.) Macmillan: New York

Reed, Elizabeth and Reed, S. C. (1965) *Mental Retardation. A Family Study.* Sanders: Philadelphia

Reeves, Joan (1969) *Thinking about Thinking.* Methuen PB: London. (1st Edit. Secker & Warburg, London, 1965)

Rhine, J. B. (1959) 'How Can One Decide about ESP?' *Amer. Psychologist,* **14,** 606-8

Rhine, J. B. (1969) 'Psi Missing Re-examined'. *J. Parapsych.,* **33,** 1-38

Rhine, Louisa (1970) *Mind over Matter: Psychokinesis.* Macmillan: London

Rieff, Philip (1959) *Freud: The Mind of the Moralist.* Gollancz: London

Rieff, Philip (1966) *The Triumph of the Therapeutic.* Chatto & Windus: London

Rock, I. (1966) *The Nature of Perceptual Adaptation.* Basic Books: New York

Roe, Ann (1952) *The Making of a Scientist.* Dodd Mead: New York

Roe, Ann (1952a) 'A Psychologist Examines Sixty-four Eminent Scientists'. *Scientific American,* **187,** 21-25. (Reprinted in Vernon (ed.) (1970))

Rogers, C. R. (1954) 'Towards a Theory of Creativity'. *E.T.C.: A Review of General Semantics,* **11,** 249-60. (Reprinted in Vernon (ed.) (1970))

Roll, W. G. (1973) *The Poltergeist.* New American Library: New York

Rose, R. (1952) 'Experiments in ESP and PK with Aboriginal Subjects'. *J. Parapsych.*, **16**, 219-20

Rose, R. (1955) 'Experiments in ESP and PK with Aboriginal Subjects: A Second Report'. *J. Parapsych.*, **19**, 92-98

Rosenberg, M. J. (1965) 'When Dissonance Fails'. *J. Personal. & Soc. Psych.*, **1**, 28-42

Rosenblueth, Arturo (1970) *Brain and Mind*. M.I.T. Press: Cambridge, Mass.

Rosenthal, R. (1966) *Experimenter Effects in Behavioural Research*. Appleton-Century-Crofts: New York

Rosenzweig, M. R. *et al.* (1972) 'Brain Changes in Response to Experience'. *Scientific American*, **226**, 22-30

Rowland, L. W. (1939) 'Will Hypnotized Persons Try to Harm Themselves or Others?' *J. Ab. & Soc. Psych.*, **34**, 114-17

Rushton, W. A. H. (1971) 'First Sight—Second Sight'. (Presidential Address.) *Proc. Soc. Psychic. Res.*, **55**, 177-88

Russell, Bertrand (1948) *Human Knowledge*. Allen & Unwin: London

Russell, Clare and Russell, W. M. (1968) *Violence, Monkeys and Man*. Macmillan: London

Rutter, M. (1972) *Maternal Deprivation Reassessed*. Penguin.

Rycroft, Charles (1966) 'Causes and Meaning'. *See* Rycroft (ed.) (1966)

Rycroft, C. (ed.) (1966) *Psychoanalysis Observed*. Constable PB: London

Ryle, Gilbert (1949) *The Concept of Mind*. Hutchinson: London

Ryzl, M. (1970) *Parapsychology: A Scientific Approach*. Hawthorn: New York

Sarbin, T. R. (1962) 'Attempts to Understand Hypnotic Phenomena'. *See* Postman (ed.) (1962)

Schaffer, H. R. (1971) *The Growth of Sociability*. Penguin

Schmidt, H. (1969) 'Precognition of a Quantum Process'. *J. Parapsych.*, **33**, 99-109. 'Clairvoyance Test with a Machine'. *Idem*, 300-307

Schmidt, H. (1969b) 'Quantum Processes Predicted'. *New Scientist*, **44**, 114-16

Schmidt, H. (1971) 'Mental Influences on Random Events'. *New Scientist*, **50**, 757-58

Sears, R. R. (1944) 'Experimental Analysis of Psychoanalytic Phenomena'. *See* Vol. I of Hunt (ed.) (1944)

Sears, R. R. (1951) *A Survey of Objective Studies of Psychoanalytic Concepts*. Social Science Research Council: Ann Arbor, Michigan. (Compiled 1942)

Semeonoff, B. (ed.) (1970) *Personality Assessment*. Selected Readings. (2nd Edit.) Penguin. (1st Edit. 1966)

Shapiro, D., *et al*. (1969) 'Effects of Feedback and Reinforcement on the Control of Human Systolic Blood Pressure'. *Science*, 163, 588-89

Shaw, M. E. and Costanzo, P. R. (1970) *Theories of Social Psychology*. McGraw-Hill: New York

Sherif, M. (1963) *The Psychology of Social Norms*. (2nd Edit.) Harper & Bros: New York. (1st Edit. Harper & Row, New York, 1936)

Sherrington, Charles (1940) *Man on his Nature*. Cambridge University Press

Shor, R. and Orne, M. (eds) (1965) *The Nature of Hypnosis: Selected Basic Readings*. Holt, Rhinehart & Winston: New York

Shuey, Audrey (1966) *The Testing of Negro Intelligence*. (2nd Edit.) Social Sciences Press: New York

Sinclair, Upton (1962) *Mental Radio*. (Rev. Edit.) C. C. Thomas: Springfield, Ill. (1st Edit. 1930)

Skinner, B. F. (1953) *Science and Human Behaviour*. Macmillan: New York

Skinner, B. F. (1957) *Verbal Behavior*. Appleton-Century-Crofts: New York

Skinner, B. F. (1961) *Cumulative Record*. (2nd Edit.) Appleton-Century-Crofts: New York. (1st Edit. 1959)

Skinner, B. F. (1966) 'The Physiology and Ontogeny of Behaviour'. *Science*, 153, 1205-13. (Reprinted in Endler, Boulter and Osser (eds) (1968))

Skinner, B. F. (1971) *Beyond Freedom and Dignity*. Knopf: New York

Slater, Eliot (1968) Review of Hansel (1966). *Brit. J. Psychiatry*, 114, 653-58

Sluckin, W. (1965) *Imprinting and Early Learning*. Aldine: Chicago. (2nd Edit. Methuen: London 1972)

Smith, K. and Smith, W. (1962) *Perception and Motion*. Sanders: Philadelphia

Smythies, J. R. (ed.) (1965) *Brain and Mind: Modern Concepts of the Nature of Mind*. Routledge: London

Smythies, J. R. (ed.) (1967) *Science and ESP*. Routledge: London

Soal, S. G. and Goldney, K. Mollie (1943) 'Experiments in Precognitive Telepathy'. *Proc. Soc. Psychic. Res.*, **47**, 21-151

Soal, S. G. and Bateman, F. (1954) *Modern Experiments in Telepathy*. Faber: London

Solomon, R. L. and Wynne, L. C. (1953) *Traumatic Avoidance Learning: Acquisition in Normal Dogs*. Psych. Monogr., **67**, No. 354

Spearman, C. (1904) ' "General Intelligence" Objectively Determined and Measured'. *Amer. J. Psych.*, **15**, 201-92. (Reprinted in Jenkins and Paterson (eds) (1961) and in Butcher and Lomax (eds) (1972))

Spigel, I. (ed.) (1965) *Readings in the Study of Visually Perceived Movement*. Harper & Row: New York

Stafford-Clark, D. (1967) *What Freud Really Said*. Penguin. (Macdonald: London, 1965)

Stanford, R. (1971) 'EEG Alpha Activity and ESP Performance: A Replicative Study'. *J. Amer. Soc. Psychic. Res.*, **65**, 144-55

Stanford, R. and Lovin, Carole (1970) 'EEG Alpha Activity and ESP Performance'. *J. Amer. Soc. Psychic. Res.*, **64**, 375-85

Steiner, George (1969) 'The Tongues of Men'. *The New Yorker*, Nov. 15, 217-36

Stevens, S. S. (1957) 'On the Psychophysical Law'. *Psychol. Rev.*, **64**, 153-81

Stevens, S. S. (1967) 'The Market for Miracles'. *Contemp. Psych.*, **12**, 1-3

Stevenson, Ian (1967) 'An Antagonist's View of Parapsychology'. Review of Hansel (1966). *J. Amer. Soc. Psychic Res.*, **61**, 254-68

Stevenson, I. and Pratt, J. G. (1968/69) 'Exploratory Investigation of the Psychic Photography of Ted Serios'. *J. Amer. Soc. Psychic. Res.*, **62**, 103-29 and *J. Amer. Soc. Psychic. Res.*, **63**, 352-65

Stewart, W. A. (1969) *Psychoanalysis: The First Ten Years 1888-1898*. Allen & Unwin: London

Storr, Anthony (1966) 'The Concept of a Cure'. *See* Rycroft (ed.) (1966)

Storr, Anthony (1968) *Human Aggression*. Allen Lane: London

Sutcliffe, J. P. ' "Credulous" and "Skeptical" Views of Hypnotic Phenomena'. *See* Shor and Orne (eds) (1965)

Szasz, T. S. (1962) *The Myth of Mental Illness*. Secker & Warburg: London

Taylor, Charles (1964) *The Explanation of Behaviour*. Routledge: London

Taylor, C. W. and Barron, F. (eds) (1963) *Scientific Creativity: Its Recognition and Development*. (Proc. of the Utah Conferences 1956/57/59) Wiley: New York

Tenhaeff, W. (1966) 'Some Aspects of Parapsychological Research in the Netherlands'. *Internat. J. Neuropsychiatry*, (Special ESP Issue), **2**, 408-20

Terman, L. M. (1947) 'Psychological Approaches to the Study of Genius'. *Papers on Eugenics*, No. 4. (Reprinted in Vernon (ed.) (1970))

Terman, L. and Miles, Catherine (1936) *Sex and Personality*. McGraw-Hill: New York

Thorndike, E. L. (1911) *Animal Intelligence: Experimental Studies*. Macmillan: New York

Thorndike, E. L. (1966) *Human Learning*. M.I.T. Press PB: Cambridge, Mass. (1st Edit. 1931)

Thorpe, W. H. (1963) *Learning and Instinct in Animals*. (2nd Edit.) Methuen: London

Tiger, Lionel (1969) *Men in Groups*. Nelson: London

Tiger, Lionel and Fox, Robin (1972) *The Imperial Animal*. Secker & Warburg: London

Tinbergen, N. (1951) *The Study of Instinct*. Oxford University Press

Titchener, E. B. (1897) *An Outline of Psychology*. Macmillan: New York

Tolman, E. C. (1932) *Purposive Behavior in Animals and Men*. Appleton-Century-Crofts: New York. (University of California Press 1949)

Torrance, E. P. (1962) *Guiding Creative Talent*. Prentice Hall: Englewood Cliffs, N.J. (First Chapter reprinted in Vernon, (1970))

Tyler, L. E. (1965) *The Psychology of Human Differences*. (3rd Edit.) Appleton-Century-Crofts: New York

Ullmann, M. and Krippner, S. (1970) *Dream Studies and Telepathy*. Parapsychol. Foundat. Monogr.: New York

Ullman, M., Krippner, S. and Feldstein, S. (1966) 'Experimentally-Induced Telepathic Dreams: Two Studies using EEG-REM

Monitoring Technique'. *Internat. J. Neuropsychiatry*, (Special ESP Issue), **2**, 420-39

Ullman, M., Krippner, S. and Vaughan, A. (1973) *Dream Telepathy*. Macmillan: New York. Turnstone: London

Van Over, R. (ed.) (1973) *Psychology and Extrasensory Perception: A Basic Reader*. New American Library PB: New York

Vernon, P. E. (1950) *The Structure of Human Abilities*. Methuen: London. (*See also* Wiseman (ed.) (1967))

Vernon, P. E. (1963) *Personality Assessment: A Critical Survey*. Methuen: London

Vernon, P. E. (1969) *Intelligence and Cultural Environment*. Methuen: London. (Summary reprinted in Butcher and Lomax (eds) (1972))

Vernon, P. E. (ed.) (1970) *Creativity*. Selected Readings. Penguin

Vowles, D. M. (1970) *The Psychobiology of Aggression*. (Inaugural Lecture) University of Edinburgh Press

Wallach, M. A. and Kogan, N. (1965) 'A New Look at the Creativity-Intelligence Distinction'. *J. Personal.*, **33**, 348-69. (Reprinted in Vernon (ed.) (1970))

Walmsley, D. M. (1967) *Anton Mesmer*. Robert Hale: London

Wann, T. E. (ed.) (1964) *Behaviour and Phenomenology*. University of Chicago Press. (Phoenix PB 1965)

Wason, P. C. and Johnson-Laird, P. N. (eds) (1968) *Thinking and Reasoning: Selected Readings*. Penguin

Watson, J. B. (1930) *Behaviourism*. (2nd Edit.) University of Chicago Press and Phoenix PB. (1st Edit. 1924)

Webb, W. B. (ed.) (1968) *Sleep*. (Part I: Inquiry and Argument. Part II: Selected Readings.) Macmillan: New York

Weick, K. E. (1965) 'When Prophecy Pales: The Fate of Dissonance Theory'. *Psychol. Reprints*, **16**, 1261-75

Welford, A. T. (1968) *The Fundamentals of Skill*. Methuen: London

Wertheimer, Max (1961) *Productive Thinking*. (Edited by Michael Wertheimer.) Tavistock: London

West, D. J. (1971) 'Reasons for Continuing Doubt about the Existence of Psychic Phenomena'. *See* Parapsychology Foundation (1971)

Wheeler, Ladd (1970) *Interpersonal Influence*. Allyn & Bacon PB: Boston, Mass.

White, Rhea (1964) 'A Comparison of Old and New Methods of Response to Targets in ESP Experiments'. *J. Amer. Soc. Psychic. Res.*, **58**, 21-56

Whiting, J. W. and Child, I. L. (1953) *Child Training and Personality: A Cross-Cultural Study*. Yale University Press: New Haven

Whyte, L. L. (1960) *The Unconscious Before Freud*. Basic Books: New York

Wiener, Norbert (1961) *Cybernetics*. (2nd Edit.) M.I.T. Press: Cambridge, Mass. (1st Edit. 1948)

Wiener, Norbert (1964) 'Dynamic Systems in Physics and Biology'. *New Scientist*, **21**, No. 375. (Reprinted in Vol. I of N. Calder (ed.) *The World in 1984*. (2 vols) Penguin 1965

Wisdom, J. O. (1970) 'Situational Individualism and Emergent Group Properties'. In Borger and Cioffi (eds) (1970)

Wiseman, S. (ed.) (1967) *Intelligence and Ability: Selected Readings*. Penguin

Wissler, Clark (1901) 'The Correlation of Mental and Physical Tests'. *Psychol. Rev. Monogr. Suppl.*, **3**, No. 6. (Reprinted in Jenkins and Paterson (eds) (1961))

Wittgenstein, Ludwig (1953) *Philosophical Investigations*. Blackwell: Oxford

Wollheim, R. (1971) *Freud*. Fontana/Collins PB: London

Wolman, B. (ed.) (1968) *Historical Roots of Modern Psychology*. Harper & Row: New York

Woodworth, R. S. (1958) *The Dynamics of Behaviour*. Holt, Rhinehart & Winston: New York

Woodworth, R. S. and Sheehan, Mary R. (1964) *Contemporary Schools of Psychology*. (3rd Edit.) Ronald Press: New York

Young, P. C. (1949) 'Antisocial Uses of Hypnosis'. *See* le Cron (ed.) (1948)

Young, P. T. (1959) 'The Role of Affective Processes in Learning and Motivation'. *Psychol. Rev.*, **66**, 104-25. (Reprinted in Bindra and Stewart (eds) (1966))

Zajonc, R. B. (1968) 'Cognitive Theories in Psychology'. *See* Vol. I of Lindzey and Aronson (eds) (1968)

Zilboorg, G. and Henry G. (1941) *A History of Medical Psychology*. Norton: New York

Zubek, J. P. (ed.) (1969) *Sensory Deprivation: Fifteen Years of Research*. Appleton-Century-Crofts: New York

Name Index

General Index

Abilities, human 95-107, 119
  class structure and 99-100
  heredity or environment and 96-100, 106, 107, 119, 125
  racial and ethnic differences 100-101, 119, 121
  testing 95-6
Academy of Sciences, French 268
Act Psychology 52, 63, 162
Aesthetics, experimental 25
Aggression 86-7
American Association for the Advancement of Science 240, 309
American Psychoanalytic Association 250
American Psychological Association 34, 65, 133, 208
Animal minds 69-78, 88-9
  'behaviouristic' study of 69, 73-5
  'ethological' study of 70, 75-7
  'mentalistic' study of 69, 70-3
Associationism, Associationists 23, 29, 43, 51, 61, 73, 132
Aversion therapy 145-7, 155, 160

Behaviour 1-2, 3, 30
  as requiring interpretation 260-61
  study of pathological 244

Behaviour therapy 141-53, 155
  aversion therapy 145-7, 155, 160
  operant conditioning therapy 147-53, 155
  reciprocal inhibition 143-5, 155
Behaviourism 28, 29, 46, 49, 55, 56, 71, 153, 162, 176, 256
  and instinct theory 81, 89
  in comparative psychology 69, 73-5
Behaviouristics x, 127-55
  behaviour therapy 141-53, 155
  conditioning 128-41, 154-5
  two truths behind 154
Benthamites 122
Berlin 36, 53, 54
Binet-Simon Scale 104-5
Brain 20, 317
  changes in 120

California, University of, Berkeley 204
  Institute of Personality Assessment 192-3
Cambridge University 201
Causality effect, Michotte's 59-61
Chicago University 36, 190
Christian Science 269
'Church of the True Word' 225-6
Clairvoyance 298, 308, 318